Structures and Transformations in Modern British History

This major collection of essays challenges many of our preconceptions about British political and social history from the late eighteenth century to the present. Inspired by the work of Gareth Stedman Jones, twelve leading scholars explore both the long-term structures – social, political and intellectual – of modern British history, and the forces that have transformed those structures at key moments. The result is a series of insightful, original essays presenting new research within a broad historical context. Subjects covered include the consequences of rapid demographic change in the eighteenth and nineteenth centuries; the forces shaping transnational networks, especially those between Britain and its empire; and the recurrent problem of how we connect cultural politics to social change. An introductory essay situates Stedman Jones's work within the broader historiographical trends of the past thirty years, drawing important conclusions about new directions for scholarship in the twenty-first century.

DAVID FELDMAN teaches history at Birkbeck, University of London, where he is director of the Pears Institute for the Study of Anti-Semitism. He has written on Jewish history as well as on the history of migration, immigration and emigration in early modern and modern Britain. He is the author of *Englishmen and Jews: Social Relations and Political Culture, 1840–1914* (1994) and co-editor of *Paths of Integration: Migrants in Western Europe 1880–2004* (with Leo Lucassen and Jochen Oltmer, 2006).

JON LAWRENCE lectures in modern British history at the University of Cambridge and is a Fellow of Emmanuel College. He has written widely on the social, political and cultural history of modern Britain, and is the author of *Speaking for the People: Party, Language and Popular Politics in England, 1867–1914* (1998) and *Electing Our Masters: The Hustings in British Politics from Hogarth to Blair* (2009).

Structures and Transformations in Modern British History

Edited by

David Feldman and Jon Lawrence

CAMBRIDGE
UNIVERSITY PRESS

CAMBRIDGE
UNIVERSITY PRESS

The Edinburgh Building, Cambridge CB2 8RU, UK

Published in the United States of America by Cambridge University Press, New York

Cambridge University Press is part of the University of Cambridge.

It furthers the University's mission by disseminating knowledge in the pursuit of education, learning and research at the highest international levels of excellence.

www.cambridge.org
Information on this title: www.cambridge.org/9781107679641

© Cambridge University Press 2011

First published 2011
First paperback edition 2013

A catalogue record for this publication is available from the British Library

Library of Congress Cataloguing in Publication data

Structures and transformations in modern British history / edited by David Feldman and Jon Lawrence.
      p. cm.
    ISBN 978-0-521-51882-6 (Hardback)
1. Great Britain–Politics and government–19th century.   2. Great Britain–Politics and government–20th century.   3. Great Britain–Politics and government–21st century.   4. Great Britain–Social conditions–19th century.   5. Great Britain–Social conditions–20th century.   6. Great Britain–Social conditions–21st century.   7. Great Britain–Intellectual life–19th century.   8. Great Britain–Intellectual life–20th century.   9. Great Britain–Intellectual life–21st century.   I. Feldman, David, 1957–   II. Lawrence, Jon.   III. Title.
DA530.S87 2011
941.08–dc22

                                                    2010028673

ISBN 978-0-521-51882-6 Hardback
ISBN 978-1-107-67964-1 Paperback

Structures and transformations in modern British history: essays for Gareth Stedman Jones

Contents

List of figures   *page* ix
Notes on contributors   x

Introduction: structures and transformations in British
historiography   1
DAVID FELDMAN AND JON LAWRENCE

1   Coping with rapid population growth: how England fared
    in the century preceding the Great Exhibition of 1851   24
    E. A. WRIGLEY

2   The 'urban renaissance' and the mob: rethinking civic
    improvement over the long eighteenth century   54
    EMMA GRIFFIN

3   Forms of 'government growth', 1780–1830   74
    JOANNA INNES

4   Family formations: Anglo India and the familial proto-state   100
    MARGOT FINN

5   The commons, enclosure and radical histories   118
    ALUN HOWKINS

6   Engels and the city: the philosophy and practice of urban
    hypocrisy   142
    TRISTRAM HUNT

7   The decline of institutional reform in nineteenth-century
    Britain   164
    JONATHAN PARRY

8   British women and cultures of internationalism,
    *c.*1815–1914   187
    ANNE SUMMERS

9   Psychoanalysis, history and national culture   210
    DANIEL PICK

10 Labour and the politics of class, 1900–1940   237
    JON LAWRENCE

11 The dialectics of liberation: the old left, the new left and
    the counter-culture   261
    ALASTAIR J. REID

12 Why the English like turbans: multicultural politics in
    British history   281
    DAVID FELDMAN

Index   303

Figures

Figure 1.1 Annual rates of growth of population
and of a real wage series.   *page* 27
Figure 1.2 The geographical distribution of hundreds
grouped by the size of population growth
between 1791 and 1831.   41

Notes on contributors

DAVID FELDMAN is Professor of History and Director of the Pears Institute for the Study of Anti-Semitism at Birkbeck, University of London. Gareth Stedman Jones taught him as an undergraduate and also supervised his doctoral thesis on Jewish immigration to the East End of London. Together with Stedman Jones he co-edited *Metropolis – London: Histories and Representations since 1800* (1989) and he is the author of *Englishmen and Jews: Social Relations and Political Culture 1840–1914* (1994) He has been an editor of the *History Workshop Journal* since 1996.

MARGOT FINN is Professor of Modern British History at the University of Warwick. Her 1987 Columbia University doctoral dissertation benefited from supervision provided by Gareth Stedman Jones during his visiting professorship at that institution. Finn is the author of *After Chartism: Class and Nation in English Radical Politics, 1848–1874* (1993) and *The Character of Credit: Personal Debt in English Culture, 1740–1914* (2003). She is currently writing a book on the families of the East India Company.

EMMA GRIFFIN is Senior Lecturer in Modern British History at the University of East Anglia. Her PhD thesis, supervised by Gareth Stedman Jones, was published as *England's Revelry: A History of Popular Sports and Pastimes, 1660–1800* (2005). She has published two further books: *Blood Sport. A History of Hunting in Britain* (2007) and *A Short History of the British Industrial Revolution* (2010). She is currently working on a study of working-class autobiography and life-writing.

ALUN HOWKINS is Professor Emeritus of Social History at the University of Sussex. He first met Gareth Stedman Jones through politics in the late 1960s and has worked with him in History Workshops and the *History Workshop Journal* ever since. His main publications include *Poor Labouring Men* (1985), *Reshaping Rural England* (1991) and *The*

Death of Rural England (2003). He is currently working on commons and commoners after 1845.

TRISTRAM HUNT is Lecturer in History at Queen Mary, University of London. He read history at Trinity College, Cambridge before a year's postgraduate fellowship at the University of Chicago. He returned to Cambridge to undertake his PhD on Victorian civic pride with Gareth Stedman Jones. His main publications include *Building Jerusalem: The Rise and Fall of the Victorian City* (2004) and *The Frock-coated Communist: The Revolutionary life of Frederich Engels* (2009). He is a regular broadcaster, a Trustee of the Heritage Lottery Fund and was elected MP for Stoke-on-Trent Central in May 2010.

JOANNA INNES was an undergraduate, graduate student and research fellow at Cambridge 1972–1982, and for several years co-organised the Cambridge Social History Seminar with Gareth Stedman Jones. She has been a Fellow of Somerville College, Oxford since 1982. A collection of essays pulling together her work on British social policy in the eighteenth century was published in 2009, under the title *Inferior Politics*. She is now working on a study of changes in the modes and objects of social policy in late eighteenth- and early nineteenth-century Britain: *Enlightenment, War and Social Policy.*

JON LAWRENCE teaches modern British history at the University of Cambridge and is a Fellow of Emmanuel College. Gareth Stedman Jones taught him as an undergraduate and supervised his PhD on popular politics in Wolverhampton (1989). His main publications are *Speaking for the People: Party, Language and Popular Politics in England, 1867–1914* (1998) and *Electing our Masters: The Hustings in British Politics from Hogarth to Blair* (2009). He is currently working on a history of class and self-identity in Britain since the 1880s.

JONATHAN PARRY is Professor of Modern British History at the University of Cambridge, where he has been a colleague of Gareth Stedman Jones since 1992. He is a Fellow of Pembroke College, and author of four books on nineteenth-century British history, including *The Politics of Patriotism: English Liberalism, National Identity and Europe, 1830–1886* (CUP, 2006). He is currently writing about Henry Layard.

DANIEL PICK is Professor of History at Birkbeck College and is a Fellow of the British Psychoanalytical Society. His doctoral research in the History Faculty, Cambridge, supervised by Gareth Stedman Jones, was the basis for his book *Faces of Degeneration* (1989). Other publications include *Svengali's Web* (1993), *Rome or Death: The Obsessions of General Garibaldi* (2005), and, as co-editor (with Lyndal Roper), *Dreams and History* (2004). He is an editor of the *History Workshop Journal*.

ALASTAIR J. REID is a Fellow of Girton College, Cambridge where he teaches modern British social history. Gareth Stedman Jones supervised his PhD on the division of labour and politics in the British shipbuilding industry. His principal publications are *United We Stand: A History of Britain's Trade Unions* (2005) and *The Tide of Democracy: Shipyard Workers and Social Relations in Britain, 1870–1950* (2010). He is currently working on aspects of counter-culture in Britain since 1945 and is a co-founder and editor of *History and Policy*.

ANNE SUMMERS is Honorary Research Fellow at Birkbeck, University of London, having retired as a Curator of Modern Historical Manuscripts at the British Library in 2004. She has worked with Gareth Stedman Jones as a member of the editorial collective of the *History Workshop Journal* since its founding in 1975. Her publications include *Angels and Citizens: British Women as Military Nurses 1854–1914* (1988 and 2000) and *Female Lives, Moral States: Women, Religion and Public Life in Britain 1800–1930* (2000). She is currently researching relations between Christian and Jewish women in Britain, 1840–1940, with support from the British Academy.

SIR TONY WRIGLEY was formerly Professor of Economic History in Cambridge; Master of Corpus Christi College, Cambridge; and President of the British Academy. His books include *Population and History* (1969), *People, Cities and Wealth* (1987), *Continuity, Chance and Change* (1988) and (with R. S. Schofield) *The Population History of England* (1981). *Energy and the English Industrial Revolution* is currently in press.

Introduction: structures and transformations in British historiography

David Feldman and Jon Lawrence

The travails of social history

'Social history is at present in fashion', Eric Hobsbawm observed in 1971, when the popularity of the subject was also becoming allied to grand intellectual ambitions.[1] This was reflected five years later with the arrival of a new journal: *Social History*. In the first issue its editors announced confidently, and with a certain degree of belligerence, that social history was 'not a new *branch* of historical scholarship' but rather 'a new kind of history' whose mission was 'to make incursions into all fields of historical analysis'. Social history was to transform historical practice by generating a new, more holistic understanding of past societies – a 'total' history.[2] The same editorial recognised the significance of precursors such as the *Annales* School in France and British Marxist historiography, but declared, 'social history has no orthodox repertoire, no dominant central "core" around which revolve a score of minor interests and enthusiasms'.[3] Not even class. And this despite the fact that the journal rapidly became known for publishing a series of important interventions that dealt centrally with class formation, class-consciousness and class struggle in eighteenth- and nineteenth-century Britain.[4]

---

[1] E. J. Hobsbawm, 'From social history to the history of society', *Daedalus*, 100, (1971), pp. 20–45, at p. 20. Appropriately enough, 1971 was the year when *Outcast London* by Gareth Stedman Jones was first published by Oxford University Press.

[2] 'Editorial', *Social History*, 1, (1976), pp. 1–3, at p. 1. The contrast with the cautious, pluralist tone struck by Peter N. Stearns in 1967 at the launch of the American-based *Journal of Social History*, 1, (1967), pp. 3–6, is striking.

[3] 'Editorial', *Social History*, 1, (1976), p. 1.

[4] For British examples from the later 1970s see, F. K. Donnelly, 'Ideology and early English working-class history: Edward Thompson and his critics', *Social History*, 1, (1976), pp. 219–238; A. E. Musson, 'Class struggle and the labour aristocracy, 1830–60', *Social History*, 1, (1976), pp. 335–356; John Foster, 'Some comments on "class struggle and the labour aristocracy"', *Social History*, 1, (1976), pp. 357–366; H. F. Moorhouse, 'The Marxist theory of the labour aristocracy', *Social History*, 3, (1978), pp. 61–82; E. P. Thompson, 'Eighteenth-century English society: class struggle without class?', *Social History*, 3, (1978), pp. 133–165; Alastair J. Reid, 'Politics and

Despite its centrality to the debates of the 1980s and early 1990s that would signal the retreat of social history as a 'totalising' project, in the 1960s, and for much of the 1970s, class occupied a contested place in modern British social history. It was present only unevenly. It did figure, for example, in histories of social movements and popular politics. Characteristically, historians claimed that it was not possible to understand the actions of political elites without taking account of 'pressure from below' and often invoked the terminology of class as they did so. This tendency extended well beyond the ranks of Anglo-Marxists. To be sure, it can be found in Edward Thompson's argument that it was the working-class radical movement that drove the Reform crisis of 1832 to its conclusion, but it is also there in John Vincent's ground-breaking account of *How Victorians Voted*.[5] But the advance of social history meant not only writing the history of politics 'from below', it also meant expanding the subject matter of history itself. The history of material life was significantly present in this body of research. In part, this work developed from within the tradition of labour history where Marxism and class analysis were important. But economic history was equally significant and here, with few exceptions, Marxism and class analysis remained marginal in a sub-discipline still shaped by the Cold War. Taking their cue from economic history and social science, and sometimes located in distinct departments of economic and social history, historians made use of quantitative methodologies to gauge changes in the standard of living, in fertility and mortality, the crime rate and in the operation of labour markets. Writings on social policy, notably those of R. H. Titmuss, were another source of inspiration generating work on the Poor Law and the origins of the welfare state.[6]

Social history encompassed a close interest in the conditions of daily life. Historians strived to get close to the texture of lived experience in the household and the home, in patterns of consumption, in the worlds

economics in the formation of the British working class', *Social History*, 3, (1978), pp. 347–361; Nicholas Rogers, 'Money, land and lineage: the big bourgeoisie of Hanoverian London', *Social History*, 4, (1979), pp. 437–454; Clive Behagg, 'Custom, class and change: the trade societies of Birmingham', *Social History*, 4, (1979), pp. 455–480.

[5] E. P. Thompson, *The Making of the English Working Class*, revised edn, (Harmondsworth, 1968), pp. 888–890, 899; John Vincent, *Pollbooks: How Victorians Voted* (Cambridge, 1967).

[6] Asa Briggs and John Saville (eds), *Essays in Labour History* (London, 1960); E. J. Hobsbawm, *Labouring Men: Studies in the History of Labour* (London, 1964); E. A Wrigley (ed.), *Nineteenth-century Society: Essays in the Use of Quantitative Methods for the Study of Social Data* (Cambridge, 1972). For Titmuss see the preface to Jose Harris, *Unemployment and Politics: A Study in English Social Policy, 1886–1914* (Oxford, 1972) and Pat Thane, 'Introduction', in *The Origins of British Social Policy* (London, 1978).

of work and leisure. They struggled to recover the choices made by the 'common people' as they made their own history and in doing so explored, for example, the history of women and histories of popular religion and belief. Some of this work, but by no means all, was shaped by the concept of class in one form or another. The eclecticism of urban history and especially of the magnificent collection of essays on *The Victorian City* provides a demonstration of the fruits of diversity.[7] Less happily, the three volumes of *The Cambridge Social History of Britain*, published in 1990 but in most respects redolent of an earlier era, provided an account of modern Britain in which class is a passing but not a structuring presence.[8] Research extended too to the history of popular culture or mentalities; on the growth of respectability, for example. For some, inspired by debates within Marxism, investigating respectability went hand in hand with a search for the aristocracy of labour. But another source was the work of G. S. R. Kitson Clark and his former research students. For Kitson Clark the rise of respectability did not express the dynamic of class relations so much as the outcome of engaged Anglican social leadership. As this suggests, the diversity of social history extended also to the intellectual and political influences that social historians carried with them in these years.[9]

Yet despite these wide-ranging origins, the debates which marked the diminishing authority of social history neglected the baggy heterogeneity of the field.[10] They often focused narrowly on the issue of class – and class in the nineteenth century, at that. Contributors moved quickly from their concern with the salience of 'class' for particular historical developments – the character of Chartism, for example, or the reasons for the emergence of the Labour Party – to assess 'the claims of specifically social historical explanation'. At this point, the fate of a certain interpretation of class in a particular period stood for the viability of

[7] Harold James Dyos and Michael Wolff (eds), *The Victorian City: Images and Realities*, 2 vols (London, 1973).

[8] F. M. L Thompson (ed.), *The Cambridge Social History of Britain, 1750–1950*, 3 vols (Cambridge, 1990).

[9] Robert Q. Gray, *The Labour Aristocracy in Victorian Edinburgh* (Oxford, 1976); Geoffrey Crossick, *An Artisan Elite in Victorian Society: Kentish London 1840–80* (London, 1978); F. M. L. Thompson, *The Rise of Respectable Society: A Social History of Victorian Britain, 1830–1900* (London, 1988); also Brian Harrison, *Peaceable Kingdom: Stability and Change in Modern Britain* (Oxford, 1982); see Miles Taylor, 'The beginnings of modern British social history?', *History Workshop Journal*, 43, (1997), pp. 155–176, which traces the broader contours of this non-Marxian post-war social history.

[10] These debates did arise elsewhere, however. See, for example, Jane Rendall, '"Uneven developments": women's history, feminist history and gender history in Great Britain', in Karen Offen, R. R. Pierson and Jane Rendall (eds), *Writing Women's History: International Perspectives* (London, 1991).

social history in general.[11] If we keep in mind the pluralism of social history in the 1960s and 1970s, this was a strikingly narrow denouement.

Class could perform this role, in part, because it brought together so many facets of the new social history. This was despite – or perhaps because of – continuing debate over what the term meant, how the phenomenon was constituted and where it could be found. In British historiography, the central question for many social historians had been why, under the impact of rapid industrialisation, the disorder, popular protest and acute anxiety of the propertied classes in the first half of the nineteenth century had given way to the contained conflicts and relative stability of 'the age of equipoise' and the successes of popular liberalism. These questions inspired influential approaches to class as diverse as those of Harold Perkin – who constituted classes and the dynamics of conflict through contending class ideals – and John Foster – who sought to vindicate Marxism–Leninism in his account of *Class Struggle and the Industrial Revolution*.[12] The narrative of crisis, containment and development inspired a vast corpus of research work on the labour aristocracy, respectability, popular culture and social control.

Beyond this, however, class has a special relevance for what seemed to be the central, epoch-defining, event in modern British history – the Industrial Revolution. In part this is because Friedrich Engels's account of conditions in Manchester and other cities made a vital contribution to Karl Marx's theory of history and programme of revolution driven by class struggles.[13] More generally, the combination of urbanisation, commercial growth and factory industry led many contemporaries to contemplate the impact of these changes on social relations and political stability, and as they did so they often used the terminology of class.[14] Historians of nineteenth- and twentieth-century Britain are able to find the terminology of class in their source materials in ways that historians of earlier periods do not. Moreover, because of the centrality of class to both Marxist and non-Marxist accounts of modern society, these references seemed to be especially significant.

---

[11] Robert Gray, 'Class, politics and historical revisionism', *Social History*, 19, (1994), pp. 210–211. For a similar formulation see Marc W. Steinberg, 'Culturally speaking: finding a commons between post-structuralism and the Thompsonian perspective', *Social History*, 21, (1996), pp. 193–214, at p. 194. See also Patrick Joyce 'The end of social history?', *Social History*, 20, (1995), pp. 73–91.

[12] Harold Perkin, *The Origins of Modern English Society, 1780–1880* (London, 1969); John Foster, *Class Struggle and the Industrial Revolution: Early Industrial Capitalism in Three English Towns* (London, 1974).

[13] See Tristram Hunt's chapter in this volume.

[14] Asa Briggs, 'The language of class in early nineteenth-century England', in Briggs and Saville, *Essays in Labour History*.

As mention of Marx indicates, social history was also shaped by its political engagements. The partisan energy generated by the highly technical debate on the standard of living in the late eighteenth and early nineteenth centuries was due in large measure to the way these exchanges were not only about a confined historical problem but also concerned, in the context of the Cold War, the historic effects of capitalism and the free market more generally.[15] Increasingly it was by researching and interrogating class that historians developed a reciprocal relationship between their political beliefs and scholarly expertise. These were, indeed, the years of the forward march of labour in which the trade union movement achieved unprecedented numerical strength and political influence, in which the Labour Party claimed to represent, among other things, the interests of 'labour', and when debate on the left focused on whether these interests were best advanced from within that party or outside it. In this context the relationship between working-class formation and working-class politics in the nineteenth century held a special significance. For the emergence of class and the development of an organised labour movement appeared to be the lasting legacy of the nineteenth century, one that disclosed the historic trajectory of the British left and that continued to shape the present. The History Workshop movement and the first appearance of *History Workshop Journal: A Journal of Socialist Historians* in 1976 made these connections overt. Several of the exchanges in these years – on the history of trade unionism, for example, or on the relationship between class and sexual difference – had resonances in, or even clear implications for, the present.[16]

Yet even before social history came under radical theoretical attack its explanatory power was weakening. In part this arose from its own success. Notably, the pursuit of 'experience', inspired by some of Edward Thompson's programmatic statements and by history from below more broadly, brought to light a whole range of experiences that could not be contained within the class paradigm (or sometimes even within left politics). Here the impact of feminism and women's history

[15] Peter Mathias, 'Preface' in Arthur J. Taylor (ed.), *The Standard of Living in Britain in the Industrial Revolution* (London, 1975), pp. vii–viii.
[16] Richard Price, *Masters, Unions and Men: Work Control in Building and the Rise of Labour* (Cambridge, 1980); Jonathan. Zeitlin, 'The emergence of shop steward organisation and job control in the British car industry', *History Workshop Journal*, 10, (1980), pp. 119–137; Dave Lyddon, 'Workplace organisation in the British car industry', *History Workshop Journal*, 15, (1983), pp. 131–140; Barbara Taylor, *Eve and the New Jerusalem: Socialism and Feminism in the Nineteenth Century* (London, 1983); Sally Alexander, 'Women, class and sexual difference', *History Workshop Journal*, 17, (1984), pp. 125–149.

was crucial. But the general point extended more widely as historians' exploration of experience revealed just how diverse this had been.[17] New histories of the Industrial Revolution were also corrosive. Both quantitative and qualitative studies now revealed that industrialisation was a slower and longer process than had been imagined in the 1960s.[18] Yet this now discredited view of the Industrial Revolution had underpinned the work of Perkin, Foster and others. These difficulties were most keenly felt and understood by those historians who had turned to social history to generate histories of society as a whole. The idea that social history might generate such a total history began to appear less and less likely as diversity made synthesis, at the societal level, more problematic, and as the foundational concept of the Industrial Revolution appeared a less dependable basis for the edifice. Finally, in 1979 the left in Britain experienced the first in a historic series of political defeats. It had not only been historians of the left who had been drawn to social history or to the history of class, but undoubtedly they had exerted a huge influence on discussion and debate. For these figures, the repeated defeats of the 1980s and 1990s prompted radical questioning about the direction of history, the role of the labour movement and the historical significance of 'class'.

Most fundamentally, in the early 1980s social history came under attack from historians who questioned the place of material life in historical explanation and who focused instead on the ways identities and interests are created *within* culture. This shift from society to culture, from an exploration of experiences and structures to meanings and identities, registered not only in history but across the humanities and social sciences. One salutary effect was to renew and extend the field of study. Historians were now able to ask how identities which appeared to be 'natural' or a part of 'common sense' had, in fact, been invented, sustained and transformed discursively. The work of Michel Foucault was hugely influential here, leading historians to focus on the relationships between these discursive structures and the operation of power. Accordingly, the burgeoning field of women's history now turned, not to the recovery of women's experiences, but to the processes through which

[17] The growing attention to the history of immigrants and of antipathy towards immigrants is just one area where the pursuit of experience burst the bounds of class. Kenneth Lunn (ed.), *Hosts, Immigrants and Minorities: Historical Responses to Newcomers in British Society, 1870–1914* (Folkestone, 1980) was a path-breaking collection. Roger Swift and Sheridan Gilley (eds), *The Irish in the Victorian City* (London, 1985) also helped to define the trend.

[18] Raphael Samuel, '"The workshop of the world": steam power and hand technology in mid-Victorian Britain', *History Workshop Journal*, 3, (1977), pp. 6–72; G. N. Von Tunzelmann, *Steam Power and British Industrialization* (Oxford, 1978); Nicholas F. R. Crafts, *British Economic Growth during the Industrial Revolution* (Oxford, 1985).

gender differences were made. This shift registered more widely as similar questions extended to sexual identities and the politics of the body, to national identities, to tradition, to race and ethnicity, and of course to class itself.[19]

The turn to culture, discourse and meaning thus opened new horizons but obscured others. As early as 1991, Raphael Samuel wrote alarmed by 'the self-conscious drive to make representation the only significant field of study'.[20] In 1995 Patrick Joyce argued that 'the salutary effect of postmodernist thought might be said to lie in its invitation to question the idea of a clear distinction between representation and the "real"'. He suggests that our perception of the reality of the past can never be apprehended apart from the discursive categories of the texts we study. The role of the historian is then to 'trace the discursivities of the social' and in this way histories of 'society' and of 'class' may still be written.[21] This suggestion did not go unanswered, but the interests of succeeding cohorts of historians have moved away from social history as it was once conceived. It is not that social history is no longer practised but, contrary to the hope expressed in 1976, it is now firmly established as one branch of historical scholarship among many. In place of the ambition for a 'total' social history, the emphasis is now very much on the reconstruc-tion of 'the social' at the micro level: on the careful analysis of the small-scale and the immediate – on how human beings interact with each other and with the material world. This new 'material' turn comes in many forms, from the resolutely post-modern to the stubbornly empiricist, but it is striking how a common lexicon of keywords seems to dominate – 'everyday life', 'material culture', 'place', 'practice' and 'network' stand out.[22] Across a range of topics, from the family and sexual practices, to

---

[19] Jeffrey Weeks, *Sex, Politics and Society: The Regulation of Sexuality since 1800* (London, 1981); Gareth Stedman Jones, *Languages of Class: Studies in English Working Class History, 1832–1982*, (Cambridge, 1983); Joan Scott, 'On language, gender, and working-class history', *International Labor and Working-Class History*, 31, (1987), pp. 1–13; Robert Colls and Philip Dodd, *Englishness: Politics and Culture* (Beckenham, 1986); Denise Riley, *'Am I that Name?' Feminism and the Category of 'Women' in History* (Basingstoke, 1988); Judith R. Walkowitz, *City of Dreadful Delight: Narratives of Sexual Danger in Late-Victorian London* (London, 1992); Dror Wahrman, *Imagining the Middle Class: The Political Representation of Class in Britain, c.1780–1840* (Cambridge, 1995); Catherine Hall, *Civilising Subjects: Metropole and Colony in the English Imagination 1830–67* (Cambridge, 2002).

[20] Raphael Samuel, 'Reading the signs', *History Workshop Journal*, 32, (1991), pp. 88–101, at p. 96.

[21] Joyce, 'The end of social history?', pp. 78, 83–84.

[22] Patrick Joyce (ed.), *The Social in Question: New Bearings in History and the Social Sciences* (London, 2002); Frank Trentmann, 'Materiality in the future of history: things, practices and politics', *Journal of British Studies*, 48, (2009), pp. 283–307.

the domestic interior and the neighbourhood, social history therefore remains dynamic and innovative, even if there is much less confidence that a holistic picture can be constructed from these fragments of the past.[23] Much of this work now eschews speculating on connections between the social and political, although particularly among the more empirically minded there remains an underlying emphasis on the determining role of material life.[24] At the same time, in their emphasis on language and the techniques of 'governmentality', many political historians have continued to speculate on connections with society and social change, though for the most part now in contingent or particular, rather than structural ways.[25]

Stedman Jones and British history

This broad story of historiographical change is also Stedman Jones's story, but not, it must be stressed, in any simple sense. Stedman Jones's relationship to social history was always that of the critical outsider. He admired it for challenging the narrowness and conservatism of mainstream historical practice, but his own principal interests and enthusiasm often lay elsewhere: in reconstructing the interrelated history of economic structures, ideas and politics, rather than in the popular cry to write new histories 'from below'. From his student days Stedman Jones had been a strident advocate of the need to reject the complacent traditions of empiricism and positivism in British historiography, and he consistently challenged the illusion that empiricist history was somehow non-ideological and non-theoretical.[26] In this he was allied to key

---

[23] Simon Szreter, *Fertility, Class and Gender in Britain, 1860–1940* (Cambridge, 1996); Leonore Davidoff, Megan Doolittle, Janet Fish and Katherine Holden, *The Family Story: Blood, Contract and Intimacy, 1830–1960,* (London, 1999); Kate Fisher, *Birth Control, Sex and Marriage in Britain, 1918–1960* (Oxford, 2006); Deborah Cohen, *Household Gods: The British and their Possessions* (New Haven, CN, 2006); Trevor Griffiths, *The Lancashire Working Classes, c.1880–1930* (Oxford, 2001); Marc Brodie, *The Politics of the Poor: The East End of London, 1885–1914* (Oxford, 2004); Selina Todd, *Young Women, Work, and Family in England, 1918–1950* (Oxford, 2005).

[24] E.g. Griffiths, *Lancashire*; Brodie, *Politics of the Poor*.

[25] Patrick Joyce, *Visions of the People: Industrial England and the Question of Class* (Cambridge, 1991) and *The Rule of Freedom: Liberalism and the Modern City* (London, 2003); James Vernon, *Politics and the People: A Study in English Political Culture, c.1815–1867* (Cambridge, 1993) and *Hunger: A Modern History* (Cambridge, MA, 2007). For an attempt to explore the inter-connection of structure and discourse, see Jon Lawrence, *Speaking for the People: Party, Language and Popular Politics in England, 1867–1914* (Cambridge, 1998); Geoff Eley, *A Crooked Line: From Cultural History to the History of Society* (Ann Arbor, MI, 2005), adopts a similar position.

[26] Stedman Jones, 'The pathology of English history', *New Left Review* [hereafter *NLR*], 46, (November–December 1967), pp. 29–43; reprinted as 'History: the poverty of

figures of the new 'New Left' in the early 1960s; notably writers such as Perry Anderson, Stuart Hall and Tom Nairn, who were also engaging with the work of European intellectuals, including Antonio Gramsci, Georg Lukács, Jean-Paul Sartre and, somewhat later, Louis Althusser, in an attempt to challenge what they perceived to be the insularity of the older generation of English socialist intellectuals including Marxists such as Edward Thompson and Raymond Williams, as well as more orthodox 'Labourist' figures such as Margaret Cole and Henry Pelling.[27] In 1967, Stedman Jones declared that socialist historians must abandon the 'safe pastures of labour history' and the 'cosy humanitarian niche which liberal historians have always been all too happy to accord to them'. Instead they should 'establish the *theoretical* foundations of any history, they should advance into the structure and history of the ruling class, into the interpretation of the historical morphology of whole cultures. They should follow the example of perhaps the most successfully revolutionary group of modern historians – the *Annales* school.'[28]

Looking back on this period in 1984, Stedman Jones recalled being attracted by the 'cultural iconoclasm' of the *New Left Review*, and acknowledged that 'the political and cultural positions pioneered by the *New Left Review*' had been an important influence on him in the 1960s.[29] Stedman Jones first wrote for the *New Left Review* in November 1964, when he was just 21 (reviewing Donald Read's *The English Provinces c1760–1960*) and he served on the journal's editorial board continuously from 1965 to 1983.[30] But although Stedman Jones shared the New Left's emphasis on the relevance of current political dilemmas for the writing of history, he nonetheless always privileged the demands of

empiricism' in Robin Blackburn (ed.), *Ideology in Social Science: Readings in Critical Social Theory* (London, 1972); Stedman Jones, 'From historical sociology to theoretical history', *British Journal of Sociology* 27, (1976), pp. 295–305, at p. 296; also his 'History in one dimension', *NLR*, 36, (March–April 1966), pp. 48–58, reviewing A. J. P. Taylor, *English History, 1914–1945*.

[27] Chun Lin, *The British New Left: A Critical History 1957–1977* (Edinburgh, 1993); Dennis Dworkin, *Cultural Marxism in Postwar Britain: History, the New Left, and the Origins of Cultural Studies* (Durham, NC, 1997); Duncan Thompson, *Pessimism of the Intellect?: A History of New Left Review* (Monmouth, 2007); Madeleine Davis, 'The origins of the British New Left' in Martin Klimke and Joachim Sharloth (eds), *1968 in Europe: A History of Protest and Activism, 1956–1977* (Basingstoke, 2008). See also Stedman Jones, 'Anglo-Marxism, neo-Marxism and the discursive approach to history' in Alf Lüdtke (ed.), *Was bleibt von marxistischen Perpektiven in der Geschichtsforschung?* (Göttingen, 1997), at pp. 159–163.

[28] Stedman Jones, 'Pathology of English history', p. 43.

[29] Gareth Stedman Jones, *Outcast London: A Study in the Relationship between Classes in Victorian London* (1971: London, 1984), 'Preface to the 1984 edition', pp. xiii–xiv.

[30] Thompson, *Pessimism?*, pp. 10, 123–124, 172; *NLR*, 29, (January–February 1965), 'Editorial Board'.

professional historical scholarship over immediate political purposes – his was neither a didactic history to inspire the present generation, nor an overarching meta-history, such as that associated with the *New Left Review*, with its emphasis on the supposedly arrested political and intellectual development of Britain compared with continental Europe.[31] Hence his early interest in reconstructing the micro-contexts that had sustained the latent Toryism of an apolitical working class in late nineteenth-century London, as well as his emphasis on the fragility of radical sub-cultures and the inherent difficulties of mass mobilisation. Significantly, he recalls that his original intention as a graduate student had been to recast the *New Left Review*'s central question 'Why no British revolutionary tradition?' by asking instead the more overtly historical question: 'Why the triumph of liberal ideas and assumptions among the mass of the population?'[32] As this determination to recast the New Left's pessimistic, counter-factual analysis suggests, Stedman Jones was never wholly aligned with the Anderson/Nairn circle, nor was he ever as comfortable as them with history as sweeping polemic laid down by a New Left clerisy. Perhaps significantly, *Outcast London*, published in 1971 when Stedman Jones was 28, included thanks both to Edward Thompson and to Perry Anderson. But, by then, it was already clear that Stedman Jones's closest intellectual ties were to Raphael Samuel, a central figure in the first New Left of the late 1950s and, like Stedman Jones, subsequently an intellectually restless and un-doctrinaire member of the broad 'New Left' (though, after the 'restructuring' of 1961–1962, crucially *not* part of Anderson's inner circle at the *Review*).[33]

Perhaps most importantly, Samuel was the founding spirit of the History Workshop movement at Ruskin College, Oxford in 1966 (when Stedman Jones was a graduate at Nuffield College). From the outset, the ethos of Samuel's history workshops was radically different from the self-consciously intellectual spirit that characterised the *New Left Review*. Though never overtly populist, the History Workshop movement was avowedly popular – its aim was to promote grass-roots historical practice within a broadly socialist–feminist culture (though *History Workshop* only

---

[31] See esp. Perry Anderson, 'Origins of the present crisis', *NLR*, 23, (January–February 1964), pp. 19–45, and 'Components of the national culture', *NLR*, 50, (July–August 1968), pp. 3–57.

[32] Stedman Jones, *Outcast London*, '1984 Preface', pp. xiv–xv; also in his 'History and theory: an English story', *Historein: A Review of the Past and Other Stories* [Athens], 3, (2001), pp. 103–124, at pp. 109–110 [available at www.nnet.gr/historein/historeinfiles/histvolumes/hist03/hist03stedman.htm].

[33] Stedman Jones, *Outcast London* [1971 edn], pp. v–vi, and 'Raphael Samuel: obituary', *The Independent*, 11 December 1996; Michael Kenny, *The First New Left: British Intellectuals after Stalin* (London, 1995), p. 29; Thompson, *Pessimism?*, pp. 7–8.

became explicitly a journal of socialist 'and feminist' historians in 1982).[34] Writing in 2001, Stedman Jones observed that 'Its most important characteristic is the pluralism that was built into it from the start' (in contrast to what he termed 'the furtive mandarin Leninism that increasingly informed the perspectives of the *Review*').[35] For three decades, until his premature death in 1996, Raphael Samuel personified not only the History Workshop movement, but the possibility of combining the humanism and popular sympathies of older English radical traditions with the theoretical sophistication and intellectual openness of the New Left at its best.

Throughout the 1960s and 1970s, Stedman Jones still identified himself with the project of a new social history, but even at this point he understood this project as almost the antithesis of the dominant forms of social history then becoming established in both British and American academia. True, he long acted as the co-ordinator of a dedicated 'Social History Seminar', first at Oxford with Raphael Samuel and Tim Mason, and then for many years at Cambridge (only in the mid-1990s was it finally renamed the 'Themes in Modern History Seminar').[36] As he later recalled, the aim of these seminars had been to bring together champions of a broad range of new historical methods who were 'united mainly by a common ambition to break out from the narrow confines of political and constitutional history'.[37] But, like Tony Judt and Geoff Eley, two early members of the Cambridge Social History Seminar, Stedman Jones was already a fierce critic of social history's tendency either to ignore politics and the state, or to understand both through ill-digested and essentially ahistorical social science paradigms.[38] By contrast, Stedman Jones argued that social history should aspire to be a totalising, theoretically

---

[34] *History Workshop Journal*, 1, (1976), pp. 1–3 [editorial statement], and 13 (1982), pp. 1–2 ['History Workshop Journal and feminism']; Raphael Samuel, 'History workshop, 1966–80' in Samuel (ed.), *People's History and Socialist Theory* (London, 1981), at pp. 410–417; Dworkin, *Cultural Marxism*, pp. 184–205.

[35] Stedman Jones, 'History and theory', pp. 115–116 – he had resigned from the *New Left Review* board in 1983, see *NLR*, 142, (November–December 1983), p. 5 [editorial].

[36] The seminar continued under this title until 2001, but Stedman Jones's principal energies had by then long been devoted to the seminar series organised by the Centre for History and Economics which he had established with Emma Rothschild at King's College in 1991.

[37] Stedman Jones, 'History and theory', p. 111.

[38] Stedman Jones and Raphael Samuel, 'Sociology and history', *History Workshop Journal*, 1, (1976), pp. 6–8; Stedman Jones, 'From historical sociology', and 'Class expression versus social control: a critique of recent trends in the social history of leisure', *History Workshop Journal*, 4, (1977), pp. 162–170, reproduced in *Languages of Class*; Tony Judt, 'A clown in regal purple: social history and the historians' *History Workshop Journal*, 7, (1979); Geoff Eley and Keith Nield, 'Why does social history ignore politics?', *Social History*, 5, (1980), pp. 249–271.

informed historical method – not something that sought to analyse the 'social' in supposed isolation from politics, economics or culture (including, of course, ideas). It was this 'totalising' version of the social history project that informed *Outcast London*. In it, he brought together urban history, economic history (including the analysis of labour markets and poverty), social anthropology (through his focus on 'the deformation of the gift') and the history of ideas and social policy. But unlike historians influenced by E. P. Thompson, he displayed relatively little interest in reconstructing the 'experience' of poverty. Rather, his concern was to understand how those with social, economic and political power had responded to the perceived challenge of poverty (and of the poor) at the heart of Britain's imperial capital. True, the book was sub-titled 'a study in the relationship between classes in Victorian society', but this was understood largely in ideological and social policy terms, rather than as a call to reconstruct day-to-day interactions across the class divide.

But then, as he made clear in the celebrated essay 'Working-class culture and working-class politics' (1974), which did attempt to open up the question of 'experience', Stedman Jones perceived the culture of the London poor to be largely sealed off from outside influences by the late nineteenth century.[39] In this essay, Stedman Jones sought to make sense of the cultural and political gulf between E. P. Thompson's early nineteenth-century radical working class of *The Making of the English Working Class* (1963) and Richard Hoggart's conservative, inward-looking, mid-twentieth-century working class of *The Uses of Literacy* (1957) – hence the essay's subtitle – 'notes on the remaking of a working class'.[40] He sought to reconcile 'the cultural, economic and political history of the working class' by portraying London workers' 'estrangement from political activity' as rooted in the material realities of their lives (notably casual labour and increased domesticity) and the 'enclosed and defensive' culture that this bred: a culture of the pub, sport and music hall.[41] In many ways the essay captured the zeitgeist of the early 1970s, as historians reflected on contemporary debates about working-class 'reformism' and 'instrumentalism'.[42] It also represented Stedman

---

[39] Stedman Jones, 'Working-class culture and working-class politics in London, 1870–1900: notes on the remaking of a working class', *Journal of Social History*, 7, (1974), pp. 460–509 (reprinted in *Languages of class*).

[40] Stedman Jones, 'History and theory', p. 116, where he confesses to not having 'read through' Thompson's masterpiece before writing *Outcast London*.

[41] Stedman Jones, 'Working-class culture', pp. 462–463, 498–500.

[42] For example John Goldthorpe, David Lockwood, Frank Bechhofer and Jennifer Platt, *The Affluent Worker*, 3 vols (Cambridge, 1968–1969); Robert Roberts, *The Classic Slum: Salford Life in the First Quarter of the Century* (Manchester, 1971); Ross McKibbin, *The Evolution of the Labour Party, 1910–1924*, (London, 1974).

Jones's most developed attempt to sketch out the social and cultural dimensions of a structural 'total history'. Although a *tour de force*, this was not a stable intellectual terminus. As Stedman Jones later reflected, it was not clear why districts still dominated by broadly the same social and economic structures as those of the 1890s should, a few decades later, generate radical political movements including 'Poplarism' and communism. Writing in the early 1980s, he explained that at this stage, 'I did not possess a clear conception of the limits of social explanation, i.e. in what senses the political could not be inferred from the social'.[43]

One consequence of his 'linguistic turn' has been that Stedman Jones, like so many others, has become much more uncertain about the possibility of writing history that claims to be 'total' in this earlier sense. In the preface to the 1984 edition of *Outcast London* he recalls the strong influence of the *Annales* school on his early work, and how this shaped the ambition 'to reconstruct historical totalities – a rather grandiose ambition which I had conceived from a blending of the theories of Lukacs and the historical work of Braudel'.[44] By 2001, he recalled this period as one in which he had been gripped by 'the fantasy that it was possible to construct some structuralist version of *l'histoire totale*'.[45] But as these comments suggest, not only were Stedman Jones's theoretical interests always diverse, they were also always shaped by substantive historical questions. Theory was a tool to be used heuristically, not something that should enslave the historian, closing off, rather than opening up, new questions. As he stressed in a 1976 essay on 'theoretical history', 'like any other "social science"', history 'is an entirely intellectual operation which takes place in the present and in the head'. The historian, he argued, combines technical skills for evaluating 'the residues of the past' with the 'more important . . . active intellectual' task of determining which residues possess 'historical significance, and what significance they possess' for answering specific 'historical problems'.[46] In this sense, not only did all history depend on 'some explicit or implicit theory of social causation', but the 'adequacy' of any theory was to be judged by the significance of the problems it helped one to formulate, not the conceptual neatness of the answers it supplied. In this respect, we would argue, Gareth Stedman Jones has always been a methodological pluralist, even if at times his declamatory style has rather obscured this

---

[43] Stedman Jones, *Languages of Class*, pp. 10–11; also *Outcast London*, '1984 Preface', p. xvi.

[44] Stedman Jones, *Outcast London* '1984 Preface', p. xiv; see also his 'The Marxism of the early Lukács: an evaluation', *NLR*, 70, (November–December 1971), pp. 27–64.

[45] Stedman Jones, 'History and theory', p. 111.

[46] Stedman Jones, 'From historical sociology', p. 296.

flexibility. In the 1960s, his determination to challenge the perceived English phobia about theory tended to obscure his own intellectual eclecticism, while more recently his advocacy of a 'discursive' approach to history has sometimes been couched in a dogmatic language which appears all but to preclude the possibility of writing other forms of history.[47]

But these texts are not typical, nor, crucially, are they reflective of how Stedman Jones has worked as a practising historian. For one thing, Stedman Jones has generally worn theory lightly. Even in *Languages of Class* the closest he came to claiming theoretical legitimacy for his decisive break with the Thompsonian emphasis on 'experience' and 'class consciousness' was a rather elliptic reference to the polemics of French post-structuralism:

What this [the Thompsonian] approach cannot acknowledge is all the criticism which has been levelled at it since the broader significance of Saussure's work was understood – the materiality of language itself, the impossibility of simply referring back to some primal anterior reality, 'social being', the impossibility of abstracting experience from the language which structures its articulation.[48]

Perhaps not surprisingly, Stedman Jones has been taken to task for the partial nature of his linguistic turn in the 1980s.[49] By contrast, we would argue that Stedman Jones was using structuralist linguistic theory for a specific purpose: to redefine the 'historical problem' of Chartism's rise and fall and, more broadly, of the relationship between industrialisation and the politics of radical protest. Not only was he happy to acknowledge the limiting role of the 'social realm', and the continued validity of 'social interpretation', but his whole argument about the declining purchase of Chartist discourse hinged on an essentially realist conception of the central state that would be broadly recognisable to social-science historians such as Theda Skocpol.[50] Reviewing the reception of *Outcast London* in 1984, a year after *Languages of Class* appeared, Stedman Jones was still happy to defend his earlier use of poverty studies and other

[47] Stedman Jones, 'Pathology of English history', esp. pp. 29 and 43; *Languages of Class*, pp. 21, 24; Stedman Jones, 'The determinist fix: some obstacles to the further development of the linguistic approach to history in the 1990s', *History Workshop Journal* 42, (1996), pp. 19–35, esp. pp. 28–30 (an abridged version of the essay in Lüdtke, *Was bleibt?*).
[48] Stedman Jones, *Languages of Class*, p. 20.
[49] For instance Scott, 'On language'; Peter Schöttler, 'Historians and discourse analysis', *History Workshop Journal*, 27, (1989), pp. 37–65, at pp. 45–48.
[50] Stedman Jones, *Languages of Class*, pp. 95, 242; Jon Lawrence, *Speaking*, pp. 50–52; Theda Skocpol, *States and Social Revolutions: A Comparative Analysis of France, Russia and China* (Cambridge, 1979).

conventional socio-economic sources as referent points against which to decode 'middle-class mythologies about the casual poor' – rejecting more purist post-structural arguments that such sources should only be studied discursively.[51] In doing so, he observed that, 'It is a problem inescapably faced by any critical history of social or economic policy' – i.e. any history not content merely to describe past discourses. Indeed, at the end of this retrospective essay he concedes only that, 'if I were attempting to write *Outcast London* today, I would attempt to formulate the problem in a *slightly* different fashion' (although it has to be acknow-ledged that there are few clues either here, or in *Languages of Class*, as to how this might be done in practice).[52] Similarly, *Metropolis – London*, the collection of essays he co-edited in 1989, contains many contributions with a strong social historical content, while his own essay on the changing representations of the 'cockney' arguably owes more to Hobs-bawm's work on the invention of tradition than to post-structuralism.[53] But then Stedman Jones has never displayed that suspicion of the quan-tifiable and the structural which is characteristic of more avowedly 'cultural' advocates of the linguistic turn. Indeed, since 1991 he has acted as the co-director of the Centre for History and Economics at King's College, Cambridge, which proclaims its aim as being to promote scholarly co-operation 'through the application of economic concepts to historical problems, through the history of economic and social thought, or through economic history'.[54]

In deciding what are the most salient historical questions of the moment Stedman Jones has always been driven, first and foremost, by his perception of what history can tell us about present politics. Down to the late 1970s, this meant, above all, testing the adequacy of the Marxist understanding of both historical change and the dynamics (and contra-dictions) of capitalism as an economic and social system. One has to take seriously Stedman Jones's frequently restated calls throughout this period for a theoretically and historically informed socialist practice. Moreover, this political dimension to his work has not evaporated with his break from Marxism. Throughout the 1980s he continued to write

[51] Samuel had made a similar point about the Victorian census in 1981 in his essay 'History and theory' in *People's History*, p. xlvii.

[52] Stedman Jones, *Outcast London* '1984 Preface', p. xxiv (emphasis added); he was responding to the criticisms of Gertrude Himmelfarb and Karel Williams; Lawrence, *Speaking*, pp. 51–53.

[53] David Feldman and Gareth Stedman Jones (eds), *Metropolis – London: Histories and Representations since 1800* (London, 1989), including his 'The "cockney" and the nation, 1780–1988'.

[54] Centre for History and Economics at www-histecon.kings.cam.ac.uk/index.html.

about the dilemmas of the British and European left, always insisting on the need for an adequately theorised understanding of the historical trajectory of socialist movements as the essential starting point when asking the old Leninist question 'What is to be done?'.[55] With the decline of the European socialist left in the 1990s, Stedman Jones's attention focused more on historicising the myths of globalised liberal economics, and tracing the history, and crucially the continued salience, of past socialist and social democratic aspirations. In *An End to Poverty?* (2004), Stedman Jones explores how and why it became possible, in the late eighteenth century, for thinkers such as Paine and Condorcet to marry the new science of political economy to a radical vision of a more egalitarian society in which human want would be unknown.[56] This is a rigorous case-study in the history of ideas at the birth of the modern, industrial world, and it links directly to his life-long concern to understand the social and intellectual context that shaped radical and revolutionary responses to industrial capitalism.[57] But it was manifestly also conceived as an attempt to historicise the 'truths' of global liberal capitalism, and to restate the intellectual coherence of a radically social-democratic politics aimed at realising the full potential of modern, commercial society. Hence his *Guardian* article 'A history of ending poverty', which explicitly linked the book's themes to the idealistic aspirations of those hoping to see Western governments commit themselves to harness the resources of international commerce to 'end world poverty'.[58] Hence, too, his claim that studying the intellectual history of Europe during and after the French Revolution is not only 'relevant to current political conflict', but can offer a 'helpful contribution to the battles of the present' against the 'age-old sources of greed, exploitation and misery'.[59]

Since the 1990s, Stedman Jones has registered an explicit engagement with the so-called 'Cambridge School' of the history of ideas, associated with Quentin Skinner, J. G. A. Pocock and his colleague at King's

[55] For instance, 'Why the Labour Party is in a mess' *New Socialist*, January–February 1983, reprinted in *Languages of Class* as 'Why is the Labour party in a mess?'; '"Tawneyism" is not enough', *New Statesman*, 21 December 1984, pp. 31–33; 'The rise and fall of French Marxism' in Institute for Contemporary Arts, *Ideas from France* (London, 1985); 'Paternalism revisited: the future of socialism', *Marxism Today* (July 1985), pp. 25–28.
[56] Stedman Jones, *An End to Poverty? A Historical Debate* (London, 2004).
[57] See esp. Stedman Jones, 'Introduction' to Karl Marx and Friedrich Engels, *The Communist Manifesto* (London, 2002), pp. 3–187.
[58] Stedman Jones, 'A history of ending poverty: Tom Paine's ideas are still ahead of today's campaigners', *The Guardian*, 2 July 2005.
[59] Stedman Jones, 'History and theory', pp. 121–122.

College, John Dunn. In his 1996 essay attacking the determinist fallacies of Foucauldian cultural history, Stedman Jones deploys key concepts from this tradition such as 'language games' and 'intentionality', although his emphasis is again on using its methods and insights heuristically to help find 'new ways of connecting social and intellectual history free from the problems embodied in the Marxian notion of ideology'.[60] Hence, too, his declared ambition 'to extend the procedures and discriminations developed in the study of intellectual and cultural history to encompass the broader domains of social and political history'.[61] Writing in 2001, Stedman Jones acknowledged that working on the history of political economy and its adversaries in the 1980s[62] had led him to find 'many points of convergence between my own approach and that of the study of intellectual history and the history of political thought, as they had developed in England and especially in Cambridge from the 1960s'. But he also suggested that in its comparative neglect of both religious and economic thought this tradition had proved ill-suited to understanding the dynamic new intellectual and cultural forces at work in the eighteenth and nineteenth centuries.[63]

There can be no doubt that the history of political ideas has dominated Stedman Jones's work since the 1980s. When 'Rethinking Chartism' was published in the early 1980s he was already working (and teaching) primarily on the history of Marxism and other forms of early European socialism.[64] Appointed to a Readership by the University of Cambridge in 1986, Stedman Jones took the title 'Reader in Social Thought', and from 1997 he was Professor of Political Science and a senior member of the university's Political Thought subject group. In one sense the journey from casual labour markets and music hall to the visionary radicalism of Condorcet and Paine may seem a long one, but in truth there has been a remarkable consistency in Stedman Jones's historical interests and analysis. *An End to Poverty?* may start by analysing late eighteenth-century radical interpretations of political economy which sought to overthrow monarchical and aristocratic power, but it

[60] Stedman Jones, 'Determinist fix', p. 20.   [61] Ibid., p. 28.

[62] Notably through the King's College research project that led to Istvan Hont and Michael Ignatieff (eds), *Wealth and Virtue: The Shaping of Political Economy in the Scottish Enlightenment* (Cambridge, 1983).

[63] Stedman Jones, 'History and theory', p. 119.

[64] Significant texts include, 'Engels and the genesis of Marxism', *NLR*, 106, (1977), pp. 79–104; 'Utopian socialism reconsidered', in Raphael Samuel (ed.) *People's History and Socialist Theory* (London, 1981); and his book-length introduction to Marx and Engels, *Communist Manifesto*.

ends with the triumph of a much more conservative variant of social reform in the era of *Outcast London* – an era epitomised by the work of Samuel Barnett and Arnold Toynbee, and by the politics of the early Labour Party.[65] Indeed, in writing of 'Labour's singular ability to combine within one credo a commitment to socialise all means of production, distribution and exchange, with an almost Burkean respect for monarchical and aristocratic institutions', one could argue that he comes close to synthesising the New Left positions of Thompson and Anderson.[66] What is clear is that, as in the 1960s, his work remains firmly focused on understanding the connections between economic change and political radicalism – though where once he assumed this relationship to be socially determined, his focus now is much more squarely on how thinkers, and political actors, have understood the changes taking place around them. 'Structures' and 'transformations' remain central to Stedman Jones's work, even if understanding structural change in society and economy is no longer assumed to hold the key to understanding transformations in politics and culture.

Where we are now

One thing is surely clear: as we write there is no new 'total history' on the horizon, straining to resurrect social history's brief moment of imperial ambition in the 1970s. Together, the undimmed influence of the 'cultural turn', social history's shift from macro- to micro-analysis, and political history's focus on questions of language and institutional practice, underscore the limited prospects for any return to 'total history' in this earlier sense. There is, however, growing recognition of the need to interrogate connections between politics and culture on the one hand, and society and economy on the other. Indeed, this is merely part of a broader trend in recent scholarship stressing the need to reconstruct patterns of *interconnection*. Within political history one finds an emphasis on studying the interaction between politicians and public, often shaped by an explicit desire to bridge unhelpful distinctions between 'high' and 'low' politics.[67] There is also a growing interest in tracing the processes whereby political ideas make the transition from intellectual debate to

---

[65] Stedman Jones, *End to poverty?*, pp. 207–235.   [66] Ibid., p. 230.
[67] Martin Francis, 'Tears, tantrums and bared teeth: the emotional economy of three Conservative Prime Ministers, 1951–1963', *Journal of British Studies*, 41, (2002), pp. 354–387; Jon Lawrence, 'Political history' in Stefan Berger, Heiko Feldner and Kevin Passmore (eds), *Writing History: Theory and Practice*, 2nd edn. (London, 2010), and *Electing our Masters: The Hustings in British Politics from Hogarth to Blair* (Oxford, 2009).

practical politics.[68] Perhaps most significantly, there has been a new-found determination to explore (rather than simply assert) the global connections that have shaped modern British history. The interconnections between colony and metropole have naturally received particular attention,[69] but there has also been a growing interest in tracing both the interconnections between the four nations of the 'British Isles',[70] and also the ways in which Britain's global engagements have shaped both society and polity.[71]

Accordingly, there is now probably more talk of 'process' than 'structure' among those keen to knit together the historical fragments. Where 'structure' is still invoked, the emphasis tends to be on a plurality of 'structures', rooted more in discourse (structures of meaning) or techniques of governance (structures of practice), rather than a single, grand structure rooted in society and economy. The vogue for discussing the distinctive discourses and practices of 'liberal modernity' or 'post-modernity' reminds us that these more pluralistic structures are still assumed to be linked to broad processes of epochal change, but the precise nature of this connection is generally assumed to be either contingent or irrecoverable.[72] Instead, the focus tends to be on reconstructing discourses or practices, and charting their change over time (description rather than explanation predominates, reflecting the diminished role for claims of 'causality' since the cultural turn). The twelve essays collected in this volume naturally reflect many of these recent historiographical trends – they are, after all, the product of their time. Claims about causation tend to be cautious, and couched in terms of plausibility rather than certainty; discourses and state practices loom large, and no one writes as

---

[68] E. H. H. Green and D. M. Tanner (eds), *The Strange Survival of Liberal England: Political Leaders, Moral Values and the Reception of Economic Debate* (Cambridge, 2007), 'Introduction'; Frank Trentmann, *Free Trade Nation: Commerce, Consumption and Civil Society in Modern Britain* (Oxford, 2008).

[69] Miles Taylor, 'The 1848 revolutions and the British empire', *Past & Present*, 166, (2000), pp. 146–180; Kathleen Wilson (ed.), *A New Imperial History: Culture, Identity and Modernity in Britain and Empire, 1660–1840* (Cambridge, 2004); Catherine Hall and Sonya O. Rose (eds), *At Home with the Empire: Metropolitan Culture and the Imperial World* (Cambridge, 2006); Susan D. Pennybacker, *From Scottsboro to Munich: Race and Political Culture in 1930s Britain* (Princeton, NJ, 2009); Vernon, *Hunger*.

[70] Colin Harvie, *A Floating Commonwealth: Politics, Culture, and Technology on Britain's Atlantic Coast, 1860–1930* (Oxford, 2008); Eugenio Biagini, *British Democracy and Irish Nationalism, 1876–1906* (Cambridge, 2007).

[71] David Armitage and Michael J. Braddick (eds), *The British Atlantic World, 1500–1800*, 2nd edn. (Basingstoke, 2009); David Armitage, *Greater Britain, 1516–1776: Essays in Atlantic History* (Aldershot, 2004); Trentmann, *Free Trade Nation*.

[72] Joyce, *Rule of Freedom*; Vernon, *Hunger*; Chris Otter, *The Victorian Eye: A Political History of Light and Vision in Britain, 1800–1910* (Chicago, IL, 2008).

though a single, overarching structure might provide the key to historical explanation. On the other hand, as the title suggests, there is a strong emphasis not just on change, but on the close examination of key transformative moments or 'conjunctures'. One also finds a sustained interest in exploring connections – between society and culture, between colony and metropole, between economy and politics, though always from a non-determinist perspective. Indeed, one of the key themes ranging across otherwise quite diverse chapters is a determination to reopen old questions about the relationship between long-term socio-economic change and changes in culture and practice.

This takes four distinct forms. A number of chapters deal directly with the nature and the consequences of rapid demographic change between the mid-eighteenth and mid-nineteenth centuries (Wrigley, Griffin, Hunt); others explore transnational networks, especially those between Britain and its empire, within the context of long-term socio-economic change (Finn, Summers, Feldman); or the specific problem of how we connect cultural politics to social change (Pick, Reid). Finally, as befits a book in honour of Gareth Stedman Jones, there is a clutch of chapters exploring the relationship between radical politics and changes in society and state across the nineteenth and twentieth centuries (Innes, Parry, Howkins, Hunt, and Lawrence).

Tony Wrigley's powerful essay reminds us how the work of the Cambridge Population Group on the demography of early modern and modern England effectively rehabilitates the notion of rupture, but associated now, not with industrialisation per se, but with the extraordinary pressure of population growth between the 1790s and the 1830s. Wrigley brings out both the unprecedented nature of this sustained population growth and its highly concentrated character, and he concludes that only the transition to a new type of economy, based on the utilisation of inorganic energy sources, allowed England to escape the subsistence crisis predicted by contemporaries such as Thomas Malthus and the classical economists. Wrigley acknowledges that the crisis was accentuated by the French Revolution and the long years of counter-revolutionary warfare that it sparked, but he reminds us that beneath these political and cultural upheavals lay a dramatic rupture in the population history of England. It was this rupture that created the all too real backdrop for anxious discussions about the possibilities of state amelioration (Innes), or about how to deal with the consequences of rapid, often chaotic, urbanisation (Griffin on the politics of urban 'improvement' and Hunt on the politics of urban social segregation). Indeed, Wrigley's chapter should perhaps be viewed as a reminder of the largely untapped potential of the

Cambridge Population Group's work for reformulating questions in the social and political history of modern Britain.[73]

The second group of essays shifts the focus to Britain's global connections through trade, empire and cultural exchange (in the process reminding us that alongside the inorganic economy it was almost certainly the growth, and the terms, of global trade that allowed Britain to escape demographic crisis). These chapters also remind us that this is one of the key sites where politically engaged historical scholarship remains normative. In their different ways, the chapters by Finn, Summers and Feldman each sets out to challenge some of the instinctive assumptions of that politicised history, but not the idea that developing an adequate understanding of Britain's changing role in the world is intrinsically political. Finn focuses on the ways in which making the empire was intricately connected with the strategies of British families to accumulate economic, social and cultural capital at home. She explores how the regular flow of letters between colony and metropole served both to maintain connections and also to construct an idealised, imaginary version of each. Summers focuses on transnational networks of communication, but her central interest lies in understanding the religious, moral and feminist discourses shaping a distinctive, if fractured, female internationalism during the triumphal decades of British imperialism in the second half of the nineteenth century. In the process, she insists that we do great violence to the complexities of this movement if we insist on understanding it solely from a post-colonial perspective in which privileged British women are assumed to be advancing their own identity claims by objectifying a colonised 'Other'. Finally, Feldman focuses on the moment that 'empire strikes back' by exploring the conservative roots and reflexes of Britain's late twentieth-century politics of 'multiculturalism'.

In the chapters by Daniel Pick and Alastair Reid cultural politics themselves are centre-stage. Pick's chapter explores the reception of Freud and psychoanalysis among British intellectuals, and argues that the indifference and/or hostility displayed by historians was unusual, reflecting the distinctive features of the profession's formation, rather than the wider 'defects' of the national culture. Reid, by contrast, focuses on a particular moment in the late 1960s when debates about how the mind is constituted spilled over into radical politics, rather than remaining the preserve of a small intellectual elite. Indeed, one could argue that without this moment it would be hard to imagine Pick's

---

[73] For two major works seeking to explore this potential for the modern period, see David Levine, *Reproducing Families: The Political Economy of English Population History* (Cambridge, 1987) and Szreter, *Fertility, Class and Gender*.

chapter being written at all. Reid focuses on reconstructing the connections between politics and broader mentalities at this defining moment, and is concerned less with how and why counter-cultural radicalism flourished when it did, than with analysing the centripetal forces that destabilised it almost as soon as it exploded on to the scene.

In this sense, whilst Pick and Reid's chapters are distinctive for their sustained focus on cultural politics, they share an interest in exploring the contours of British radicalism that runs through many of the chapters in this volume, as it does through much of Stedman Jones's scholarship. Like Reid, Howkins and Lawrence foreground discourses of radicalism, though in both cases paying close attention both to the historical changes they sought to make sense of, and the plausible alternative worlds they sought to construct through language. Howkins examines the tensions that developed between an older radical politics, rooted in custom and memory, which was determined to uphold the ancient rights of commoners, and a new, more urban politics that celebrated preservation and rational recreation in the name of an idealised 'people'; often in opposition to the concrete people whose livelihoods depended on the commons. Lawrence seeks to explain why in 1939–1940 the political vision constructed by Labour between the wars suddenly appeared not just plausible, but actively desirable to millions of people who had previously remained aloof from Labour politics. By contrast, Innes and Parry focus more squarely on changing expectations about the institutional make-up, and legitimate activities, of the state. But they, too, foreground the vital question of the factors opening up, or closing down, what is perceived to be possible in politics – what historians working in a different tradition might call transformations in the political imaginary.[74]

Finally, we would argue that these chapters are shaped in the spirit of Stedman Jones's own scholarship. Like him, they display wariness towards fads in historical scholarship, and a determination to place substantive historical problems to the fore. More fundamentally, like Stedman Jones, they display a strong interest both in deep structures and in transformative moments, though no longer anchored to the sort of 'totalising' project that shaped works such as *Outcast London* in the early 1970s. For Stedman Jones, the deep structures that are now most explanatory are discursive and imaginary, rather than socio-economic, but it remains vital to grasp their structural dimension – the way that they underpin apparently contingent processes of historical change. For

---

[74] See Cornelius Castoriadis, *The Imaginary Institution of Society* (Cambridge, MA, 1998); Charles Taylor, *Modern Social Imaginaries* (Durham, NC, 2004).

Stedman Jones, the linguistic turn was never about the triumph of contingency. Rather, it signalled his determination to identify the linguistic and imaginary structures in which a radical oppositional politics had developed in Western Europe in the first half of the nineteenth century. For Stedman Jones, we would argue, developing such an understanding represents a political act in itself, since sound political action can only be constructed on the basis of a sound understanding of the conditions that have shaped present conceptions of what is, and is not, possible in politics.

1 Coping with rapid population growth: how England fared in the century preceding the Great Exhibition of 1851

E. A. Wrigley

The population history of England as a whole has been charted in detail from 1541 onwards. In 1538 a royal injunction was issued requiring Anglican churches to maintain registers of baptisms, burials and marriages. For the next three centuries the Anglican registers provide the prime source of information about the population history of the country until decennial census taking began in 1801 and civil registration of births, deaths and marriages followed in 1837. It proved possible to use the information recorded in a large sample of parish registers, despite their various defects, to generate estimates of many demographic variables, including both national population totals and a wide range of measures of fertility, mortality and nuptiality.[1] Thus for a period totalling more than four-and-a-half centuries there is reliable information about the size of the English population and its characteristics. At no time in this period has the population growth rate approached the level reached in the last decades of the eighteenth and the early decades of the nineteenth centuries. In all probability, indeed, the peak reached then was not equalled in any previous era of English history.

The intrinsic growth rate (IGR) measures the rate at which a population will eventually grow assuming that the fertility and mortality rates current at a given point in time are maintained indefinitely. It is thus a convenient summary measure of the comparative demographic situation of two or more populations at the same time or of the same population at different dates. Not only was the IGR at its early nineteenth-century

The work embodied in this chapter is closely related to research supported by two ESRC research grants (RES-000-23-0131 and RES-000-23-1579) and two made by the British Academy (SG-40833) and (SG-42909).

I should like to thank Dr Max Satchell of the Cambridge Group for the History of Population and Social Structure for producing the map in Figure 1.2 in GIS. Thanks also to Philip Stickler for post-GIS image processing.
[1] E. A. Wrigley and R. S. Schofield, *The Population History of England, 1541–1871: A Reconstruction*, pbk edn with new intro. (Cambridge, 1989): E. A. Wrigley, R. S. Davies, J. E. Oeppen and R. S. Schofield, *English Population History from Family Reconstitution 1580–1837* (Cambridge, 1989).

peak higher than at any earlier period since the inception of parochial registration, the difference was also marked. If measured over thirty-year periods to minimise the impact of short-term influences, the IGR at its peak stood at 1.61 per cent per annum for the period centring on 1816.[2] In no comparable period before the late eighteenth century had the rate even reached 1.00 per cent per annum. Except for a relatively brief period in the late sixteenth and early seventeenth centuries, it did not exceed 0.6 per cent per annum until the later eighteenth century. A population growing at an annual rate of 1.61 per cent will double in just less than forty-five years. After the peak reached in 1816 the rate declined steadily. In the thirty-year period centring on 1851, for example, it stood at 1.15 per cent per annum, well below its peak three decades earlier.[3]

The object of this chapter is to call attention to the scale of the achievement implied in coping with such an unprecedented rate of population growth.[4]

The period running from c.1760 to c.1840 is often described as the classic period of the Industrial Revolution. Almost half a century ago Deane and Cole's groundbreaking exercise in national income accounting gave a new dimension to the study of the period.[5] It appeared to confirm the received wisdom that economic growth accelerated sharply over this period. Subsequent work, especially that of Crafts, while continuing to use the same analytic framework, has substantially changed the prevailing view of growth rates.[6] It is now widely accepted that economic growth was substantially less rapid than earlier supposed. If that was the case, and given that estimates of the size of the economy c.1850 have not changed significantly, it necessarily follows that the economy must have been much larger c.1750 than was once supposed,

---

[2] The amount by which a population actually increases may vary somewhat from that suggested by the IGR because of the influence of the age structure of the population at the time the IGR is calculated and of the impact of net migration. But in this instance the scale of increase suggested by the IGR is not greatly different from the empirical increases which took place. In the thirty-year period 1801–1831 the population grew from 8.671 to 13.254 million, an increase of 52.8 percent. An IGR of 1.6 percent would suggest a rise of 61.0 percent over a thirty-year period.

[3] All the population data quoted in this paragraph may be found in Wrigley *et al.*, *English Population History*, Table A9.1, pp. 614–615.

[4] It is of interest that the stresses produced by rapid population growth are a recurring theme in Boyd Hilton's recent survey of English history over much the same period covered in this essay: Boyd Hilton, *A Mad, Bad, and Dangerous People? England 1783–1846* (Oxford, 2006).

[5] P. Deane and W. A. Cole, *British Economic Growth 1688–1959: Trends and Structure* (Cambridge, 1962).

[6] N. F. R. Crafts, *British Economic Growth During the Industrial Revolution* (Oxford, 1985). See also J. Mokyr (ed.), *The British Industrial Revolution: An Economic Perspective* (Boulder, 1993).

in turn suggesting that in the period preceding 1750 there were already important changes in train in the economy.[7] Recent work in reconstructing the history of the changing occupational structure of England appears to confirm this. Preliminary results suggest, for example, that the proportion of the male labour force in Lancashire engaged in manufacture may have been as high in 1750 as it was a century later.[8]

Although what was once the conventional view of the nature of economic change between 1750 and 1850 no longer commands widespread support, it does not follow that this period was lacking in drama and notable achievement. It deserves still to be seen as one of outstanding interest, crucial to the appreciation of the nature of the new economic system which was replacing its predecessor. Figure 1.1 sets the scene. It is a variant of a graph published a quarter of a century ago in the *Population History of England* which was designed to bring out the striking change in the relationship between the rate of population growth and the rate of growth in the real wage which took place as the eighteenth century drew to a close.[9] In the original graph the Phelps-Brown and Hopkins (PBH) series was used to measure real wage change.[10] Their series was a remarkable pioneering exercise. Since then, however, several alternative series of wages and prices have been published which have remedied some of the limitations and defects in the PBH series.[11] Rather than republish the original graph, therefore, it seemed preferable to use a more recent estimate of real wage change and to take advantage of the construction of a slightly modified population series produced by the technique of inverse projection in constructing a revised version of the original graph.

---

[7] E. A. Wrigley, 'The quest for the industrial revolution', *Proceedings of the British Academy*, 121, (2003), pp. 147–170.

[8] Among the findings of an early analysis of militia list and parish register material carried out at the Cambridge Group for the History of Population and Social Structure under the ESRC grant RES-000-23-0131. For additional information see www.geog.cam.ac.uk/research/projects/occupations.

[9] Wrigley and Schofield, *Population History of England*, Figure 10.4, p. 410.

[10] The price and wage data in question may be found in two articles by E. H. Phelps Brown and S. V. Hopkins, 'Seven centuries of building wages' and 'Seven centuries of the prices of consumables compared with builders' wage rates' in E. M. Carus-Wilson (ed.), *Essays in Economic History*, vol. 2 (London, 1954–1962).

[11] In some cases, the new estimates have suggested solutions to old puzzles. They suggest, for example, that the apparent lag between changes in the real wage and changes in nuptiality which caused much discussion when the *Population History of England* was published disappears when an improved wage series is used. See Wrigley and Schofield, *Population History of England*, Figure 10.9, p. 425 and E. A. Wrigley, 'British population during the "long" eighteenth century, 1680–1840' in R. Floud and P. Johnson (eds), *The Cambridge Economic History of Modern Britain*, vol. 1, *Industrialisation 1700–1860* (Cambridge, 2004), Figure 3.7, p. 78, and associated text.

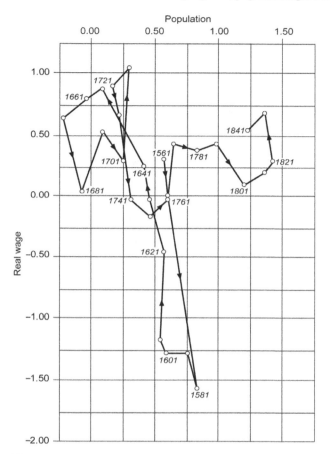

Figure 1.1 *Annual rates of growth of population and of a real wage series.*
Source: Wrigley *et al., English Population History*, Table A9.1, pp. 614–615.
The real wage series is that used in Wrigley, 'British population during the
"long" eighteenth century', Figure 3.7, p. 78.

Figure 1.1 plots the annual rate of change in the population total
against the annual rate of change in real wages. The points on the graph
are ten years apart and each point represents change over a thirty-year
period centring on the date shown. Thus, for example, the population in
1546 was 2,908,465, in 1576 3,447,944, an increase of 18.55 per cent,
which equates to a rate of annual increase of 0.57 per cent. The mid-
point of this period is 1561, the earliest date shown on the graph. The
real wage change was taken as the rate of increase or decrease between

two readings thirty years apart, each of which represents the average real wage over a ten-year period. The average real wage over the period 1571–1580 was 11.4 per cent higher than it had been in 1541–1550, which equates to an annual rate of growth of 0.36 per cent over the thirty-year period centring on 1561. The location of the point on the graph representing 1561 is determined by these two readings.

For the first two centuries the graph displays the classic pattern to be expected in an organic economy in a long-settled land. All pre-industrial economies were organic. An organic economy was one in which not only food but almost all the raw materials which entered into material production were either vegetable or animal in origin. This in turn meant that the process of photosynthesis on which all vegetable growth depends set limits to the scale of material production which could be attained and to the quantity of energy which any economy could secure. It implies that the very process of growth in an organic economy produces problems which will arrest and may reverse further growth.[12]

The band of points representing change during this period intersects with the line at which real wage change is zero in a manner which suggests that an annual population growth rate of approximately 0.5 per cent could be sustained without detriment to living standards, or, in other words, that output was rising sufficiently quickly to sustain a modest rate of growth of population without penalty. This is itself a tribute to the vigour of the early modern English economy. In most organic economies the comparable point would have been much closer to a zero population growth rate. If, however, the population growth rate exceeded this level, real wages were apt to fall sharply. This occurred during the later decades of the Tudor period and appeared to be happening again during the early and middle decades of the eighteenth century. In contrast, when population growth fell below about 0.5 per cent per annum, real wages improved, though the pattern was irregular, since the periods when population was declining most rapidly were not those when real wages were rising fastest. Despite this asymmetry, experience prior to the mid-eighteenth century clearly suggests that if the rate of population growth soared it would exact a heavy price in living standards. Indeed, assuming that earlier experience could be extended linearly, an annual rate of population growth of, say, 1.25 per cent might be expected to result in the real wage falling by at least 1.50 per cent per annum. In all likelihood, however, the fall would be still

---

[12] The concept of an organic economy is discussed at length in E. A. Wrigley, *Continuity, Chance, and Change: The Character of the Industrial Revolution in England* (Cambridge, 1988), esp. pp. 17–32.

greater since the logic of the connection between the population growth rate and the real wage suggests a curvilinear relationship between them if the population growth rate rises to a level well above its normal range. Yet during the final quarter of the eighteenth century and throughout the first half of the nineteenth century the line of points on the graph wandered further and further from its 'normal' path. Exceptionally rapid population growth was associated with *rising* rather than *falling* real wages. Whereas previously there was a marked and consistent negative relation between rates of population growth and rates of real wage growth, in the new regime the relation turned positive. As one rose the other also increased, a feature fundamentally at odds with all previous experience.

It should not be thought that the placing of the points on the graph precisely reflects the experience of the generations of men and women who lived in England between the mid-sixteenth and mid-nineteenth centuries. Other wage and price series result in real wage series which differ somewhat from that used in constructing Figure 1.1. The use of different data sources is bound to have this effect. However, even if exactly the same price and wage data are used, different assumptions about the relative weights given to the components in a cost of living series can produce significantly different results. Furthermore, changes over time in the relative size of different occupational groups can make a significant difference to average earnings overall even if the relative level of incomes of the several occupational groups remains unchanged. And this list of factors which widen the error bands of measurement could be considerably extended. For example, what determined the living standards of the members of a family was the sum of the earnings of all its members, whereas wage data usually relate only to male wage earners. Despite these reservations about the accuracy of historical real wage series, however, it would be quixotic to call in question the validity of the dramatic break from their accustomed pathway displayed by the points on Figure 1.1 in the later eighteenth century. Experiments with other real wage series results in graphs which show a markedly similar overall pattern to that in Figure 1.1, though the placing of the individual points may differ somewhat.

All organic economies laboured under the same constraints. Ricardo depicted the basic problem in terms of the limited supply of land. Economic growth invariably meant an increased demand for animal and vegetable raw materials. Indirectly this was true even of mineral raw materials since a large quantity of thermal energy was needed to obtain metals from minerals by smelting, and this was normally achieved by burning wood or charcoal. In an organic economy the ineluctable tension which concerned Ricardo was never far away. An increase in the output of wool, for example, must entail setting aside a larger acreage for sheep pasture, which in turn must mean less land available to produce food or animal and vegetable raw materials. Hence the words penned by Sir Thomas More when contemplating one aspect of this problem: 'your sheep, that were wont to be so meek and tame and so small eaters, now, as I hear say, be become so great devourers, and so wild, that they eat up and swallow down the very men themselves.'[13] Ricardo caught the essence of the problem by noting that each increase in production must mean either taking in new land which would be, on average, less productive than the land already in cultivation, or working existing land more intensively. In either case the return to land and labour would tend to decline, eventually reaching the point where no further expansion would be undertaken. Moreover, he argued that it was beyond the powers of man to change this situation, remarking of the end result: 'This will necessarily be rendered permanent by the laws of nature, which have limited the productive power of the land.'[14] Every success carried within it the seeds of subsequent failure. A generation earlier Adam Smith had come to much the same conclusion:

In a country which had acquired that full complement of riches which the nature of its soil and climate, and its situation with respect to other countries, allowed it to acquire; which could, therefore, advance no further, and which was not going backwards, both the wages of labour and the profits of stock would probably be very low. In a country fully peopled in proportion to what either its territory could maintain or its stock could employ, the competition for employment would necessarily be so great as to reduce the wages of labour to what was barely sufficient to keep up the number of labourers, and, the country being already fully peopled, the number could never be augmented.[15]

The third of the great triumvirate of classical economists, Malthus, reasoned similarly. He contrasted the halcyon days following the initial settlement of good land with what must eventually follow: 'But the accumulation of capital beyond the means of employing it with the same returns on lands of the greatest natural fertility, and the most

---

[13] T. More, *Utopia* and *A Dialogue of Comfort*, Everyman's Library, rev. edn (London, 1951), p. 26. More was protesting chiefly against enclosure: 'Therefore that one covetous and insatiable cormorant and very plague of its native country may compass about and enclose many thousand acres of ground together within one pale or hedge, the husbandmen be thrust out of their own' with dire consequences (p. 26).

[14] David Ricardo, *On the Principles of Political Economy and Taxation* in *The Works and Correspondence of David Ricardo*, ed. P. Sraffa with the collaboration of M. H. Dobb, 11 vols (Cambridge, 1951–1973), I, p. 126.

[15] A. Smith, *An Inquiry into the Nature and Causes of the Wealth of Nations*, ed. E. Cannan, 5th edn (London, 1961), I, p. 106.

advantageously situated, must necessarily lower profits; while the rapid increase of population will tend to lower the wages of labour.' As a result, 'In the natural and regular progress of a country towards its full complement of capital and population, the rate of profit and the corn wages of labour permanently fall together'.[16]

The shape of the belt of points shown in Figure 1.1 covering the period from the mid-sixteenth to the mid-eighteenth century exemplifies the problem which concerned the classical economists. Because it was so difficult to match any but the most modest of population rises by a commensurate increase in production, living standards suffered in periods of rapid population growth but recovered when the rate of growth fell. The mould was broken, however, at the end of the eighteenth century, paradoxically at much the same time as the classical economists were writing. Real incomes in the early nineteenth century were rising only slowly by the standards of later generations but they were not falling precipitately in the manner which might have been expected in the light of earlier experience. In order to appreciate the extraordinary turn which events had taken, it would perhaps be more illuminating to measure the rate of growth of real wages in the early decades of the nineteenth century not against a zero rate of growth, as is perhaps conventional, but against what past experience suggested would happen with population growing at more than 1.25 per cent per annum. Measured in this way, the annual rate of growth in real wages in the early nineteenth century, which averaged c.0.5 per cent (Figure 1.1) measured against zero, should rather be judged as the difference between 0.5 per cent and −1.5 per cent, or −2.0 per cent, a truly remarkable achievement. I have discussed elsewhere the nature of the changes which made possible the escape from the normal constraints of an organic economy.[17] In this chapter I shall concentrate on the way in which some aspects of the population changes of the period reflect the progressive transformation of the economy.

If the problems which had plagued communities experiencing over-rapid population growth in earlier centuries were to be avoided, it was essential that the structure of aggregate demand should change, that a decreasing proportion of such demand should be devoted to the necessities of life and more to what the classical economists termed comforts and luxuries, the products of secondary and tertiary industry: otherwise

---

[16] T. R. Malthus, *The Principles of Political Economy Considered with a View of its Past and Present Effects on Human Happiness*, 2nd edn [1836] in *The Works of Thomas Robert Malthus*, ed. E. A. Wrigley and D. Souden, 8 vols (London, 1986), V, pp. 121, 128.

[17] Wrigley, *Continuity, Chance and Change*.

pressure on the land was bound to increase. The occupational structure will mirror changes in the structure of aggregate demand. The income elasticity of demand for food is characteristically less than unity. As an illustration, suppose that a family's income rises from 100 units to 150 units, or by 50 per cent. In the former situation 75 units are spent on food, 25 units on other commodities; in the latter situation spending on food may rise to, say, 100 units, but on other commodities to 50 units. On food the rise is 33 per cent, on other items 100 per cent. Since the percentage increase in expenditure on food is less than the overall increase, the income elasticity for this good is said to be less than unity.

When incomes rise, therefore, a smaller proportion of aggregate demand will be devoted to food. Reflecting this, employment in agriculture is likely to fall as a percentage of the workforce, while manufacture and services will employ increasing percentages. Symmetrically, a decline in average real incomes will tend to lead to a rise in the proportion of the labour force in agriculture since an increasing proportion of limited budgets will be spent on food, reinforcing the existing pattern of population distribution over the land surface. In an organic economy it was normal for about three-quarters of the labour force to be engaged in agriculture. This is an inescapable concomitant of low average real incomes because by far the biggest element in family expenditure was the purchase of food. With rising real incomes, the geographical distribution of the population will change progressively and, in the longer term, radically, since secondary and tertiary production is much more spatially concentrated than agricultural production.[18] Lopsided growth was to be a key feature of the escape from past perils.

Rising real incomes and a change in the structure of aggregate demand is, of course, only a necessary but not a sufficient cause of escape from the constraints of an organic economy. As long as a marked rise in the output of the secondary sector, like that of the primary sector, increased pressure on the land, as in Sir Thomas More's aside, the problem remained. It was essential that inorganic sources of energy and raw materials should increase steadily in relative importance if growth were no longer to carry with it the seeds of failure. The development of a mineral-based energy-rich economy was a prerequisite of long-term success as the structure of aggregate demand changed.

If population growth takes place without significant change in the aggregate structure of demand it is likely at best to take the form which

---

[18] E. A. Wrigley, 'Country and town: the primary, secondary, and tertiary peopling of England in the early modern period' in P. Slack and R. Ward (eds), *The Peopling of Britain: The Shaping of a Human Landscape*, The Linacre Lectures 1999 (Oxford, 2002).

Geertz, writing about Indonesia, described as *agricultural involution* which, he remarked, 'resembles nothing so much as treading water. Higher-level densities are offset by greater labour inputs into the same productive system, but output per head (or per mouth) remains more or less constant.'[19] The pool grows larger, but the numbers treading water in it increase at least as quickly.[20] Geertz's model had much in common with that of Boserup. She envisaged advances in agricultural technology taking place in response to rising population pressure, enabling a larger population to be supported without material change in living standards but at the cost of decreasing leisure as the working day lengthened, or there were fewer days of rest, or both.[21] In practice, for the reasons set out by Ricardo, in a European context it is more likely that output per head will decline in these circumstances. This appears to have happened in Belgium, for example, in the early modern period when output per acre increased substantially, matching the highest levels anywhere in Europe, but the land was increasingly subdivided and output per head in agriculture declined.[22] Lopsided growth, in contrast, occurs when the aggregate structure of demand changes in a way which gives rise to a differentially rapid growth in non-agricultural employment, which in turn will cause changes in the geographical distribution of the population.

The beginnings of change in England lay in its unusually successful agriculture, a success closely linked to rising urbanisation by a process of positive feedback.[23] Between the end of the sixteenth and the beginning of the nineteenth centuries the proportion of the male labour force engaged in agriculture almost halved, falling from c.70 to c.40 per cent of the total, though the country remained largely self-sufficient in food. Over the same period the population rose from c.4 million to

---

[19] C. Geertz, *Agricultural Involution: The Process of Ecological Change in Indonesia* (Berkeley, 1963), p. 78.

[20] Ibid., p. 95.

[21] E. Boserup, *The Conditions of Agricultural Growth: The Economics of Agrarian Change under Population Pressure* (London, 1965), p. 43.

[22] G. Dejongh and E. Thoen, 'Arable productivity in Flanders and the former territory of Belgium in long-term perspective (from the middle ages to the end of the Ancien Régime)' in B. J. P. Bavel and E. Thoen (eds), *Land Productivity and Agro-systems in the North Sea Area (Middle Ages – 20th Century)*, CORN publication, ser. 2 (Turnhout, 1999), p. 58. At the same time the percentage of the Belgian population living in towns and cities declined, as might be expected in view of labour productivity trends in agriculture. The urban percentage fell from 23.9 percent in 1700 to 18.9 percent in 1800. J. de Vries, *European Urbanization 1500–1800* (Cambridge, MA, 1984), Table 3.7, p. 39.

[23] E. A. Wrigley, 'Urban growth and agricultural change: England and the continent in the early modern period' in E. A. Wrigley, *People, Cities and Wealth* (Oxford, 1987).

c.8.7 million but the size of the labour force engaged in agriculture rose little if at all.[24] Given that the country remained largely self-sufficient in food, it is obvious that labour productivity in agriculture must have risen greatly over the two centuries in question. The proportion of the labour force employed outside agriculture doubled from 30 to 60 per cent. Since the population more than doubled, this implies that the numbers engaged in secondary and tertiary occupations must have more than quadrupled. Lopsided growth began as the population adjusted to a changing pattern of job opportunities. Initially, the most striking aspect of the changed situation was the rapid growth of London which ended the seventeenth century as the most populous city in Europe. London's growth itself provoked differential growth elsewhere. The fastest growing county in the seventeenth century was, of course, Middlesex, which included the bulk of London, but the second fastest growing county is perhaps a surprise. It was Northumberland, and the third fastest was Durham.[25] An illustrative calculation suggests that this was probably associated with the effect on Tyneside of the massive expansion in the burning of coal in London.[26] In the eighteenth century the pattern changed. London no longer increased its share of the national population total. The most frenetic increase occurred in the towns and cities of the north and the Midlands, which radically changed the rank order of urban places in England by the end of the eighteenth century.[27] In both centuries the urban percentage rose substantially, from 8.25 per cent in 1600 to 17.0 per cent in 1700 and 27.5 per cent in 1800, at which date England was the most heavily urbanised country in Europe apart from the Netherlands, whereas in 1600 it had been among the least urbanised. The contrast between England and the rest of Europe became so pronounced that in the second half of the eighteenth

---

[24] E. A. Wrigley, 'The transition to an advanced organic economy: half a millennium of English agriculture' *Economic History Review*, 59, (2006), pp. 435–480.

[25] E. A. Wrigley, 'Rickman revisited: English county growth rates in the early modern period', *Economic History Review*, 62, (2009), pp. 711–735.

[26] As Langton remarked, 'London relied on vast quantities of waterborne coal from the north-east from the sixteenth century, and the early prominence of Newcastle as the largest town of highland England in the seventeenth century was a reciprocal of that'. J. Langton, 'Urban growth and economic change: from the late seventeenth century to 1841' in P. Clark (ed.), *The Cambridge Urban History of England*, II, *1540–1840* (Cambridge, 2000), p. 481. The illustrative calculation is described in Wrigley, 'Rickman revisited'.

[27] On the transformation of the whole urban system in the north between Tudor times and the nineteenth century, see J. K. Walton, 'North' in Clark (ed.), *Cambridge Urban History of England*, II, *1540–1840*. On the links between urban growth and economic growth over the same period, Langton, 'Urban growth and economic change'.

century about 70 per cent of all the urban growth across the continent was taking place in England alone.[28]

At the beginning of the sixteenth century England had been a purely organic economy. By the end of the eighteenth century it was already part way towards a mineral-based energy economy, the type of economy which has allowed the modern world largely to escape the constraints which dogged all organic economies. The change had been in train throughout the seventeenth and eighteenth centuries. This development brought in its wake profound change in almost every aspect of social and economic life. These in turn greatly altered the demographic map of the country. The rest of this chapter is in part a description of the ways in which demographic change reflected the gradual supplanting of the old economic system by the new and in part a discussion of the impact of greatly accelerated population growth on some aspects of this process.

It is possible to paint a new picture of the changes taking place over the century before the Great Exhibition because recent work has resulted in the construction of new population series for each of the 610 English hundreds at decennial intervals from 1761 to 1851 (the hundred was the ancient administrative unit intermediate in size between the county and the parish). The census provides totals for each hundred from 1801 onwards.[29] The earlier totals are estimates based on the number of marriages recorded in parish registers for each year from 1754 to 1800. These marriage totals were collected and published as part of the 1801 census operation under the direction of John Rickman.[30] The returns for individual parishes were grouped into hundred totals when the *Parish Register Abstract* (PRA) was published and therefore the hundred is the smallest unit for which a continuous series of population totals can be constructed using the PRAs.[31]

Was the growth lopsided? At one extreme, if growth were uniform throughout the country it would mean that rural agricultural areas were

[28] Wrigley, 'Urban growth and agricultural change', Table 7.2, p. 162 and Table 7.7, p. 179, and de Vries, *European urbanization*, Table 3.7, p. 39.

[29] Details of the steps taken to correct the various deficiencies in the published census totals may be found in E. A. Wrigley, *The Early English Censuses*, forthcoming.

[30] The reason for basing the hundred population estimates on the marriage returns and details of the methods used are described in E. A. Wrigley, 'English county populations in the later eighteenth century' *Economic History Review*, 60, (2007), pp. 35–69.

[31] The nineteenth-century censuses provide population data for many more than 610 hundreds but in 1801 the PRA quite frequently grouped into a single unit hundreds for which there were later separate returns. For example, the town of Macclesfield was treated as part of the hundred of Macclesfield in the PRA but was separately distinguished in census returns. To enable continuous series to be constructed the 610 PRA hundreds were retained throughout so that the Macclesfield hundred always included the town of Macclesfield.

experiencing a rapid increase in numbers and would suggest that agricultural involution was taking place. The productivity of the agricultural workforce would be in decline, in part no doubt because employment was unavailable or discontinuous for many agricultural labourers. In this scenario areas dependent largely on secondary or tertiary employment would be failing to provide sufficient opportunity for the rural population surplus to find alternative employment by moving to centres of industry and commerce. At the other extreme there would be a marked contrast between rates of growth in the deep countryside, which would be close to zero, and dramatic rises in the populations of the most successful industrial and commercial centres.

In constructing the following tables, which are designed to answer the question posed in the last paragraph, each hundred was ranked according to its contribution to overall population growth. Growth was very unevenly spread among the hundreds. Consider initially the period as a whole, the subject of Table 1.1. Over the ninety years in question the English population grew by 169.8 per cent, representing an annual growth rate of 1.11 per cent. The top 10 per cent of hundreds accounted for 65.7 per cent of the growth occurring, although their starting population had formed only 32.4 per cent of the national total. The top quarter of hundreds provided more than four-fifths of the total growth occurring, while the top half accounted for 92.5 per cent of the total. The starting population of the bottom quarter of hundreds formed only 11.1 per cent and growth in this group was so modest that only 2.1 per cent of the growth overall took place in this group. In individual hundreds there were even more extreme contrasts. For example, the hundred in which population growth was greatest was Salford in Lancashire, where the population increased by 616,827 in the ninety-year period, from 81,194 to 698,021, an increase of more than 750 per cent. In contrast the twenty hundreds in which growth was least, increased by a combined total of 866 people, or by less than 1 per cent of their combined population of 110,305 in 1761. Such growth patterns leave no room for doubt that England was much closer to the second than to the first of the two extreme possibilities outlined above.[32]

It is, however, only when the ninety-year period is divided into sub-periods that some of the most interesting features of the pressures exerted by rapid population growth can be studied. Table 1.2 mirrors

---

[32] It is worth noting that the patterns which emerge when using *absolute growth* as the criterion in ranking parishes are not greatly different from those which are visible if the criterion used is the *growth rate*. I have constructed a table based on this criterion paralleling Table 1 which substantiates the point but judged it excessive to present both in a short chapter.

Table 1.1 *Population growth in 610 English hundreds 1761–1851*

	Starting population	Growth	Per cent growth overall	Per cent growth p.a.	Average population of hundred in 1761	Share of population in 1761	Share of growth 1761–1851
1761–1851 England	6,310,340	10,717,140	169.8	1.11	10,345		
Top 10%	2,043,341	7,037,289	344.4	1.67	33,497	32.4	65.7
Top quarter	3,316,056	8,750,556	263.9	1.45	21,674	52.5	81.7
Second quarter	1,340,543	1,167,276	87.1	0.70	8,819	21.2	10.9
Top half	4,656,599	9,917,832	213.0	1.28	15,268	73.8	92.5
Bottom half	1,653,742	799,307	48.3	0.44	5,422	26.2	7.5
Bottom quarter	700,577	227,478	32.5	0.31	4,609	11.1	2.1

Source: Wrigley, *The Early English Censuses*, Table A2.7.
Note: The Scilly Islands are not included since they were not covered in the early censuses.

Table 1.2 *Population growth in 610 English hundreds in three sub-periods, 1761–1791, 1791–1831 and 1831–1851*

	Starting population	Growth	Per cent growth overall	Per cent growth p.a.	Average population of hundred	Share of population in 1761	Share of growth 1761–1791
1761–1791 England	6,310,340	1,535,336	24.3	0.73	10,345		
Top 10%	2,102,967	1,066,851	50.7	1.38	34,475	33.3	69.5
Top quarter	3,236,908	1,339,885	41.4	1.16	21,156	51.3	87.3
Second quarter	1,179,685	177,575	15.1	0.47	7,761	18.7	11.6
Top half	4,416,593	1,517,460	34.4	0.99	14,481	70.0	98.8
Bottom half	1,893,748	17,876	0.9	0.03	6,209	30.0	1.2
Bottom quarter	1,040,023	−47,974	−4.6	−0.16	6,842	16.5	−3.1
1791–1831 England	7,845,676	5,405,865	68.9	1.32	12,862		
Top 10%	3,059,119	3,295,732	107.7	1.84	50,149	39.0	61.0
Top quarter	4,551,212	4,225,949	92.9	1.66	29,746	58.0	78.2
Second quarter	1,504,725	698,169	46.4	0.96	9,900	19.2	12.9
Top half	6,055,937	4,924,118	81.3	1.50	19,856	77.2	91.1
Bottom half	1,789,740	481,746	26.9	0.60	5,868	22.8	8.9
Bottom quarter	804,275	128,446	16.0	0.37	5,291	10.3	2.4
1831–1851 England	13,251,541	3,775,939	28.5	1.26	21,724		
Top 10%	6,054,295	2,801,342	46.3	1.92	99,251	45.7	74.2
Top quarter	8,496,295	3,325,023	39.1	1.66	55,531	64.1	88.1
Second quarter	2,178,806	311,923	14.3	0.67	14,334	16.4	8.3
Top half	10,675,101	3,636,946	34.1	1.48	35,000	80.6	96.3
Bottom half	2,576,440	138,993	5.4	0.26	8,447	19.4	3.7
Bottom quarter	1,349,849	10,950	0.8	0.04	8,881	10.2	0.3

Source: Wrigley, *The Early English Censuses*, Table A2.7.
Note: The Scilly Islands are not included since they were not covered in the early censuses.

the information in Table 1.1 for each of three sub-periods. The general pattern found for the whole period is also visible in the three sub-periods but there are instructive differences between them which suggest that rapid population growth created greater difficulty in the middle period, when the growth rate peaked, than in the other two. In the initial period from 1761 to 1791 the annual rate of national population growth was 0.73 per cent, a high rate by comparison with any earlier comparable period other than the peak years of the Elizabethan growth surge, but only a little more than half the rate in the middle period, 1791–1831, when the rate jumped to 1.32 per cent. In the final, shorter period from 1831 to 1851 the annual growth rate, though still very high at 1.26 per cent, had begun its long decline.

In both the first and third sub-periods, the top quarter of hundreds was growing so swiftly that close to nine-tenths of the national increase took place in this limited group (87.3 and 88.1 per cent in the two sub-periods). The top 10 per cent of hundreds accounted for 69.5 and 74.2 per cent of all growth respectively. The bottom half therefore contributed very little to overall growth. The population of the bottom quarter of hundreds in the first and third sub-periods was effectively stationary (the annual rate of growth was –0.16 per cent in the first period; 0.04 per cent in the third), and even taking all the hundreds in the bottom half, growth rates were still notably modest (0.03 per cent per annum in the first period; 0.26 per cent in the third).

In the middle sub-period, however, the contrast in growth rates was substantially less marked than earlier or later, which, in the model adumbrated above would suggest more signs of strain than in the other two periods. The top quarter of hundreds absorbed less than 80 per cent of the overall increase compared with almost 90 per cent in 1761–1791 and 1831–1851. About 9 per cent of the overall rise took place in the bottom half, a much higher figure than in the other two sub-periods and there was even modest growth rather than virtual stasis in the bottom quarter of hundreds. Comparison of the annual rates of growth in the different hundred groupings tells the same story. In all periods growth in the top half of the table was much higher than in the bottom half, but in the middle period the contrast between the top and bottom elements was substantially less marked. This is clearly seen, for example, by comparing the middle sub-period with its successor. The overall annual growth rate in the former was only modestly higher than in the latter but the annual growth rates for each successive hundred grouping reveal some instructive differences. The rates for the top 10 per cent and the top quarter were very similar in the two sub-periods (the rates in question were 1.84 in 1791–1831 and 1.92 in 1831–1851 for the top 10 per cent, and 1.66 and 1.66 for the top quarter). For the second quarter, however, the rate in the earlier sub-period was 43 per cent higher than in the later one (0.96 and 0.67), while in the bottom half the contrast was even more marked. In the bottom half overall the annual population growth was more than twice as high in 1791–1831 as in 1831–1851 (0.60 and 0.26), while in the bottom quarter it was almost ten times as high (0.37 and 0.04).

The composition of each group shown in Table 1.2 varied somewhat from one sub-period to another, though many hundreds were in the same group throughout the whole period.[33] To provide an indication of the geography of relative population growth, Figure 1.2 shows the distribution of the hundreds in the several groups in the middle sub-period 1791–1831. The map mirrors the Tables 1.1 and 1.2 in dividing all the hundreds into five groups; the top ten per cent, the rest of the top quarter, and the second, third and fourth quarters. Thus, since there were 610 hundreds, the first group consists of 61 hundreds, while each of the full quarters consists of either 152 or 153 hundreds. The hundreds are ranked by the absolute size of the increase taking place. A full discussion of the patterns visible in the map is beyond the scope of this chapter. However, to illustrate the possibilities which it offers, consider one prominent feature. There is a large red block covering much of the north-west and the west Midlands. It is not quite a solid block since there are hundreds in south Derbyshire and a neighbouring area in Staffordshire which interrupt what would otherwise be an almost completely uniform area, but it is nonetheless a striking phenomenon: it forms a tract of land consisting of most of the West Riding and Lancashire, north and east Cheshire, much of Derbyshire, one hundred in Nottinghamshire, much of Staffordshire, the north-west corner of Leicestershire and the north of Worcestershire. This area alone accounted for 31 per cent of the whole national population growth over the forty-year period, and more than half of the total for the top ten per cent group of hundreds.

The next most significant contributor to the national growth total was the 'metropolitan' red area consisting of London and its hinterland but extending to almost the whole of Kent and the eastern half of Sussex. This area accounted for 19 per cent of the rise in the national population total over the period. Almost exactly half of the overall national increase, therefore, took place in these two areas.

---

[33] For example, there were 61 hundreds in the top 10 percent of hundreds; almost two-thirds of these (39 in all) were in the top 10 percent in all three sub-periods.

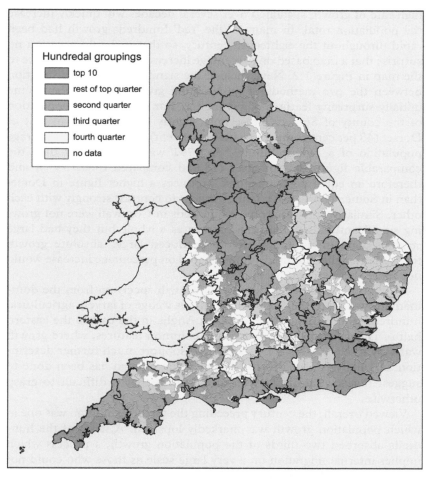

Figure 1.2 *The geographical distribution of hundreds grouped by the size of population growth between 1791 and 1831. Source:* See Table 1.2.

In a more extensive analysis of the changes summarised in Table 1.2 it would be illuminating to consider also a map which was based not on the absolute size of the increase taking place in each hundred but on the percentage rise in population. At first sight one might expect the two maps to differ markedly because a hundred with a small initial population has no chance of making the top ten per cent group if ranked by the absolute size of the increase taking place. However, it is also true that a high rate of growth sustained over several decades will quickly increase the population total. In many of the 'red' hundreds growth had been rapid throughout the eighteenth century, so that it should occasion no surprise that a map based on percentage increase shows a resemblance to the map in Figure 1.2. Nevertheless, the significance of the distinction between the two methods of representing growth does explain some initially surprising features of Figure 1.2. For example, the population of the county of Somerset rose only slightly less rapidly than that of Dorset (48 per cent compared with 51 per cent), but because the average population of a Dorset hundred in 1791 was much larger than the comparable figure for Somerset (18,026 compared to 6,733[34]), and therefore an equal percentage rise produces a higher figure in Dorset than in Somerset, the two counties appear to contrast strongly with each other. Similarly, the westernmost hundreds in Cornwall were not growing significantly faster than the country as a whole but they had large starting populations and therefore produced larger absolute growth totals than smaller hundreds. A map based on percentage increase would not cause these areas to stand out.

At the other end of the population growth spectrum from the dominant growth areas there was an enormous wedge of largely agricultural hundreds from Lincolnshire and East Anglia in the east to the eastern half of Devon in the west with many common features, where growth was very modest. This area, too, would support much further description and analysis. But it is to be hoped that enough has been done to suggest that spatial display can reveal much that is difficult to grasp otherwise.

Viewed overall, the century preceding the Great Exhibition was one in which population growth was markedly lopsided. A tenth of the hundreds absorbed two-thirds of the population growth, a process which implies internal migration on a very large scale as those who could not find gainful employment locally moved to the places in which industry and commerce provided them with the living wage not available in their native parishes. During the troubled middle period, however, the demographic evidence suggests the possibility that the adjustment process was less well able to cope with the challenge than either earlier or later.

---

[34] In calculating these averages I have excluded towns and boroughs. Many cities, towns and boroughs were treated as hundreds in the early censuses. They were relatively numerous in Dorset compared to Somerset (seven as against three). The Dorset towns were all small and their increases over the period were modest. Because their 'footprint' was also small they are barely visible on the map.

The challenge itself, of course, was more severe because population growth rates reached a peak in these decades.

An excessively simplified 'model' of the nature of the process of accommodating the surge in population growth rates experienced by England in the later eighteenth and early nineteenth centuries might run as follows. The more purely rural parts of the country, where agriculture provided the great bulk of employment opportunities for the labour force, could play little or no part in providing work for the rapidly rising number of adult males. If the population in such areas rose significantly it would result in increasing unemployment and more intermittent employment. Fewer days in work would cause annual incomes to decline, other things being equal, the equivalent in a capitalist farming system to the decline in output per man which would characterise a peasant farming system experiencing similar pressures.

The potential problem, however, need never materialise provided that elsewhere in the country employment opportunities were increasing quickly enough to absorb the surpluses which would otherwise build up in the rural, agricultural communities. England had long been accustomed to high rates of internal migration.[35] It was often the case that only a minority of men and women who reached adult years died in the same parish in which they had been born and, although most migration was over relatively short distances, longer distance movement had long been commonplace. The point is vividly illustrated in the notes made by Richard Gough of Myddle, a village close to Shrewsbury, about his fellow parishioners in the later seventeenth century. Myddle was about 160 miles distant from London. In his 'Introduction' to an edition of Gough, Hey remarks that, 'He frequently mentions London in passing as if it were commonplace that his neighbours should have been there. Men and women from all sections of his community went to the capital in search of fortune or excitement or to escape from trouble at home.'[36]

---

[35] The high frequency of internal migration in England during the early modern period is extensively treated in D. Souden, 'Pre-industrial English local migration fields', unpublished PhD thesis, University of Cambridge (1981). See also P. Clark, 'Migration in England in the late seventeenth and early eighteenth centuries' in P. Clark and D. Souden (eds), *Migration and Society in Early Modern England* (London, 1987).

[36] R. Gough, *The History of Myddle*, ed. D. Hey (London, 1983), p. 19. The scale of movement to London from distant parts of the country in the sixteenth century is vividly clear from the registers of freemen on the rolls of the London livery companies. S. Rappaport, *Worlds within Worlds: Structures of Life in Sixteenth-century London* (Cambridge, 1989), esp. pp. 76–86.

The rise in the intrinsic growth rate for the country as a whole to which reference was made earlier occurred in all types of parish.[37] This in turn implies that the virtual absence of growth in those hundreds in the country in which growth was least (the bottom half of hundreds in Table 1.1) must reflect a heavy net out-migration from the 305 hundreds in question. Young men and women finding future prospects of employment (and therefore, among other things, of marriage) were bleak, moved to the relatively small group of hundreds in which job opportunities were rising fast because the local economy was expanding vigorously.[38] In these circumstances the population trends in the agricultural hundreds would act as a barometer of the success of the economy as a whole in coping with accelerating population growth rates.[39] As long as numbers barely altered in such hundreds any difficulties would be minor but if numbers began to rise it would suggest that difficulties were increasing.

It might seem paradoxical to suggest that the absence of population growth in half the hundreds in the country could be a marker of success but that is the implication of the argument. Its validity can be tested by considering another body of data relating to the English hundreds. The high and rising cost of the Poor Law was a major source of concern to contemporaries and gave rise to furious argument. His advocacy of their abolition made Malthus many bitter enemies. The poor laws attracted much heated political debate and the wish to secure reliable evidence about their operation caused Parliament to require the collection of a wealth of statistical information on the subject. The evidence presented in Table 1.3 is drawn from the periodic parliamentary reports in which the data were presented.

Table 1.3 compares expenditures on the poor in fast- and slow-growing hundreds. The hundreds were ranked according to the absolute size of the increase in population taking place between 1791 and 1831, the middle period of Table 1.2. The information for the group of fast-growing hundreds was obtained from a random sample of thirty hundreds drawn from the top 10 per cent of hundreds (sixty-one hundreds

---

[37] Wrigley et al., English Population History, pp. 501–507.

[38] P. Kitson, 'Family formation, male occupation, and the nature of parochial registration in England, c. 1538–1837', unpublished PhD thesis, University of Cambridge (2004), esp. chs 4 and 6.

[39] The ability to provide employment for a rapidly growing population may, of course, explain in part the growth itself by a feedback mechanism in which early and almost universal marriage is encouraged by a vigorous demand for labour. This causes population growth rates to rise, which in turn limits any rise in the cost of labour. A closely related range of issues is discussed in J. Goldstone, 'The demographic revolution in England: a re-examination' Population Studies, 40, (1986), pp. 5–33.

Table 1.3 *Population growth and poor law expenditure*

	Fast-growing hundreds			Slow-growing hundreds		
	1781	*1801*	*1816*	*1781*	*1801*	*1816*
Population	1,249,128	1,755,313	2,298,433	165,546	154,487	166,829
	1783–1785	*1803*	*1813–1815*	*1783–1785*	*1803*	*1813–1815*
Expenditure on the poor (£s)	305,622	664,790	979,741	37,001	83,118	110,259
Expenditure per head of population (£s)	0.245 (100)	0.379 (154.8)	0.426 (174.2)	0.224 (100)	0.538 (240.7)	0.661 (295.7)
	1783–1785	*1803*	*1813–1815*	*1783–1785*	*1803*	*1813–1815*
Ratio of expenditure per head in slow-growing to fast-growing hundreds	91.4	142.1	155.0			

Sources: Population data: Wrigley: *The Early English Censuses*, Table A2.7. Poor law data for 1783–1785 and 1803: Abstract of the answers and returns under an Act for the Procuring Returns relative to the Expence and Maintenance of the Poor in England, *PP*, Accounts and Papers 1803–1804 (175). For 1813–1815: Abridgement of the abstract of the answers and returns under an Act for Procuring Returns relative to the Expence and Maintenance of the Poor in England, *PP*, Accounts and Papers 1818 (82).

Notes: The figures in parentheses on the line for expenditure per head of population index the later totals to the 1781 figure.
The thirty randomly selected fast-growing hundreds were as follows: *Cambridgeshire*, Isle of Ely (including City of Ely, Wisbech, Witchford North and Witchford South); *Cheshire*, Macclesfield (including Macclesfield town); *Cornwall*, Kerrier, Penwith; *Derbyshire*, Derby Borough, Highpeak; *Durham*, Chester; *Gloucestershire*, Bristol and Barton Regis, Cheltenham; *Hampshire*, Isle of Wight, Portsdown, Portsmouth Borough; *Kent*, Aylesford, St Augustine, Sutton at Hone (including Woolwich, Deptford and Greenwich); *Lancashire*, Liverpool Borough; *Salford*; *Leicestershire*, Leicester Borough; *Middlesex*, Ossulstone Finsbury, Westminster; *Northumberland*, Newcastle-on-Tyne Town; *Staffordshire*, Offlow, Pirehill; *Surrey*, Southwark Borough; *Sussex*, Brighton, Hastings; *Warwickshire*, Birmingham Town; *Worcestershire*, Halfshire; *Yorkshire*, *West Riding*, Agbrigg, Leeds Town.
The thirty slow-growing hundreds were as follows: *Berkshire*, Charlton; *Cambridgeshire*, Flendish; *Devon*, Halberton; *Dorset*, Poole Town; *Gloucestershire*, Cleeve, Tewkesbury; *Herefordshire*, Ewyas Lacy, Webtree; *Norfolk*, Clavering; *Northamptonshire*, Chipping Warden, Polebrook, Rothwell, Willybrook; *Oxfordshire*, Dorchester; *Rutland*, East, Wrandike; *Somerset*, Milverton, Portbury, Whitestone; *Wiltshire*, Frustfield, Mere, Ramsbury, Salisbury City, Westbury, Whorwelsdown; *Worcestershire*, Blackenhurst, Doddingtree, Evesham Borough; *Yorkshire*, *East Riding*, Ainsty of York, Whitby Strand.

in all); the information for the slow-growing group was again taken from a random sample of thirty hundreds drawn from the 100 slowest-growing hundreds. The poor law expenditure data refer to the average of the three years 1783–1785, to 1803 and to the average of the three years 1813–1815. The population totals are those for 1781, 1801 and 1816 (taken as the mean of the totals for 1811 and 1821). The information is much condensed since the totals refer to all thirty hundreds in each group treated as an aggregate of the individual hundreds. Thus the population of the 'fast' group rose from 1,249,128 in 1781 to 2,298,433 in 1816, or by 84 per cent, whereas the population of the 'slow' group was virtually stationary, rising only marginally from 165,546 to 166,829 over the same period, an increase of less than 1 per cent.

The names of the hundreds in each sample are shown at the foot of Table 1.3. The hundreds in the fast-growing group were chiefly centres of commercial activity, manufacture or mining, but include a few hundreds where numbers increased substantially even though they were largely rural. The example of the Isle of Ely shows how this might happen. The estimation of hundred populations before the first census is possible because of the collection and publication of *Parish Register Abstracts* in the 1801 census. The *Parish Register Abstract* for the Cambridgeshire hundred of the Isle of Ely included not only the city of Ely, but three hundreds which were later treated separately (Wisbech, North Witchford and South Witchford). The 'hundred' therefore had a much bigger population than most rural hundreds and the absolute rise in population was large even though its rate of growth was only about average for the country as a whole.[40]

The slow-growing hundreds, in contrast, were primarily agricultural areas but included a few towns (Poole, Salisbury, Evesham) where growth was limited in these decades.

The total expenditure on the poor rose by a broadly similar percentage in the two groups. Over the first period from 1783–1785 to 1803, the difference was immaterial, being close to 120 per cent in each case. In the second period 1803 to 1813–1815, the rise was somewhat larger in the 'fast' group but the difference was not large. The case was very different, however, when measured by expenditure per head of population. Given the unfamiliarity of pounds, shillings and pence in the twenty-first century it is convenient to express the totals in question as

---

[40] Both the Isle of Ely and England as a whole grew by about two-thirds over the forty-year period. For a largely agricultural area, however, its rate of growth was exceptionally high, attributable in large measure, no doubt, to the more effective drainage of the Fens which became feasible with steam drainage.

fractions of a pound. In 1783–1785 the annual expenditure per head of population in the two types of hundred was similar, £0.245 in the 'fast' group, £0.224 in the 'slow' group (just under five shillings in each case in the currency of the day). In 1803 the figure had risen by 55 per cent in the 'fast' group to £0.379, an increase which agrees fairly closely with the rise in the cost of living for poor people. The price of bread, for example, rose by 65 per cent over the two decades. In the 'slow' group the rise was markedly greater. The 1803 figure was £0.538, a rise of 141 per cent. Over the second period from 1803 to 1813–1815 the changes were more modest. In the 'fast' group the cost per inhabitant rose by 13 per cent to £0.426; in the 'slow' group by 23 per cent to £0.661. Over the whole thirty-year period from 1783–1785 to 1813–1815, therefore, the rise in the former case was 74 per cent (once again a broadly similar figure to the increase in the price of bread which rose by 101 per cent[41]), but it was very different in the latter case where the rise was far greater at 195 per cent. Whereas the burden per head was slightly lower in the slow-growing hundreds than in the fast-growing hundreds at the start of the period, by the end of the French wars it was 55 per cent higher than in the hundreds where population growth was rapid.

The pattern of change suggests that, despite the fact that agriculture was prosperous during the war period, the demand for labour faltered in rural areas even though population growth was still modest in the middle period 1791–1831, whereas the places experiencing very rapid growth, chiefly engaged in secondary and tertiary production, did not find that the burden of the poor increased any faster than the rise in the price of bread.

This brief examination of the possibility that when population growth was rapid overall it may have created greater difficulties in hundreds where the growth was modest than where it was swiftest has a limited purpose. A far wider and more searching analysis is needed to establish the reasons why a broad uniformity in the poor rate burden was replaced by wide discrepancies between different types of hundred. It will shortly be possible, for example, to specify the occupational structure of each hundred c.1815 and thereby to avoid making the crude assumption that very slow growth indicates a heavy dependence on agriculture as a

---

[41] The bread prices are London prices for the quartern loaf. On the assumption that the poor relief payments would reflect both current and recent prices, the bread price was calculated over a trailing three-year period including the current year. Thus the bread price for 1783–1785 was taken as the average for the years 1781–1785, that for 1803 as the average for 1801–1803, and that for 1813–1815 as the average for 1811–1815. Mitchell, *British Historical Statistics* (Cambridge, 1988), Prices, Table 2.2, pp. 769–770.

source of employment.[42] A wider study should, of course, also include information about the course of the poor law burden in the post-war period in different types of hundred. And the fact that England was at war for much of the middle period, 1791–1831, when growth was fastest, should not be ignored. At the time of the 1811 census the armed forces may have claimed approximately 15 per cent of the adult male population aged 18–45.[43] This represents a large annexation of manpower from the most productive age group and the fact that the period of warfare lasted for two decades prolonged this situation to an extent unknown in other wars before or since. A full discussion of this issue is beyond the scope of this chapter, but it is reasonable to suppose that the absence of men in the armed forces and other dislocations brought about by war affected the ability of the economy to adjust rapidly and flexibly to rising numbers.

The poor law data throw additional light on the contrast between the middle period and the two periods on either side of it, visible in the hundred population data. They serve to draw attention to an important aspect of the problems which England encountered when attempting to absorb the shock of a marked peak in the population growth rate.

The transition from an organic economy to one where traditional constraints on growth had become largely irrelevant also transformed the occupational structure of an economy and with it the distribution of population. In an organic economy where the land provides both food and the raw materials for secondary industry, agriculture is the predominant employer and the location of the bulk of the population is likely to reflect the varying value of the land for agricultural purposes. The northwest of England, where hills and moorland cover much of the land surface, will support a much sparser population than can make a living in East Anglia. If the national population total rises it is unlikely greatly to change the *relative* size of the populations of different regions. Disproportionate increases in secondary and tertiary employment may qualify this generalisation somewhat but violent change is unlikely.

---

[42] Under the provisions of Rose's Act (52 George III c. 146) the occupation of the father was to be set down when a baptism was recorded in an Anglican register. The occupational data for all ten thousand English parishes for the eight-year period 1813–1820 have been secured by the Cambridge Group for the History of Population and Social Structure under a grant from the ESRC (RES-000-23-0131). When the raw data have been processed the occupational structure of each parish and hundred will be known.

[43] See Wrigley *et al.*, *English Population History*, Table A9.1 pp. 614–615 for the age breakdowns on which this estimate is based. At the time of the 1811 census there were estimated to be a total of 273,021 men in the army, navy and merchant service. *1851 Census*, Population tables, I, Number of inhabitants, vol. I, Report, p. xxiii, tab. II.

During the transition to a mineral-based energy-rich economy the boot is on the other foot. When thermal and mechanical energy became available on a scale and at a price which slowly transformed the industrial production landscape, and as technical innovation permitted their effective harnessing to increase productivity per head, a radical reordering of the relative size of regional populations followed. For example, at one extreme the population of Lancashire increased from 324,126 in 1761 to 2,063,437 in 1851, while at the other that of Wiltshire over the same period increased from 181,295 to 260,895. In the former case the 1851 total was more than six times greater than in 1761, in the latter case the rise was only a little more than 40 per cent.[44] Growth is necessarily lopsided because it is concentrated in the secondary and tertiary sectors. The paradigmatic sequence is from an original situation in which primary, secondary and tertiary employment is divided in the approximate ratio 80:15:5, to an intermediate situation following the rapid expansion of secondary industry where the ratio may run, say, 40:50:10, which in turn is ultimately replaced by a situation, found in the wealthier countries today, where tertiary activity dominates the scene and the ratio may be 5:15:80.

Secondary and tertiary employment, unlike primary employment, is not largely determined by the distribution of productive land and therefore as population grows its geographical balance is radically changed. If productivity per head in agriculture is rising, the proportion of the workforce in agriculture will tend to fall, and the absolute numbers of men in agriculture may remain roughly stable. Only if total agricultural output rises even faster than output per head will there be an opportunity to employ more men on the land. Otherwise any further accumulation of population in rural areas will be an indication of stress. In general, England escaped severe difficulty under this head but the behaviour of the poor rate in hundreds in which occupational structures were very different during the period of peak growth rates suggests that the country flirted with the problem for a time.

The population of England in 1751 was 5,921,905; in 1851 17,030,147, not far short of a tripling over the century.[45] The annual rate of growth was little more than 1 per cent, modest compared with that reached in much of the world in the second half of the twentieth century, but rare to a degree in the pre-industrial world if sustained over a full century. It contrasted sharply with other west European countries in the same period, as may be seen in Table 1.4. As a result, though still

---

[44] Wrigley, *The Early English Censuses*, Table A2.6.   [45] Ibid.

Table 1.4 *Population growth in England compared with other countries in Western Europe 1750–1850*

	Population (millions)			Relative size	
	c.1750	*c.1850*	*1850/1750 x 100*	*c.1750*	*c.1850*
England	5.92	17.03	287.7	100	100
France	24.60	36.30	147.6	416	213
Germany	17.00	35.40	208.2	287	208
Italy	15.80	24.70	156.3	267	145
The Netherlands	1.90	3.10	163.2	32	18
Spain	8.60	14.80	172.1	145	87
Sweden	1.78	3.48	195.5	30	20

Note: In several cases the national units was a nineteenth-century creation. Livi-Bacci's estimates refer to the units which came into being after unification.
Sources: England: Wrigley, *The Early English Censuses*, Table A2.6. Other countries: M. Livi-Bacci, *The Population of Europe: A History* (Oxford, 2000), Table 1.1, pp. 8–9.

much smaller in population than the most populous European countries, the relative position of England changed considerably. Despite the rapidity of population growth in England, however, the number of men engaged in agriculture changed very little, whereas in other countries agricultural employment continued to grow. The absolute number of men employed in agriculture in England began to decline from the 1840s at the latest and probably from an earlier date.[46] The decline was continuous thereafter, whereas the comparable totals continued to rise until a much later date elsewhere. Reliable comparative data for this period are scarce but it is worth noting that the number agriculturally employed was rising in France in the second half of the nineteenth century, peaking in 1896; in Italy the number increased until 1921; in the Netherlands until 1930; in Sweden until 1920.[47]

---

[46] E. A. Wrigley, 'The occupational structure of England in the mid-nineteenth century', in E. A. Wrigley, *Poverty, Progress, and Population* (Cambridge, 2004), Table 5.8, p. 166, and E. A. Wrigley, 'Men on the land and men in the countryside: employment in agriculture in early nineteenth-century England' in L. Bonfield, R. M. Smith and K. Wrightson (eds), *The World We Have Gained: Histories of Population and Social Structure* (Oxford, 1986). A conventional reading of the census totals suggests the number was still rising between 1841 and 1851 but there is good reason to suppose that a change in census practice meant that the published totals are misleading.

[47] All data taken from B. R. Mitchell, *European Historical Statistics 1750–1975*, 2nd rev. edn (London and Basingstoke, 1981), Table C1, pp. 161–173. It should be noted that changes in registration practice and conventions make the reliability and comparability of the series uncertain.

The recent construction of population estimates for each hundred covering the whole period of the classic Industrial Revolution makes it possible to view the nature of the changes taking place in a new light. There were fifteen times as many hundreds as counties. This enables patterns of change to be traced more clearly. The marked concentration of growth in a small fraction of the total number of hundreds and the very modest growth in fully half of them brings home the scale of the contrast with earlier times and with other countries at the same time. Comparing the path of real wages during a period of unprecedented population growth rates with what was to be expected in the light of the experience of earlier periods leaves no doubt about the extent of the change in the economic constitution of the country, enabling it to meet successfully a challenge which would have spelled disaster in earlier centuries. Markedly lopsided growth was a key element in this success. Rising productivity per head in agriculture limited the opportunity for increased employment in agricultural areas, other than in some types of tertiary activity, so that slow growth in such areas was a mark of the success of industry and commerce in providing jobs elsewhere for those who could not find work locally. This in turn implied spectacular growth where the new opportunities were being created, with two-thirds of all the population growth taking place in one-tenth of the hundreds.

There remains the question of why the population growth rate in England should have peaked towards the end of the eighteenth century and in the early decades of the nineteenth century. The proximate cause of the increased rate of growth is clear. It was primarily due to a rise in fertility rather than any marked decline in mortality. The fertility rise occurred because marriage age fell, and fewer men and women remained single. Fertility within marriage also rose with a decline in the average interval between births, probably due to a marked fall in the stillbirth rate.[48] Furthermore, despite the fact that women were marrying earlier and fewer remained single, there was an increase in the proportion of all births which were illegitimate.[49] But many aspects of the feedback occurring between economic change, prevailing social conventions and individual behaviour which underpinned the rising fertility trend remain poorly understood. The scale of the surge in population growth rates is clear, together with its strikingly uneven geographical impact. The

[48] E. A. Wrigley, 'Explaining the rise in marital fertility in the "long" eighteenth century', *Economic History Review*, 51, (1998), pp. 435–464.
[49] E. A. Wrigley, 'Marriage, fertility and population growth in eighteenth-century England' in R. B. Outhwaite (ed.), *Marriage and Society: Studies in the Social History of Marriage* (London, 1981), esp. pp. 146–163.

severity of the challenge which it entailed is also evident. But much remains to be done to account more fully both for the rise in the growth rate and its later decline.

This chapter should be viewed as a *ballon d'essai*. It presents material for discussion rather than providing conclusive evidence for the thesis advanced. It is potentially vulnerable to new empirical findings. For example, if it can be shown that during the middle period of fastest population growth agricultural employment was increasing to match population growth in rural areas, the inferences which I have made about a relative failure to cope with population pressure are called in question. Similarly, the evidence of poor law expenditure trends in fast- and slow-growing hundreds, though suggestive, will only become conclusive when the occupational structures of each hundred can be specified.[50] And it would be illuminating to analyse poor law expenditures for all hundreds and over a longer period, rather than using only a relatively small random sample of hundreds. There are also some more general issues which are covered largely by implication rather than being directly confronted. The escape from the constraints associated with organic economies which is portrayed in the graph in Figure 1.1 suggests that incomes were rising throughout the whole period 1761–1851. There is no sign in the graph that this advance was thrown off course during the period of fastest population growth between 1791 and 1831. In a lengthier treatment of the impact of the period of fastest population growth, these issues and others linked to them would need much fuller consideration.

I trust that the main thesis of this chapter is, however, both clear and beyond reasonable doubt. The pace of population growth during the later eighteenth and early nineteenth centuries was without parallel in English history or in contemporary experience elsewhere other than in areas of recent settlement. Past experience suggested that such a rapid rate of growth must involve great suffering and a severe depression in living standards. The assumptions made by the classical economists implied a similar outcome. It is against this backcloth that the economic record of the period should be judged. This has not always been the case. For example, the conventional discussion of trends in real incomes sometimes embodies the assumption that the absence of clear evidence of increase in some sense implies failure, especially as there is much clearer evidence of advance in the second half of the nineteenth century. But if comparison is made not with the future but with the past, the

---

[50] See footnote 42.

degree of success achieved must appear far greater. This becomes clearer when population trends are considered not just at the national level but using small units such as the hundred. The stark contrast between areas growing far faster than the national average and those where there was little or no growth suggests a massive reshaping of economic activity without which rapidly rising numbers would have spelled deep misery. There is suggestive evidence that as growth rates reached a peak the strain became severe, but overall the scale of the achievement in coping with rapid population growth was striking.

2 The 'urban renaissance' and the mob: rethinking civic improvement over the long eighteenth century

Emma Griffin

The 'urban renaissance' and the mob

Few concepts in urban history have been so influential in recent years as that of the 'urban renaissance'. The expression was formulated by Peter Borsay in the early 1980s, and taken to denote the process by which civic leaders sought to bring greater order, decorum and beauty to civic centres by demolishing some of their densely packed, vernacular buildings and replacing them with wide open thoroughfares and new buildings made from modern materials.[1] And despite the emergence of a large and growing literature on the eighteenth-century town in the past two decades, the existence of the urban renaissance still remains largely undisputed.[2] Much of this work has focused on the physical improvements made to the urban infrastructure by the construction of new streets and buildings,[3] the creation of parks, walks and gardens,[4] and the introduction of street lighting.[5] At the same time,

---

[1] Peter Borsay, *The English Urban Renaissance. Culture and Society in the Provincial Town, 1660–1770* (Oxford, 1989); M. Girouard, *The English Town* (New Haven, 1990); Carl B. Estabrook, *Urbane and Rustic England. Cultural Ties and the Social Spheres in the Provinces, 1660–1780* (Manchester, 1998); R Sweet, *The English Town, 1660–1840* (Harlow, 1999), pp. 219–255. For Scotland, see Bob Harris, 'Towns, improvement and cultural change in Georgian Scotland: the evidence of the Angus burghs, c. 1760–1820', *Urban History*, 33(2), (2006), pp. 195–212.

[2] See, however, A. McInnes, 'The emergence of a leisure town; Shrewsbury, 1660–1760', *Past & Present*, 120, (1988), pp. 53–87; J. Jefferson Looney, 'Cultural life in the provinces: Leeds and York, 1720–1820' in A. L. Beier, David Cannadine and James M. Rosenheim (eds), *The First Modern Society* (Cambridge, 1989); Leonard Schwarz, 'Residential leisure towns in England towards the end of the eighteenth century', *Urban History*, 27(1), (2000), pp. 51–61.

[3] Michael Reed, 'The transformation of urban space, 1700–1840', in Peter Clark (ed.), *The Cambridge Urban History of Britain, 1540–1840*, ii (Cambridge, 2000).

[4] Peter Borsay, 'The rise of the promenade; the social and cultural use of space in the English provincial town, 1660–1800', *British Journal of Eighteenth-century Studies*, 9, (1986), pp. 125–140.

[5] Malcolm Falkus, 'Lighting in the dark ages of English economic history', in D. C. Coleman and A. H. John (eds), *Trade, Government and Economy in Pre-industrial England: Essays Presented to F. J. Fisher* (London, 1976).

however, this literature has shown itself sensitive to cultural components of urban change, stressing also the social opportunities offered by new urban amenities such as assembly rooms, inns and coffee houses and the role urban improvement played in forging a new civic identity.[6] Furthermore, this account of the blossoming eighteenth-century town complements remarkably well a number of other themes that currently dominate the historiography of this period – the importance of politeness, for example,[7] the rise of consumerism and shopping,[8] and the emergence of the 'public sphere'.[9] Together these various historiographical strands present a coherent picture of eighteenth-century urban life, pointing to the existence of an improving physical environment which formed the locus of polite sociability and middle-class consumerism and political discourse.

Yet for all the internal consistency of this account of the Georgian town, it does not fit so well with a largely unrelated body of literature concerned with various elements of street life over the long eighteenth century. Frank O'Gorman, for example, has reminded us that a large part of every late-eighteenth-century election was conducted out in the streets, despite the frequent brawling and rioting they encouraged.[10] It was not simply formal politics that took place in the streets. David Cressy and Ronald Hutton have demonstrated civic elites busy at work organising political celebrations and commemorations in the streets of

---

[6] A. Vickery, *The Gentleman's Daughter: Women's Lives in Georgian England* (New Haven, 1998); Peter Clark, *The English Alehouse: A Social History, 1200–1830* (London, 1983); Peter Clark, *British Clubs and Societies 1580–1800: The Origins of an Associational World* (Oxford, 2000); R. Sweet, *The Writing of Urban Histories in Eighteenth-century England* (Oxford, 1997); Joyce Ellis, '"For the honour of the town": comparison, competition and civic identity in eighteenth-century England', *Urban History*, 30(3), (2003), pp. 325–337; Paul Elliott, 'The origins of the "creative class": provincial urban society, scientific culture and socio-political marginality in Britain in the eighteenth and nineteenth centuries', *Social History*, 28(3), (2003), pp. 361–387.

[7] Lawrence E. Klein, 'Politeness and the interpretation of the British eighteenth century', *Historical Journal*, 45(4), (2002), pp. 869–898; Paul Langford, 'The uses of eighteenth-century politeness', *Transactions of the Royal Historical Society*, 6th ser., 12, (2002), pp. 311–331.

[8] Ian Mitchell, 'The development of urban retailing 1700–1815' in P. Clark (ed.), *The Transformation of English Provincial Towns, 1600–1800* (London, 1984); Jon Stobart, 'Shopping streets as social space: leisure, consumerism and improvement in an eighteenth-century county town', *Urban History*, 25, (1998), pp. 3–21; John Beckett and Catherine Smith, 'Urban renaissance and consumer revolution in Nottingham, 1688–1750', *Urban History*, 27(1), (2000), pp. 31–50.

[9] James Van Horn Melton, *The Rise of the Public in Enlightenment Europe* (Cambridge, 2001); Hannah Barker and Simon Burrows (eds), *Press, Politics and the Public Sphere in Europe and North America, 1760–1820* (Cambridge, 2002).

[10] Frank O'Gorman, 'Campaign rituals and ceremonies: the social meaning of elections in England, 1780–1860', *Past & Present*, 135, (1992), pp. 79–115.

Stuart England, and my own work has revealed that these practices continued long into the eighteenth century.[11] And alongside these political expressions of the elite, a wide range of plebeian political activities was to be found in the public spaces of the eighteenth-century town. A large historiography concerned with the political actions of those excluded from formal political processes has drawn attention to a range of popular street politics running from choreographed and orderly processions and demonstrations at the one end to riots at the other.[12] Certainly these studies do not suggest that plebeian street politics remained unchanged through the eighteenth century, and some offer convincing evidence for the taming of some aspects of political street culture, yet none suggest that these practices had disappeared by the century's end. A century of civic improvement may have altered the form of the more boisterous manifestations of street politics, but it did not bring about their demise.

At the same time, research into the history of popular entertainments has indicated the existence of a plebeian counterpoint to the walks, balls and music festivals enjoyed by the well-to-do, most of it located right in the middle of the town's improved streets and squares. Eighteenth-century popular entertainments ranged from the occasional annual events, such as matches of football through the town centre or the children's blood-sport of throwing at cocks on Shrove Tuesday, to events such as bull-baitings or fairs held on a more regular basis throughout the year, to the informal entertainment offered by quacks, mountebanks and itinerant musicians on an almost daily basis.[13] Studies of London's street life and underworld point to the presence of street selling,[14]

---

[11] David Cressy, *Bonfires and Bells. National Memory and the Protestant Calendar in Elizabethan and Stuart England* (London, 1989); Ronald Hutton, *The Rise and Fall of Merry England. The Ritual Year, 1400–1700* (Oxford, 1994); Emma Griffin, *England's Revelry. A History of Popular Sports and Pastimes, 1660–1830* (Oxford, 2005). See also Robert Poole, 'The march to Peterloo: politics and festivity in late Georgian England', *Past & Present*, 192, (2006), pp. 109–153.

[12] Ian Gilmour, *Riot, Risings and Revolution: Governance and Violence in Eighteenth-century England* (London, 1992); Nicholas Rogers, *Crowds, Culture, and Politics in Georgian Britain* (Oxford, 1998); Mark Harrison, *Crowds and History: Mass Phenomena in English Towns, 1790–1835* (Cambridge, 2002); Robert Shoemaker, *The London Mob: Violence and Disorder in Eighteenth-century England* (London, 2004), esp. pp. 111–152.

[13] Griffin, *England's Revelry*; Charles Phythian-Adams, 'Milk and soot: the changing vocabulary of a popular ritual in Stuart and Hanoverian London' in D. Fraser and Anthony Sutcliffe (eds), *The Pursuit of Urban History* (London, 1983); Brenda Assael 'Music in the air: noise, performers and the contest over the streets in the mid-nineteenth-century metropolis' in Tim Hitchcock and Heather Shore (eds), *The Streets of London: From the Great Fire to the Great Stink* (London, 2003).

[14] James H. Winter, *London's Teeming Streets* (London, 1993), pp. 100–117.

prostitution[15] and begging[16] – all to be found somewhere in the open spaces of the eighteenth-century city, and usually in the nineteenth-century city as well. Once again, these studies do not present the eighteenth century as a period of unchanging cultural practice, indicating that some at least of these customs – bull-baiting, organised football and street-walking, for example – had been either suppressed or relocated by the century's end. Yet despite these developments we still seem very far from the world of politeness. Large civic fairs and their swarms of low-class pleasure-seekers continued to engulf the market-place on a periodic basis, and itinerant quacks, performers and musicians continued to entertain (and annoy) on the public streets long into the nineteenth century. Tim Hitchcock has concluded his history of begging by arguing that 'a long-standing culture of mutual obligation and charity ensured that beggars were able to retain their freedom to ... stand at street corners'.[17] The fortunes of different aspects of plebeian street culture were highly uneven, and whilst urban improvement certainly forced an end to some customs, it did not lead to the elimination of all in a clear and linear fashion.

This brief survey of the literature on popular street politics, entertainment and the urban underworld suggests, at the very least, that there is something incomplete about the standard account of the urban renaissance. Just as the eighteenth-century civic reformer sought to remove anything that was loud, smelly, dirty or noisy from the streets, so too have urban historians been hard at work excising the rubbish and racket from their histories. In reality, however, the areas that civic reformers sought to improve were not empty and unused spaces, but spaces already used by others, largely excluded from the improving process. The poor may not have influenced planning design, but they still had the power to subvert the visions of those who ruled them, and they need to be reintegrated in some way into our historical narratives of the eighteenth-century town.

Improving the market-place

At the same time as there is an apparently unnoticed gap in much recent work on the eighteenth-century town between contemporary visions of civic improvement and the reality of street life, there is also an absence.

---

[15] Tony Henderson, *Disorderly Women in Eighteenth-century London. Prostitution and Control in the Metropolis, 1730–1830* (London, 1999), pp. 52–75.
[16] Tim Hitchcock, 'Begging on the streets of eighteenth-century London', *Journal of British Studies*, 44(3), (2005), pp. 478–498.
[17] Ibid., p. 479.

It is something of a surprise that the most central, the most iconic, the most public and the most used of all civic spaces – the market-place – is also a blind spot in recent urban history. The market-place was not only an important part of the physical landscape of the town, subject to improvement and upgrading in the same way as other elements of the urban landscape. It was also, in fact, the location of much of the political activity and street entertainment enjoyed by the poor. Sitting at both the physical and cultural centre of the town, the market-place is therefore an excellent place to attempt to connect the hitherto largely unconnected histories of civic improvement and urban street life.

Most English markets already had a very long history by the eighteenth century. Some were in existence prior to the Norman Conquest of 1066; many more were created in the thirteenth and fourteenth centuries, when well in excess of a thousand new markets were licensed.[18] And with markets came market-places. Medieval trade regulations required that markets should take place in an open and public space with defined boundaries: all goods should physically pass through this space, and trading should occur at a set time. Bulk purchase of material outside the market-place was prohibited and many markets were restricted to small-scale purchases at 'reasonable prices'.[19] Confining buying and selling to a certain time and place enabled the proper regulation of trade and assisted in the monitoring of illegal practices, such as forestalling (buying goods before they reached the markets), regrating (buying and then reselling goods at market) and engrossing (buying up goods in large quantities). A physical market-place was fundamental if these ideals were to be upheld, so the granting of medieval market charters was also accompanied by the creation of many new market-places.

If the medieval market-place was primarily a place to conduct trade, however, it was also much more than this. Any space which could be guaranteed to draw large crowds of people at defined times inevitably also enjoyed a broader cultural significance, and medieval historians have recently begun to consider the social as opposed to purely economic dimension of the medieval market.[20] James Masschaele has drawn attention to how medieval market-places were embedded within the formal structures of power and were used by both Church and state

---

[18] R. H. Britnell, 'The proliferation of markets in England, 1200–1349', *Economic History Review*, 2nd series, 34, (1981), pp. 209–221.

[19] E. P. Thompson, 'The moral economy of the English crowd in the eighteenth century', *Past & Present*, 50, (1971), pp. 76–136.

[20] James Masschaele, 'The public space of the market place in medieval England', *Speculum*, 77(2), (2002), pp. 383–421.

to disseminate news about politics and government, and for punishment.[21] The exact uses to which the market-place was put had certainly undergone some change by the early eighteenth century, yet a recognisably medieval pattern of political and social activity still endured. The extent to which they survived the urban renaissance forms one of the central concerns of this chapter.

A successful market-place is always a heavily used space, and wherever evidence about markets has survived, it points to the owners of market charters engaging in a continuous process of repairing, improving and modifying the fabric of their market-places. As many historians have suggested, however, the eighteenth century witnessed a quickening of the pace of urban improvement, and this renewed effort is clearly discernible in the history of market-places. In keeping with the spirit of improvement, a few towns even built a new market-place. In the ancient borough of Sandwich, for example, a new market-place was laid out 'in an elegant, airy stile';[22] and the growing coastal town of Brighton built a new market-place in the 1770s.[23] In most towns, however, improvements to the market-place were more piecemeal, and involved a gradual process of clearing, updating and modifying the market-place that already existed.

This process can be seen with particular clarity in the county town of Gloucester. Here the markets were held in four wide streets crossing at the centre of the town and, like many market-places, this space was filled with numerous encroachments by the eighteenth century. At the centre of the town was situated a covered market for butter and cheese known as the Kings Board, and the High Cross – an ornate cross adorned with the statues of several monarchs. The butchers' shambles and mercery both had fixed stalls on the streets. Two market houses had been built in the middle of the streets during the seventeenth century – the Barley-Market House and Wheat-Market House.[24] In addition to this collection of covered markets, market crosses and buildings, the four central streets that served as a market-place were filled with statues of George I and Queen Anne, a large and ornate water conduit, a pillory and the stocks.[25]

---

[21] Ibid., p. 421.

[22] Edward Hasted, *The History and Topographical Survey of the County of Kent*, vol. 11, (Canterbury, 1797–1801), p. 115.

[23] Frederick George Fisher, *Brighton New Guide* (London, 1800), p. 6.

[24] Samuel Rudder, *The History and Antiquities of Gloucester; A New History of Gloucester* (Cirencester, 1781), p. 34. See also M. D. Lobel (ed.), *Historic Towns: Maps and Plans of Towns and Cities in the British Isles with Historical Commentaries, from Earliest Times to 1800*, i, (Oxford, 1969).

[25] Rudder, *History of Gloucester*, pp. 17–36.

In the second half of the eighteenth century, most of these edifices were taken down in an attempt to enhance the appearance of the centre of the town and to improve the flow of traffic. The High Cross, condemned for 'greatly [interrupting] the passage for carriages' was removed in 1750 by Act of Parliament.[26] The Kings Board and a number of houses 'which project inconveniently' onto the streets were also removed by this Act. A second Act of 1781 provided a new market house for the dairy market and ordered the removal of the remaining street furniture: the statues, the water conduit, the pillory and stocks, and the two market houses were all swept away by this Act. Within a little more than thirty years, the appearance of the centre of Gloucester had changed beyond recognition. The disordered jumble of buildings located in the city's centre had been demolished, leaving a clear, empty space, which was pleasing to the eye and enabled the free flow of carriages and people.

Though few towns saw quite so much street furniture removed from the market-place in such a short space of time, the processes at work in Gloucester were not atypical. In Halifax, for example, an antique market cross, the pillory, the stocks and a maypole were all cleared from the market-place in the early nineteenth century.[27] In Chesterfield, an old market house and a row of buildings between the market-place and New Square were taken down in the early nineteenth century, thereby opening up and considerably extending the market-place, and rendering it, in the opinion of one resident, 'one of the most commodious in the kingdom'.[28] The length and breadth of the country, civic authorities were involved in making piecemeal improvements to their marketing spaces. As part of the process of eighteenth-century civic improvement that Borsay has described, civic authorities were attempting to enhance their market-places by removing old and dilapidated buildings, and laying forth a clean, open space.

Improvements to market-places should not, however, be understood simply as a process of demolition, and the changes witnessed in provincial market-places goes deeper than the framework of an 'urban renaissance' allows. At the heart of this movement was a more subtle endeavour, involving not simply the removal of buildings and edifices,

---

[26] Ibid., p. 31.

[27] The cross, pillory, stocks and maypole were all removed at some point between the publication of Watson's history of 1775 and White's of 1837. See John Watson, *History and Antiquities of the Parish of Halifax, in Yorkshire* (London, 1775), p. 203; William White, *History, Gazetteer, and Directory, of the West-riding of Yorkshire*, i, (Sheffield, 1837), p. 400.

[28] George Hall, *The History of Chesterfield* (London, 1839), p. 182.

but also an attempt to redefine the way central marketing spaces were both used and perceived. One element of this was effacing the rural appearance of many urban market-places. Consider, for example, the market-place in seventeenth-century Nottingham: according to John Evelyn it had 'a pond in the centre, a mouldering stone wall down its midst, trees, saw-pits . . .' .[29] In addition, it was unpaved and during bad weather the market-place resembled a muddy country fair more than a modern civic centre. The market-place in neighbouring Leicester had a similarly rural appearance. It contained 'the Pigeon Tree, under which country women sat to sell pigeons', and a horse pond 'where the porters from the Crowns and the Cranes washed their horses'.[30] In both of these towns, improvement involved removing these rural features and fashioning a more modern, commercial and civic space. These improvements were designed not simply to remove clutter and set forth an open space. They were intended to make the market-place feel more like a civic space, to look like a place more suited to business.

Along with the traditional rural features of provincial market-places went many of the medieval market crosses that civic authorities had built and maintained for several centuries. Besides being used for markets, crosses were also used by the ruling elites as a place to proclaim public notices and disseminate political messages. They were consequently a focal point in many towns with both practical and symbolic significance, and they were accordingly situated in the most central parts of the town.[31]

Many fell victim to the modernising spirit that swept through towns in the second half of the eighteenth century. In both Nottingham and Leicester, for example, the removal of the old market crosses formed part of the modernisation process just described. In Nottingham there were no fewer than five market crosses in the early eighteenth century.[32] All had been removed by the early nineteenth century. The Butter Cross and Monday Cross were the first to go.[33] Next the Malt Cross was taken down, it 'being of no kind of Use and Productive of nothing

---

[29] Quoted in J. Holland Walker, 'An itinerary of Nottingham', *Transactions of the Thoroton Society of Nottinghamshire*, 35, (1931), at p. 78.

[30] William Gardiner, *Music and Friends, or Pleasant Recollections of a Dilettante*, iii, (London, 1853), p. 11.

[31] See Russell Chamberlin, *The National Trust. The English Country Town* (London, 1983), pp. 79–84.

[32] Charles Deering, *The History of Nottingham* (Nottingham, 1751; facs. repr. Wakefield, 1970), pp. 8–9.

[33] The cross must have been removed between 1721, when the corporation paid for 'mendings up at the Cros', and the publication of Deering's *History* in 1751. See *Records of the Borough of Nottingham, 1702–1760*, vi, (Nottingham, 1914), p. 84; Deering, *History of Nottingham*, 8; Holland Walker, 'Itinerary of Nottingham'.

but Inconvenience and Expence', and a few years after that both the Hen Cross and the Weekday Cross were likewise removed.[34] The High Cross in neighbouring Leicester was stripped to one pillar in the 1770s in order to improve the flow of traffic.[35] This final remnant was removed in the 1830s.

Such actions were by no means unusual. Across the country, civic authorities, who for centuries had regarded their market crosses as the focal point of the town, began to view their crosses very differently. Certainly some towns continued the investment required to keep their market crosses in good repair – the fine fifteenth-century cross at Chichester, for example, was 'spared the odium' of demolition in the early nineteenth century thanks to the preservation efforts of some of the town's residents.[36] In many places, however, the market cross was now perceived as an obstruction without utilitarian or aesthetic value. One after another, civic authorities concluded their crosses were not worth the expense or bother of their upkeep.

Along with rural features and market crosses, went many of the sheds, tenements and encroachments that seemed to appear inexorably on market-places with the passing of time. At Wolverhampton, for example, Improvement Acts of 1777 and 1814 removed 'unseemly buildings and obstructions' making instead 'fine openings ... to the Market-place and some of the streets, which were before close and confined'.[37] In part, no doubt, civic authorities wished to see the removal of sheds and encroachments simply in order to improve the flow of traffic. Certainly, most towns had expanding populations in the century after 1750 and the consequent growth in trade and in traffic caused a problem that many authorities needed to address. But it would be mistaken to assume that it was only, or even primarily, concerns about the movement of traffic that motivated town leaders to purchase and take down the many sheds, tenements and stalls that cluttered their market-places. As well as

---

[34] For the Malt Cross, see *Records of the Borough of Nottingham, 1760–1800*, vii, (Nottingham, 1947), p. 282. For the Hen and Malt Cross, see *Records of the Borough of Nottingham, 1760–1800*, vii, (Nottingham, 1947), p. 391; Holland Walker, 'Itinerary of Nottingham', p. 81. For the Weekday Cross, see Holland Walker, 'Itinerary of Nottingham', 32 (1928), p. 66. In the 1850s, all three crosses were remembered by name. See Nottinghamshire Archives, 'Diary of Samuel Collinson', M382, p. 63.

[35] Gardiner, *Music and Friends*, iii, p. 10; John Throsby, *The History and Antiquities of the Ancient Town of Leicester* (Leicester, 1791), pp. 364–365; [Susannah Watts], *A Walk through Leicester; Being a Guide to Strangers* (Leicester, 1804), pp. 28–29.

[36] *Antiquarian and Topographical Cabinet*, vi, (London, 1809), [no page]. See also the photographs of the fine market crosses still standing in Chichester and Salisbury in Chamberlin, *National Trust*, p. 80.

[37] William White, *History, Gazetteer, and Directory of Staffordshire* (Sheffield, 1834), p. 170.

improving traffic flows, civic authorities were consciously removing some of the messier, dirtier and noisier aspects of trade and commerce. The market people's sheds and tenements not only blocked the flow of traffic, they were also an eyesore – a constant visual reminder of the working nature of the market. Civic elites were certainly keen to see improved traffic flows, but they were also seeking to create a pleasant civic space when the markets were quiet or closed.

In this attempt to improve and modernise market-places, butchers' shambles were a particular target. In Carlisle, for example, the shambles on the market-place were condemned for having 'a very grotesque and antique appearance': they were purchased and taken down in the 1790s.[38] In the first half of the nineteenth century, many more towns followed suit: Stockton upon Tees in 1825, for example,[39] and Chester in 1828.[40] And once again, there was more to these clearances than a simple desire to remove clutter and set forth an open space; at the heart of these endeavours was an attempt to create a more dignified urban centre. Thus in Hereford, a local writer objected not simply to the appearance of the shambles – a 'large and irregular cluster of wooden buildings' – but more seriously to the 'indecency' of the public slaughter of animals, an attraction to 'children, especially'.[41] The overall trend is unmistakable. Civic leaders were striving to create cleaner and more orderly market-places, and the removal of butchers' shambles was an integral part of this process. The demolition of shambles formed part of a more far-reaching attempt to transform the market-place from a place of workaday business to something altogether more edifying.[42]

With the removal of crosses, butchers' shambles and the traders' sheds and tenements, many provincial market-places changed dramatically in appearance over the long eighteenth century. The disorganised, cluttered market-places of old were gradually replaced by clear, open, harmonious spaces. In many towns, this process of change was completed with the construction of new buildings – corn exchanges, market houses and halls, and shambles – specifically designed to house some of the marketing activity that earlier demolitions had displaced. In place of the market people's unauthorised sheds and vernacular buildings, fine

---

[38] William Hutchinson, *The History and Antiquities of the City of Carlisle* (Carlisle, 1796), pp. 77–78.

[39] John Brewster, *The Parochial History and Antiquities of Stockton upon Tees.* (Stockton upon Tees, 1829), p. 223.

[40] Joseph Hemingway, *History of the City of Chester*, ii, (Chester, 1831), pp. 14–16.

[41] John Price, *An Historical Account of Hereford* (Hereford, 1796), p. 62.

[42] See also Ian MacLachlan, 'A bloody offal nuisance: the persistence of private slaughter-houses in nineteenth-century London', *Urban History*, 34(2), (2007), pp. 227–254.

modern buildings paid for by the public purse went up. This was a conscious attempt not only to enhance the appearance of the provincial town, but also to impose a greater degree of order and control within it. Some aspects of outdoor marketing were unavoidably noisy and chaotic, and providing new modern buildings for trading helped to create the appearance of a more decorous town centre. At the same time, the new public buildings were a visible symbol of civic leaders' wealth and power; these were imposing structures that helped to reinforce the message of a ruling body firmly in control.[43]

There can be little doubt that the eighteenth century witnessed a significant refashioning of the market-place in provincial towns, as one town after another sought its own improvement Act, each involving some attempt to clear or smarten up the market-place. The extent of this transition, however, is not fully comprehended by our standard account of the 'urban renaissance'. Demolitions and new buildings did help to enhance the appearance of the town in the way that many architectural and urban historians have demonstrated, but they also had a deeper symbolic and cultural significance. This was not simply an attempt to beautify the provincial town, it was also a systematic and far-reaching attempt to clean up the innately messy, noisy and disordered world of marketing.

It is perhaps worth underscoring this final point. These attempts to improve the market-place were intended to enhance and improve the traditional outdoor market: they were not part of an attack on the existing system of markets. Certainly improvements were often accompanied by the reorganisation of markets, and sometimes with the removal of some markets from one part of town to another. The most dirty and inconvenient markets – usually those of horses, sheep and cattle – were frequently moved to streets at the edge of town at the time of improvement, but this still left the markets of meat, fish, fruits, vegetables, dairy, earthenware, leather and clothes at their traditional locations in the centre of town. Sheffield's Improvement Act of 1784, for example, removed all livestock from the central streets of the Wicker: the cattle and pigs markets were moved to the edge of the town, and the sites they vacated became hay and fruit markets instead.[44] Civic authorities were not seeking to reform, reduce or interfere in any other way with traditional market processes, which remained intact well into the

[43] For market halls, see, in particular, James Schmiechen and Kenneth Carls, *The British Market Hall. A Social and Architectural History* (New Haven, 1999).

[44] David Hey, *Fiery Blades of Hallamshire: Sheffield and its Neighbourhood, 1660–1740* (Leicester, 1991).

nineteenth century. Improvements were designed to facilitate marketing, not to suppress it.[45] Indeed, it is more helpful to consider these changes as part of a desire to separate marketing from other facets of urban life. Part of the improving process in towns involved the creation of areas where polite citizens did not have to walk through muddy, unpaved streets, slip on the detritus of food markets, and mix with farmers, pigs and chickens. The goal was not to eliminate mud, food and animals. Eighteenth-century civic leaders knew such things were part and parcel of any economically vibrant town; they simply wished to create a few pleasant spaces without them. Seen in this context, the urban renaissance appears a far more pragmatic and limited phenomenon than its more enthusiastic proponents suggest.

Improving the populace?

Whilst urban improvement did rather little to alter markets and marketing, it did have significant ramifications on some of the social, cultural and political practices that had graced the early modern market-place. It should already be clear that these improvements were not simply about the beautification of urban space. The redesigned spaces contained a message about the appropriate and legitimate uses to which civic spaces might be put, and urban elites underscored this message by gradually changing the way in which they organised and managed political and recreational events in their public market-places. Some of these developments are already well known. Studies of civic celebrations and entertainments, for example, have shown urban elites withdrawing their support for bonfires and barrels of ale in the market-place, and replacing them with much more carefully orchestrated events.[46] During the course of research for my PhD, I uncovered another, rather less-well-known, example: the bull-bait. At the start of the eighteenth century many town authorities paid for the upkeep of a bull-ring at which butchers could bait their bulls before slaughter; some even upheld local medieval by-laws prohibiting the slaughter of unbaited bulls. Their support for these by-laws and bull-rings had largely evaporated by the middle of the century – this chaotic plebeian pastime was incongruous in the new urban environment they were aiming to achieve.

---

[45] On this point, see Steve Poole, 'Scarcity and the civic tradition: market management in Bristol, 1709–1815' in Adrian Randall and Andrew Charlesworth (eds), *Markets, Market Culture and Popular Protest in Eighteenth-century Britain and Ireland* (Liverpool, 1996).

[46] Nicholas Rogers, 'Crowds and political festival in Georgian England' in Tim Harris (ed.), *The Politics of the Excluded, c. 1500–1850* (Basingstoke, 2001).

Alongside these examples we might also consider the case of public punishment. The market-place had traditionally been the location of numerous different punishments, ordered by both the spiritual and secular courts. At the most serious end was the pillory – its use was reserved for those convicted of notorious crimes, such as forgery, perjury and sexual crimes. Less serious crimes were punished by public whippings, either at the whipping post, or at the 'cart's tail', which involved the offender being flogged whilst following a cart around the market-place. A range of minor crimes, usually involving public disorder – drunkenness, swearing or vagrancy, for example – or the failure to perform public duties, were punished by a stint in the stocks. There was consequently a variety of different structures – pillories, whipping posts and stocks – maintained at public expense in the market-place for the punishment of offenders throughout much of the eighteenth century.[47] The consequences of civic improvements for this culture of public punishment were varied and complex, though in general terms urban improvement was accompanied by a gradual process of elimination of punishment from the market-place.

A brief examination of the decline of the pillory illustrates some of the forces at work. Before the close of the century, many towns had abandoned its use altogether and had set about dismantling and removing their pillories. We have already noted two casualties in the pages above, at Gloucester and Halifax. In Nottingham, the pillory had been taken down at some point in the eighteenth century, and when Robert Calvin was sentenced to stand in the pillory for assaulting two girls in 1808, a new one needed to be built and assembled in the market-place especially for the purpose.[48]

Elsewhere pillories survived into the early nineteenth century, though their use was becoming ever-more infrequent. The Kendal Quarter Sessions ordered the use of the pillory for the final time in 1801, when it found the innkeeper Peter Towers guilty of an indecent assault against a girl less then ten years old.[49] It was perhaps in acknowledgement of the unusualness of the punishment that the magistrates

---

[47] See Dave Postles, 'The market place as space in early modern England', *Social History*, 29(1), (2004), pp. 41–58; Greg T. Smith, 'Civilised people don't want to see that kind of thing: the decline of public physical punishment in London, 1760–1840' in Carolyn Strange (ed.), *Qualities of Mercy. Justice, Punishment and Discretion* (Vancouver, 1996); R. McGowen, 'Civilising punishment: the end of the public execution in England', *Journal of British Studies*, 33(3), (1994), pp. 257–282.

[48] James Orange, *History and Antiquities of Nottingham*, ii, (London, 1840), p. 873.

[49] Cumbria Record Office, Kendal, Westmorland Quarter Sessions Records, WQ/SR/580/12.

in St Albans remitted the part of John Wallis's sentence requiring him to stand in the 'Pilory' in 1809.[50]

Documenting the decline in the use of the pillory is inevitably more straightforward than explaining the reasons for this decline.[51] Certainly, the reasons are many and complex and go beyond the themes of civic space that inform this chapter. Historians have drawn attention to a cluster of beliefs – humanitarianism, changes in the relationship between the state and the individual, and a new faith in the power of prisons to reform the criminal – that underpinned a growing unease about punishment upon the body.[52] Equally, the power of the crowd to subvert the court's sentence, by either cheering offenders or seriously harming, on occasion even killing, them conflicted with the emergence of a well-documented desire for more uniform punishment at the close of the eighteenth century.

Nonetheless, one cannot fully appreciate the decline of the pillory without returning to its location – the market-place – and the changes in the way in which this space was being used. Consider, for example, what the bookseller and writer William Hutton witnessed in Derby when the notorious Mrs Beare, recently acquitted of assisting in a poisoning, was condemned to stand in the pillory for her role in procuring an abortion. The pillory being out of repair, the unfortunate Mrs Beare managed to release herself and ran through the town in an attempt to escape the angry mob. According to Hutton, she was 'pelted all the way; new kennels produced new ammunition; and she appeared a moving heap of filth'.[53] Far from displaying the majesty of the state, the punishment descended into a chaotic and disordered spectacle involving an excrement-covered escaped prisoner and an angry mob in hot pursuit.

Admittedly, an escape from the pillory was a rare event, but the general chaos and disorder that were associated with its use was not, and reports of punishment at the pillory abound with tales of an angry mob only scarcely under control. Two culprits taken down from the pillory in Chelmsford, for example, were 'begrimed with rotten eggs' and as they were escorted back to the gaol 'assailed with the indignant

[50] *St Albans Quarter Sessions Rolls, 1784–1820*, ed. David Dean. Hertfordshire Record Publications, 7, (1991), p.111.

[51] Parliament confined the pillory to the single crime of perjury in 1816, and its use was formally abolished altogether in 1837. 56 Geo. III c 138 (1816); 1 Vict. c.23 (1837). See Peter Bartlett, 'Sodomites in the pillory in eighteenth-century London', *Social and Legal Studies* 6(4), (1997), pp. 553–572.

[52] Martin Wiener, *Reconstructing the Criminal. Culture, Law and Policy in England, 1830–1914* (Cambridge, 1990); Michael Ignatieff, *A Just Measure of Pain. The Penitentiary in the Industrial Revolution* (London, 1978).

[53] W. Hutton, *History of Derby* (London, 1817), pp. 211–213.

shouts and execrations of the populace'.[54] At Charing Cross, a man
convicted of assaulting a drum boy was pelted with 'mud, eggs, turnips,
and other missiles' until he was 'completely enveloped with mud and
filth', and it was only with 'the utmost difficulty that the peace officers
could prevent him from being torn to pieces by the mob'.[55] Not only did
unruly spectacles such as these fit ill with new ideals about civic
decorum, they also tilted perilously close to a breakdown of order. The
pillory was sure to attract a large crowd of men and women, drawn
largely from the lower sections of society, with the consequent risk that
disorder was never far away. It was all sharply at odds with the neat and
ordered market-place that civic elites were attempting to fashion.

Once again, it is more appropriate to view the decline of the pillory as
part of an endeavour to separate various elements of urban life rather
than as an instance of suppression. Corporal punishment continued long
into the nineteenth century in private prison yards, as did the use of the
stocks (along with flying mud and stones) in rural areas. Nor indeed was
the public execution under any serious threat through the eighteenth
century, the gallows being always constructed at the edge of town rather
than the centre.[56] The decline of the pillory marked the end of punishment in *the market-place*, not the end of public punishments or of
punishment on the body, and was part of the process of creating an
orderly and civilised space at the heart of the town where ladies and
gentlemen need not be troubled by the messier and baser aspects of life.
At the same time, the decision of ruling elites to abandon their pillories
dovetails neatly, in both chronology and spirit, with a wide range of other
choices they made about the appropriate uses to which their market-
places might be put.

It is clearly much easier to record the improvers' visions of the properly
ordered market-place than to describe how these improvements were
perceived at street level. Urban histories and local archives provide a wealth
of information about the process of civic improvement, but these and other
sources offer only the most sketchy account of how these initiatives were
greeted by those lower down the social scale. From the evidence that
survives, however, one cannot fail to be struck by the conservatism of
market traders in the face of improvement and change. When markets were
moved, traders frequently kept as close to their old places as they could.
This spirit was captured by the great eighteenth-century antiquary
John Thorsby. Having described the manifold changes in Nottingham's

---

[54] *Ipswich Journal*, 4 July 1807.   [55] Ibid., 4 August 1810.
[56] V. A. C. Gatrell, *The Hanging Tree. Execution and the English People 1770–1868* (Oxford,
1994).

markets, he added that 'Notwithstanding all these alterations the several dealers or market people keep to the same spots or as near to them as they can, where they used to vend their different commodities'.[57]

The conservatism of market people in the face of change is most apparent with butchers, who not infrequently refused altogether to move to the new accommodation provided for them. In Exeter, for example, a new row of slaughter houses built outside the town on the banks of the river was 'soon deserted, and the building was converted into a brew-house'; meanwhile the butchers returned to their old patch. Such was the 'force of habit', despaired the town's historian, 'that the inhabitants cannot be prevailed on to remove such a nuisance'.[58] The authorities in Newark had similar difficulties, battling for two decades to get the butchers 'dislodged from the Market Place'.[59] When market places were improved and markets reorganised, market people had little choice but to comply, but these examples remind us that the elites' enthusiasm for improvement and for change was not shared by all in the urban community. They also indicate that the urban renaissance was not a linear or one-way process of improvement, but one side of a continuing dialogue between leisure and trade, patricians and plebs.

Furthermore, although civic improvement certainly changed the physical environment of many market-places, it did little to quell the traditional buoyant and festive atmosphere of a busy market. Eighteenth-century markets continued to gather crowds looking for something to buy and a little entertainment just as they ever had. Market day might see the appearance of itinerant quack doctors, for example, ready to pull teeth, cure eyes, sell medicines and diagnose any number of ailments.[60] Quacks were frequently accompanied by a musician, and might even erect a small wooden stage on which to perform – as well as dispensing medical care of rather doubtful value they provided entertainment for the crowd.[61] Puppet shows – usually featuring Punch and 'Joan' – remained popular throughout the nineteenth century: the bookseller Charles Knight thought they could still often be found 'at the corner of some street' at mid-century.[62] In addition, a ragbag of mountebanks,

[57] John Throsby, *The History and Antiquities of the Town and County of the Town of Nottingham* (Nottingham, 1793), p. 136.
[58] Alexander Jenkins, *The History and Description of the City of Exeter* (Exeter, 1806), p. 388.
[59] R. P. Shilton, *The History of the Town of Newark* (London, 1820), pp. 372–373.
[60] C. J. S. Thompson, *Quacks of Old London* (London, 1928).
[61] Fiona Haslam, *From Hogarth to Rowlandson. Medicine in Art in Eighteenth-century Britain* (Liverpool, 1996).
[62] Charles Knight, *London* (London, 1851), p. 422. See, more generally, George Speaight, *The History of the English Puppet Theatre* (New York, 1956).

entertainers, songsters and beggars wandered the markets on busy market days looking to turn a few pennies. Market-goers might even occasionally witness something more out of the ordinary, such as the sale of a wife, or the cart 'actually *driven by four large hogs*' that circuited the market-place in St Albans, or the 'small balloon' launched from the market-place in Huddersfield in 1814.[63] A busy market day was all bustle and conviviality and was the occasion of a plebeian 'consumption' and 'sociability' that has been largely omitted from the standard account of an urban renaissance. Despite improvements to the physical structure of the market-place, it also remained the location of a straggly, semi-regulated street life that simply does not fit the urban renaissance thesis. The urban renaissance, it seems, is perhaps best regarded as a powerful civic ideal, rather than a social reality.

In the realm of political activity there is also abundant evidence to suggest that popular perceptions of the market-place changed more slowly than those of the civic elite and that improvements proceeded only through a process of conflict and compromise. The tradition of political protest in the market-place was already centuries old by 1800 and it showed no sign of disappearing in the wake of civic improvement. For example, in the outbreaks of food rioting triggered by provisions scarcities between the years 1799 and 1801 and again between 1810 and 1813, angry protestors drew on established custom when they descended on the market-place to air their complaints.[64] Nor was it just food riots that took place in market-places; rioters with a range of industrial and other grievances also choose to demonstrate there. In Nottingham in 1794, for example, 'a mob' assembled in the market-place to protest about working conditions in a local cotton factory.[65] In Clare, Suffolk, agricultural labourers transported a threshing machine to the market-place where they proceeded to burn it.[66] In Dover, a crowd of 'above a thousand people' collected in the market-place, in order to try and rescue a gang of smugglers being conveyed to the

---

[63] For wife sales, see, in particular, E. P. Thompson, 'Wife sales', in his *Customs in Commons* (London, 1993). See also reports of wife sales such as the following: *Ipswich Journal*, 13 June 1812; *Hull Packet*, 28 August 1810; *Hull Packet*, 18 May 1813; *Examiner*, 15 January 1815. See also *Aberdeen Journal*, 6 November 1811; *Leeds Mercury*, 10 December 1814.

[64] *Ipswich Journal*, 6 September 1800 (Nottingham); *Jackson's Oxford Journal*, 20 September 1800 (Smithfield, London); *Derby Mercury*, 14 August 1800 (St Ives, Cambridge); *Leeds Mercury*, 9 June 1810 (Birmingham); *Derby Mercury*, 16 April 1812 (Bristol); *Leeds Mercury*, 25 April 1812 (Manchester, Rochdale and Macclesfield).

[65] Abigail Gawthern, *The Diary of Abigail Gawthern of Nottingham, 1751–1810*, ed. Adrian Henstock, (Thoroton Society Record Series, 33, 1978–1979), 2 July 1794, p. 61.

[66] *Morning Chronicle*, 16 May 1816.

town's gaol.[67] Certainly there was a range of other spaces in which riots sometimes occurred, yet the market-place stands out as a prime location for demonstrators with a wide range of grievances, many of them having little to do with markets or food.

There was clearly a symbolic dimension to the appropriation of the public market-place for popular protest – a symbolism that was perhaps even heightened by several decades of civic improvement. Well-organised demonstrations frequently assembled in, or processed around, the market-place, as if passing through the market-place helped to emphasise the legitimacy of the protestors' complaints. Thus industrial rioters often assembled in the market-place before marching to factories, mills and warehouses outside the town; whereas food rioters might meet at the edge of town and march in en masse.[68] In Sheffield in 1812, angry food rioters 'came marching through the corn market in wooden clogs, down the shambles, through the butter market, up the other side of the shambles, and into the potato market, where . . . they began to throw the potatoes in every direction'.[69] In parading around the market-place in an almost orderly fashion, protestors aped the processions of civic elites and the parades and exercises of the cavalry; in throwing potatoes, however, they demonstrated their adherence to a very different set of principles. More generally, changes in the built environment did rather little to alter working people's perceptions of the market-place. No matter what improvements civic leaders made to their markets, those they governed continued to understand the market-place as a site of fair exchange and as the rightful location for airing legitimate grievances many decades after improvement had taken place. Indeed, when placed in the context of an improved market-place, these riotous actions have yet greater significance. Some of these examples imply a more confident, more autonomous and less deferential working class and a slight rebalancing of the relationship between rulers and ruled. No less significantly, they also reveal some of the limitations of the concept of an urban renaissance. The civic improvers did not in fact carry all before them; social change in the urban context was the outcome of negotiation and compromise, and the improvers' visions were mediated by actions of the plebs.

---

[67] *Jackson's Oxford Journal*, 14 March 1807.

[68] *Caledonian Mercury*, 18 March 1811, 23 May 1816, 13 April 1812; *Morning Chronicle*, 26 April 1815.

[69] *Morning Chronicle*, 17 April 1812. See also Mark Harrison, 'Symbolism, "ritualism" and the location of crowds in early nineteenth-century English towns' in Denis Cosgrove and Stephen Daniels (eds), *The Iconography of Landscape. Essays on the Symbolic Representation, Design and Use of Past Environments* (Cambridge, 1989); Adrian Randall, *Riotous Assemblies: Popular Protest in Hanoverian England* (Oxford, 2006).

The suggestion that the market-place remained a site of political significance is finally reinforced by evidence concerning the evolution of more peaceful forms of plebeian political activity. In the late 1810s, and in a departure from traditional campaigning methods, radicals began organising peaceful mass meetings, at which speakers addressed audiences of several thousand from moveable stages and hustings erected in various open spaces – usually the moors outside towns, but occasionally at market-places instead.[70] These mass meetings were effectively curtailed following the Peterloo Massacre of 1819, yet by the 1830s the Chartists were once more staging smaller open-air meetings, often in urban market-places.[71] In the following decades the tradition of outdoor meetings passed to the temperance reformers, travelling from town to town in their placarded carts delivering speeches to anyone who would listen.[72] The nineteenth century saw a gradual decline in the frequency with which the market-place was used for public speech. No less significantly, however, it also witnessed a subtle shift in the way it was used. The market-place, the market cross in particular, had historically been the place where civic or Church leaders addressed those they ruled. By the nineteenth century, it no longer formed a significant element of the ruling body's government and at this point, public speaking in the market-place passed into the hands of those who had traditionally listened. The market-place had become the location of dialogue between working people rather than between rulers and ruled. This provides further evidence of the emergence of a more confident and autonomous working class, now appropriating for themselves a space that had for centuries been their rulers' domain. And it also reinforces the suggestion that the working classes helped to determine the outcome of the urban renaissance and need therefore to be incorporated into our understanding of the eighteenth-century town.

---

[70] See, for example, accounts of the meeting at Smithfield market in *Morning Chronicle*, 7 July 1819; *Morning Chronicle*, 15 October 1819. See also Malcolm Chase, *Chartism: A New History* (Manchester, 2007).

[71] Michael Lobban, 'From seditious libel to unlawful assembly: Peterloo and the changing face of political crime c1770–1820', *Oxford Journal of Legal Studies* 10(3), (1990), pp. 307–352. See also *Leicester Journal*, 3 August 1832; *Leicester Chronicle*, 24 November 1838, 30 September 1843; *Northern Star*, 31 July 1841.

[72] Brian Harrison, *Drink and the Victorians: The Temperance Question in England, 1815–1872* (London, 1971). See also Anna Davin, 'Socialist infidels and messengers of light: street preaching and debate in mid-nineteenth century London' in Hitchcock and Shore (eds), *Streets of London*.

Conclusions

I opened this chapter by observing that much recent writing about Georgian England is polarised between two quite different versions of the eighteenth century. On the one hand there is the shopping, assemblies and fine Georgian buildings of social elites; on the other the world of the 'mob', colourful street customs and beggars. Looking at the public spaces that everybody shared provides an alternative way of conceptualising some of these phenomena and offers the possibility of bridging these seemingly unconnected elements of eighteenth-century urban life.

This study of the market-place certainly lends some support to the concept of an urban renaissance: clearing, widening, straightening, rebuilding – it all occurred somewhere in the eighteenth-century market-place. The urban renaissance thesis is not 'wrong': the physical appearance and cultural life of towns were enhanced during the eighteenth century, and the concept of improvement will continue to inform our understanding of the eighteenth-century town, and indeed of 'the eighteenth century' more widely. At the same time, however, even the most comprehensive account of urban improvement provides no more than a partial account of changes in the fabric of civic life. Urban historians have confused the language of civic improvement, which certainly did emerge in the eighteenth century, with historical reality, which in fact changed far more slowly. They need to look beyond the smooth words penned by those in power and consider the messy and disordered spaces themselves.

The history of the eighteenth-century market-place clearly demonstrates the emergence of a divergence between plebeians and elites concerning the legitimate uses of public spaces. The urban renaissance was not the outcome of a one-way process of improvement, but an uneven and complex process that proceeded through compromise and conflict between all those with any stake in the urban environment. Urban improvement certainly involved the harmonious enhancement of civic life, but it also triggered conflicts over the proper uses and rightful owners of public spaces. Clearly, it is only by considering the actions of the 'mob' that a proper appreciation of the nature and extent of the 'urban renaissance' will ever be gained.

3   Forms of 'government growth', 1780–1830

Joanna Innes

During the 1960s and 1970s, when government accounted for some 15–20 per cent of UK employment and public expenditure stood at about 40 per cent of GDP, and when the welfare state seemed firmly set in place, the question when and how 'government growth' had originated seemed to an up-and-coming generation of historians both topical and compelling. By trying to answer this question, they hoped to create a historical context for scholarly and public understanding of the present.[1]

It was generally accepted that the late nineteenth and early twentieth centuries had seen an important shift in gear. At that time, the civil service expanded considerably, and was reshaped so as roughly to resemble a Weberian rational bureaucracy. Elementary education was made first compulsory (1880) and then free (1891). The central as opposed to

I would like to thank Simon Devereaux for sharing with me the draft of his survey article, 'The historiography of the English state during "the long eighteenth century": Part I – decentralized perspectives', *History Compass*, 7 (March 2009): www.blackwell-compass. com/subject/history/; his emphases, however, differ from mine.

[1] Estimates from David Heald, *Public Expenditure. Its Defence and Reform* (Oxford, 1983), pp. 16, 30–31, 206. Heald – whose book was written after the political tide had turned, to defend public expenditure against the assumption that it was necessarily 'bad' – also stresses complexities of measurement. The doyen of 'government growth' historiography was Oliver Macdonagh: see esp. 'The nineteenth-century revolution in government: a reappraisal', *Historical Journal*, 1, (1958), pp. 52–67; *A Pattern of Government Growth 1800–60: the Passenger Acts and their Enforcement* (London, 1961); and *Early Victorian Government 1830–1870* (London, 1977). For a critical re-inspection of the subject of his original case-study, with references to the wider discussion provoked by his work, Peter Dunkley, 'Emigration and the state 1803–1842: the nineteenth-century revolution in government reconsidered', *Historical Journal*, 23, (1980), pp. 353–380. Other surveys dating from this period include Derek Fraser, *The Evolution of the British Welfare State. A History of Social Policy since the Industrial Revolution* (London, 1973) and (with an emphasis on the early part of the period) Ursula Q. R. Henriques, *Before the Welfare State. Social Administration in Early Industrial Britain* (London, 1979). Geoffrey F. Fry, *The Growth of Government. The Development of Ideas about the Role of the State and the Machinery and Functions of Government in Britain since 1780* (London, 1979) unusually surveyed a wide range of central government institutions, including those concerned with foreign policy, empire and economic as well as social policy.

the local state acquired a role in financing welfare, with the establishment first of Old Age Pensions (1908) and then National Insurance (1911). All these developments attracted attention. It was, however, also common for writers of surveys and texts to look somewhat further back in search of the origins of 'government growth', at least to the 1830s – a decade which saw the first Privy Council grants in support of education, the establishment of a royal commission to look into the Poor Law (1833), the creation of the Poor Law Commissioners to administer the New Poor Law, and of Home Office appointed factory inspectors to monitor the implementation of the 1833 Factory Act. Normally some attention was directed yet further back: to the first years of the nineteenth century, when dim prefigurings of later shifts were discerned. The first Factory Act passed in 1802; the first parliamentary debates about the merits of public elementary schooling took place in 1807; by the 1810s, there were already exchanges in Parliament about the pros and cons of the 'principle of interference'.

In suggesting that the origins of a trend towards 'government growth' could be traced back to the early nineteenth century, historians of the 1960s and 1970s had to square up to an older periodisation, most influentially set out by the jurist Albert Venn Dicey. Dicey's Harvard *Lectures on the Relations between Law and Public Opinion in the Nineteenth Century* were first published in 1905, republished in a second edition in 1914 – and then (tellingly) reprinted in 1962. Dicey distinguished three phases in the relationship between law and public opinion: an 'old Tory' phase, lasting till the 1830s; a phase of 'Benthamism' or 'individualism', lasting from about 1825–1870; and finally a 'collectivist' phase, beginning in about 1865. Richard Cosgrove claims that, of Dicey's most notable works, '*Law and Opinion* suffered the greatest loss of influence in the twentieth century'.[2] Yet this 'loss of influence' was a result of his book being widely read and vigorously debated. And in fact, his periodisation was not entirely rejected. Proponents of the view that the trend towards government growth marked the century as a whole saw Dicey's 'individualist' phase as transitional. They accepted that the case against government intervention was strongly urged, that key initiatives depended on the energy and commitment of a few enthusiasts, and that forms of intervention were experimental, limited and cautious. 'Benthamites' were (contrary to what Dicey had held) not wholly opposed to state intervention, these historians argued – but they did not suggest that they were indiscriminately in favour of it. What

---

[2] Richard A. Cosgrove, 'Dicey, Albert Venn (1835–1922)', *Oxford Dictionary of National Biography*, (Oxford, 2004) – henceforth *ODNB*.

they affirmed nonetheless was that important changes took place in this period, changes whose roots in social pressures, pressure-group processes, ideological change and political manoeuvring it was worth trying to trace.[3]

Since the 1980s, these topics have ceased to be central to historical enquiry. This has surely been the result in part of a larger waning of interest in 'the state', in the face of the 'cultural turn in the human sciences', but also of changes in attitudes to government, and on the part of government, in the present. The late twentieth century saw efforts to shrink the state: to reduce its presence as an employer and to cut back on its role in the economy and as a provider of welfare services – or at least, to reduce the extent of its *direct* control in these sectors, often at the same time increasing its *indirect* control, through the construction of elaborate systems for enforcing accountability. A result of these changes has been the derailing of the traditional 'government growth' teleology. Historians have responded by developing new sensitivity to the ways in which 'the state' not only now acts, but has always acted through a complex series of partnerships with other public or private bodies, more or less formally constituted. Charting the changing form of the state has, in this context, come increasingly to be approached as a matter of locating its changing place within a 'mixed economy' of provision.[4]

Within early modern and modern British historiography, there has meanwhile been an intensification of interest in *certain* aspects of the history of the state, though not the same ones as previously. Instead of the welfare state, what John Brewer has influentially termed the 'fiscal-military state' has floated towards the centre of at least some historians' fields of vision.[5] Historians have enquired, not merely about what sums of money governments have been able to extract from time to time, but also about how their ways of mobilising funds have been shaped by, and

[3] A particularly reflective collection of essays was Gillian Sutherland (ed.), *Studies in the Growth of Nineteenth-Century Government* (London, 1972).

[4] A historian who used the phrase early was Geoffrey Finlayson, *Citizen, State, and Social Welfare in Britain 1830–1990* (Oxford, 1994), p. 6.

[5] John Brewer, *The Sinews of Power: War, Money and the English State* (London, 1989). Two collections prompted by his work are Lawrence Stone (ed.), *An Imperial State at War: Britain from 1689 to 1815* (London, 1983) and John Brewer and Eckhart Hellmuth (eds), *Rethinking Leviathan. The Eighteenth-Century State in Britain and Germany* (London, 1999). For critical responses, see Paul Langford, *A Polite and Commercial People* (Oxford, 1989), ch. 14; John Cookson, *The British Armed Nation 1793–1815* (Oxford, 1997), pp. 1–15. Stephen Conway attempts to strike a balance in *The British Isles and the War of American Independence* (Oxford, 2000), pp. 347–353 and *War, State and Society in Mid-Eighteenth-Century Britain and Ireland* (Oxford, 2006), ch. 1.

in return helped to shape, relations with the public.[6] Government's role in mobilising military force has been approached with similar questions in mind.[7] There has been a growth of interest in ways in which the British state has managed its simultaneous but in some ways different relationships with different parts of the British Isles. Also, in the roles governments have been asked to play in shaping national, ethnic, religious and gender identities, and in regulating morals.[8]

When, in the early 1990s, three British historians revisited the issue of 'government growth' in the early nineteenth century, their exchange both illustrated and dramatised some of these changes of view. First into the field was Peter Jupp, who, in an article entitled 'The landed elite and political authority in Britain, c. 1760–1850', offered a restatement of the 'government growth' story.[9] Jupp was less concerned than most earlier writers in this line with specific policy initiatives, more interested in charting broader developments in the scale and shape of governmental and parliamentary activity. He argued that between 1760 and 1830 – that is, even before the passage of the first Reform Act – British government became more independent of the monarch; more businesslike, handled a greater volume of business and played a greater role in regulating economy and society. It drew more key personnel – even at the highest levels – from outside the traditional landed classes, and these men interacted more intensely with each other and forged a clearer sense of group identity. Moreover, governmental and parliamentary business was increasingly reported to a broad public.[10] Jupp's effort to sketch the 'government growth' story on a broad canvas laid him open to vigorous challenge from Philip Harling and Peter Mandler.[11] Their views were

---

[6] Very much in this vein is Martin J. Daunton, *Trusting Leviathan: The Politics of Taxation in Britain, 1799–1914* (Cambridge, 2001).

[7] For one recent such study, Nicholas Rogers, *Naval Impressment and its Opponents in Georgian Britain* (London, 2008).

[8] For the 'British Isles' agenda, see contributions to the *Oxford History of the British Isles* in volumes edited by Paul Langford, Colin Matthew and Keith Robbins. Linda Colley's *Britons: Forging the Nation 1707–1837* (New Haven, 1992) has been the most influential 'identity' study; see also Kathleen Wilson (ed.), *A New Imperial History: Culture, Identity and Modernity in Britain and the Empire 1660–1840* (Cambridge, 2004). For a particularly impressive history of seventeenth-century Britain constructed around the whole agenda sketched in this paragraph, see Michael Braddick, *State-Formation in Early Modern England c1550–1700* (Cambridge, 2000).

[9] Jupp, 'Landed elite', *Journal of British Studies*, 29, (1990), pp. 53–79.

[10] I will not develop here Jupp's arguments about government personnel and the role of the landed classes (a less prominent theme in his article than one might have expected from his title), nor will I engage with Mandler and Harling's response to this part of his argument.

[11] 'From "fiscal-military" state to laissez-faire state, 1760–1850', *Journal of British Studies*, 32, (1993), pp. 44–70.

clearly influenced by their own research: by Harling's work on early nineteenth-century reforms in British central administration, in the context of growing intolerance of 'corruption', and Mandler's work on the mutations of aristocratic Whiggery during the 1830s decade of reform, and the cultural and intellectual context out of which those new policies emerged.[12] But their response was also crucially informed by John Brewer's account of the development, across the later seventeenth and eighteenth centuries, of a British 'fiscal-military state'.[13] Brewer had shown (Harling and Mandler said) that the British state *had* grown, markedly increasing its capacity to mobilise money and men, and on that basis emerging as a European and increasingly global 'great power'. But (they argued) the state thus conceived had not *continued* to grow after 1815; on the contrary, it had shrunk, as public spending was slashed at the end of a quarter of a century of warfare, and peacetime conditions made it possible to cut back on 'placemen' (officials) in a manner that not only radical but even moderate public opinion increasingly favoured. As chastened by these reforms, the state machine – never, even at its height, very extensively or directly concerned with matters of domestic government – was quite a limited entity.

The object of the present chapter is to probe some of the conceptual problems involved in assessments of 'government growth', with special reference to the case of Britain in the late eighteenth and early nineteenth centuries. In its concluding section, the chapter returns to questions which interested welfare-state historians of the 1960s and 1970s, and offers some thoughts on the limited and specific, but nonetheless important ways in which the role of 'government' on the domestic front could be said to have 'grown' both during the era of the French Revolutionary and Napoleonic Wars and beyond.

Defining the state

An initial problem for anyone trying to characterise developments in 'the state' or in 'government' is that these are elusive objects of study. Both in the early nineteenth century and now, it is very possible for two people, each using these words appropriately, nonetheless to be talking about quite different things. Philip Abrams effectively rehearsed the issues in

---

[12] For Harling, see Philip Harling, *The Waning of 'Old Corruption': The Politics of Economical Reform in Britain, 1779–1846* (Oxford, 1996); for Mandler, *Aristocratic Government in the Age of Reform: Whigs and Liberals 1830–1852* (Oxford, 1990) and 'Tories and paupers: Christian political economy and the making of the New Poor Law', *Historical Journal*, xxxiii, (1990), pp. 81–103.

[13] See footnote 5.

his 1977 'Notes on the difficulty of studying the state'.[14] First, even considered as a cluster of institutions, each with their own more or less well-defined powers and responsibilities, 'the state' or 'government' is by no means a coherent thing: at best, it is an assemblage of parts, each with its own character and history. Practice also varies in terms of which institutions are and are not counted in. Are courts of law parts of 'the state'? 'The state' and 'the government' often connote the *central* state and *central* government. But it is not obvious which agents of 'government' operating in the localities should and shouldn't be counted as agents of that centre. Even if we distinguish some particularly 'local' layer of government, why should this not be considered an element of 'the state'? It seems odd to treat matters falling under the purview of local government as on a par with other matters left entirely unregulated.

It is worth bearing in mind that usage changed over our period. Eighteenth-century discussions of 'the state' and 'government' were generally *constitutional* discussions, concerned with characterising the institutional framework within which the practice of governing took place. In the early nineteenth century, by contrast, it became common to conceive of 'the government' or 'the state' as an active force, doing or choosing not to do particular things. The King's ministers, though normally referred to as 'the ministry' or 'the administration', were sometimes dubbed 'the government' even in the early eighteenth century, but from the later eighteenth century this became increasingly common. From about the time of the younger Pitt, the prime minister came to be conceived of as heading a 'government': Pitt's government, Liverpool's government, and so forth – a locution which survives in English usage to this day, but which has never caught on in the United States, where the President still presides over an 'administration'. Protestors complaining about 'the government' in the early nineteenth century, and MPs arguing about whether or not 'government' should 'interfere', were framing their thoughts in ways that their forefathers would not have done.[15]

Similarly, around 1800, the terms 'central' and 'local' government, which now seem natural antonyms, were not used as we use them now. In the eighteenth century, the closest distinction was that between 'officers of state' and 'inferior officers of government'. In the early nineteenth century, when the phrase 'local government' was used, it

---

[14] First published in the *Journal of Historical Sociology*, 1, (1988), pp. 59–87.
[15] I first offered some thoughts on terminology in 'Changing perceptions of the state in the late eighteenth and early nineteenth centuries', *Journal of Historical Sociology*, 15, (2002), pp. 107–113, but my research on this topic remains patchy, and my conclusions to some extent impressionistic.

normally – initially almost exclusively – connoted governing institutions operating in British territories overseas: India, Australia and so forth. Only from the 1830s did the phrase start to be applied to people exercising power within specific British regions. Even by the 1850s that usage was not dominant, though the 'Local Government Act' of 1858 must have gone some way towards entrenching it (it was further entrenched in 1871, with the setting up of the supervisory 'Local Government Board').[16] Barely had the term been given this domestic application than it started to be championed as an age-old principle of the British constitution! The tradition of 'local self-government' (another neologism) was widely averred to have provided the foundations upon which English liberty had been built.[17] Clearly, a name had been found for something thought long to have existed – and there is no reason to dismiss this notion. But we should be aware that by the mid-nineteenth century, people were imagining the institutional landscape in which they lived through a grid of concepts many of which had only recently found their current applications.

If 'the state' can be conceptualised as an assemblage of institutions, it can be understood in other ways too. For example, as a set of processes, whose content is determined by choices people make: by the ways in which they invoke and try to deploy 'the state'.[18] The business of government is generated by the choices both of officials and of private persons. As either take more or fewer initiatives, as officials are more or less diligent, or private parties see more or less point in calling 'the state' to their aid, so the reach and effective power of the state expands or contracts. Of course, the state's reach and power are also determined by the things that make 'it' more or less capable of responding to these wishes: that is, inasmuch as others accept or contest these attempts, or inasmuch as 'it' has at its disposal more or less in the way of human or material resources. But that is in the end essentially to say that many

---

[16] Anyone who searches on the phrase 'local government' within the 'full-text only' corpus of *The House of Commons Parliamentary Papers* (ProQuest 2005–8: http://parlipapers. chadwyck.co.uk/home.do) will be able to replicate this finding.

[17] This phrase was first used in *Parliamentary Papers* in 1835. It was first cited in *Hansard* in 1836 (see http://hansard.millbanksystems.com/). There are earlier uses in print, but the context is very commonly colonial, or refers to the component kingdoms of the UK. Joshua Toulmin Smith did most to popularise it in a British context: see his *Government by Commission Illegal and Pernicious ... the Rights, Duties, and Importance of Local Self-Government* (London, 1849). For Smith, L. T. Smith, 'Smith, Joshua Toulmin (1816–1869)', *ODNB*, and Peter Claus, 'Languages of citizenship in the City of London 1848–1867', *London Journal*, 24, (1999), pp. 23–37.

[18] See on roughly this theme, Michael Braddick, 'State formation and social change in early modern England: a problem stated and approaches suggested', *Social History*, 16, (1991), pp. 1–17.

different kinds of process and personal choice are involved in any one 'government' action. Of course, if we conceptualise the state as a set of processes, or indeed, as a complex of behaviours, then its boundaries become very fuzzy. 'State power' proves to be difficult to distinguish from the power of the individuals or collectivities who collaborate with the state. But that is how it is: the competent, well networked, officious or corrupt official, the company or voluntary society which does or does not put its resources and expertise at the state's disposal do help to determine its character and effective power.[19]

Inasmuch as it is a set of processes, or a complex of more or less voluntarily chosen behaviours, the state is also an idea: it exists because it is imagined, and because imagination shapes behaviour. Castaways adrift on the ocean are an improbable arm of the British state, but in so far as their behaviour is shaped by ideas about what they may and may not legitimately do and expect – what aid they may expect on what terms from passing ships, under what circumstances they may kill and eat each other – 'the state' has a dim and latent presence even within their boat.[20]

States of all periods can and in some circumstances should be conceptualised in all these ways. It is, however, particularly important to consider processes and ideas when considering pre-modern states. Older states were often lightly staffed and resourced by late modern (late nineteenth-century or later) standards. Yet a purely institutional approach may tend to underestimate their power. Pre-modern states were sometimes able to achieve surprising things with relatively little official involvement and next-to-no public spending: for example, creating patchy but non-trivial networks of local schools.[21] Swelling numbers of officials and inflating budgets do not always mean (don't we all know it?) more effective state action: they may rather reflect changes in the way that the state operates.

---

[19] For two accounts stressing the dependence of 'the state' on those who deploy it or nominally represent it: Paul Langford, *Public Life and the Propertied Englishman 1689–1798* (Oxford, 1991); Peter King, *Crime and Law in England, 1750–1840: Remaking Justice from the Margins* (Cambridge, 2006).

[20] A. W. B. Simpson, *Cannibalism and the Common Law: the Story of the Tragic Last Voyage of the Mignonette and the Strange Legal Proceedings to Which it Gave Rise* (London, 1984). In a rather different style, historians inspired by Michel Foucault's writings about the dependence of power on ways of thinking also stress the role of imagination in constructing the state: e.g. Patrick Joyce. *The Rule of Freedom: Liberalism and the Modern City* (London, 2003).

[21] For an overview of European developments, Mary-Jo Maynes, *Schooling in Western Europe: A Social History* (Albany, NY, 1985).

Quantifying government growth

Accounts of 'government growth', in Britain or elsewhere, focusing on the late modern period – from say 1850 – have often put public spending and public employment at their heart. These indices also figured prominently in debates about 'overgrown government' in the 1970s and 1980s. Late twentieth-century opponents of the over-mighty state sought to cut spending (and in this way, to lighten the burden of taxation), to reduce the government's role as a provider of goods and services, and its role as employer. Historians have their own reasons for finding spending and employment indices attractive. On the one hand, they promise to offer a holistic picture: to provide a *general* sense of whether and to what extent government was growing (or shrinking).[22] On the other hand, they appear to do this in rigorous and precise ways. In fact, of course, all such indices are complex artefacts: the result of a series of decisions (often made by a wide variety of people, at various reporting stages) about what to count and how.

In the context of the Jupp–Harling and Mandler exchange, Harling and Mandler appeared to win the argument on the numbers: Jupp offered as evidence for his case a variety of numerical series, rather desultorily reported, not all of which plainly evidence the growth he sought to document.[23] Harling and Mandler, by contrast, focused on a few key indices: above all relating to public spending, though also to public employment and to numbers of Acts passed. They argued on this basis that overall public spending shrank; that, even setting war-related expenditure aside (it is scarcely surprising that, with the war's end, this should have shrunk), 'civil government' expenditure per head did not exceed eighteenth-century levels until the 1840s, and, finally, that numbers of public Acts passed per parliamentary session shrank. These numerical series did much of the work of making plausible their claim of shrinkage.

---

[22] See, e.g., Bernard Harris, *The Origins of the British Welfare State: Society, State, and Social Welfare in England and Wales, 1800–1945* (Basingstoke, 2004), pp. 12–13; or Theodore S. Hamerow, *Birth of a New Europe. State and Society in the Nineteenth Century* (New York, 1983), ch. 10. For a discussion of some of debatable features of modern estimates, see Heald, *Public Expenditure*.

[23] Thus, Jupp cited figures showing growth in numbers of papers lodged with the Treasury, though these ended disconcertingly in 1815 – leaving him open to Harling and Mandler's counter-claim that this was an effect of war. ('Landed elite', p. 63). To demonstrate growth in legislative activity, he cited totals of 'all bills' – yet numbers of public bills passed each session *declined* from the 1820s (as Harling and Mandler rightly point out); continuing increase in total acts passed was sustained by continuing growth in local (increasingly railway) acts (Jupp, 'Landed elite', p. 68; Harling and Mandler, 'From "fiscal-military state"', pp. 50–51).

Yet all these indices are problematic. Changing numbers of statutes often reflect something of interest – but they are a crude measure of governmental or parliamentary activity, since modes of processing proposals, their scope and their significance may all vary, from Act to Act and over time.[24] Parliament now passes fewer public Acts per session than its late eighteenth-century precursor; this reveals little about relative exertion, ambition or impact. In fact the decline in numbers of public Acts issuing from Parliament in the 1820s had much to do with improvements in legislative planning and process, particularly fiscal planning and process.

Harling and Mandler's claims about trends in public expenditure are even more problematic. The figures they cite are seriously inadequate for their purpose. First, in the small print that accompanies their tables, Harling and Mandler note that what they report are actual expenditure figures, with no allowance for the changing value of money.[25] Julian Hoppit has, however, noted in an important corrective article that, once changes in the value of money are taken into account, the wartime peak in spending, which corresponded with a peak in inflation, becomes much less pronounced. There was indeed a fall in real expenditure after the war – yet during both peace and war thereafter, spending (appropriately adjusted) consistently stood at higher levels than before the French Revolution, proportionate to, in fact slightly more than proportionate to, new levels of national income.[26] This is less surprising when we remember that, though in retrospect the century after Waterloo seems to have been a peaceful century for Britain, it was less so for continental Europe. British governments were constantly alert to wars and rumours of wars, and mindful that they might need to rearm and remobilise.

When they analysed trends in spending on 'civil government', Harling and Mandler deflated totals by population. Given the era's rapid population growth, this is a powerful deflator. It is difficult to see it as appropriate. In fact, if one probes further into the forms of spending within the category 'civil government', it emerges that they consisted in great part of the expenses of the royal court and royal family; certain

---

[24] I write as someone who has counted as assiduously as anyone: Julian Hoppit and Joanna Innes, 'Introduction' to Hoppit (ed.), *Failed Legislation. Compiled from the Commons and Lords Journals 1660–1800* (London, 1997), pp. 1–24; Innes, 'Legislating for three kingdoms; how the Westminster Parliament legislated for England, Scotland and Ireland 1707–1830' in Hoppit (ed.), *Parliaments, Nations and Identities in Britain 1660–1850* (Manchester, 2003).

[25] Harling and Mandler, 'From "fiscal-military state"', p. 56.

[26] Julian Hoppit, 'Checking the Leviathan, 1688–1832' in Donald Winch and Patrick K. O'Brien (eds), *The Political Economy of British Historical Experience 1688–1914* (Oxford, 2002), at pp. 280–285.

public salaries (for example the salaries of diplomats, sheriffs and judges); and miscellaneous supply grants, including spending on public works. In the eighteenth century, expenditure on the lottery represented the second largest expenditure per head.[27] Not much of this spending could have been expected to grow with population: even expenditure on law and justice, which includes those costs of the penal system that were borne by central funds (a small part of the total) should be assessed in the context of what was by the 1830s a declining rate of prosecutions and convictions.

As this breakdown suggests, 'civil government' meant something less than might be supposed. A relatively small part of the costs of domestic government was borne upon central funds: much was paid for out of local rates; some was unremunerated. Magistrates, for example, central figures especially in county but also in town government, usually served without pay. We know that significant cuts were made in some forms of local spending – notably in money spent on the relief of the poor, after the New Poor Law of 1834 – so, at least from that date, adding local spending data might strengthen the case for shrinkage.[28] But the reader needs to be aware not merely that locally funded expenditure is excluded from this series, but that that accounts for most of what we might be interested in. (Moreover, trends in local spending differed in different parts of the British Isles: in both Scotland and Ireland, expenditure on the poor increased following reforms in the 1830s and 1840s).[29]

What Harling and Mandler are effectively capturing in their enquiry into civil expenditure – though the point remains largely implicit – is that early and mid-Victorian Britain operated with a very different *kind* of system of domestic government from that which developed in the late Victorian period, and further developed in the twentieth century. By the standards of these subsequent periods, the restricted role of central government, and low levels of spending, especially spending from central funds, are notable. But it is not clear that the sorts of calculations which capture that contrast are well adapted to capturing the character and extent of change from the eighteenth into the early nineteenth century, when central spending on such matters was consistently small, and marginal to the larger pattern of effort.

---

[27] Harling and Mandler draw on B. R. Mitchell, *British Historical Statistics* (Cambridge, 1988), pp. 578–580, 587, which in turn draws on *British Parliamentary Papers* (1868–9), p. xxxv, where more detail about the make-up of annual spending totals can be found.

[28] Karel Williams collects the figures – and discusses some problems in their interpretation: *From Pauperism to Poverty* (London, 1981).

[29] For Scotland, Rosalind Mitchison, *The Old Poor Law in Scotland: The Experience of Poverty, 1574–1845* (Edinburgh, 2000); for Ireland, Peter Gray, *The Making of the Irish Poor Law 1815–43* (Manchester, 2009).

None of this means that such numerical series – if cautiously and critically employed – are without interest. They can provide a helpful framework for thinking; they suggest questions to ask, and set limits to what we can plausibly assert. But – picking up further threads from our earlier discussion of various ways of conceptualising 'the state' and 'government' – they are best adapted to illuminating certain aspects of institutional functioning. They are not well adapted to illuminating change in processes of government, in how government is experienced or in its role in changing patterns of conduct. General indices are, moreover, by their nature likely to obscure changes in *what* government does.

Varieties of liberalism

As Harling and Mandler note, the pattern of 'government shrinkage' which they claim their figures illustrate conforms to something one might expect to find if one took as one's starting point early nineteenth-century discussion of the role of government. There was certainly a lot of talk in the early nineteenth century about the need to restrict the role of government: to cut expenditure and reduce tax burdens, to reduce ministers' opportunities to exercise illegitimate influence through appointments to public jobs, and to put an end to various demeaning and destructive forms of government 'interference'. In Dicey's account, these new currents of thought gradually eroded 'old Tory' modes of governance, opening the way to an era of individualism. Undoubtedly the most influential recent writer on these themes has been Boyd Hilton. Hilton's *Age of Atonement* developed the view that the broad diffusion of these ideas within Britain owed less than scholars such as Dicey had supposed to Benthamite utilitarianism and political economy, much more to a form of providentialist Christianity which attributed to God the intention – manifest, to those who had eyes to see, in the internal logic of society – of subjecting human beings to a set of probationary tests, to develop and reveal qualities of will and spirit. It is to this cultural context that we should chiefly look, Hilton has argued, to understand the roots of early nineteenth-century liberalism. In his recent volume in the *Oxford History of England*, focusing on the period 1783–1846, he has developed and refined this account, identifying two, imperfectly aligned, forms of 'liberalism', one focusing on civil rights, the other 'a socio-economic version based on market values'.[30]

---

[30] Boyd Hilton, *The Age of Atonement: The Influence of Evangelicalism on Social and Economic Thought 1785–1865* (Oxford, 1988), esp. chs 1–6, and *A Mad, Bad and Dangerous People? England 1783–1846* (Oxford, 2006), esp. pp. 30, 314–328, 518–524.

In Hilton's re-imagining of the early nineteenth century, Adam Smith and David Ricardo, Jeremy Bentham and Edwin Chadwick dwindle in size, while the figure of Scottish evangelical divine Thomas Chalmers looms large. Hilton is surely right to join other recent scholars in emphasising the significance, the influence and cultural resonance, of this once neglected figure, and of the idioms of political and social discourse that he favoured.[31] However, pervasive patterns of thinking probably normally become pervasive because they fit with a variety of world views; in this context, any attempt to identify one key source for early nineteenth-century liberalism may be misdirected. Hilton himself concedes that theology does not get him very far in accounting for Whig views. His attempts to make the case for the influence of theology even on individual Tory politicians have not been wholly persuasive – not least because, all too often, we simply lack good evidence as to what their leanings were.[32]

More fundamentally still, I would want to question how far we should expect to be able to read active politicians' record of political choices off their ideological dispositions, however these are conceived. Though, when a politician is first confronted with an issue, ideology may well predispose him (or her) to see that issue in a particular way, it is surely the rare practical political problem to which ideology suggests a clear response; more commonly, issues are complex and confusing, and require that some principles be compromised to protect others – or indeed require fresh thinking, adjustments in the grid through which the politician sees the world. Politicians' views commonly evolve and change as they wrestle with issues and enlarge their understanding of their practical and political implications. They may, for their own private satisfaction or for purposes of public presentation, gloss the position they ultimately decide to endorse in terms of (what they can persuade themselves or others are) their more enduring principled commitments. But this ultimate fit is more commonly the result of a creative, negotiative process than it is the reflection of any clear and compelling logic.

Take the case of the repeal of the Combination Acts, agreed by Parliament in 1824 after a failed attempt in the preceding year.[33] Repeal

---

[31] See esp. S. J. Brown, *Thomas Chalmers and the Godly Commonwealth in Scotland* (Oxford, 1982).

[32] For the Whigs, *Mad, Bad and Dangerous People*, p. 520. Hilton's first and still most sustained exercise in these terms was 'Peel: a reappraisal', *Historical Journal*, xxii, (1979), pp. 585–614. Hilton, 'Whiggery, religion and social reform: the case of Lord Morpeth', *Historical Journal*, iv, (1994), pp. 829–859 (which runs a similar analysis for one Whig) includes, in its opening sections, probably the best exposé extant of the difficulties of this kind of analysis.

[33] This episode has been most fully explored from the perspective of its radical supporters: see Iorwerth Prothero, *Artisans and Politics in Early Nineteenth-Century London*

was most consistently championed by Whigs and radicals with links to labour. They saw a need to free workers to get the best bargains the market would allow. Some supporters of this measure realised that it opened the way to tests of collective strength – but believed that, since the market would set limits to what could be achieved, this would prove a learning process. Others seem to have imagined that free bargaining would be individualised, and were disappointed by the collective actions which ensued. There followed debate as to whether it was necessary to place constraints on workers to prevent intimidation and coercion, and, if that were desirable, how it was best effected. A prevailing disposition to cut back on the role of government must have helped to make repeal possible; the fact that key ministers in some ways shared that disposition also mattered. Yet one could have this disposition and still wrestle with the problem of how to give it effect. As William Huskisson was reported to have said in moving the modification of the repeal bill (29 March 1825): 'As a general principle, he undoubtedly thought that every man had a fair inherent right to carry his own labour to whatever market he liked; and so to make the best of it ... But then, on the other hand, he must as strenuously contend for the perfect freedom of those who were to give employment to that labour.'[34] There was plenty of scope for debate as to the implications of such potentially conflicting general principles.

If ideologies usually do more to determine the language and character of debate than the precise conclusions of those who subscribe to them, then historians need to be cautious about looking to ideology to do much explanatory work.

A final note of caution. Hilton characterises as 'liberal' a range of attitudes and ideas only some of which were commonly so termed by contemporaries. He equates liberalism broadly with the desire to reduce – or enlighten people as to the necessary limits of – government's role, activities and impact. In a socio-economic context more specifically, he equates it with the notion that society and economy have their own logic, which should be left to work itself out; socio-economic 'liberals', as Hilton characterises them, held that government, in so far as it acted at all, should act mechanically, in accordance with clearly stated rules, not in an ad hoc, or (as he terms it) 'managerialist' fashion.

(Folkestone, 1979), ch. 9; Ronald K. Huch and Paul K. Ziegler, *Joseph Hume, the People's MP* (Philadelphia, 1985), ch. 3. For Huskisson's role, Alexander Brady, *William Huskisson and Liberal Reform* (London, 1967), pp. 106–109.

[34] *Parliamentary Debates*, xii, p. 1292 (29 March 1825).

Historians are not bound to abide by usage in the periods they study. But it is worth underlining something that Hilton himself is very clear about: that in this period the term 'liberal', though diversely applied, was applied less broadly, and not at all in some of the ways that he applies it.[35] It was applied primarily to what he distinguishes as one strand of liberalism: civil rights liberalism. 'Liberals' so understood were people who questioned the scale of privileges enjoyed by churchmen, and the need for restrictions on rights of assembly and expression. To hold those views was to stand in a distinct position on the political spectrum, if one not perfectly represented by any party or faction; those who held it recognised their kinship with others who held such views. Contemporaries also sometimes characterised as 'liberal' those who opposed interference with trade or economic activity more generally – and adherents of political economy as a system of ideas assessed other MPs as more or less 'sound' in their views.[36] By contrast, it's not clear that Hilton's 'socioeconomic liberals' would have recognised themselves as a group, or indeed understood the criterion that Hilton employs to distinguish them as a group.

Interest in cutting back on the role of government took many other forms, and in some of these other forms attracted very wide support. Thus, at the end of the Napoleonic Wars there was general agreement on the need to cut back on government spending and patronage; few if any would have denied that these were desiderata; dissent tended to focus on issues of scale and speed.[37] Similarly there was broad agreement on the need to cut spending on the poor: by far the largest local spending head – though this desire was often associated with interest in intensifying efforts to shape popular attitudes and conduct (through the processes by which the relief system was scaled back, through schooling, or the penal system).[38] Most people probably favoured *some* freeing of industry and commerce, not least through the lightening of tax burdens, though detailed debate tended to be shaped by the perceived interests of lobby

---

[35] His starting point was undoubtedly the long-standing historians' practice of distinguishing post-war Tories into 'liberal' and other (Hilton calls them 'high') Tories. Index entries under 'Liberalism' in *Mad, Bad and Dangerous People* index contemporary uses of the term, and contrast with more broadly conceived index entries under 'Liberal and high Toryism' and 'Liberalism, ambiguities of'. For a general survey of usage, Jorg Leonhardt, *Liberalismus: zur historichen Semantik eines Deutungsmusters* (Munich, 2001), chs 4–5.

[36] See, e.g., David Ricardo, *The Works and Correspondence of David Ricardo*, ed. Piero Sraffa, 11 vols, (Cambridge, 1951), pp. vii, 19.

[37] Harling, *Old Corruption*; Daunton, *Trusting Leviathan*, chs 2–3; J. E. Cookson, *Lord Liverpool's Administration* (Edinburgh, 1975).

[38] J. R. Poynter, *Society and Pauperism* (London, 1969), chs 6–8.

groups, and the nature of MPs' local power bases.[39] So widely diffused was enthusiasm for reducing government activity in these respects that it was represented, if in varying ways, among Tories, Whigs and radicals, in Parliament and in the constituencies. Equally there was general enthusiasm – again, in the context of many otherwise different world views – for the promotion of personal independence and self-reliance. If the object is to capture the 'spirit of the age', then there may be a point in looking for common ideas sustaining this broad body of thought, and in giving it a generic name – for example, 'liberalism'. But the baggy amorphousness of the object of study needs to be appreciated. Meanwhile, we should not lose sight of the fact that those whom contemporaries were most likely to term 'liberal' did not earn that title by calling for reductions in public spending or in government activity across the board, or indeed for more individual self-reliance, but rather by urging a reconsideration of very particular elements of government's interaction with society.

The role of government in promoting social welfare

Let us finally turn to the kinds of issues which interested 1960s and 1970s historians of 'government growth': to the role of government as a provider of public services, especially services relating to justice, police and welfare, and ask whether, and if so in what senses, a case for government growth can be made in these regards. In this final part of my chapter, I will confine my attention to England, because English, Scottish and Irish arrangements differed in important ways, and there is not space here to do justice to these differences.[40]

Historians of the 1960s and 1970s worked against the background of a tradition of writing about eighteenth-century English domestic government, and its deficiencies, with roots in the nineteenth century itself, in the critical writings of would-be 'reformers'. The reformers' perspective informed the most influential early twentieth-century account, Beatrice and Sidney Webb's multi-volume 'History of English Local Government', most of which focused on the period 1688–1835. The Webbs' work was distinguished by its extraordinarily broad empirical base, and its analytical ambition; it was nonetheless deeply marked by reformers'

---

[39] As Hilton himself stressed in *Corn, Cash and Commerce*, ch. 6 and in 'The political arts of Lord Liverpool', *Transactions of the Royal Historical Society*, 5th ser., 38, (1988), pp. 150–153.

[40] I have written about them elsewhere, esp. in 'Governing diverse societies' in P. Langford (ed.), *Oxford History of the British Isles: the Eighteenth Century* (Oxford, 2002), and in 'Legislating for three kingdoms'.

critical emphases, and therefore consistently emphasised the limits of eighteenth-century governmental capacity and achievement.[41]

In the past few decades, historians have revisited these critical assessments. The more general development of early-modern historiography has enabled them to place eighteenth-century practices within a broader early-modern perspective, and to identify ways in which they were themselves innovative, embodying attempts at 'improvement'; also to compare them laterally with practices prevailing at the time in other European states. When they are set in this context, three features of eighteenth-century English arrangements are notable. First, the apparatus of domestic government was relatively tightly integrated: statute laws applied everywhere, and were broadly (certainly not perfectly) given local effect. Second, the policy-making process was notably open, inasmuch as statute law was generated in Parliament, whose proceedings were not secret (they could indeed be followed in published 'Votes'). Local representatives played a prominent part in the making of laws; Parliament provided an arena in which domestic issues could be discussed even when they could not be resolved; a significant body of pamphlet literature was produced by way of contribution to and commentary on these discussions. Third, public services were relatively lavishly financed. Money for the building of bridges and maintenance of streets, building and maintenance of prisons, transport of vagrants and relief of the poor was siphoned from householders and occupiers of land through local rates. As property values increased, on the back of growth in the national economy, so public resources increased. Historians have also shown that there was a good deal of innovation and experimentation: practice was by no means hidebound.[42] For all these reasons, most specialists would now be inclined to represent English domestic governmental systems at the start of the nineteenth century as standing on a relatively high base. Nor in this context does it now seem necessary to seek out exogenous sources of energy – in, for example, evangelicalism or utilitarianism – to explain why in the early nineteenth century there should have been interest in improvement or reform.

---

[41] S. and B. Webb, *English Local Government from the Revolution to the Muncipal Corporations Act.* 9 vols, (London, 1906–1929).

[42] I developed these arguments in a general way in 'Parliament and the shaping of eighteenth-century English social policy', *Transactions of the Royal Historical Society*, 5th ser., xl, (1990), pp. 63–92, now republished in my collection *Inferior Politics: Social Problems and Social Policies in Eighteenth-Century Britain* (Oxford, 2009). See also, for the English poor laws in European perspective, Innes, 'The state and the poor: eighteenth-century England in comparative perspective' Brewer and Hellmuth (eds), *Rethinking Leviathan*.

Two things that did not happen much in the eighteenth century nonetheless deserve remark. First, ministers and other central officers of central executive government did not do much to shape laws relating to justice, police or welfare: they tended to leave such matters to backbenchers. Occasionally they helped to shape criminal laws in periods of anxiety about crime levels – but this was the exception, not the rule. Their failure to engage energetically in making such laws partly arose from the fact that they equally left these laws' execution largely to magistrates and other 'inferior' officers: as a result, they had little expertise in these matters, and concluded that MPs active in their communities had a better basis for judging what was needed than they. Second, perhaps in part because ministers did not take the lead, Parliament was unadventurous in tackling *new* issues. Effort tended to focus on improving existing bodies of law: criminal law, laws against 'vice and immorality', poor and vagrancy laws, laws governing imprisonment for debt. Moreover, though there were some significant changes of policy under these heads – there were major shifts in penal policy; workhouse building was encouraged; procedures were developed to facilitate the release of imprisoned debtors – difficulties in building consensus under this regime meant that some ambitious schemes (for the reform of the poor laws, for example), though repeatedly debated, were never agreed.[43]

Between 1780 and 1830, the basic shape of the apparatus of English domestic government did not change much: not until the 1830s and after was the institutional order that took shape between the later Middle Ages and the early seventeenth century significantly restructured. Criminal justice continued to be administered in the localities by roving circuit judges and by magistrates; magistrates also played key roles in county and to some extent borough administration; constables offered a variety of support services, and were supplemented in towns by nightwatch forces. At parish level, if there was a central forum, it was the parish vestry, where ratepayers developed a policy framework for parish officers. Traditionally, those who filled local offices received little if any pay, perhaps expenses; people acted out of a sense of obligation, perhaps hoping to gain local status. Some changes can be identified. As growing amounts of money cycled through lower levels of government – expenditure on the poor increased threefold between 1783–1785 and 1829,

---

[43] Innes, 'Parliament and the shaping'. See also my 'Domestic face of the military fiscal state' in Lawrence Stone (ed.), *An Imperial State at War: Britain 1688–1815* (London, 1993), also reprinted in *Inferior Politics*.

expenditure funnelled through county rates fivefold[44] – a trend to pay salaries to local officials can be discerned. Some big-town magistrates were put on salaries; it became more common for parishes to retain a salaried overseer of the poor, and normal for the night watch to be performed by disciplined bodies of publicly paid men. The trend was patchy, but a trend nevertheless. Partly as a corollary of increased public spending, there were moves to improve administrative oversight – systems of reporting and inspection – and calls for more transparency, to improve public accountability. Ideas that were implicit in these shifts would inform subsequent, structural change. Still, those more radical changes lay ahead.[45]

More notable in this period were certain forms of change that did not involve the formal restructuring of institutions, or major increases or shifts in patterns of expenditure, or even notable changes in the balance of tasks on which paid or unpaid officials spent their time. The changes that took place nonetheless roughly correspond to some things that historians of the 1960s and 1970s had in mind when they premised 'government growth'. They entailed change in the two features of the eighteenth-century scene that I have just noted as qualifying the general picture of engagement and movement. First, around the turn of the eighteenth/nineteenth centuries, ministers and other central office-holders enlarged their role in the shaping of policy across the domestic front. Even when 'government' in the very broadest sense did not extend its reach, there was a re-gearing in the relationship between its levels and parts. Second, in some respects, government broadly conceived *did* extend its role. Its agenda broadened. Parliament extended its remit to issues which it had previously largely ignored – education, public health – or with which it had not concerned itself for several generations – the spiritual health of the nation; it deepened its engagement with some issues with which it had previously only lightly engaged – with questions of the standard of living of the employed population, and occupational welfare. These discussions did not always result in action. When the Commons agreed to the establishment of parochial schools in 1807, the Lords threw the bill out. When legislation was passed, it was often cautious, and meagre in its effects: the first, 1802 Factory Act, for example, was said within a decade to be widely ignored, when not

---

[44] *British Parliamentary Papers* (1830–1831), pp. ix, 287. Poor-law expenditure across England and Wales increased from £2m to £6.33m in this period; expenditure from county rates from £0.25m to £1.28m.

[45] The best brief overview is David Eastwood, *Government and Community in the English Provinces 1700–1870* (Basingstoke, 1997).

altogether forgotten. Still, something had happened: much of the Victorian social agenda had been adumbrated, even if in some cases decades more would pass before discussion bore fruit in significant public programmes.[46]

How did these changes happen? There is much still to be learnt on this score. I will outline a few hypotheses. First, what made ministers and other central-government officeholders willing to play a more active role? Change in the wider European context should be borne in mind. The late eighteenth century was an age of active reforming monarchs (Joseph II, Catherine II); the French Revolution brought into being a reforming republic and empire, whose activities in turn stimulated innovation in some surviving princely states such as Prussia and Bavaria. The French Revolution certainly led some in Britain to abjure 'reform'. But others responded differently. Pitt's cousin Grenville argued, in relation to plans for Church reform that he and Pitt were hatching, that the rule 'quieta non movere' no longer applied; '[t]hese things are all stirred up by the restless spirit of the times, and our duty is to give them a right direction'.[47]

A parallel stimulus to bold thinking was provided by 'enlightened' texts exploring aspects of what it became fashionable to call 'the science of legislation'. Adam Smith's *Wealth of Nations* and T. R. Malthus's *Essay on the Principle of Population* provide examples of British works in this genre.[48] Both recognised that legislative innovation was likely to cause trouble. Both nonetheless suggested that large principles were at stake. In this context, it could be concluded that the kind of cautious, experience-based tinkering that backbenchers had traditionally gone in for no longer represented a plausible way forward.

British ministers and officeholders were not formed in a political culture that encouraged an intellectual approach to politics. But this does not mean that they did not read. Pitt was supposed to be and

---

[46] This discussion draws on my work in progress on the reshaping of social policy in the UK, 1780–1830. I hope that the first fruits of this might be available in the next few years in the form of a book, *Enlightenment, War and Social Policy: George Rose and the State of the People 1784–1818*. For the first factory act, see Innes, 'Origins of the Factory Acts: the Health and Morals of Apprentices Act 1802' in N. Landau (ed.), *Law, Crime and English Society 1660–1840* (Cambridge, 2002), pp. 230–255.

[47] Cited in H. M. C. Fortescue (*The manuscripts of J. B. Fortescue, Esq., preserved at Dropmore*, 10 vols, (London, 1892–1927)), VI, at p. 6. For similar general argument, David Eastwood, 'Patriotism and the English state in the 1790s' in Mark Philp (ed.), *The French Revolution and British Popular Politics* (Cambridge, 1991).

[48] Smith's work, which first appeared in 1776, went through six editions by 1791 (Smith died the previous year); Malthus's *Essay* first appeared in 1799; it likewise went through six editions before his death in 1834.

probably was influenced by his reading of Adam Smith (who advised government, and was given a position in the Scottish customs service as a reward). Pitt's Secretary to the Treasury, George Rose, read Malthus, and struggled to formulate an effective response. John Rickman, recruited by Rose to run the first, 1801 census (he became a clerk of Parliament, and managed all subsequent censuses, down to 1831), read avidly on social and economic themes; he thought that British government needed to change its ways quite smartly if it was to compete against the Continental powers.[49]

Individual temperament mattered. British political institutions and culture encouraged cautious attention to what Parliament and public opinion would accept. Pitt did not break the mould – many of his successors were cautious tinkerers – but he himself was unusually undaunted by the difficulties of engineering change, and his efforts helped to change expectations. By the early 1790s, he had in view a significant measure of Church reform (reforming the tithe system, seen as discouraging agricultural improvement, and pressing the clergy to be more diligent in the discharge of pastoral duties), and reform of the poor laws – again, partly with an eye to fostering economic development, by removing obstacles to labour mobility. Less programmatically, and more as particular problems emerged, he also pressed for the modernisation of labour laws: for the removal of barriers to growth and innovation, and the development of alternative means of promoting workers' welfare, more compatible with the demands of a competitive global economy than older systems of regulation and protection. The British political system, and the onset of war, combined to limit his achievements. He did lay before Parliament a proposal for significant change to the poor laws in 1796–1797, but this failed to command support; he worked with Grenville on Church reform plans through 1799–1800, but these were lost when he resigned from office in 1801 – in poor health, and because forbidden by the King to pursue his plan of combining Irish union with 'Catholic Emancipation'.[50]

---

[49] R. F. Teichgraeber, '"Less abused than I had reason to expect": the reception of *The Wealth of Nations* in Britain, 1776–90', *Historical Journal*, xxx, (1987), pp. 337–366; George Rose, *Observations on the Poor Laws, and on the Management of the Poor* (London, 1805). For Rickman, David Eastwood, 'Rickman, John (1771–1840)', in *ODNB* and O. C. Williams, *Life and Letters of John Rickman* (London, 1912), pp. 116–117 (and see also p. 37, for Smith and Pitt).

[50] Grayson Ditchfield, 'Ecclesiastical legislation during the ministry of the Younger Pitt, 1783–1801', *Parliamentary History*, 19, (2000), pp. 64–80; Poynter, *Society and Pauperism*, pp. 62–76. Pitt's attempts to develop a form of labour policy have not yet been charted, though for some glimpses see J. L. and Barbara Hammond, *The Skilled Labourer* (first pub. 1919, new edn, London, 1979), pp. 45–67.

Yet these issues remained on the agenda, and the (often to-be-disappointed) expectation that 'government' might take the lead in tackling them also survived. Grenville during the next few years complained in Parliament about the pusillanimity of Addington's approach to Church reform; Perceval did plan to move ahead on that front, but his assassination put paid to that. Representatives of industrial workers who had had the experience (or knew that their counterparts had had the experience) of sitting down with Pitt to hammer out ways forwards remained hopeful that they might come to terms with ministry and Parliament well beyond the period in which anyone had the will or power to meet them half-way.[51]

Among Pitt's successors as prime minister, Lord Liverpool seems to have been especially troubled by the rising expectations of ministers and central government officeholders. He was well aware that the central executive remained poorly equipped to generate ambitious domestic policies; he, moreover, did not believe that *any* public policy could do much to resolve manifold problems with roots deep in society and economy. However, leaving policy-making to backbenchers was decreasingly credible. In the immediate post-war period, as poor rates pressed hard upon a depressed economy, his administration declined calls to take the lead in reforming the poor laws – but in practice the select committees which met for several years thereafter, whose recommendations resulted in some changes to the law, were well stocked with ministers and other officeholders. The kinds of men who would have taken the lead had government owned the task did get involved, even though they operated wholly within a parliamentary framework.[52]

[51] Grenville in House of Lords debate, 2 June 1802: [Debrett] *The Parliamentary Register; or, History of the Proceedings and Debates of the House of Commons* (18 vols, London, 1802), pp. xviii, 587–579. Harrowby in House of Lords debate 1818: [Hansard], *Parliamentary Debates* (First series, 41 vols., 1812–1820), pp. xxxvii, 718; *British Parliamentary Papers* 1834 (556) pp. x, 421–422.

[52] Hilton, 'The political arts of Lord Liverpool', provides an interesting analysis of Liverpool's (at first sight, odd) preference for keeping policy issues at arm's length from the cabinet. MPs named to poor law committees 1816–1819 included the Chancellor of the Exchequer (Vansittart), the Vice President of the Board of Trade (Robinson), Castlereagh (then Foreign Secretary), Bathurst (former President of the Board of Trade, then secretary of state for war and colonies), Huskisson (whose talents the government had recently recruited by making him First Commissioner of Woods and Forests) and T. P. Courtenay (a former secretary to the Treasury, then at the Board of Control). Courtenay, *Copy of a Letter to the Rt. Hon. William Sturges Bourne, Chairman of the Select Committee of the House of Commons Appointed for the Consideration ...* (London, [1817]), attributed special importance to proposals made to the committee by Huskisson and Castlereagh.

A younger generation of politicians, who grew up with new expectations, sometimes adjusted accordingly. Peel provides a case in point. He served as Irish Chief Secretary (1812–1818) at a time when Irish backbenchers, frustrated by their inability to make progress with reforms, looked to help from the executive. Peel came to accept that he must bring forward each session a series of measures. He carried over that cast of mind into the Home Secretaryship, when he held that post from 1822. He then, for example, worked at unblocking the tangle into which metropolitan communities had got themselves in finding a way forward for metropolitan policing – and managed to broker agreement on what became the Metropolitan Police Act of 1829.[53]

I am suggesting that ministers and officeholders enlarged their ideas about the scope and character of their responsibilities. Yet certainly change was limited. Indeed, throughout the nineteenth century, social-policy proposals continued often to emanate from backbenchers; not until the twentieth century did ministers establish a near monopoly of initiative.[54] Changes in this period, though real, were only incidents in a longer process.

At the same time, though, another, partly overlapping but distinct change was taking place: a broadening of the central state, in the sense now of *Parliament*'s agenda. To explain this, we will need to look beyond ministers and officeholders, to backbenchers and indeed to the wider society, out of which emerged many of the ideas and projects which were then funnelled through backbenchers. Certain social issues which did not figure on the relatively narrowly conceived eighteenth-century parliamentary agenda nonetheless engaged much public interest, developing under voluntary auspices. Education provides an instance: the eighteenth century saw the formation of societies and the launching of public appeals to establish charity schools and Sunday schools. Health provides another: infirmaries and dispensaries were launched in their dozens without governmental or parliamentary encouragement or regulation. Smallpox inoculation over the same period became common practice, and was administered across whole communities, without the involvement of any officials other than overseers of the poor.[55] The

[53] For Ireland, see Innes, 'Legislating for three kingdoms', pp. 32–33; for police, Elaine Reynolds, *Before the Bobbies: The Night Watch and Police Reform in Metropolitan London 1720–1830* (Stanford, CA, 1998), chs 7–8.

[54] See generally Valerie Cromwell, 'The losing of the initiative by the House of Commons, 1780–1914', *Transactions of the Royal Historical Society*, 5th ser., xviii, (1968), pp. 1–23.

[55] For a now dated but still exceptionally wide-ranging review of voluntarism, David Owen, *English Philanthropy 1660–1960* (Cambridge, MA, 1965), esp. chs 1–3; for smallpox inoculation similarly, P. E. Razzell, *The Conquest of Smallpox* (London, 1977) remains the most general introduction.

piecemeal appearance of legislative proposals bearing on such matters on the early nineteenth-century parliamentary agenda can be conceptualised as the result of a maturation process, as activists in these fields came to believe that parliamentary endorsement would help them to achieve more – though a formulation of that kind leaves issues of timing unaccounted for. Proposals sometimes emerged out of developing relationships between particular promoters and officials or MPs. Some issues came to Parliament in the first place on the coat-tails, as it were, of more traditional issues – education on the back of the poor laws; health (especially in the form of what could be done to prevent fever epidemics) on the back of prisons. The making of such linkages to some extent reflected the prior forging of links both between issues, and between species of activist, at a local level.

I think there is a broader story to tell too, however, about the development in the late eighteenth century of a new problematic – 'the state of the people' – creating a context for new thinking about what public and parliamentary agendas *should* be. The 1780s provided a crucible for this new thinking. In that decade, men – and women – who prided themselves on their public spirit, jarred by Britain's loss of her American colonies in consequence of what some viewed as an unnecessary, others as an ill-managed, war, operating in a period saturated with ideas about possible 'improvements' and 'reforms', addressed themselves to the task of what was sometimes (in an established phrase) termed 'reforming manners', sometimes (more neologistically) 'bettering society'. To this end they encouraged the establishment of friendly societies and Sunday schools, sustained industry (especially by training young people) and promoted temperance (by closing pubs).[56] To aim to 'reform manners' was to aim to tackle social problems at the root: to tackle causes, not symptoms. That project had last attracted widespread innovative effort in the late seventeenth and early eighteenth centuries; it provided a theme for many flurries of localised effort thereafter. Two striking features of the late eighteenth-century reformation of manners movement were first that it was associated with, and helped to popularise, many relatively new institutional forms – reformed prisons, Sunday schools, spinning schools, elite-sponsored savings schemes – in this way helping to launch new lines of improving enterprise, and second that it was particularly associated with initiatives designed to help members of the

---

[56] Innes, 'Politics and morals: the reformation of manners movement in later eighteenth-century England' in E. Hellmuth (ed.), *The Transformation of Political Culture in Late Eighteenth-Century England and Germany* (Oxford, 1990), also now republished in *Inferior Politics*.

working population to help themselves. It was not merely culture-changing in intent, but aimed more particularly at the creation of a culture of independence and self-improvement. These developments took place against the background of a long-term rise in food prices that was believed to be creating particular difficulty for the working population. And they took place too in the context of burgeoning enthusiasm for empirical social enquiry, which gave rise to many local statistical studies of conditions bearing on popular health and welfare.[57]

These developments cross-fertilised to encourage innovative forms of thinking and writing about the 'state of the people'. They also created a context for rethinking both the scope and the purpose of public policy. Writers and their readerships, local and central officials and MPs all began to envision a new public-policy agenda whose primary object would be to promote individual independence, self-reliance and enterprise. If the mass of the population were indisputably struggling with difficult circumstances (then being characterised by empirical enquirers with unprecedented detail and precision), that merely helped to focus the question: What could be done to help people to better themselves and, ultimately, improve on those circumstances? What, if any, mix of removing unnecessary economic constraints, supplying education, addressing background health issues, facilitating saving, improving spiritual leadership at parish level and subjecting the errant to reformative penal regimes might do the trick?

I think that it is in the context of this new vision that we should set the broadening of the content of the early nineteenth-century parliamentary agenda – a broadening initially entailing for Parliament more talk than action. This new vision encouraged the reconceptualisation of old policies as well as new approaches. Pitt, alongside other would-be poor-law reformers of the era, showed little interest in the old, Elizabethan system of rate-based cash relief, more interest in developing complementary support systems: schools, systems of work provision, savings schemes. Debates on penal policy were in parallel recast around issues of health and education.[58]

Proponents of these initiatives did not clearly conceive of themselves as enlarging the role of government within society. They sought rather to foster individual effort. Government activity and legislation were for

---

[57] Innes, 'Power and happiness: empirical social enquiry from political arithmetic to moral statistics' in *Inferior Politics*.

[58] Poynter, *Society and Pauperism*, pp. 62–76. For penal policy, the most interesting overview is Robin Evans, *The Fabrication of Virtue: English Prison Architecture 1780–1840* (Cambridge, 1982).

them merely tools – the tools they had to hand – to promote culture change. However, new forms of state activity *were* in practice implied: activity to effect change, but then also to maintain new cultural patterns. These reforming efforts consequently, if inadvertently, helped to fuel debate about what were proper – and possible – roles for government: about what government could and should do.[59] No more in this context than in many others did they prove easy to resolve.

Conclusion

'Government' is a term with a variety of meanings. If government is understood as an assemblage of institutions, yet more or less institutions can be included. It can also be understood to refer to a set of functions, perhaps discharged in part by officials, but usually on the basis of some form of collaboration with the public. Or it can be conceived in terms of a set of ideas informing conduct. The metaphor of 'growth' is easier to apply to some of these understandings than others. Through the eighteenth and early nineteenth centuries, recurrent wars jacked up spending, and added to the national debt and the cost of servicing that debt. There was consistent concern, always sharpest during and immediately after the end of wars, to contain and reduce these costs, as also to contain and reduce the cost of relieving the poor. But much nineteenth-century debate about setting limits to government focused not on these issues, but rather on particular ways in which government used its power, to restrict civil or religious liberties, or to act *for* people when (it was argued) it was better to leave people to act for themselves. Nineteenth-century arguments against 'government interference' did not always focus on costly or labour-intensive forms of 'interference'; instead, they often focused on the putative effects of government action on the individual psyche or on social dynamics – or, as contemporaries more commonly expressed it, upon 'morals'. In the late twentieth century, when much public spending and public employment arose from the provision of services, all of these issues could be seen as tightly interrelated. But in the period that we are considering, though these concerns did overlap, they overlapped less. Focusing on spending patterns is probably not a good way of getting to grips with the changing scale and range of governmental activity on the domestic front; we need to use different tools to achieve that.

---

[59] For some reflections on this complicated theme, Innes, 'Central government interference: changing conceptions, practices and concerns 1688–1840' in Jose Harris (ed.), *Civil Society in British History* (Oxford, 2003).

4   Family formations: Anglo India and the familial proto-state

Margot Finn

For Marxist, functionalist and feminist historians alike, the family figures as a cornerstone of capitalist modernity. From Friedrich Engels's *Origins of the Family, Private Property and the State*, through Talcott Parsons's theorisation of the nuclear family's role in sustaining industrialisation to Hall and Davidoff's analysis of the gendered construction of Victorian class identities, the close nexus between family formations and economic development has remained a constant of the historical analysis of eighteenth- and nineteenth-century British society.[1] To be sure, scholars have disagreed fundamentally as to the nature of this pivotal relationship. For Alan Macfarlane, it was precisely because its marriage system was highly individualised and dis-embedded from kin networks that capitalism flourished in England; for Richard Grassby, in sharp contrast, capitalist development required the property of London's business classes to be 'vested and consolidated in the family, not the individual'.[2]

Although older traditions of imperial history remained largely insulated from these historiographical debates, the emergence of 'new' imperial histories has fostered an efflorescence of scholarship on the part played by family relationships in shaping the conflicted modernities of the British empire.[3] In this context, arguments about the pivotal role of the family as an instrument of 'bourgeois' capital formation have gained new purchase, becoming imbricated with Foucauldian histories of race,

---

[1] For an excellent overview of this literature, see Leonore Davidoff, Megan Doolittle, Janet Fink and Kathleen Holden, *The Family Story: Blood, Contract and Intimacy, 1830–1960* (Harlow, 1999), pp. 19–25.

[2] Alan Macfarlane, *Marriage and Love in England: Modes of Reproduction 1300–1840* (Oxford, 1986), pp. 322–323; Richard Grassby, *Kinship and Capitalism: Marriage, Family, and Business in the English-Speaking World, 1580–1740* (Cambridge, 2001), p. 385.

[3] For the 'new' imperial history and its engagement with gender and the family, see, for example, Kathleen Wilson (ed.), *A New Imperial History: Culture, Identity and Modernity in Britain and the Empire 1660–1840* (Cambridge, 2004).

biopower and colonial governmentality.[4] Enriching our understanding of the social origins of economic and political change, the new imperial history of the British family has focused overwhelmingly on problems of racial alterity and exclusion. Thanks to studies by Chatterjee, Ghosh and Hawes, for example, we now know a great deal about the mixed-race progeny of British fathers in colonial India, illegitimate children whose problematic position in the family has become emblematic of a wider racialisation of British power relations under East India Company rule.[5] In contrast, we know little about how governing-class families in India reproduced themselves as white and British prior to the onset of Crown rule in 1858, by forming legitimate marriage alliances through which property and patronage could safely be channelled into capital accumulation and political power. Whereas the extant literature on mixed-race children born to British fathers underlines the governing class's imperative to exclude these liminal members from the imperial family fold, the literature on British national identity among the imperial governing elite instead highlights this class's willingness to encompass ethnic others from within the United Kingdom. Thus Colley and Bayly draw attention to the ease with which 'intermarriage between Celtic and English dynasties' yielded 'a new unitary ruling class' that shared a 'collective mentality' and was fired by 'a sharper sense of British national and Imperial mission' in the late eighteenth and early nineteenth centuries.[6]

In this chapter, I use the marital histories of a prominent governing-class family in early nineteenth-century India to explore the British family's function at the interface between the public and the private sphere in a colonial setting. In Britain itself, family solidarity played a crucial role in enabling economic expansion by providing an effective mechanism for managing financial risk. 'Loyalty to kin had functional and symbolic importance', Margaret Hunt has argued of eighteenth-century England, for 'it helped people to make sense of a society in which bureaucratic structures were few, authority was for most intents and purposes lodged in households, and social valuations at all levels of society were often more related to blood and ancestry than to individual

---

[4] Ann Laura Stoler's *Race and the Education of Desire: Foucault's History of Sexuality and the Colonial Order of Things* (Durham, NC, 1995) established key lines of analysis. For British elaborations, see esp. Durba Ghosh, *Sex and the Family in Colonial India: The Making of Empire* (Cambridge, 2006).

[5] Indrani Chatterjee, *Gender, Slavery and Law in Colonial India* (Oxford, 1999); Ghosh, *Sex and the Family*; Christopher Hawes, *Poor Relations: The Making of a Eurasian Community in British India 1773–1833* (Richmond, 1996).

[6] Linda Colley, *Britons: Forging the Nation 1707–1837* (London, 1992), p. 161; C. A. Bayly, *Imperial Meridian: The British Empire and the World 1780–1830* (London, 1989), p. 134.

merit'.[7] R. J. Morris's detailed analysis of British property relations underlines the persistence throughout the nineteenth century of familial strategies for managing risk, a reliance that reflected both the restricted purchase of life insurance and limited liability and the effect of welfare structures that focused overwhelmingly on the poor.[8]

Kin-based financial mechanisms likewise underpinned British and European economic and political expansion on the subcontinent.[9] In the century that stretched from Clive's military victories to the Mutiny of 1857–1858, the East India Company shed its commercial privileges and operations and fitfully assumed increasing burdens of state power. The limited size of its civil service, the protracted lapse of time that characterised communication with London and the persistence of myriad indigenous sovereign political formations all reinforced the close ties between the Company's proto-state and governing-class families in India in this period. The directors' monopoly over scarce appointments to the covenanted civil service also ensured that 'Connections with the Company tended . . . to be hereditary', a characteristic further underlined by the great prevalence of intermarriage among its leading families.[10] Under Company rule, Ghosh suggests, British families mediated 'the relationship between the state and its subjects'.[11] Indigenous South Asian bureaucratic structures further bolstered this colonial confluence of kinship and governmentality: the *cutcherries* that functioned as the nerve centres of Company business were shaped fundamentally by patrimonial familial practices.[12]

By examining the marital fortunes of a prominent imperial kin network, I seek to illuminate British governing-class families' accommodation of the social, cultural and economic demands and opportunities of empire. Navigating between perceptions of difference and constructions of similarity was an essential colonial family strategy, vital to the reproduction of wealth and power across the generations. Meaningful analysis of British hostility to racial *métissage* on the subcontinent requires an understanding of the norms and expectations that governed family formation and the

---

[7] Margaret Hunt, *The Middling Sort: Commerce, Gender, and the Family in England, 1680–1780* (Berkeley, CA, 1996), p. 24.

[8] R. J. Morris, *Men, Women and Property in England, 1780–1870* (Cambridge, 2005), p. 371.

[9] The Dutch instance is detailed by Julia Adams, *The Familial State: Ruling Families and Merchant Capitalism in Early Modern Europe* (Ithaca, NY, 2005).

[10] P. J. Marshall, *East Indian Fortunes: The British in Bengal in the Eighteenth Century* (Oxford, 1976), pp. 11–12.

[11] Ghosh, *Sex and the Family*, pp. 12–13.

[12] Bhavani Raman, 'The familial world of the compnay's *kacceri* in early modern Madras', *Journal of Colonialism and Colonial History*, 9, (Fall, 2008).

disposition of family property among the British metropolitan political elite, as well as attention to the ways in which these norms and expectations were challenged by the emergence of an increasingly global marriage market. To this end, I explore the imperial family fortunes of Gilbert Elliot (1751–1814), the first Earl of Minto, who served as Governor General of India from 1806–1813. Minto's domestic life in India with his younger sons and the parallel lives of his wife, his daughters and his heir in Britain are chronicled in dense detail in the family's voluminous correspondence. These private letters offer a counter-narrative to the dominant history of imperial *métissage*. For although their correspondence is replete with racial stereotypes and cross-cut by sexual tension and innuendo, Minto and his younger sons made few references to indigenous women in their correspondence, and they appear not to have sired illegitimate children with Indian slaves or concubines. The great burden of their epistolary effort was directed not at the threat of perceived racial others, but rather to the challenges posed by a succession of white interlopers seeking access to the family circle and its considerable resources. Animated by impecunious daughters-in-law of problematic white ethnicity, by creole wives of dubious European parentage and by bastard British sons, this counter-narrative boasts only fictive and metaphorical racial half-castes, yet it too is nonetheless fundamentally concerned with the technologies of social and textual power that prohibited or allowed the mixing of bloodlines within imperial society.[13]

I

Minto's private correspondence testifies abundantly to the centrality of family in the Earl's political stratagems, financial dealings, social activities and emotional life. The eldest son of a Scottish baronet, Gilbert Elliot had married Anna Maria Amyand in 1777. Four sons and three daughters born to the couple survived to adolescence, requiring substantial capital investment by their parents but also fuelling their dynastic ambitions. Minto's elevation to the peerage upon his appointment as Governor General of India represented the culmination of a concerted campaign that he and his wife had pursued relentlessly since the 1780s. The sorrow occasioned by their physical separation during his tenure in office was alleviated by a constant stream of correspondence between colony and metropole. From his departure for India in 1807 on board the *Modeste* – which sailed under the command of his son George – until his return to England with George and his younger brother, John, in

---

[13] For the simultaneous power and fragility of 'bloodlines' in British conceptions of kinship, see esp. Davidoff *et al.*, *The Family Story*, pp. 4, 51–52, 78–80.

1814, the Earl dispatched hundreds of lengthy letters to his wife and children at the Minto estate in the Scottish Borders. Lady Minto and her remaining offspring in turn unleashed a continuous cascade of correspondence to the Elliot menfolk, linking the distant Earl through letters to family, community, party and nation at home. As Colonel John Drinkwater – a family friend and in-law who served the Elliots as a trustee and confidant for decades – later wrote, when urging the second Earl to publish selections from Minto's family correspondence, 'His private letters to your mother alone would be invaluable to the Historian as communicating the secret springs of many publick occurrences which are but obscurely if at all known at present'.[14]

Marriage lay at the very heart of the 'secret springs' that shaped the course of the Earl's public life in India. Minto had inherited an estate saddled with debt, which his parliamentary ambitions, cosmopolitan tastes and rapidly expanding brood of progeny magnified over time. His desire to secure his children's fortunes and to rebuild the family mansion at Minto (to create a residence capable of accommodating three generations of the Elliot clan under a single roof) form dominant leitmotifs of his letters, providing the key justification for his extended Asiatic exile. Writing from Calcutta in 1807, Minto commented facetiously that he would continue to augment his daughters' portions 'till the beauties are ten thousand pounders & can afford to be ugly and stupid'. The prospective alliances of his sons also figured prominently in his Asiatic marital calculus. 'George has brought such loads of fine things from China that he may purchase all the young Ladies in England', he observed contentedly to his wife in 1808.[15] Minto's family-orientated distribution of the spoils of empire radiated out from this nuclear core through siblings and in-laws to a vast, insatiable army of retainers, friends and potential patrons. His obvious pleasure in marking the nuptials of his family and friends with timely gifts of Indian patronage shines through the pages of Minto's letters home. 'Pray tell Lord Somerville that his brother is on the point of marriage, & that as a wedding gift ... I have appointed him to the *Collectorship* of *Dacca*', he wrote to the Countess in 1807.[16]

In this connubial environment, the marriage in India of the Earl's younger sons John Elliot (to Amelia Casamaijor) and George Elliot

---

[14] Colonel John Drinkwater to the 2nd Earl, 18 February 1835, National Library of Scotland (hereafter NLS), Minto Papers, MS 11803, fol. 248 verso.

[15] Minto to the Countess, 4 December 1807, NLS, Minto Papers, MS 11063, fol. 50 verso; Minto to the Countess, 25 January–15 February 1808, NLS, Minto Papers, MS 11063, fol. 71 verso.

[16] Minto to the Countess, 18 December 1807, NLS, Minto Papers, MS 11063, fols. 57 verso–58. The estimated revenue of the appointment was £3,000 per annum.

(to Eliza Ness) appear at first glance to be unproblematic. As John's godmother wrote to the Earl from London on learning of his match, 'I can't say that the news much surprised me, as . . . we all know what a friend you are to Marriage'.[17] The immediate reactions of Minto and the Countess to their sons' successive love matches were, however, decidedly unenthusiastic. Eager to distribute the Company-state's political favours to foster the marriages of other men's sons in India, Minto was loath to encourage John and George to follow in their footsteps. Capital accumulation for marriage – not marriage itself – was the prime purpose of their service in India. Nor did Amelia Casamaijor and Eliza Ness constitute strategic choices for Minto's younger sons. Lacking dowries and bereft of exalted connections, they also threatened to bring worryingly hybrid genealogies into the Elliot lineage. The processes by which Minto, the Countess, and their children in Scotland came to accept these distant daughters as their own kin illuminate not only the shifting markers that demarcated race, class and nation in this period but also the pragmatic mechanisms by which these boundaries were policed, breached or maintained by imperial families.

Eighteen years old when she married the twenty-one-year-old John Elliot in 1809, Amelia was a daughter of James Casamaijor, a senior Company civilian. The young couple first met as adolescents in 1805, when John set forth for India in advance of his father and brother. On shipboard, Casamaijor and his wife befriended John, inviting him to dine at their table, lending him money as needed and introducing him to their adolescent daughters. Although John Elliot repeatedly denied any attachment at the time, describing the Casamaijor sisters in one letter home as 'not being over clean and I don't think particularly agreeable', the shared voyage appears to have sown seeds of abiding affection.[18] Serving as his father's private secretary four years later, John accompanied Minto to Madras, where he and Amelia precipitously declared their love. They were married within a matter of weeks, and returned to Calcutta with the Earl, with whom they set up residence at Government House.

Amelia's lack of a marriage portion and her paternal bloodlines posed potential obstacles to the union. Casamaijor was of tripartite British, Portuguese and Malay descent. This mixed patrimony – at once financially inadequate and racially other – had proved a major impediment to the marriage of Amelia's older sister Jane to the Company servant Henry

[17] Eleanor Drinkwater to Minto, 23 March 1810, NLS, Minto Papers, MS 11141, fol. 66.
[18] John Elliot to the Countess, 28 July 1805, NLS, Minto Papers, MS 11094, fol. 19.

Russell.[19] John Elliot's determination to marry Jane's sister Amelia is intriguing in this context, for his father was fully aware of Sir Henry Russell's objections to the union of his eldest son and heir with a Casamaijor.[20] John Elliot himself evinced an enduring antagonism to India's indigenous population. Writing to the Countess in 1809, Minto remarked of the Asians 'swarming' about him that 'I am not at all annoyed by their black skins, as John is. He has no charity for a dark complexion.'[21] The Earl's opposition to John's match with Amelia, although fierce, proved short-lived. 'I confess that I emptied a terrible volley of grief & dismay & despair upon the unfortunate ambassador', he reported to his wife, but within '*an quarter of an hour* after my stomach had been thus relieved, I was as happy as a bridegroom, & within an hour, was in the Casamaijor house joining their hands'.[22] The rapidity with which Minto's resistance to this marriage crumbled and the complete absence of references to Amelia's mixed ancestry in the family's private correspondence suggest contemporaries' willingness to suspend racial sensibilities when it suited their broader purposes to do so. Philosophical predisposition may have complemented this familial pragmatism. Minto's attitude was consistent with the universalising tendencies of the conjectural history that had been formative in his education (and which he actively promoted as a patron of Oriental scholarship), a historiographical tradition in which race figured as a mutable historical artefact rather than a changeless biological identity.[23]

More pragmatically, Amelia's acceptance by her Scottish in-laws was effected by a strategic onslaught through the imperial post. In a letter to his mother written soon after his marriage, John Elliot represented Amelia's social and cultural identity as a *tabula rasa*, an epistolary strategy that underscored his father's authority to determine his wife's fitness to join the family. 'I say nothing about Amelia as all I can tell you about her would be like speaking of some unknown person in Iceland . . . and . . . I think you will receive good accounts of her from everybody who mentions her to you amongst others I suspect my Father as one of her

---

[19] Sir Henry Russell to Charles Russell, 20 November 1808, Bodleian Library, MS Eng. lett. c. 152, fol. 92 verso. See also William Dalrymple, *White Mughals: Love and Betrayal in Eighteenth-Century India* (London, 2002), pp. 452–460.

[20] Minto to the Countess, 28 October 1809, NLS, MS 11064, fols. 184–185 verso.

[21] Minto to the Countess, 8 June 1809, NLS, Minto Papers, MS 11064, fol. 60.

[22] Minto to the Countess, 12 October 1809, NLS, Minto Papers, MS 11064, fol. 172 verso.

[23] For Minto's philosophical dispositions, see Jane Rendall, 'Scottish orientalism: from Robertson to James Mill', *Historical Journal*, 25, (March, 1982), pp. 43–69, esp. pp. 45, 48, 50–51.

admirers', he observed.[24] Minto's recognition that John's marriage to an unknown so-called 'Indian' woman would cause consternation at home was matched by his determination to ensure that the family would accept Amelia as an Elliot relation by return of post. To achieve this goal, he ignored her racial background entirely and discounted the significance of her penury, highlighting instead her feminine attractions and her status as a genteel person of cultivated sensibilities. Acknowledging that 'Mr Casamajor [sic] is not Crosus' and estimating Amelia's dowry as 'not less than five dozen of shifts', he claimed that John's additional expenditure as a married man would be modest and noted that he himself would be able to augment his son's income with the gift of another government office. Femininity and sociability trumped race and economic class in this analysis. 'Amelia Casamajor [sic] is really a very sweet & good girl, & worthy of the cousinry & even of the Sister-hood', he wrote. 'Her education has been good, & the manner & habits of her Mothers [sic] house quite exemplary.'[25] Gender stereotypes and idealised conceptions of home were central to the Earl's fashioning of Amelia's image for domestic consumption at home, where she was destined (he hoped) to join the extended family unit as a co-resident at Minto. 'I think it is an excellent & essential thing . . . that she is likely . . . to fall in with all the family tastes & fancies, so that she will be really one of us & not a stranger at home', he advised the Countess.[26] Silent on her father's background, Minto instead constructed a genealogy in which Amelia acquired a quintessential Englishness through the maternal line. 'No girls can have been better brought up [than the Casamaijor daughters], & they are the only persons I have seen in India really like young English Gentlewomen', he commented to his wife.[27]

The ground prepared by Minto's epistolary representation of her feminine virtues and class status was cultivated assiduously by Amelia, whose skills as a letter-writer appear to have been essential to her acceptance into the family circle in Scotland years before her return to Britain. Amelia's letters to her in-laws successfully combined personal modesty, solicitude for the Elliots' domestic interests, and a crafty deployment of maternal imagery. 'There is not a fine phrase or an affectation or in short anything but good sterling happy nature in the whole letter', Minto's heir, Gilbert Elliot, commented when he informed

[24] John Elliot to the Countess, 24 December 1809, NLS, Minto Papers, MS 11094, fol. 173 verso.

[25] Minto to the Countess, 12 October 1809, NLS, Minto Papers, MS 11064, fols. 173 verso–174.

[26] Minto to the Countess, 19 October 1809, NLS, Minto Papers, MS 11064, fol. 178.

[27] Minto to the Countess, NLS, Minto Papers, MS 11064, fol. 179.

his brother John that the family had now 'passed judgement' on Amelia's initial correspondence to them.[28] Writing to his mother, Gilbert was more explicit: 'Amelia's letter is worth her weight in gold and I am perfectly satisfied that John was quite right to marry her ... in short I confess it is a great relief to me tho' I had no doubt of her being better than the generality of Indian Ladies, yet not knowing Mrs Cas: ... I did feel a little afraid of the genteels [sic]', he confided.[29] The Countess herself informed Minto that John's 'marriage came upon me like a flash of lightening & I will be honest enough to own that I felt a Bone in my throat for some minutes', but she too was rapidly won over by John and Amelia's letters. 'The only *fault* John has committed was *falling in Love*, & when I look back to former days, I cannot but acknowledge his Mother did so before him, & I must add this little bit of encouragement, that to this hour I have never repented this heinous sin', she admitted.[30] Amelia and John, relieved by their receipt of congratulatory letters from Scotland, hastened to send correspondence that would confirm Amelia's identity as a prospective British matron at Minto. 'No one detests India and loves Home more than I do', Amelia asserted, assuring the Countess that she would 'find that Johns [sic] expences have not increased by marrying, notwithstanding the arrival of that little darling ... which we are now every hour expecting'.[31]

Opposition to John's marriage from his relatives in Britain diminished sharply as Amelia's identity shifted from 'a native of India' to an 'English gentlewoman'.[32] But the spectre of alterity raised by this union soon extended from John to his brothers George and William, officers in the Royal Navy who had accompanied Minto to India. The Countess's sister warned Minto that his countenance of the match would encourage his unmarried sons to follow their brother's example, 'as after your ready consent to John you cannot refuse them, if they choose *even a Chinese wife*'.[33] In the event, George Elliot met Eliza Ness while engaged in

---

[28] Gilbert Elliot to John Elliot, 16 July 1810, NLS, Minto Papers, MS 11752, fol. 91 verso.

[29] Gilbert Elliot to the Countess, 14 July 1810, NLS, Minto Papers, MS 11081, fol. 162.

[30] Countess Minto to Minto, 13 March 1810, NLS, Minto Papers, MS 11081, fols. 73–73 verso.

[31] Amelia Elliot to the Countess, 3 October 1810, NLS, Minto Papers, MS 11094, fol. 261.

[32] Lady Malmesbury described Amelia to the Countess as 'a native of India' in March 1809. By 1811, however, she was reconciled to the match: 'I saw a letter of Amelia's that delighted me it was so natural, clear, lively & pleasant & as I find she really contributes to the Comfort of your Exile, I no longer lament Johns [sic] having married so early'. Lady Malmesbury to Minto, 29 March 1809, 19 April 1811, NLS, Minto Papers, MS 11110, fols. 86, 131, 162.

[33] Ibid., 27 March 1810, fol. 132.

protecting the Company's Chinese trade, and married her without parental consent. Lady Minto reported to her husband that George's letter announcing the match 'came like a thunder ball'. Like Amelia, Eliza was of hybrid ancestry: her father was a Yorkshire man, but her mother was Irish. Whereas Amelia's paternal Malay great-grandmother had been effectively erased in the Elliot family consciousness by her mother's reputation as 'a good specimen of an English gentlewoman', Eliza's associations with her Irish female kin occluded the Englishness of her paternal lineage. 'To *you* I cannot help saying the *connections* seemed very far from what one should have wished for & you know my prejudices to be strong against the Irish', the Countess wrote unhappily to her husband.[34] Eliza's Irishness clearly encompassed far more than a merely national affiliation, figuring in Lady Minto's outraged sensibilities as a symbol of all that was vulgar, uneducated and untouchable in the female sex. If Eliza proved 'not vulgar', the Countess ruminated, 'It must be from nature, not Education or Example', for 'the accounts of [her] Mama ... are not very pleasing'. Abetted by her sister, her eldest son and her daughters, the Countess dispatched letters to friends and family in Harrogate, Limerick and Liverpool, seeking clarification of Eliza's social status. Eliza's mother, sister and female cousins, Lady Minto reported, appeared to have blameless 'Characters, but their manners & conversation seems [sic] to be that of very *underbred* & vulgar people ... truly Irish, of the 2nd rank ... with strange expressions & sort of *cant* words'.[35] Lapses in epistolary courtesy compounded these improper familial associations, as Eliza's failure to write promptly from India to her in-laws at Minto reinforced her identity as an alien other. 'I really feel perfectly acquainted and delighted with Amelia ... [but] as to Eliza she has kept herself to herself ... & not laid herself before us as Amelia boldly ventured to do at first', Lady Minto commented censoriously to her spouse.[36]

To combat the pernicious influence of Eliza's Irish female kin, the Countess advocated a form of domestic apartheid. Urging that Eliza must be segregated from her natal family, Lady Minto ultimately took comfort in the very depth of the Ness clan's social distance from her own. As she wrote to Lord Minto in 1811, 'her family must be kept in the Background ... & it is lucky they are so *decidedly* out of the question as society, rather than only halfway between the right & the wrong'.[37]

---

[34] Countess to Minto, 23 September 1810, NLS, Minto Papers, MS 11081, fols. 196–196 verso. Eliza's paternal lineage is noted in *OxDNB*, vol. 18, p. 166.
[35] Countess to Minto, 13 June 1814, NLS, Minto Papers, MS 11083, fol. 211.
[36] Countess to Minto, 13 May 1811, NLS, Minto Papers, MS 11081, fol. 308.
[37] Countess to Minto, 27 March 1811, NLS, Minto Papers, MS 11081, fol. 275 verso.

The Earl, who had taken the now pregnant Eliza under his paternal wing at Government House, dispatched conciliatory letters in triplicate to the Countess, urging the folly of a precipitate policy of exclusion. Predictably, Minto's efforts to reconcile his wife to George's marriage sought both to highlight her paternal, English bloodline and to use the evidence of epistolary niceties to deflect attention from the failings of her maternal kin. 'George shewed me ... a full & very clear note of the whole family drawn up in the form of a Pedigree; on one side the paternal branch, & on the other the maternal from the grand Fathers downwards with all the collateral relations', he reported in 1812. Noting that both sides of Eliza's family boasted connections with 'persons of fortune indeed opulence & consideration in England as well as Ireland', he concluded by observing that he had read examples of the Ness family's private letters and saw in them 'a great deal of good family affection, uniformly the best possible sentiments upon all subjects'.[38]

If Lady Minto's antagonism had been directed at Amelia Casamaijor rather than Eliza Ness, the Elliots' imperial marital woes might substantiate the contention that nineteenth-century British women played a crucial role in precipitating the hardening of racial consciousness that marked this period. In this interpretation, sexual antagonism between white and indigenous women mounted sharply as greater numbers of British wives accompanied their husbands on duty to the subcontinent, crystallising hitherto fluid conceptions of racial difference into rigid, hierarchical theories of racial superiority and inferiority.[39] The racialised processes of inclusion and exclusion described in the colonial correspondence of Minto's nuclear family depart, however, from this model in significant ways. To be sure, Lady Minto (even from Scotland) played a central role in policing the boundaries of difference, writing obsessively to family and friends in Britain and India to obtain information that would allow her to assign fixed social and cultural identities to the 'Indian' wives acquired by her sons in the Orient. Yet the Countess's conceptions of acceptable in-laws fit only imperfectly with the Orientalist stereotypes familiar from the secondary literature on British India: the image of the vulgar, lower-class Irish adventuress loomed far larger in her fears than did indigenous women, mixed-race *métis* and creoles from the subcontinent. By far the most strident antagonism to 'black' racial

---

[38] Minto to the Countess, 17 November 1812, NLS, Minto Papers, MS 11083, fols. 124–125 verso.

[39] Discussions of the relative merits of this interpretation include Ronald Hyam, *Empire and Sexuality* (Manchester, 1990), esp. pp. 118–121 and Ann Laura Stoler, 'Rethinking colonial categories: European communities and the boundaries of rule', *Comparative Studies in Society and History*, 31, (1989), pp. 134–161, esp. pp. 146–147.

others in the Elliot family correspondence, indeed, was to be found not in the Countess's letters but in those associated with her son John, whose wife was one-sixteenth Malay.

II

As elaborated thus far, the Elliots' imperial family romance conforms to the contours of the first Earl's last will and testament (witnessed in Madras in 1813), which defined his family unit in terms of marriage, legitimate offspring and sibling relations. The will, typical of a genre of writing that was calculated to present the family as 'an enclosed universe', specified eight bequests to members of his family circle, leaving the remainder of the Earl's considerable estate in Britain and India to his eldest son, Gilbert.[40] Whereas the will recognised responsibilities for the welfare of his wife, their six surviving children, a loyal family retainer, and the progeny born to two Elliot brothers by their wives, his private letters in contrast acknowledged Minto's paternal obligations to a broader family circle that encompassed eight British bastard offspring. Marked by fluid distinctions between black and white, savage and civilised, these letters also displayed significant slippage within white categories of distinction along the axes that divided public from private, legitimate from illegitimate and European from creole identities. Carefully shielded from public view by Minto in Britain, the existence and status of his bastard sons was exposed to scrutiny in India, forcing his legitimate family to renegotiate the borders that demarcated their conceptions of dependent kin.

Minto sired eight white children upon his British mistress, Mrs Barry. The relationship dated from at the very least the early 1780s until 1794, when Minto took up his appointment as viceroy of Corsica.[41] Mrs Barry's background and social status are opaque, but she appears to have had lower-middle-class origins at best.[42] Robert, George and Alexander Barry alone of Minto's bastards survived to adulthood, and only Alexander outlived their father. The boys were educated above their mother's station, but below that of the Earl's legitimate sons. In 1792,

---

[40] Morris, *Men, Women and Property in England*, p. 100 highlights the use of language in wills to enclose the family. For Minto's will, see Oriental and India Office Collections, L/AG/34/27/13–20, British Library.

[41] Copy of Colonel John Drinkwater to William Elliot, 14 September 1814, NLS, Minto Papers, MS 11135, fol. 29 verso.

[42] The single letter written by Mrs Barry that remains in the Minto correspondence attests to her literacy, but she was clearly perplexed by the niceties of grammar, spelling and punctuation. Mrs Barry to Sylvester Douglas, August 1792, NLS, Minto Papers, MS 11196, fols. 59–59 verso.

George and Alexander Barry were learning Latin, Greek and French under the tutelage of a Church of Scotland minister; Minto's legitimate sons Gilbert, George and John Elliot were educated at Eton. In their teens, the Barry boys joined the rapidly expanding naval and military forces that enabled Britain's governing elite to exert a newly global dominion in these years. Like Minto's legitimate son George Elliot before him, George Barry was put to sea under the care of Captain Thomas Foley.[43] For Alexander and Robert Barry, Minto purchased military appointments. Rendered marginal to the Elliot lineage by their illegitimacy, both Alexander and Robert looked to the penumbra of the British empire for their professional advancement. Robert embarked for Ceylon in 1798 as an ensign in a regiment of Malay troops.[44] His brother Alexander, anxious to secure rapid advancement, recognised that his promotion would also be eased by a willingness to forgo a commission in 'an old established' corps. 'With regard to promotion I shall only repeat my request that a Company in a black Corps may be purchased for me, should a more desirable advancement prove impracticable', he wrote to Minto in 1800.[45]

Minto's affection for the boys is evident from his correspondence, but so too is his desire that knowledge of their paternity should be restricted to a select circle of intimates. He conducted financial transactions with the brothers, their mother and their maternal aunts only indirectly, through trusted intermediaries. In early youth, the boys themselves were unaware that Minto was more to them than a generous male patron, as an especially poignant letter from Robert to Alexander Barry in 1802 attests. 'I beg you will do me the favour if you well can, to write me who my father was and what employ he had, for every thing was kept so extremely secret, that to this day I don't know whose son I am', Robert wrote from Colombo. 'You will by giving me the history of our family oblige me very much.'[46]

Knowledge of the Barrys within Minto's legitimate family circle was fragmented and strictly controlled. His wife was fully aware of the boys' existence. During Minto's prolonged absences from Britain, she assisted with the oversight of their upbringing, writing to Minto in 1800 that Captain Foley spoke well of their son George Elliot and of George Barry: 'the only fault *I* have to find with him [Barry] is being much more expensive than George, which should not be the case, & I think you should write to him & confine him within certain limits', she

[43] Captain Thomas Foley to Minto, 30 December 1797, NLS, Minto Papers, MS 11136, fols. 1–2 verso.
[44] NLS, Minto Papers, MS 11136, fols. 5–5 verso, fols. 13–13 verso.
[45] Alexander Barry to Minto, 18 November 1800, NLS, Minto Papers, MS 11133, fol. 27.
[46] Robert Barry to Alexander Barry, 27 February 1802, NLS, Minto Papers, MS 11133, fol. 33 verso.

counselled.[47] Knowledge of the Barrys' identity increased sharply among Minto's younger legitimate sons from 1807, when the Earl established his residence at Government House. Minto seized this opportunity to attach Alexander to his Calcutta household, appointing this by now sole surviving natural son to his personal staff. Both George and John Elliot learned of Barry's intimate tie to them in consequence, as too (upon marriage) did their wives. The subject of bastardy – long a leitmotif in Minto's correspondence with his wife – now emerged as a topic of open ribaldry in the Governor General's household. The household jokes on this topic suggest the ease with which the class-based alterity inherent in white illegitimacy could shade into racial thinking. John Elliot played practical jokes on his new Indian sisters-in-law in which he and his brother George Elliot figured as their father's sons by supposedly having sired spurious sons of their own. In one such incident, John convinced George's wife Eliza that both brothers had fathered bastards in Scotland – white lads destined to be trained up as shoemakers. In another variation on this theme, John and Amelia conspired to prove to Amelia's sister Elizabeth that John was the father of a black Indian infant, a claim that they sought to substantiate by producing a local toddler for her inspection.[48]

Alexander Barry was as acutely conscious as his legitimate half-brothers of the ways in which bastardy compromised personal identity. In both his public military career and his private life, Barry was far more deeply immersed in the creole, *métis* and indigenous sectors of colonial society and culture than were his legitimate Elliot siblings. His problematic paternity ensured that Barry, white and British by birth, was a hybrid European by professional and personal association. His military and marital opportunities thus lay at the margins of the South Asian empire rather than at its nodal points in London and Calcutta. Seconded from his Malay company in 1807 to join Minto's family circle at Government House, Barry by 1810 had turned his attention towards new territories outside Bengal. Outposts such as Batavia and Bourbon, wrested from the French and Dutch as the Napoleonic Wars were played out in Asian military theatres, opened new professional vistas for officers such as Barry whose ambitions outweighed their family status. Minto had sought unsuccessfully since 1807 to purchase Barry a Majority;

[47] Countess to Minto, 22 January 1800, NLS, Minto Papers, MS 11074, fol. 177.
[48] Amelia Elliot to Minto, 18 August 1811, NLS, Minto Papers, MS 11095, fols. 127–127 verso; John Elliot to Minto, 3 April 1810, MS 11094, fols. 228–229. For the role of jokes in domestic relations at this time, see Carolyn Steedman, 'Servants and their relationship to the subconscious', *Journal of British Studies*, 42, (July, 2003), pp. 316–350, esp. pp. 330–333, 348–350.

thwarted in this fond hope, in 1810 he instead appointed his illegitimate son secretary to the new British government at Bourbon.[49]

Once safely ensconced in his government office, Barry followed the example set by his half-brothers in Bengal and plunged, without paternal approval, into an impolitic love match with a girl of problematic creole ancestry. Leonore Auclair was the daughter of a French officer who had served for years in the East Indies, and was now rumoured to be a colonel of cavalry at Corfu. Her mother (apparently also French) had died in Leonore's infancy; her father had abandoned his family of young daughters before Leonore had formed distinct memories of him. Like Barry himself, she thus possessed a compromised birthright, a characteristic that her future husband evidently found appealing. 'She is *almost an Orphan*, & I do not like her the less for that', he informed Minto in 1811.[50] In his letters to his father, Barry laboured to reveal his fiancée's preternatural fitness to become the wife of a social outrider such as himself while working to present Leonore to Minto in ways that rendered her a suitable spouse for an imperial Briton. Barry acknowledged that her nationality had initially given him pause. Although 'the girl's partiality for anything in the shape of an Englishman' had led her to welcome his attentions, she was neither truly British nor fully French. Indeed, as a creole, she was only imperfectly European. 'The *resemblance* ... (for they are not the same) which the Creole character here naturally bears to the French, and to which I am less a friend than ever, had hitherto in every instance held me back, & secured me against the influence of beauty, even strengthened by accomplishments, as long as these advantages were accompanied by a style of manners, *nearly* or completely *what the English* call *foreign*', Barry admitted to his father. He then proceeded to justify his identification of Leonore as an ideal proto-European by invoking Enlightenment conceptions of nature.[51] Barry elaborated an environmentalist model of identity formation, in which his fiancée would shed her French and creole character under his manly English tutelage. Commenting on Leonore's sickly pallor and extreme bashfulness when he first proposed to her, Barry noted that their engagement had 'materially raised her spirits & improved her looks'. 'She has

---

[49] For Minto's efforts to purchase Barry's Majority, see, for example, Minto to Colonel John Drinkwater, 6 November 1807, NLS, Minto Papers, MS 11133, fol. 144–144 verso.

[50] Alexander Barry to Minto, 14 May 1811, NLS, Minto Papers, MS 11134, fols. 39–50 verso, citation fols. 41.

[51] See, for example, a letter of 30 July 1811: 'In short when I married her she was a child of nature & I hope she will long continue so, at the same time you will understand by this expression, that I mean to describe her rather as a colonial *Virginie* than as an English *Dairy-maid*.' NLS, Minto Papers, MS 11134, fol. 80.

now a beautiful European complexion, & a glow [of] health on her cheeks, that would do credit to any County in England', he opined. The departure of her two sisters to join their father after the marriage, Barry concluded (in tones that recall Lady Minto's determination to segregate Eliza Ness from her Irish maternal kin), would leave Leonore 'unencumbered by relatives of any description, or at least [none] sufficiently proximate to lay claim to the right to embarrass me. And as *French folks*, I am not sorry for this.'[52] Of necessity a canny strategist of family relations, Barry clearly recognised that his wife – unlike Amelia Casamaijor and Eliza Ness – was not destined to enjoy full integration into the Elliot kin network in India, much less at home in Britain. When he proposed a visit to Calcutta to introduce Leonore to the Earl in 1812, he underlined that the couple would not expect to lodge at Government House. 'You must not . . . think, that I shall bring a little French wife, and perhaps a *squalling* brat within the precincts of the great *House* at Calcutta, if I do undertake the excursion', he assured Minto.[53]

III

The marital histories of Minto's legitimate and illegitimate sons are illuminating precisely because they help to situate the tensions of empire that derived from race within a broader context, one that recognises the inherent frictions that marked family relations (irrespective of empire) in the British metropole. As Leonore Davidoff has argued, the complex combination of social, sexual, financial and psychological functions performed by propertied families in nineteenth-century Europe and the co-existence in many families of age cohorts that included a bewildering mix of full- and half-brothers and sisters, uncles, aunts, cousins, in-laws and step-parents generated ideal conditions for intense familial conflict, even as they underpinned capitalist development in the West.[54] These tensions could be (and often were) exacerbated by perceptions of racial alterity, as the Elliot family history in India amply attests. But this imperial family story also demonstrates that the perception of racial difference was no more a required ingredient for sibling rivalry and sexual conflict among relations than an inevitable barrier to the resolution of these tensions when it reared its ugly head above the domestic parapets. For Alexander Barry's alterity derived not from his racial difference – he was as fully

[52] Alexander Barry to Minto, NLS, Minto Papers, MS 11134, fols. 44, 44 verso–45, 48 verso.
[53] Alexander Barry to Minto, 28 October 1812, MS 11133, fols. 192 verso–193.
[54] Leonore Davidoff, 'The legacy of the nineteenth-century bourgeois family and the wool merchant's son', *Transactions of the Royal Historical Society*, 6th ser., XIV, (2004), pp. 25–46.

white and British as his half-brothers – but rather from his illegitimacy, and from his reluctance to inhabit that subordinate identity only on the edges of the Indian empire. Nor did the perceived ethnic difference of Amelia Casamaijor and Eliza Ness preclude their full incorporation – as daughters-in-law, mothers, sisters and wives – into the Elliot family bloodline. Like Alexander Barry when contemplating his French creole wife, Minto and later his family in Scotland proved capable of re-imagining these 'Indian ladies' as fully British kin.

The fluid patterns of exclusion and inclusion to which the Elliots subjected Minto's illegitimate sons and his creole and colonial daughters-in-law provide a revealing counterpoint to the experiences of the mixed-race progeny of British officers and their indigenous concubines, for they remind us that whiteness and legitimacy, like blackness and bastardy, were unstable, fractured and manufactured categories of belonging. More than this, the Elliots' colonial engagement with the family politics of empire offers a salutary reminder that the construction of ideologies of inclusion and exclusion was at once a social and a textual process. Kin relations were integral to the development of racial consciousness, for the family (as contemporaries fully recognised) lay at the heart of imperial politics. Until the early twentieth century, English dictionaries consistently defined 'race' in terms of family lines, rather than ethnographic groups: to Samuel Johnson, race was thus defined as 'A family ascendancy', 'A family descendancy', 'A generation; a collective family'.[55] Race and family were likewise inextricably bound in the private correspondence of the first Earl Minto, for letter-writing played a central role in mediating the marital relations through which the family's households at home and abroad experienced *métissage* within and across racial boundaries. Epistolary expression was the key mechanism by which knowledge of alterity – whether based on colour, class or culture – was transmitted to (or withheld from) the Elliot family at Minto by their menfolk on the subcontinent. In this, the Elliot family story reflects not only the normative behaviours of the Company elite but also wider communicative practices that allowed eighteenth- and nineteenth-century Britons to flourish economically, socially and politically in global arenas that stretched from the Atlantic to the Indian Ocean worlds.[56]

As in contemporary printed literature, concepts of natural difference and scientific metaphors were vital to the construction of white,

---

[55] Nicholas Hudson, 'From "nation" to "race": the origin of racial classification in eighteenth-century thought', *Eighteenth-Century Studies*, 29, (Spring, 1996), pp. 247–264.

[56] See esp. Sarah M. S. Pearsall, *Atlantic Families: Lives and Letters in the Later Eighteenth Century* (Oxford, 2008).

black and creole identities in the Elliot family correspondence. Amelia Casamaijor's mother was 'a good specimen of an English gentlewoman', Amelia's letters to her in-laws exemplified her 'good sterling happy nature', Eliza Ness's freedom from vulgarity derived 'from nature, not Education or Example', and the Barry brothers, as illegitimate offspring, were of course Minto's 'natural' sons.[57] This natural imagery could erect barriers between whites and blacks, but it also divided whites from whites and provided grounds for the inclusion within the Elliot family of individuals marked as other by their birth status, their supposed bloodlines or their putative nation of origin. Family letters thus reflected the complexity of race, class, ethnicity and legitimacy as boundaries of difference, but more fundamentally the epistolary process enabled and elaborated the family's negotiation of these human frontiers. Less rigid and determinist than the historical, anthropological and scientific treatises that were later to foment Victorian racial stereotypes, the personal correspondence of governing-class families had provided a key testing ground on which the antinomies of British identity were first explored, policed and refashioned in the empire's global marriage market.

[57] Colonel Drinkwater, writing to Gilbert Elliot on 14 August 1813, described Leonore Barry as 'the most natural & unsophisticated piece of animal life I ever saw'. NLS, MS 11803, fol. 25 verso. Gilbert Elliot to John Elliot, 16 July 1810, NLS, Minto Papers, MS 11752, fol. 91 verso; Countess to Minto, 23 September 1810, NLS, Minto Papers, MS 11081, fols. 196–196 verso.

5   The commons, enclosure and radical histories

Alun Howkins

Few events in recent English social history have had such a central, and controversial, place as the enclosure of the common lands. Accounts of what E. P. Thompson once described as 'a plain enough case of class robbery',[1] have divided historians in a way few other recent historical arguments have. This is not the place to go into these arguments in detail but we can separate two different elements. The first 'strand' is the idea that enclosure, by ending the open field system of agriculture, destroyed a peasant or yeoman class. This argument, it seems to me, is concerned mainly with the open fields. The second strand is that the common land or 'waste', which was part of the open field system of agriculture, was used by a much larger group than the 'yeomen' or peasant class, and this gave them a degree of economic independence. Enclosure, by removing the commons, economically damaged this group, reducing them to wage labour. In this chapter I am concerned only with the enclosure of the common or waste and its effect on the 'labouring poor'.

As with the arguments about the end of a peasantry, most of this debate has centred on the period c. 1700–1850, and concentrated on the English Midlands. Looking at these areas and this period the argument has divided between those who saw the commons, and especially the common waste, as a resource for all the community, and those who focus on the so-called 'commoners'. The former were simply residents of the manor with no land holdings at all. The latter were property holders in the manor where the enclosure was taking place who had common right by virtue of those holdings. By definition these could, and did, range from the lord of the manor, who could hold or own thousands of acres, to tiny freeholders and even copyholders who held only a few acres.

At one level the argument is simply resolved. Legally the only people who had common rights, unless there were specific provisions to the

[1] E. P. Thompson, *The Making of the English Working Class* (Harmondsworth, 1968), p. 237.

118

contrary in the manorial courts or in leases, were those who held property. However, the Hammonds argued in their classic account of enclosure published in 1911:

Were there any day labourers without either land or common rights in the old village? It is difficult to suppose that there were many ... rights that were enjoyed by the occupiers of small holdings or of cottages by long prescription, or by encroachments tacitly sanctioned, must have been very widely scattered.[2]

This view was the one broadly held by representatives of the 'new' social history in the 1970s and 1980s. For example, E. P. Thompson, in a passage from the *Making of the English Working Class* writes: 'in village after village, enclosure destroyed the scratch-as-scratch-can subsistence economy of the poor'.[3] This view, in a much more complex form, was argued at greater length in Chapter 3 of his *Customs in Common*.[4]

Against this there is a quite different set of arguments, which probably now hold sway within academic circles. Many contemporaries argued that enclosure, particularly of the commons, was desirable, and from at least the 1880s many historians have taken the same line.[5] Indeed, the founding texts of English economic history, most notably Sir John Clapham's *An Economic History of Modern Britain* of 1926, argued for this view. However, it was work by David Chambers and Gordon Mingay, published between the 1940s and the late 1960s, which created the twin orthodoxies that eighteenth-century enclosure did not destroy an English peasantry, it had already vanished, and that the commons and wastes were little used by the 'poor' in the pre-enclosure period.[6] This view continues to hold sway in most standard accounts.[7] Nevertheless, there continued to be important challenges to the orthodoxy, most notably from the work of Jeanette Neeson. Neeson's *Commoners* of 1993,[8] based on detailed studies of the South Midlands, argues that

---

[2] J. L. and Barbara Hammond, *The Village Labourer* (1911, pbk edition, London, 1966), p. 25.

[3] Thompson, *The Making*, p. 237.

[4] E. P. Thompson, *Customs in Common*, (London, 1991), pp. 97–185.

[5] Most famously, see Arnold Toynbee, *Lectures on the Industrial Revolution in England* (London, 1884).

[6] See J. D. Chambers and G. E. Mingay, *The Agricultural Revolution 1750–1880* (London, 1966), ch. 4, for the fullest account of their work.

[7] For example, Mark Overton, *Agricultural Revolution in England. The Transformation of the Rural Economy 1500–1850* (Cambridge, 1996), pp. 147–167. For a different account, but one which does not directly affect this chapter, see Robert C. Allen, *Enclosure and the Yeoman. The Agricultural Development of the South Midlands 1450–1850*, (Oxford, 1992).

[8] J. M. Neeson, *Commoners: Common Right, Enclosure and Social Change in England 1700–1820* (Cambridge, 1993).

common rights, and especially common rights on the waste, were a central part of the political economy of the rural poor for as long as the lands lay unenclosed. Although Neeson does not argue for a pre-enclosure peasantry, she does make a strong case for a sub-class of workers who got a living only partly by wage labour, a view held also by Alan Everitt for a much later period.[9] In turn, Neeson's work has been challenged by Leigh Shaw-Taylor's refinement of the orthodox view. In two important articles Shaw-Taylor argues that the poor, and particularly non-commoners, had no rights on the waste and made very little use of them. Long before the beginning of the nineteenth century, the rural poor were simply wage labourers with no stake in the land in any way.[10]

However, despite the conclusions of much academic work, at the popular level the moral power of the old radical view of enclosure remains undiminished. The image of the dispossessed yeoman driven from the land was a central part of English radical and later socialist politics from the 1840s until at least the mid-twentieth century. Given extra power by the Irish Famine, the Highland Clearances, the rediscovery of John Clare's poetry and later still by a Green movement which sought historical examples, the idea that the English poor were robbed of the land which was their birthright simply would not go away.

A great deal of this myth (if such it is) was shaped in the second half of the nineteenth century during the 'last' phase of enclosure, and it is to this period that we will now turn. Those who were involved in this phase brought to it a sense, not only of an old political economy, but of history and politics. They also brought new concerns which had little to do with the arguments and ideas of the period before the 1840s.

I

Most of the work discussed above refers to the period before the 1840s. The reasons for this are to an extent obvious. As Turner and Wordie have shown, the vast majority of land enclosed in the modern period was enclosed between c1720 and 1830 – the period of 'Parliamentary

[9] See Alan Everitt, 'Common land' in Joan Thirsk (ed), *The English Rural Landscape* (Oxford, 2000).
[10] Leigh Shaw-Taylor, 'Labourers, cows, common rights and parliamentary enclosure; the evidence of contemporary comment c. 1760–1810', *Past & Present*, 171, (May, 2001), pp. 94–126; 'Parliamentary enclosure and the emergence of an English agricultural proletariat', *Journal of Economic History*, 61(3), (September, 2001), pp. 640–662.

Enclosure by Private Bill'.[11] During this period 18 per cent of the land area of England was enclosed, most of it between 1790 and 1819.[12]

The nature of this process meant it frequently took many years, was expensive and its outcomes were far from certain. In order to address these problems attempts were made from 1801 onwards to pass general legislation. These efforts culminated in the General Enclosure Act of 1845, which created a permanent 'Inclosure Commission' with 'power to frame Provisional Orders for inclosure [sic], thus obviating the need for a special Act in each case'.[13] The provisional orders were put before Parliament in the form of an annual bill containing all approved enclosures. In practice, before the late 1860s, these bills were simply passed without discussion.[14]

The amount of common land left in England in 1845 was a matter of dispute. In 1843 a survey estimated that there were 1,860,234 acres of common waste or common field in England and Wales. Thirty years later, despite continuing enclosure, the figure was estimated at 2,368,045 acres and by 1913 at approximately 2 million.[15] Against this, the extent and effect of the 1845 General Act is clear. Basing my calculation on Tate and Turner's definitive list of enclosure awards there were, between 1845 and 1914, 883 Acts passed under the 1845 legislation enclosing just under 570,000 acres in England, plus 48,000 acres which were regulated under the Act.[16]

Compared with earlier periods, enclosure on this scale was relatively unimportant. Nevertheless, particularly in the first five years of the Act's operation, there was a flurry of bills aimed at agricultural improvement – the traditional aim of enclosure.[17] Equally the 1845 Act, and the subsequent legislation which allowed for the regulation of common or waste,

---

[11] Michael Turner, *Enclosures in Britain 1750–1830,* (London, 1984) tables p. 21; J. R. Wordie, 'The chronology of English enclosure, 1500–1914', *Economic History Review,* 36(4), (November, 1983), pp. 483–505.

[12] Michael Turner, *Enclosures,* tables p. 21.

[13] *British Parliamentary Papers,* (hereafter *BPP*) *1913 (85),* Report from the Select Committee on Commons (Inclosure and Regulation), p. 1.

[14] For a more detailed discussion of the nature and extent of enclosure after 1845, see Alun Howkins, 'Enclosure after enclosure: the use and abuse of common land 1845–1914' (forthcoming).

[15] *BPP 1913 (85),* Report from the Select Committee on Commons (Inclosure and Regulation) pp. iii–iv.

[16] W. E. Tate and M. E. Turner, *A Domesday of English Enclosure Acts and Awards* (Reading, 1978). Wales is left out as it has its own history. Scotland and Ireland were covered by different legislation. In addition, some 48,200 acres were 'regulated', including, between 1866 and 1898, some 4,100 acres in the London area under the Metropolitan Commons, *BPP 1913 (85),* Report from the Select Committee on Commons, pp. 135–149.

[17] See Alun Howkins, 'Enclosure after enclosure', for the chronology of enclosure after 1845.

had considerable local impact, especially in upland areas, mainly in the north and west of England.[18] Perhaps more importantly, the whole process of enclosure became a national, and above all an urban, political issue after 1845 in a way it had not been since the early modern period.[19] Although some continued to argue about the destruction of 'a noble peasantry', even this was seen increasingly in an urban context. Urban priorities were also central to those who saw the commons (as opposed to open fields) as a national legacy to be protected, particularly against building and urban/industrial development. Together, these debates permanently changed the ways in which enclosure, or at least the enclosure of commons or waste, was discussed. In this new political discourse the 'commoners' were increasingly marginalised and isolated. If commons were a national legacy of open space and beauty, a site of recreation, or the lungs of the cities, there was often little space or sympathy for their traditional users: the coster's donkey, the small trader's pony or the country woman's gathering of furze or firewood.

These changes meant, in turn, that the nature of opposition to enclosure, particularly the enclosure of commons or waste, changed significantly. Most importantly those involved, at all levels, became more sophisticated in their methods of opposition to enclosure. This was done mainly through the use, or attempted use, of the gradually emerging institutions of a democratic society after 1832. However, behind these there remained, until the beginning of the twentieth century, a rougher and older tradition based on folk memory and common usage.

II

Probably the most significant shift was from seeing the commons as a productive resource, to seeing them primarily as a public amenity.[20]

---

[18] See Eleanor Anne Straughton, 'Common grazing in the northern uplands; land, society, governance since *circa* 1800', unpublished DPhil thesis, University of Lancaster (2004). This is now published as *Common Grazing in the Northern English Uplands 1800–1865* (Lampeter, 2008); Brian Short, *The Ashdown Forest Dispute, 1876–1882* (Lewes, 1997); Lara Phelan, 'Economy to amenity: the commons of the New Forest and Ashdown Forest, 1851–1939', unpublished DPhil thesis, University of Sussex (2002).

[19] For the general arguments in the earlier period, see Richard Hoyle, 'Enclosure in England 1500–1750: agricultural change with and without the state', unpublished paper presented at the Anglo–French Colloquium on Agrarian History, 2008.

[20] This change has been looked at at a local level by a number of important surveys. The most interesting is unfortunately unpublished. This is Phelan, 'Economy to amenity'. Also of real importance is Neil MacMaster, 'The battle for Mousehold Heath 1857–1884: "popular politics" and the Victorian public park', *Past & Present*, 127, (1990), pp. 117–154. The subject is also touched on in Short, *Ashdown Forest Dispute*, and Straughton, 'Common grazing'.

The idea of the commons as open places where the freedom to roam was uncontrolled was not new. It was an idea which moved John Clare, even if it had no legal basis in law, and one which enclosure removed:[21]

> These paths are stopt – the rude philistines thrall
> Is laid upon them and destroyed them all
> Each little tyrant with his little sign
> Shows where man claims earth grows no more divine
> But paths to freedom and to childhood dear
> A board sticks up to notice 'no road here'

But it was not a rural impulse which picked up on these ideas, but an urban one. In 1833 a Select Committee of the House of Commons was created to consider 'the best Means of securing Open Spaces in the Vicinity of populous Towns, as Public walks and Places of Exercise calculated to promote the health and comfort of the inhabitants'.[22] Industrialisation and urbanisation, it was argued, had proceeded in a 'most surprising and rapid manner' with 'no adequate provision ... for Public Walks, or any reservations of Open Spaces, giving faculties to future improvement'.[23] The Committee urged that measures be taken to provide such provision.

Although there was little stomach for the wholesale conversion of common lands to public parks, the suggestion was put forward that in a number of areas common or waste was the possible site for 'public walks'.[24] Most obviously, two London commons, Kennington Common and Hackney Downs, were discussed.[25] However, in terms of government intervention virtually nothing was done to support public walks as a direct result of the 1833 Committee. Calls for the provisions of the 1833 Select Committee to be adopted in relation to Primrose Hill and Regents Park were ignored.[26] More substantially the radical philanthropist Joseph Brotheton, Salford's first MP, and 'Radical Dick' Potter, MP for Wigan after 1832, introduced a number of bills between 1833 and 1837 to bring the findings of the 1833 Committee into law, but they too found no favour in Russell's reforming ministry.[27]

However, the whole notion of open space and public walks re-emerged as a part of the discussion of enclosure in the mid-1840s. There was a flurry of interest in land tenure and land holding, including

---

[21] John Clare, 'The mores' in Eric Robinson and Geoffrey Summerfield (eds), *Selected Poems and Prose of John Clare* (Oxford, 1967) p. 170.
[22] *BPP 1833 (448)*, Select Committee on Public Walks, p. 2.
[23] Ibid., p. 4.   [24] Ibid., p. 7.   [25] Ibid., pp. 16, 23.
[26] *The Journals of the House of Commons*, 28 August 1833, p. 732.
[27] See, for example, *BPP 1836 (64)*, A Bill to Facilitate the Formation and Establishment of Public Walks.

copyhold and other 'antique' tenures, and in the lands of the Church, as well as ongoing debates about the tithe and its administration. It is against this background that in 1843 Peel's ministry appointed a Select Committee to enquire into Common Lands, which reported in 1844. The overwhelming reasons for enclosure, according to the Committee, were agricultural, rural and profoundly traditional:

it appears, by the evidence of competent and experienced Witnesses, that a large portion of the Waste Land of the Kingdom is capable of profitable cultivation, or other improvement.[28]

The absence in the final report of any mention of the common waste as a site of recreation was almost certainly because a private general enclosure bill was already before Parliament. This included some measures to protect the commons as a site of recreation.[29] This bill was taken up by the government and passed into law in the summer of 1845.

The 1845 legislation was seen by its proponents as an essentially enabling measure which made existing procedures simpler. However, this view was not shared by a minority within the House of Commons, nor by a substantial body of opinion outside the House. For example, radical MP Joseph Hume objected that, 'it would take away from poor men – from those who constituted the great mass of the community – the advantages which they now possessed in the enjoyment of air and exercise on these commons'.[30]

This feeling seems to have been widespread in the opposition to the bill which developed outside Parliament. For the *Bristol Mercury*, along with many other provincial papers, this was 'the landowners again legislating' in 'their public capacity for their private advantage'. The bill was 'a scheme of NATIONAL SPOILATION'. Like many other papers, including *The Times*, the *Mercury* also deplored the timing of the debate, writing that, '(t)he common lands once enclosed will be lost to the public *for ever;* and the bill which is to effect this vast and important change is being hurried through Parliament'.[31]

However, it was not only a sense of moral outrage, or even a commitment to the moral reformation of the poor through public walks, which guided the *Mercury*. The *Mercury's* position on enclosure was based on its opposition to the Corn Laws. According to the *Mercury:*[32]

One of the main pretexts for the maintenance of the present cruel and unjust corn-law is, that its repeal would throw 'the inferior soils' out of cultivation.

[28] *BPP 1844 (583)*, Select Committee on Commons Inclosure, p. iii.
[29] See *HC Debs 5 June 1844* Vol. 75 cc. 296–312.
[30] *HC Debs 4 July 1845* Vol. 82 c. 23.
[31] *The Bristol Mercury* (hereafter *BM*), 12 July 1845.   [32] Ibid.

If this be so, what then must be the inevitable result of bringing still poorer soils into cultivation? ... a tax in the shape of a bread tax – will be levied upon every man, woman and child in the United Kingdom, in order to pay the landlords for cultivating the heaths and barren moors from which they will have succeeded in excluding the people. The public will not only be deprived of breathing fresh air on many a healthy spot ... but they will actually have to pay – in the shape of a bread tax – for the raising of scanty crops of inferior corn on land which nature never intended for any such purpose.

Thus the ideas of the Anti-Corn Law League were linked to the urban ideas of the commons not as an economic resource, but as a site of leisure and, by implication, moral improvement for the urban poor. It is interesting that those who defended the bill in the Commons represented largely rural constituencies and were clearly thinking in terms of agricultural improvement. Those who opposed it were largely urban and saw the issue in terms of amenity. This shift in opposition to enclosure was a major change reflecting the moral economy of the urban middle class. In future these arguments would come to dominate discussion about enclosure.

However, in the shorter term, there were many who were prepared to weigh in with older arguments. In the House of Commons, William Sharman Crawford, MP for Rochdale, spoke at length against the bill saying that:

the interests of the poor were not provided for by the Bill before the House. If the pasturage of cows on commons was subject to proper regulations, it would be of great benefit to the poor man. The experience of past Enclosure Bills proved to him that the interests of the poor were not cared for.[33]

He argued, 'that the Bill was a landlords' Act', and 'whatever land was not now directly given up by this measure to the lords of the manor would ultimately come into their possession, because the small holders would be bought up by them, and all would thus become theirs'.[34]

Sharman Crawford, who was a Chartist and Irish nationalist, provides a link to the continuation of an older radical tradition of opposition to enclosure which still existed outside the House. He gave voice to this clearly in 1844:

In former times the rich paid the taxes; now they were paid by the poor. The Corn Laws had been maintained and the price of food kept up; and then they said to the poor man, 'Why are you in distress? Why don't you take care of yourself?' while all the while the price of provisions was kept up. By enclosure Bills the common lands had been taken away from the poor man, and continually he was driven off from spots where he had rights and immunities.[35]

---

[33] *HC Debs 4 July 1845* Vol. 82 c. 15.   [34] *HC Debs 4 July 1845* Vol. 82 c. 17.
[35] *HC Debs 4 July 1844* Vol. 76 c. 368.

This language of 'lost rights' played a central part in both popular and radical thinking. It permeates popular ballads as well as the rhetoric of Chartism.[36] For example, in May 1845, as the proposed General Act was moving slowly through the Commons a 'Meeting of the Inhabitants of Lambeth' held at the South London Chartist Hall adopted a new petition to Parliament which included the 'prayer' that the 'ten million acres' which had been 'seized by the aristocracy under the guise of law' be returned to 'the people'. To this end they prayed that 'your honourable House do repeal all Acts for the enclosure of common land, and restore them to the people, their legitimate owners'. In support of the petition, which was carried unanimously by acclamation, a Mr M'Grath drew attention to the General Act then under discussion. After repeating the peoples 'claim' to the commons he pointed out that:

one of our precious legislators appears anxious to deprive them of the remainder by enclosing the common and waste lands. (Hear, hear) It was their duty to let the house know that they were acquainted with this, and that they were resolved to resist the fell destroyer to the utmost.[37]

The commons also had their place in the concept of the 'Norman Yoke' which, according to a recent article by Malcolm Chase, lay at the heart of 'most if not all Chartist ideas about landed property'.[38] An 1844 petition against an early version of the 1845 General Act says:

That ten million acres of land were appropriated to the use of the people by England's wisest Monarch, the immortal Alfred, under the designation of the Common Lands; that these lands were preserved inviolate through the vicissitudes of the ages by the laws of the realm; and that many blessings and benefits accrued to the people from their possession.[39]

It was unclear, however, quite what 'the people' were going to do with their ten million acres. As Chase points out, apart from a shared dislike of large estates and a distrust of the state, the Chartists held different and sometimes contradictory views about landed property.[40] The position of the Chartists in relation to 'common land' was similarly confused, like that of many mid-century (and later) radicals. For instance, the

---

[36] On ballads, see Alun Howkins and Ian C. Dyck, '"The time's alteration". Popular ballads, rural radicalism and William Cobbett', *History Workshop Journal*, 23, (Spring, 1987), pp. 20–39.

[37] *The Northern Star* (hereafter *NS*), 10 May 1845.

[38] Malcolm Chase, 'Chartism and the land: "the mighty peoples question"' in Matthew Cragoe and Paul A. Readman (eds), *The Land Question in Britain, 1750–1950* (Houndmills, 2010).

[39] *NS*, 27 April 1844.   [40] Malcolm Chase, 'Chartism and the land'.

frequently quoted figure of six million acres enclosed since the reign of George II was derived from parliamentary figures for all land enclosed by private Act. This included both open fields and waste and therefore presented a problem, as no 'friend of the poor' could oppose an increase in home-produced food. As 'Bill Blades' wrote in *Reynolds Newspaper*, 'we (don't) object to commons being cultivated. A sack of good wheat is worth all the gorse bushes in creation.'[41] Apart from a strong objection, at least after the mid-1840s, to large farms, the Chartist arguments on common land seem to have simply ignored, unlike Marx, the notion of agrarian capitalism as an exploitative mode of production. Enclosure was a moral issue – it represented the conspicuous consumption of land stolen from the people by a useless aristocracy. In 1842, the *Northern Star* carried an article about northern 'proprietors' prosecuting men, women and children for gathering wimberries on recently enclosed Yorkshire moorland. The land, according to the report, had been enclosed for shooting. Here was a perfect case where a useless aristocracy was depriving the poor not only of the land but of food 'perhaps to maintain a starving perishing family'.[42]

This identification of the encloser as an idle aristocrat in fact bore little relation to most promoters of enclosure, who tended to be the most advanced, hard-headed and profit-conscious of agriculturalists. However, one area where the radical demon had more creditability was in the cities. Here, in the years after the mid-1860s, urban radical opposition to enclosure increasingly joined forces with middle-class philanthropists' concerns with the moral welfare of the poor.

III

The overwhelming concern of a small but important group in the House of Commons who opposed the General Act of 1845 was with public access to commons and waste as a site of recreation. Two major concessions, at least on paper, were made to that group. First, '(no) Land situate within Fifteen miles of the city of London ... shall be subject to be inclosed ... without the previous authority of Parliament in each particular case'. This provision was also extended on a sliding scale of distance to towns of between 20,000 and 100,000 inhabitants.[43] Second, where the land enclosed was common or waste, the Act gave the Inclosure Commissioners the right to set aside 'an appropriate

---

[41] *Reynolds Newspaper* (hereafter *RN*), 11 July 1880.   [42] *NS*, 16 July 1842.
[43] *BPP 1845 (491)*, Commons Inclosure Bill, clause 13 p. 6.

allotment for exercise and recreation for the inhabitants of the neighbourhood'. Again there was a sliding scale of the amount of land which could be allotted, based on the population of the parish.[44]

Although there was a good deal of local opposition to specific enclosure awards,[45] it was the early 1860s before a national, urban and essentially middle-class, campaign began to get under way. The focus of this campaign was, and remained for many years, London and the 'Home Counties'. It was here that the threat to open spaces was at its most palpable, and, more cynically, it was also here that the new middle-class villa-dweller could find his peace and tranquillity threatened by the enclosure of a picturesque common.

Although there is evidence, in two petitions to the House of Commons as early as 1848, of organised action in London on behalf of 'public walks' in Regents Park,[46] it was the threat to enclose Wimbledon Common in 1864, and above all, the ongoing 'fight' to preserve Hampstead Heath, which galvanised middle-class opinion. Growing out of these battles and closely linked to them was the Commons Preservation Society (CPS). The history of the CPS, although still lacking a full, published academic study, is generally well known, as are some of its early battles.[47] It was founded in July 1865 in part as a response to the attempted enclosure of Wimbledon Common, but more importantly as a result of the 1865 Parliamentary Select Committee on Open Spaces (Metropolis). The report of the Committee was clear on one thing: 'that no inclosure shall take place under the provisions of the Inclosure Act within the metropolitan area.' The committee also recognised that often ill-defined common rights were the best defence against enclosure and therefore urged that a system of regulation be introduced to protect the commons against both 'nuisance' and enclosure.[48]

---

[44] *BPP 1845 (491)*, Commons Inclosure Bill, clause 15 p. 15.

[45] See, for example, Okehampton, 1850, *Trewman's Exeter Flying Post* (hereafter *TEP*), 28 February 1850; Headington, 1850, *Jackson's Oxford Journal* (hereafter *JOJ*), 1850; Oxford, 1851, *JOJ*, 25 October 1851; Newmarket, 1851, *Ipswich Journal* (hereafter *IJ*), 8 March 1851; Hammersmith, 1855, *Morning Chronicle* (hereafter *MC*), 31 August 1855; Liversedge, 1859, *Leeds Mercury* (hereafter *LM*), 24 March 1859.

[46] *HC Debs 20 June 1848* Vol. 99 c. 879.

[47] The starting point is still G. Shaw Lefevre, *English Commons and Forests*, (London, 1894), essentially an 'official' history of the organisation up to that date. It was revised in 1910. Much more recent is Ben Cowell, 'The Commons Preservation Society and the campaign for Berkhampstead common, 1866–70', *Rural History*, 13(1), (October, 2002); David Killingray, 'Rights "riot" and ritual: the Knole Park access dispute, Sevenoaks, Kent, 1883–5', *Rural History*, 5(1), (April, 1994). There is also material on the CPS in Short, *Ashdown Forest Dispute*, and Phelan, 'Economy to amenity'.

[48] *BPP 1865 (390) (390–1)*, Select Committee on Open Spaces (Metropolis), Second report, p. vii.

In the thirty or so years after 1865, the CPS fought a number of cases in defence of commons within the metropolitan area. The most famous, and certainly the one which gained greatest popular support, was the defence of Epping Forest, which, with its humble commoners, noble, but bourgeois, defenders of the poor, and wicked aristocrats, had all the elements of a radical melodrama. However, despite using direct action such as destroying fences at Berkhampstead in 1866, the CPS normally kept well within the law. Indeed, destroying fences was legal if they were an encroachment upon common land. As G. Shaw Lefevre, one of the founders of the CPS, put it in relation to Berkhampstead, '(a)fter careful consultation . . . it was decided to resort to the old practice of abating the enclosure by the removal bodily of the fences in a manner which would be an assertion of right'. All this was done by a gang of hired navvies 'with as little damage as possible'.[49]

However, there was a different tradition. Anthony Taylor has pointed to the central importance of the commons to the London poor as places of meeting and recreation outside the control of the ruling elites, while Katrina Navickas has shown the same for areas of Lancashire and Yorkshire.[50] It was, after all, on Kennington Common that England's '1848' began and ended. To the London 'mob' and its successors, the commons were a site of recreation, but in a more active sense than that envisaged by the CPS and its supporters. To them the commons were the place for donkey racing, fairs, picnics, courting and politics. To take one example, Hampstead Heath had donkey racing and the great Easter Monday Fair as well as many less 'respectable' pastimes,[51] while Blackheath was used for the keeping of donkeys and ponies as well as a site of lewd recreations.[52] Probably less important to day-to-day life, but certainly more spectacular on occasions, the commons and wastes were also one of the decreasingly few areas in London where public politics and free speech could be practised without interference and control.

These elements came together in the 1870s as urban development began seriously to threaten a number of areas, bringing the curious and

---

[49] Ibid., pp. 64–65.

[50] Anthony Taylor, '"Commons-stealers", "land-grabbers" and "jerry builders"; space, popular radicalism and the politics of public access in London 1848–1880', *International Review of Social History,* 40, (1995), 383–408; Katrina Navickas, 'Moors, fields and popular protest in South Lancashire and the West Riding of Yorkshire, 1800–1848', *Northern History,* XLVI(1), (March, 2009), pp. 93–111.

[51] For example, see *BPP 1865 (390) (390–1),* Select Committee on Open Spaces, pp. 14, 24, 30.

[52] Ibid., p. 36.

heterodox world of London radicalism into the fight for the commons. The most striking figure here is John De Morgan, who flits through the radical world from an attempt to create a branch of the First International in Cork in 1872, through Irish and English republicanism on Teesside and in Leeds, and the campaign for the Tichbourne Claimant, to emerge in 1876 a 'leader' of the Commons Protection League (CPL) in attacks on enclosures on Plumstead Common.[53] It is not clear precisely what De Morgan or the CPL stood for. De Morgan had been involved with Charles Bradlaugh's short-lived National Republican League, which had as one of its aims a version of land nationalisation via a land tax.[54] However, despite the fact that De Morgan argued in 1877 that the commons were a productive resource capable of increasing the supply of food and reducing its costs,[55] the basic aims of the CPL seem to have been little different from those of the CPS. For instance, at a meeting in Hyde Park in 1877 it 'pledged itself to support the Commons Preservation Society to preserve the common parks and open spaces for the recreation of the people'.[56] Also, when in 1877 De Morgan formed a 'New Political Movement' called the 'People's Political Union', alongside what was basically a modified Chartist programme it included the demand for 'the preservation of all open spaces as recreation grounds'.[57] At Hackney Downs he went further still. Although he managed to attract a more plebeian crowd than the CPS normally did, and although fences were destroyed, he read a letter out from Henry Fawcett MP of the CPS, 'expressing his wish that the Society and the Commons Protection League should act in harmony'.[58] This convergence of Liberal radicalism and proto-socialist ideas was to become more pronounced in the period after the mid-1880s.

However, the CPL did differ in other ways from the CPS. As befitted De Morgan's background, its general political tone was much more militant. De Morgan himself was imprisoned at least twice as a result of his anti-enclosure activities in Plumstead and at Selson in Nottinghamshire.[59] The CPL also intervened outside the area of common

---

[53] On De Morgan, see F. D'Arcy, 'Charles Bradlaugh and the English republican movement', *Historical Journal*, XXV(2), (June, 1982), pp. 367–383; Robert Allen, 'The battle for the common: politics and populism in mid-Victorian Kentish London', *Social History*, 22(1), (January, 1977), pp. 61–77; Malcolm Chase, 'Republicanism; movement or moment?' in Malcolm Chase and Anthony Taylor (eds), *Republicanism in Victorian Society* (Stroud, 2000).

[54] *RN*, 18 May 1873.   [55] *Daily News* (hereafter *DN*), 31 March 1877.

[56] *Birmingham Daily Post* (hereafter *BDP*), 31 March 1877.

[57] *The Times*, 24 May 1877.   [58] *The Times*, 5 June 1877.

[59] See Allen, 'The battle for the common', pp. 66–67; also *DN*, 8 July 1876.

rights. In common with other radicals, for example Bradlaugh, and later Thorold Rogers and Joseph Chamberlain, De Morgan made a link between the unionisation of farm workers in the 1870s and enclosure. The CPL was involved in 1878 in defending labourers who were members of the Kent and Sussex Labourers Union who had been evicted from cottages in north Kent.[60] But perhaps the real difference was more complex and not always clear – the difference between 'defence' and 'protection' on the one hand and 'preservation' on the other. Defending or even protecting the commons has an aggressive sense in a way 'preserving' does not. Protection or defence imply an active 'enemy' who has to be resisted. Preserving is simply leaving well alone.

De Morgan seems not to have been alone. We know about him because he appears in several different places and formed an organisation which, even if short-lived, made a mark. We know less about others. John Field's study of the riots in Southsea in 1874 shows a tiny portion of common, largely used for recreation, defended by a local group of radicals, supported by a Portsmouth 'mob of roughs' and justifying their actions as defending a right that 'had existed from time immemorial'.[61] At the enclosure of Riccall in Yorkshire, a petition of fifty inhabitants of Maltby against enclosure was presented by William Askern.[62] Askern was a part-time public hangman according to his own description, but he was, according to the assistant commissioner, 'an educated man. He referred me to the works of Mr. Mill.'[63]

De Morgan, and those like him in other areas, were 'new' anti-enclosers born of the urban world of the mid and late nineteenth century. Their concerns were very different from those of earlier periods, and their methods, although still having some older elements, also took from a newer politics of proletarian democracy.[64] However, some did still oppose enclosure in the name of defending the commons and wastes as firmly economic resources.

---

[60] *The Times*, 21 December 1878.

[61] John Field, '"When the Riot Act was read"; a pub mural of the Battle of Southsea, 1874', *History Workshop Journal*, 10, (Autumn, 1980), pp. 152–163.

[62] Askern, in common with most hangmen, was a 'reformed criminal'. He was also a notorious bungler at his trade; see David Bentley, *Capital Punishment in Northern England 1750–1900* (Sheffield, 2008), p. 56. My thanks to John Chartres for this reference.

[63] Ibid., p. 68.

[64] For example, see Portsmouth in Field, 'When the Riot Act was read', and Ricall, Yorks, *BPP 1878–79 VII*, Select Committee on Provisional Orders for the Inclosure of Commons, Second Report, pp. 63–68.

IV

What little work that has been done on the defence of the commons after 1845 has a tendency to move to a new orthodoxy. This sees struggles over enclosure in the second half of the nineteenth century as entirely about preservation and access – as forerunners of the twentieth-century ecological movement.[65] But we need to remember that the vast majority of land enclosed between 1845 and 1914 was enclosed for agricultural purposes.[66] The assumption here was that the commons were not waste but simply badly farmed land. They were badly farmed because those who had rights misused them, or were incapable, because of antiquated regulations, from farming them properly. Most 'enclosers' had little interest in leisure or recreation.

The most important areas of common in 1845 were in the upland areas in the north and west of England. In addition there were some areas of waste, often associated with former forests, in southern England, for example the New Forest in Hampshire, Ashdown Forest in Sussex and the Forest of Dean. In these areas there were relatively small areas of open fields simply because the soil, herbage and terrain made arable farming either impossible or unprofitable, or most normally both.[67] Most enclosures in the north and west were to control unregulated grazing, or to stop those who had no rights grazing the commons. For example, in 1878 over 5,500 acres of Matterdale Common in Cumberland were part enclosed and part regulated under the 1876 Act. The purpose was clear. The lower parts of the moor would be enclosed, and higher parts regulated. The regulation of the higher parts would 'prevent quarrels from the hounding of sheep, and ascertain what the rights of the commoners are'. The lower-level lands, when enclosed and drained, would increase in value considerably, although they would remain as pasture.[68] The interesting point here is that the commoners,

---

[65] See Robert Hunter, 'The movements for the inclosure and preservation of open lands', *Journal of the Royal Statistical Society*, 60(2), (June, 1897), pp. 397–399; W. G. Hoskins and L. Dudley Stamp, *The Common Lands of England and Wales* (London, 1963), esp. chs 5–7; W. G. Hoskins, *The Making of the English Landscape* (Harmondsworth, 1987), ch. 6; Jan Marsh, *Back to the Land. The Pastoral Impulse in Victorian England from 1880 to 1914* (London, 1982); Peter Gould, *Early Green Politics: Back to Nature, Back to the land and Socialism in Britain 1880–1900* (Brighton, 1988); David Evans, *A History of Nature Conservation in Britain* (London, 1992).

[66] *BPP 1877 XXVI*, Inclosure Commissioner, Thirty-second Report, *passim*.

[67] See Ian Whyte, '"Wild Barren and Frightful": Parliamentary enclosure in an upland county, Westmorland, 1767–1890', *Rural History*, 14(1), (April, 2003), pp. 21–38.

[68] *BPP 1878–79 (173)*, Second report from the Select Committee on Commons, pp. 101–102.

who supported enclosure, did not want the whole area regulated despite pressure from the Parliamentary Committee. 'The enclosed part would become worth very much more, from 2s. 6d. to 20s. and therefore they naturally want that part inclosed. I do not think they would care to have a regulation of the whole.'[69]

There does not seem to have been any substantial opposition to the enclosure of most northern and western commons, although there are hints that it was not always simple. In Tavistock in 1897 there was a court case involving disputed rights of pasture over Petertavy Common on Dartmoor.[70] Similarly, regulation was little opposed, except by those who preferred the more profitable course of enclosure. However, even the light touch of regulation, increasingly the chosen route by government and the CPS, was far from unproblematic. After regulation in the New Forest, the Court of Verderers, and in Ashdown a Board of Conservators, became responsible for the day-to-day administration of the commons. The first members of these 'boards' were often those who had not only fought for commoners' rights in the past, but who had also 'previously attempted to regulate the commons without statutory powers'.[71] Phelan argues that once unity around the defence of rights passed, the commoners and their representatives began to part company. The new administrators had clear views about the 'worthy commoner', who was very different from the squatter or the semi-independent labourer, let alone the gypsy. 'They were of the opinion that they knew what was best for the commoners and . . . they could now enforce their vision of the commons' usage.'[72]

In both areas this led to problems well into the twentieth century. By the early 1890s in both the New Forest and Ashdown, committees or associations of small commoners – or even those with ill-defined use rights – had been formed and were in conflict with the official 'governors' of the forests over the actual nature of rights and who could exercise them. In this the 'little men' frequently saw themselves as the 'real commoners', put upon and regulated by the larger farmers and landowners.[73] These problems were made worse by the growth of both Ashdown and especially the New Forest as sites of middle-class residence and holidaymaking. In what Phelan calls 'the battle for social tone', a huge range of activities central to the functioning of the common land economy were attacked. Rough buildings, burning the commons, the behaviour of donkeys in the mating season and the 'welfare' of commoners' animals were the subject of constant complaint by middle-class incomers and tourists. Similarly, the development of golf

---

[69] Ibid., p. 103.   [70] *TEP,* 22 November 1897.
[71] Phelan, 'Economy to amenity', p. 148.   [72] Ibid., p. 167.   [73] Ibid., pp. 168–192.

led to clashes between commoners and golfers.[74] Golf was a problem elsewhere and led to the last of London's serious commons riots, the so-called 'Battle of One Tree Hill' in Honor Oak in 1897.[75]

The controlling of the commoners, or the plebeian visitors to commons, in 'the battle for social tone' was not restricted to the south-east. In 1880, the *Birmingham Daily Post* ran a very lengthy leader on the proposal to regulate Clent Hills in Staffordshire.

> There is a class of people who are always thinking that the public must be managed and regulated. Too much noise must not be made or too much vigour manifested by the 'lower orders' … So it is with enjoyment of freedom and holiday amusements upon the hills. Footpaths ought to be laid out, and not diverged from, a list of allowable games would probably be published, and fuss and coddle be established as controlling agencies.[76]

But it could go much further than 'rational recreation'. Neil MacMaster's fine study of the resistance to the enclosure of Mousehold Heath in Norwich shows how a well-established community, reliant on common rights, could be attacked and eventually destroyed by a 'liberal' city council's desire to create a public park.[77]

The community destroyed by the good burgers of Norwich – Pockthorpe – was by no means unusual in other respects. It is clear from the annual reports of the Inclosure Commissioners, as well as from local newspapers, that the commons and wastes continued to play a vital part in the economy of many poor households throughout the second half of the nineteenth century. In many cases such usage was legal, sanctioned by custom, or semi-legal. In these cases, those with rights often favoured, or even encouraged, enclosure. However, there was another and potentially much larger group who had no legal right, but who used the commons in a variety of ways to supplement their incomes. Here we find echoes of the debate between Shaw-Taylor and Neeson, but in a later period when the evidence of usage is much better, and seems strongly to support Neeson's argument for widespread semi-legal usage of commons and waste. As the 1913 Select Committee argued:

> in many cases … there is evidence that the neighbouring public, who are not strictly speaking commoners, have for a long period exercised with interference certain privileges, such as cutting turf, bracken, keeping geese &c. over common lands. Such privileges probably could not be at law established … but their existence is so widespread that your Committee are of the opinion that they must be respected.[78]

---

[74] Ibid., pp. 200–210.   [75] See the *Pall Mall Gazette*, 29 October 1897.
[76] *BDP,* 14 January 1880.   [77] MacMaster, 'Battle for Mousehold Heath', pp. 126–131.
[78] *BPP 1913 (85)*, Report from the Select Committee on Commons, p. 41.

Interestingly, this committee also recognised that regulation, so much favoured by the CPS, could also cause the problems which occurred in the New Forest and in Ashdown Forest when it reported that:

Persons who are not commoners, living near commons, have enjoyed privileges for which there is possibly no legal justification, such as pasturing geese, taking bracken or heath for litter, etc. [and] the deprivation of these by the operation of a regulation scheme causes undoubted hardship.[79]

To detail these rights is outside the scope of this chapter, but some basic areas of use can be indicated.[80] The annual reports of the Inclosure Commissioners list, often in some detail, the constant 'abuse' of commons by those who had no right beyond a belief that they had right, and that the practice of that right was a central part of their economic worlds. It is difficult to quantify the different categories of usage but probably the most important and most widely exercised of common 'rights', semi-legal or illegal, was loosely termed 'trespass'. This could cover a huge number of different uses ranging from the trapping or shooting of rabbits or game to the gathering of flowers and most commonly taking wood – the one thing it did not cover was simply walking across common land.

Following on from trespass, probably the next most common usage was grazing. In theory all commons were 'regulated' but in practice by the mid-century there was very little control. It is also clear that in many urban and suburban areas, those turning out had no right and certainly no other land holding. Also widespread and more serious, at least in the longer term, was the use of the commons for illegal housing – squatting – or taking in pieces of common for individual use – encroachment. Both of these represented the permanent alienation of parts of the common. There is a good deal of what we might think of as 'traditional' squatting by the poor, occasionally on a spectacular scale, as in Stamford in 1870,[81] or Withypool on Exmoor in the 1860s.[82] More prosaically, the Annual and Special Reports of the Commissioners contain numerous reports of small-scale squatting and encroachment from most areas of England, with the exception of the very mountainous regions.

Often ignored by the Commissioners, at least before the late 1860s, were encroachments by members of the local elites. It is clear that local farmers and even landowners were not averse to purloining from the common pot. Elite encroachment (or 'land-grabbing' in the language of

---

[79] Ibid., pp. 40–41.
[80] This topic will be covered in Howkins, 'Enclosure after enclosure'.
[81] *BPP 1870 (c. 39)*, Inclosure Commission, Twenty-fifth Annual Report, p. 11.
[82] *BPP 1868–9 X*, Select Committee on the Provisions of the Inclosure Act for the Labouring Poor, p. 105.

the radicals) was normally more genteel and more the experience of London and the Home Counties, where land, whether for parks and gardens or for building, was more valuable. By the 1890s, both the CPS and *Reynolds's Newspaper* thought illegal enclosure was a major problem.[83]

The final area of usage was the use of the soil of the common itself. The question of the mineral rights on commons was a vexed and complex one. However, to simplify, it is clear that the taking of gravel, stones or soil from the common or waste was widespread and often profitable. Several of the London commons were used to provide stone and gravel for road repairs by their respective vestries.[84] Elsewhere, brickfields were set up on commons, sometimes with the permission of the lord of the manor. It was brickfields which provided much of the income for the Pockthorpe commoners outside Norwich.[85] As with other usage, it is clear from the Annual Reports of the Inclosure Commissioners that this 'right' was widely abused and was frequently cited as a reason for enclosure.[86]

It should also be stressed that the use of commons was not only a feature of the rural areas. While the CPS and the radicals defended the London commons as sites of recreation for the people, the people themselves used the commons in a bewildering variety of ways. As in the rural areas, the most common use was for the pasturing of animals, especially the ubiquitous donkeys and ponies which were essential to many small tradesmen and dealers. However, the 1865 Select Committee which looked at metropolitan commons found that cattle and sheep were also kept, for example, on Hampstead Heath and Peckham Rye, as well as further out from the centre of London in Epsom and Banstead.[87]

All this points to the continuing problems of enclosure. To the CPS, and even the radicals of the CPL, the commons were the people's parks – sites of leisure and recreation. However, to many 'commoners' they remained economic units – sites of production – and as such essential to their livelihoods. This was especially so in the upland areas of the north and west, where huge areas of moorland pasture remained. However, it was also the case for many in the south and east, and even in the

---

[83] *RN*, 5 November 1893; *BPP 1913 (85)*, Report from the Select Committee on Commons, pp. 36ff.
[84] *BPP 1865 (390) (390–1)*, Select Committee on Open Spaces (Metropolis), Second report, on Hampstead Heath.
[85] MacMaster, 'The battle for Mousehold Heath'.
[86] For example, *BPP 1857 (2255)*, Inclosure Commission, Special Report, Parracombe, Devon, p. 4.
[87] *BPP 1865 (390) (390–1)*, Select Committee on Open Spaces, Second report, pp. 17, 58, 20, 54.

urban areas. Here the much less spectacular 'catch-as-catch-can' ecology persisted, and increasingly came into conflict with the idealised landscape of leisure. More publicly, the campaigns of the CPS reopened the radical debate on the commons and linked it to the wider land campaigns of the turn of the century.

V

The mobilisation of (largely) Liberal opinion by the CPS began, by the early 1880s, to move outside the simple questions of the defence of the commons. After 1876, enclosure of commons or waste in the classic sense came to an end. The question then became one of reversing the process of enclosure.

In the mid 1870s, Joseph Arch's union had picked up on the issue of commons rights, although interestingly the issue seems to have been raised most frequently at urban meetings called in support of the labourers. Speaking at Manchester and Preston during his tour of the north in 1874 to support men locked out in Suffolk, Arch linked the loss of the commons to the poverty of the labourer. With a decidedly eighteenth-century voice, he asked at Manchester where were 'the beautiful commons' the labourers had once enjoyed, and where were 'the pigs they used to turn out upon them'.[88] The enemy remained the landlord, but the solution offered pointed a way forward, which others were to pick up. When the labourers got the vote they would simply pass an Act which would 'pull the fences down'.[89]

This notion that the Enclosure Acts could be 'undone' by legislation became increasingly popular among radicals from the 1880s onwards, and eventually found its way into mainstream Liberal thought. The 1885 election, the first fought on the county householder franchise, and Chamberlain and Collings's 'Radical programme', brought 'restitution' to the fore. In a widely reported speech at Ipswich in January 1885, Chamberlain stated that Collings would bring forward a demand for a Select Committee to examine enclosures 'in the last fifty years'. If any of these were 'illegal' they would 'demand their restitution to the community or adequate compensation'.[90] Arch also made similar speeches during the campaign in 1885.[91] Building on this, Paul

---

[88] *DN*, 22 June 1874.   [89] *Manchester Times* (hereafter *MT*), 27 June 1874.
[90] *BDP,* 15 January 1885.
[91] For a brief discussion of the campaign, see Paul Readman, *Land and Nation in England. Patritism, National Identity and the Politics of Land, 1880–1914* (Woodbridge, 2008), pp. 147–148.

Readman argues that 'the conception of land reform as restitution for enclosure survived' not only within the Liberal Party after the defection of Chamberlain and Collings, but also fed into more 'extreme' causes like land nationalisation.[92] More importantly, it lay at the core of what he describes as the 'Edwardian apotheosis' of land reform after 1906. However, what is interesting about this reform movement is that it said remarkably little about the common land. All Liberal ideologues, and above all Lloyd George, were enthusiastic proponents of a lost golden age of pigs and commons, but beyond the broad panacea of land reform little was actually proposed. The Liberal 'Land Inquiry', which was supposed to provide the intellectual rationale for the land campaign, although eloquent on the iniquity of past enclosures, had virtually nothing to say about surviving commons. Indeed, the only 'practical' reference to commons was the suggestion that parish councils might acquire (through purchase) 'land ... for a village green or allotment'.[93] The idea of 'taking back' the commons, or at least those enclosed since 1845, put forward by earlier generations of Liberals and radicals, had completely vanished into the miasma of 'land reform'.[94]

The other inheritor of the radical tradition of commons defence after the 1880s was the emerging socialist movement and ultimately the Labour Party. The position here was more complicated. As Readman points out, 'scientific' socialism saw the demise of the open fields and commons as an inevitable part of the move to capitalism, and, as a result, parts of the British left were actively hostile to anything that smacked of a return to a 'pre-industrial' or peasant phase. Yet the notion of the idealised pre-enclosure village was not easily shaken off,[95] and in many respects the account given by the socialist left was similar to that given by Liberal radicals. Nevertheless, some 'socialists' and ultra-radicals continued to see commons defence as wholly separate from general land reform. An editorial in *Reynolds News* in 1897 articulated these ideas. The problems of the rural areas were the result of landlessness, and in particular the enclosure of the commons, which had been stolen 'in the most shameless manner ever known by legalized thefts'. *Reynolds* had a simple solution which harked back to an older radicalism:

---

[92] For what follows, see Readman, *Land and Nation*, pp. 148–154.

[93] Land Enquiry Committee, *The Land: The Report of the Land Enquiry Committee, Vol. 1. Rural* (London, 1913), p. 190.

[94] For a highly critical, near contemporary, view of the land campaign by a key Liberal figure, see F. E. Green, *A History of the English Agricultural Labourer, 1870–1920* (London, 1920), pp. 193–195.

[95] Readman, *Land and Nation*, pp. 182–186.

All lands enclosed since the General Enclosure of 1845 ought to be handed over to the District and parish Councils, without any compensation, by the landlords still holding them, and with reasonable compensation to innocent purchasers since that date, for the use of the rural workers.[96]

Ten years later, in slightly more measured tones, Edward Carpenter argued that the commons had been 'appropriated' by the landlords through a 'Landlord House of Parliament'.[97] Like *Reynolds*, he argued that the 'ten million acres' of common 'which Parliament voted away from the public in those days should now be voted back again'.[98]

However, as Clare Griffiths points out '(f)or most people in the Labour movement, the significance of rural history was as a prelude to the industrial economy'. The years after 1830 were seen, apart from the attempts at unionisation in the 1870s, as overwhelmingly urban.[99] Nor did early socialists see the countryside as a 'progressive' place – indeed quite the opposite. Despite the Clarion cycling and walking clubs taking the ideas of socialism into rural areas, they had very little impact before 1914 outside of small areas of East Anglia and the north-west.

As with the political discussion of the commons after 1845, the Labour Party and most early socialists saw enclosure within an urban context and tended to adopt a position similar to the CPS. In 1893, for instance, the Walworth Branch of the Social Democratic Federation opposed a sale of common land in Walworth, arguing that the vestry should use it 'as a public recreation ground for the use of the children of the district and others'.[100] Even Carpenter envisaged his 'returned' commons as having a mainly recreational function as cricket grounds, municipal parks or, in the case of the moorlands, as proto-national parks.[101] This urban context in turn shaped the views of the Labour movement. The land was 'lost', the urban poor were, in Griffiths's words 'dispossessed', and this gave a particular resonance to accounts of enclosure, and especially the account in J. L. and Barbara Hammond's *The Village Labourer* of 1911. What is important here is the way in which the left read the Hammonds. Looking at their account of the Swing Rising of the early 1830s, Griffiths writes:

---

[96] *RN,* 1 August 1897.
[97] Edward Carpenter, *The Village and the Landlord,* Fabian Tract no. 136, (London, 1907), p. 3.
[98] Ibid., p. 11.
[99] Clare V. J. Griffiths, *Labour and the Countryside. The Politics of Rural Britain 1918–1939* (Oxford, 2007), p. 30.
[100] *Lloyd's Weekly Newspaper,* 1 October 1893.
[101] Carpenter, *The Village and the Landlord,* p. 11.

their book scarcely offered an optimistic vision of the subsequent potential for revolt amongst the agricultural workers. The story of a rising suppressed in so devastating a fashion, and motivated by the desperation of a people who had not yet forgotten what it had been to have rights in the land leant itself to pathos rather than inspiration.[102]

VI

With the Hammonds we come full circle. How a historian views the Hammonds will usually indicate his or her views on enclosure, and possibly even politics generally. To Neeson, like E. P. Thompson, who in 1963 wrote of 'their great *Village Labourer*',[103] the Hammonds' book contains an essentially correct account of enclosure and the events that followed it. Interestingly, both Neeson and Thompson also quote John Clare (as I have done). Clare's sense of loss in his poems of enclosure, like the Hammond's account of Swing, is more about 'pathos than inspiration'. As such it is a strange model for a socialist. It is also a long way from the analysis of scientific socialism which saw enclosure as part of the inevitable process which marked the primitive accumulation of capital and 'freed' both land and labour for the development of capitalism as a system.[104]

The history of enclosure after 1845 brings up a number of issues. To begin with the nature of opposition changed. Those who opposed enclosure in the period before 1845 did so on the basis of social or economic grievances.[105] After 1845 much public and organised opposition to enclosure was on the quite different basis of amenity or even environment. Those involved also changed. After 1845 the organisation of much opposition to enclosure was urban and middle class, as opposed to rural and plebeian. Further, many of those involved in this protest had little or no direct interest in the commons they were defending, rather they acted 'in the interest' of the wider society. By the 1880s this view of the commons as a public amenity was shared by radical Liberals and socialists alike with few exceptions. However, this essentially philanthropic impulse, because it sought to regulate and control the commons in the wider 'public interest', increasingly tended to exclude those to whom the commons remained a vital economic asset.

---

[102] Griffiths, *Labour and the Countryside*, p. 47.
[103] Neeson, *Commoners*, p. 6; Thompson, *The Making*, p. 238.
[104] Karl Marx, *Capital, Volume 1* (Moscow, 1954) p. 685. See the whole of Chapter XXVII.
[105] For a classic statement see J. M. Neeson, 'The opponents of enclosure in eighteenth century Northamptonshire', *Past & Present*, 105, (November, 1984), pp. 114–139.

This group were seen both as increasingly marginal to mainstream economic systems and disruptive of ordered social structures.

However, it is clear that these illegal 'commoners' did use the commons and wastes to a remarkable extent. There is not a year in the Inclosure Commissioners' Annual Reports which does not report illegal usage of common land. Provincial newspapers, often in their court reports, show a plethora of cases involving claims of common right, usually in relation to stealing wood or killing rabbits. The 'waste' clearly continued to play a vital part in the lives of at least some of the poor. The word 'continued' is used advisedly, for if the use of commons, albeit illegally or semi-legally by the poor, is so widespread after the 1840s, why should it be any different in the earlier period? Indeed, in a system in which urban, industrial and market relationships were less strong, we would surely expect the exact opposite. Perhaps the evidence of the 1840s and 1850s, when evidence appears so abundant, should make us rethink the orthodox argument about commons usage between 1750 and 1840.

Engels and the city: the philosophy
and practice of urban hypocrisy

Tristram Hunt

From 'gated communities' to high-walled 'urban villages' to down-town Central Business Districts, it is now a truism of urban analysis that social relations of production dictate the spatial function of the city. Be it the security-guarded, ex-urban estates of middle-class America, the 'inner-city' compounds nestling in the heart of London and Mumbai, or the fortified suburban *laagers* which ring northern Johannesburg (modelled, it is said, on the style of Tuscan hill towns), civic space is becoming a more obviously codified commodity. Meanwhile, those urban arenas which remain open are arguably subject to an ever-more insidious process of privatisation (even militarisation) as retail districts and developers collude with councils and police authorities to lock down open parks and public squares. In Western cities, urban space has increasingly become a *sotto voce* battleground between private property interests, security functionaries and regeneration advocates. 'The Royal Institution of Chartered Surveyors [has] found that the ownership and control of public realm is shifting from the public to the private sector, replicating patterns not seen since the early Victorian era – when private landlords owned and managed vast swaths of cities', *The Guardian* recently announced.[1] Even Trafalgar Square, London's symbolic space for protest and display, is now a highly controlled zone patrolled by uniformed marshals with public drinking, feeding the pigeons and splashing in the fountains strictly outlawed.

In its modern form, much of this tradition of urban analysis as a confrontation between the means of production – the city as stage-set for the struggle between labour and capital (in varying guises) – begins with Friedrich Engels's trail-blazing 1845 publication *The Condition of the Working Class in England*. Written at the age of just twenty-four, it remains one of the defining texts for Marxist critiques of capitalism's

---

[1] 'Policing the retail republic', *The Guardian* 28 May 2008. See also Anna Minton, *Space Invaders – The Privatisation of Public Space* (Royal Institute of Chartered Surveyors, 2006).

human collateral damage as well as a profound contribution to urban thought that anticipated the approach of succeeding generations of sociologists, journalists and activists towards the built environment. One can read clear echoes of Engels's work in the 1920s Chicago School of urban theorists with their concentric zone theory or in any number of modern university courses on cultural criticism and social geography, with their derivative Henri Lefebvre influenced focus (who himself rarely deigned to mention Engels) on the production or archaeology of space.[2]

But for far too long, the *Condition* has been regarded as little more than an example of highly polemical reportage: the product of Engels's two years spent working in his father's textile mill in Salford and walking the streets of Manchester. According to Steven Marcus, 'He [Engels] was choosing to write about his own experience: to contend with it, to exploit it, to clarify it, and in some literal sense to create it and thereby himself. For in transforming his experiences into language he was at once both generating and discovering their structure.'[3] Similarly, historian Simon Gunn has described how 'Engels developed a style of grimly detailed reportage in order to extract meaning from the profusion of sense impressions'.[4] Asa Briggs has suggested that, 'If Engels had lived not in Manchester but in Birmingham his conception of "class" and his theories of the role of class history might have been very different'.[5] Manchester historian Jonathan Schofield has gone even further in stressing how Lancashire transformed Engels's thinking and, with it, the nature of communism. 'Without Manchester there would have been no Soviet Union', he declares. 'And the history of the twentieth century would have been very different.'[6]

However, Engels came to Manchester with a clear idea of the political meaning of the industrial society he was analysing. The *Condition* was not a prima facie response to 'Cottonopolis', but a carefully crafted text which sought to square the condition of 1840s England with his pre-existing philosophical certainties. As a result, Engels's 'Manchester' was as much a philosophical construct as any kind of objective, sociological depiction. And the awesome power of this polemic came as much from

---

[2] See Ira Katznelson, *Marxism and the City* (Oxford, 1992); Aruna Krishnamurthy, '"More Than Abstract Knowledge": Friedrich Engels in Industrial Manchester', *Victorian Literature and Culture*, 28, (2000), pp. 427–448; Henri Lefebvre, *The Production of Space* (Oxford, 1991).

[3] Steven Marcus, *Engels, Manchester and the Working Class* (London, 1974), p. 145.

[4] Simon Gunn, *The Public Culture of the Victorian Middle Class* (Manchester, 2000), p. 36. See also Marc Eli Blanchard, *In Search of the City* (Stanford, 1985), p. 21.

[5] Asa Briggs, *Victorian Cities* (London, 1990), p. 116.

[6] *The Guardian*, 4 February 2006.

this political architecture as its urban reportage. Moreover, it is this ideological agenda which has continued to distort understandings of the Victorian city, and its slum archipelagos, to this day.

In the summer of 1839, Engels produced a dry run for the *Condition*. Composed under the pseudonym 'Friedrich Oswald', his *Letters from Wuppertal* appeared in the pages of Karl Gutzkow's paper *Telegraph für Deutschland*, and provided an anonymous critique of the social, environmental and moral effects of industrialisation by a leading Barmen textile manufacturer's heir. Lacking much of the ideological certainty of the *Condition*, Oswald's *Letters* constituted a purer work of reportage knitted together by a teenager's fury towards his father's generation of narrow-minded, pietistic elders. With a crescendo of indignation at the misery wrought by the protestant–capitalist nexus who still governed the Rhineland towns of Barmen-Elberfeld, the *Letters* pointed to the polluted river Wupper, 'its bright red colour . . . due not to some bloody battle . . . but simply and solely to the numerous dye-works using Turkey red'; traced the plight of the weavers bent over their looms and the factory workers 'in low rooms where people breath in more coal fumes and dust than oxygen'; lamented the exploitation of children and the grinding poverty of those Engels would later term the *lumpenproletariat* ('these men are those known as *Karrenbinder*, totally demoralized people, with no fixed abode or definite employment, who crawl out of their refuges, haystacks, stables, etc., at dawn, if they have not spent the night on a dungheap or on a staircase'); and charted the rampant alcoholism amongst the leather-workers where three out of five died from excess schnapps consumption.[7]

But despite the *Letters'* sweeping condemnation of working conditions, class divisions and the social costs of industrialisation, Engels's target was not capitalism in any meaningful sense. He had as yet no real understanding of the historic dynamic of private property, the function of the proletariat or the nature of surplus labour value. His criticisms amounted, in essence, to a general lament about falling standards of living as a result of quickening industrial capitalism as well as a generational distaste for the religious sensibilities of his elders. This work constituted, if any did, exactly the kind of angry, self-fulfilling journalese which Marcus and others have read into the *Condition*. However, by 1844, that ill-focused fury had gained the sure edge of political certitude.

★★★★

Engels's journey from youthful angst towards ideological certainty was a swift one as in his late teens he abjured his father's Calvinist creed,

---

[7] *Marx Engels Collected Works* (New York, 1975), vol. 2, p. 25 [henceforth, *MECW*].

embraced Hegelianism and went on to imbibe the Young Hegelian spirit during his year's military service in Berlin (1841–1842). As Gareth Stedman Jones has suggested, central to Engels's process of communist conversion was a reading of Ludwig Feuerbach's *The Essence of Christianity*, which had posited in the mind of Engels, and other Young Hegelians confronting their loss of faith, the revelation that religion was a question of humanity not divinity.[8] In the God-head man had created a deity in his own image and likeness. Yet so replete with perfection was this objectified God that mankind started to abase himself before its spiritual authority. As such, the original power relationship was reversed. 'Man – this is the secret of religion – projects his essence into objectivity and then makes himself an object of this projected image of himself that is thus converted into a subject ...' And the more fervently man worshipped an exterior God, the more internally impoverished he became. 'Religion by its very essence drains man and nature of substance, and transfers this substance to the phantom of an other-worldly God, who in turn then graciously permits man and nature to receive some of his superfluity', as Engels put it. 'Lacking awareness ... man can have no substance, he is bound to despair of truth, reason and nature.'[9]

What was even more revolutionary about Feuerbach was that he applied the same critical template to the philosophy of his former tutor, Hegel. How, Feuerbach asked, was the University of Berlin professor's thinking – with its fanciful notion of *Geist* (or 'Spirit') making its way through history until its final, epic summation – substantively different to Christian theology? 'Speculative theology [i.e. Hegelianism] distinguishes itself from ordinary theology by the fact that it transfers the divine essence into this world. That is, speculative theology envisions, determines, and realizes in this world the divine essence transported by ordinary theology out of fear and ignorance into another world.' In terms of detaching man from the needs of existing society, there was little to choose between Hegelian philosophy and Christian religion. The idealistic Hegel had made the mistake of deriving being from thought, rather than thought from being and, as such, had turned reality on its head. What Feuerbach urged was a presaging

---

[8] Stedman Jones's 'Introduction' to Karl Marx and Friedrich Engels, *The Communist Manifesto*, Penguin Classics edn, (London, 2002), pp. 53–65; also his 'The First Industrial City? Engels' Account of Manchester in 1844', unpublished paper, Centre for History and Economics, published in French as 'Voir sans entendre: Engels, Manchester et l'observation sociale en 1844', *Genèses*, 22, (1996), pp. 4–18.

[9] Quoted in William J. Brazill, *The Young Hegelians* (Yale, 1970), at p. 146; *MECW*, vol. 3, p. 462.

of materialism over and above Hegelian idealism. In place of God or Spirit, he posited Man: anthropology not theology.

This was where Moses Hess, the Rhenish sugar refiner's son turned proto-socialist, took up the trajectory. Having spent time amongst the radical communist clubs of 1830s Paris (the world of the Saint-Simonians and Blanquists), Hess was interested in direct, political action rather than the circular philosophical debate fashionable amongst the Young Hegelians. Of course, Hess agreed with Feuerbach, man could only regain his essence by ending his obeisance towards a Christian deity. But this should not be attempted on an individual basis since a broader, communal process of associational conversion was needed. 'Theology is anthropology. That is true, but it is not the whole truth. The being of man, it must be added, is social, the co-operation of the various individuals towards a common aim ... and the true doctrine of man, the true humanism, is the theory of human sociability. That is to say, anthropology is socialism.'[10]

To reach this stage of common humanity an oppositional political stance had to be taken against the capitalist system which was the cause of man's dehumanisation: in short, the abolition of private property and, with it, an end to the alienating effects brought about by the money economy. Only then could the current culture of egoism and competition be curtailed and, in its place, a new sociability based on freedom and humanity be created. In this great historical movement towards socialism, each member of what he called the European triarchy – France, England and Germany – had a different role to play. Germany was to provide the philosophical foundations of communism; France the political activism; and industrialising England was to gather the social kindling. 'The antagonism between poverty and the aristocracy of money will reach a revolutionary level only in England, just as that opposition between spiritualism and materialism could reach its culmination in France and the antagonism between state and church could reach its apex only in Germany.'[11] With its vast manufactories, wealthy mill owners and hideously brutalised proletariat, the coming crisis was all set to emerge in this the heartland of the industrial revolution. 'The English are the nation of praxis, more than any other nation. England is to our century what France has been to the previous one.'[12]

---

[10] 'Über die sozialistische Bewegung in Deutschland', in Moses Hess, *Philosophische und sozialistische Schriften 1837–1850*, ed. Auguste Cornu and Wolfgang Mönke (Liechtenstein, 1980), at p. 293.

[11] Quoted in Shlomo Avineri, *Moses Hess* (London, 1985), at p. 61.

[12] 'Die Europaische Triarchie', in Moses Hess, *Philosophische*, at p. 117.

In 1842, this was exactly where the now politically engaged Friedrich Engels was heading – sent by his father to learn the family business at the Ermen & Engels mill in Salford, but far more interested in pinpointing the first signs of social revolution. Before departing, he popped in to see Moses Hess, who described the visit in a letter to Berthold Auerbach. Engels arrived, he recalled, as a shy, naive, '"first year" revolutionary' (*ein Anno I Revolutionär*). By the time he had finished his tutorial, Engels had been converted into 'an extremely eager communist'.[13] This mixture of Feuerbachian and primitive communist thinking was the ideological *hinterland* with which Engels confronted 'Cottonopolis'.

I

Engels's initial literary response to the state of Manchester was not the *Condition*. Instead, it was a far more considered work of early Marxist thought which sought to move Feuerbach's materialism further on from the idealistic Young Hegelian remnants which still enveloped it. In a seminal 1843 article for the *Deutsch-Französische Jahrbücher* (Marx's latest newspaper), 'Outlines of a Critique of Political Economy', he showed the fruits of his Salford apprenticeship by dropping the Berlin theorising for a hard-headed, empirical analysis of the economic contradictions and social crises coming Europe's way. He did so by following Hess in applying the notion of alienation – which Feuerbach had discussed solely in terms of religion – to the realm of political economy. For it was not just Christianity that involved a denial of man's nature: like Hess, Engels thought that competitive capitalism, through its systems of property, money and exchange, involved an equally disfiguring process of alienation from the authentic human essence. Under the aegis of political economy, man was divorced from himself. 'Through this theory we have come to know the deepest degradation of mankind, their dependence on the conditions of competition. It has shown us how in the last instance private property has turned man into a commodity whose production and destruction also depend solely on demand.'[14]

What drove this process of alienation, what stood at the root of political economy, was private property. This was the essential insight of Engels's 'Outlines'. It owed not a little to his recent reading of *What is Property?* (1840) by the French socialist-cum-anarchist Pierre-Joseph Proudhon – who had answered that question with the celebrated response, 'It is theft'. It was private property in the form of unearned interest from usury and

---

[13] Moses Hess, *Briefwechsel* (Amsterdam, 1959), at p. 103.
[14] *MECW*, vol. 3., p. 440.

rents from land which, Proudhon suggested, enabled one man to exploit another and underpinned the iniquities of modern capitalism. Proudhon's stress on the correlation of labour with ownership, alongside his conviction that political equality necessitated the abolition of private property, struck an immediate chord with the young Engels (despite the unacceptably anarchist trajectory of Proudhon's thinking). 'The right of private property, the consequences of this institution, competition, immorality, misery, are here developed with a power of intellect, and real scientific research, which I never since found united in a single volume', he wrote of Proudhon's book for the Owenite journal, *The New Moral World*.[15]

However, Engels took his conception of private property further than Proudhon had allowed himself and had it encompass all the apparatus of political economy, 'e.g., wages, trade, value, price, money, etc.', which he had seen at work in Manchester.[16] He concluded that private property was the essential prerequisite of political economy and it too had to be eliminated. 'If we abandon private property, then all these unnatural divisions disappear.' Discord and individualism would melt away and the true nature of profit and value clarified. 'Labour becomes its own reward, and the true significance of the wages of labour, hitherto alienated, comes to light – namely, the significance of labour for the determination of the production costs of a thing.' The end of private property and personal avarice would conclude, in Hegelian fashion, with the end of history and arrival of communism: 'the great transformation to which the century is moving – the reconciliation of mankind with nature and with itself.'[17]

This was the intellectual preamble for the *Condition*. Of course, what initially leaps off the page of Engels's impassioned work is the detailed account of the Manchester which he encountered with his Irish lover Mary Burns – its stink, noise, grime and human misery – as well as the statistical evidence of exploitation as regurgitated from the Blue Books and liberal press. But the polemic's deeper purpose was to bolster Engels's conviction, garnered from Feuerbach and Hess, that the capitalist system involved a process of human alienation. Engels's trawl through the slums of Salford and Little Ireland was an attempt, as Gareth Stedman Jones once put it, 'to validate, both metaphorically and literally, the Feuerbachian conception of the ontological loss of humanity associated with religious alienation and – in the radical communist gloss added by Young Hegelians – with the establishment of

---

[15] Ibid., p. 399.   [16] *MECW*, vol. 4, p. 32.

[17] ibid., pp. 431 and 424. See also Gregory Claeys, 'Engels' *Outlines of a Critique of Political Economy* (1843) and the origins of the Marxist critique of capitalism', *History of Political Economy*, 16(2), (1984).

money and private property'.[18] This accounts for the *Condition*'s curious opening with its epic account of Britain's pre-history of industrialisation – 'a history which has no counter-part in the annals of humanity'. It is a sweeping economic narrative taking in the spinning jenny, the steam engine, the digging of canals and the arrival of the railway. In true Moses Hess fashion, Engels declares 'the industrial revolution [is] of the same importance for England as the political revolution for France, and the philosophical revolution for Germany'.[19] Slowly, inexorably, the old economy of guilds and apprenticeships, with its thick social hierarchy, was dismantled in favour of class division, of 'great capitalists and working men who had no prospect of rising above their class'. The end product of this industrial process, the greatest iron hammered out on the anvil of history, was a dehumanized proletariat. 'The proletarian, who has nothing but his two hands, who consumes today what he earned yesterday, who is subject to every possible chance, and has not the slightest guarantee for being able to earn the barest necessities of life, whom every crisis, every whim of his employer may deprive of bread, this proletarian is placed in the most revolting, inhuman position conceivable for a human being.'[20]

Engels the anthropologist then discovers their habitat in the chapter entitled, 'The Great Towns', which went far further than *Letters from Wuppertal* in purporting to provide a material account of the costs of capitalism, but also echoes these earlier articles in its treatment of the cityscape. In a passage that instantly recalls his account of Barmen's ink-dyed waterways, Engels ascends Ducie Bridge to take a look at the river Irk, 'a narrow, coal-black, foul-smelling stream, full of debris and refuse which it deposits on the lower right bank. In dry weather, an extended series of the most revolting brackish green pools of slime remain standing on this bank, out of whose depth bubbles of miasmatic gases constantly rise and give forth a stench that is unbearable even on the bridge forty or fifty feet above the level of the water.' Nearby, Engels retraces the steps of the liberal Manchester physician James Phillips Kay inside some of the city's most insanitary hovels. 'In one of these courts there stands directly at the entrance, at the end of the covered passage, a privy without a door, so dirty that the inhabitants can pass into and out of the court only by passing through foul pools of stagnant urine and

---

[18] Gareth Stedman Jones, 'The first industrial City? Engels' Account of Manchester in 1844', p. 7.

[19] Friedrich Engels, *The Condition of the Working Class in England* (Harmondsworth, 1987), p. 61.

[20] Ibid., pp. 143–144.

excrement.' Surrounding it are hundreds more of these 'cattle-sheds for human beings' where men are reduced to the state of animals, pigs share sties with children, hundreds cramp into dank cellars, railways slash through neighbourhoods, and privies, rivers and water supplies all seem to merge into one deadly mix. 'Such is the Old Town of Manchester, and on re-reading my description, I am forced to admit that instead of being exaggerated, it is far from black enough to convey a true impression of the filth, ruin, and uninhabitableness, the defiance of all considerations of cleanliness, ventilation, and health which characterise the construction of this single district, containing at least 20–30,000 inhabitants.'[21]

There was worse to come. On the south side of the city, just off Oxford Road, was where some of Manchester's 40,000-strong Irish immigrants huddled. Mary Burns's confreres were the most exploited, lowly paid and abused of all the city's residents; the most *lumpen* of the proletariat.

The cottages are old, dirty, and of the smallest sort, the streets uneven, fallen into ruts and in part without drains or pavement; masses of refuse, offal and sickening filth lie among standing pools in all directions ... The race that lives in these ruinous cottages, behind broken windows, mended with oilskin, sprung doors, and rotten door-posts, or in dark, wet cellars, in measureless filth and stench, in this atmosphere penned in as if with a purpose, this race must really have reached the lowest stage of humanity.[22]

On the surface, Engels's Manchester appeared to have no purpose or structure – 'a planless, knotted chaos of houses' – but, in reality, there existed a terrible logic behind its suffocating form. The logic of hypocrisy. As Marx would later go beneath the surface of freedom, equality and property in *Das Kapital* to depict capitalism's 'hidden abode of production', so Engels, in good Hegelian fashion, did away with the appearance of the city to elucidate its true essence. Yes, slum tenements went up haphazardly on the crumbling side of river banks and railroads piled through old neighbourhoods, but these developments were part of a broader urban form which perfectly reflected the class divisions of industrial society. For like few before him, Engels appreciated the city's spatial dynamics – its streets, houses, factories and warehouses – as expressions of social and political power. The struggle between bourgeoisie and proletariat was not limited to the throstle room or Chartist rally, it was tangible in the street design, transport systems and planning process. 'The town itself is peculiarly built, so that a person may live in it for years, and go in and out daily without coming into contact with a working people's quarter or even with workers ... This arises chiefly

[21] Ibid., pp. 89, 92.   [22] Ibid., p. 98.

from the fact, that by unconscious tacit agreement, as well as with outspoken conscious determination, the working people's quarters are sharply separated from the sections of the city reserved for the middle class.'[23] Class conflict and the social divides wrought by private property were embedded in the very flagstones of the city.

Engels's pioneering analysis of class zoning begins along the main thoroughfare of Deansgate where the merchant princes and cotton lords commuted in to make their deals. Like today, the road was in the 1840s a retail and commercial hub lined with high-end shops and showy warehouses. And, as with so many modern city centres, 'the whole district is abandoned by dwellers, and is lonely and deserted at night; only watchmen and policemen traverse its narrow lanes with their dark lanterns'. But surrounding it, in the inner suburbs, lay the 'unmixed working people's quarters' of Manchester proper – Salford and Hulme, Pendleton and Chorlton – 'stretching like a girdle ... around the commercial district'.

And beyond that, outside this girdle, in the suburbs, 'lives the middle bourgeois ... in regularly laid out streets in the vicinity of the working quarters, especially in Chorlton and the lower lying portions of Cheetham Hill; the upper bourgeois in remoter villas ... or on the breezy heights of Cheetham Hill, Broughton, and Pendleton, in free, wholesome country air, in fine, comfortable homes'. And the finest part of the arrangement was that:

the members of this money aristocracy can take the shortest road through the middle of all the labouring districts to their places of business, without ever seeing that they are in the midst of the grimy misery that lurks to the right and the left. For the thoroughfares leading from the Exchange in all directions out of the city are lined, on both sides, with an almost unbroken series of shops, and are so kept in the hands of the middle and lower bourgeoisie, which, out of self-interest, cares for a decent and cleanly external appearance and can care for it ... they suffice to conceal from the eyes of the wealthy men and women of strong stomachs and weak nerves the misery and grime which form the complement of their wealth.[24]

Engels, who in his Barmen corporate village had shared his neighbourhood with the local dyers, weavers and operatives, declared himself properly shocked: 'I have never seen so systematic a shutting out of the working class from the thoroughfares, so tender a concealment of everything which might affront the eye and the nerves of the bourgeois, as in Manchester.' And this manipulation of urban form was not some accidental piece of planning. 'I cannot help feeling that the liberal

[23] Ibid., p. 86.   [24] Ibid.

manufacturers, the bigwigs of Manchester, are not so innocent after all, in the matter of this sensitive method of construction.'[25]

Of course, this Disraelian notion of two nations in one city was already a familiar one and the French journalist Léon Faucher had earlier drawn attention to Manchester's geography of class division with his account of 'two towns in one: in the one portion, there is space, fresh air, and provision for health; and in the other, every thing which poisons and abridges existence.'[26] But no one prior to Engels had managed to link it so intimately to the social relations of production: from the outskirts of Stockport and Staleybridge via the suburbs of Chorlton and Hulme to the central business district of downtown Manchester, Engels charts the connection of physical space to social class with an unwavering precision. Each concentric zone, each urban girdle, of 1840s Manchester is there to play a part in Engels's critique of industrialising England's class anatomy. But, in the process, the irregularities and contradictions of the real, existing Manchester, the wrong class in the wrong place – the difference between skilled and unskilled; employed and unemployed; migrant and indigenous – were ironed out as Engels sought to depict an inevitable clash of competing, homogenised class experience in the urban furnace of the Industrial Revolution.

Nor was this some stock, literary response to the specific state of Manchester's urban environment, for earlier in the chapter Engels had already analysed the social geography of London in markedly similar terms contrasting the overcrowded, miasmatic slums of St Giles consciously concealed by bourgeois planning from the 'gay world' of Oxford Street, Regent Street, Trafalgar Square and the Strand. 'It is a disorderly collection of tall, three or four-storied houses, with narrow, crooked, filthy streets, in which there is quite as much life as in the great thoroughfares of the town, except that, here, people of the working class only are to be seen.' Equally apparent in his comparison of the two cities was the human cost of capitalism – as evidenced in London's rookeries, cellars and garrets which 'no human being could possibly wish to live in'. Like Manchester, the price of London's greatness was the animalisation of the majority of its inhabitants. 'These Londoners have been forced to sacrifice the best qualities of their human nature, to bring to pass all the marvels of civilization which crowd their city.'[27]

For this was the ideological architecture of the *Condition*: rather than being a work of vivid reportage, Engels coalesced Britain's 'great towns' together as empirical evidence for the inevitable, unavoidable alienation

[25] Ibid., p. 87.   [26] Léon Faucher, *Manchester* (Manchester, 1844), p. 69.
[27] Engels, *Condition of the Working Class*, p. 69.

which capitalism entailed. In the industrial city, man was an alienated, de-humanised beast of burden – which explains the ubiquitous animal-istic imagery, the endless swine and cattle, which suffuse his text. As Engels says of Manchester's working-class accommodation, 'in such dwellings only a physically degenerate race, robbed of all humanity, degraded, reduced morally and physically to bestiality, could feel com-fortable and at home'.[28]

Unfortunately, such suffering was politically necessary since it was only once the impoverished masses had reached their lowest ebb, once their very humanity had been taken from them, that they began to realise their class-consciousness. 'Here humanity attains its most complete development and its most brutish; here civilization works its miracles, and civilized man is turned back almost into a savage', as de Tocqueville epically wrote of Manchester.[29] As one of the birthplaces of the labour movement, the city was thus both the scene of immense sacrifice but also redemption: through exploitation came ultimate liberation and the promise of socialism.

Through their hypocritical planning of the city, the middle classes hoped to put the working classes out of sight and out of mind. The terrible irony was that with the proletariat cooped up in its slums, the spatial configuration of the city only accelerated the Feuerbachian loss of human-ity and with it the nurturing of class-consciousness. As such, Victorian Manchester – the 'shock city' of free trade, industrialisation and bourgeois civilisation – was the scene of middle-class triumph but also doom. Every factory, slum and workhouse was a bourgeois memento mori: their glis-tening cities, tombs of the living dead. 'Hence the absurd freedom from anxiety, with which the middle class dwells upon a soil that is honey-combed, and may any day collapse.' From Glasgow to London, revolution was inevitable, 'a revolution in comparison with which the French Revolution, and the year 1794, will prove to have been child's play'.[30]

This unerring conviction in the city's historic purpose dictates Engels's seemingly rambling descriptions of 1840s Manchester as well as Britain's other industrialising cities (which, in many cases, he had not visited). As such, everything had an ideological function to fulfil: the landscape, people and industry. As a consequence, we never hear the voice of the individualised working class speak in Engels's account, nor is there any sense of the multiple divisions within Manchester's labouring masses – the street cleaners as opposed to cotton spinners, the washer-women as opposed to street vendors, Tories as opposed to

[28] Ibid., p. 100.
[29] Alexis de Tocqueville, *Journeys to England and Ireland* (London, 1958), p. 108.
[30] Engels, *Condition of the Working Class*, p. 64.

Liberals, Catholics as against Protestants. The nuances of Manchester's multiple economies – distribution; services; construction; retail; as well as the cotton mills – are subtly elided for an overarching urban confrontation between solidified labour and capital. Similarly, the city's rich working-class civil society of Mechanics' Institutes, friendly societies and working-men's clubs, of political parties and chapels, is absent. In contrast to Henry Mayhew's highly individualised account of working-class London (with its almost Linnaean taxonomy of poverty combined with verbatim interviews) or Charles Booth's later mapping of the East End poor (whose different colorations showed, in fact, just how closely gradations of rich and poor could exist between and betwixt each other), Engels depicts one codified, unified proletariat separated off from its bourgeois enemy and preordained to fulfil its historic destiny.[31] The *actualité* of Manchester – the complex gradations of the poor; the nuances of places – is sacrificed for a homogenised proletariat in conscious contradistinction to the bourgeoisie. Startlingly, he even appears to offer no credible difference between the *lumpenproletariat* and the industrial proletariat – when, in the coming years, the latter's calling as the 'universal class' would so clearly mark it out for Marx and Engels from 'the "dangerous class", the social scum, that passively rotting mass thrown off by the lowest layers of old society' which, more often than not, acts 'the part of a bribed tool of reactionary intrigue'.[32] In 1844 Manchester, they subsisted together as one undifferentiated mass bundled within their carefully codified geographical quarters.

Thus, far from being part of a new political literature revealing Marx and Engels's materialist turn and hence break with Young Hegelian idealism, the *Condition* offered a highly idealised vision of a precociously 'Marxist' Manchester. In the face of claims to transparent urban reportage or providing a true analysis of the interests of the proletariat, Engels crafts a reified, urban poor devoid of voice or autonomous agency. The philosophical idealism of the *Condition* demanded the sacrifice of empirical detail and individual personality for Engels's grander narrative of socio-economic contradiction.

II

In 1872, by which time Engels was living as a retired *rentier* in the breezy heights of London's Primrose Hill, he returned to the issue of town planning with a series of articles entitled *The Housing Question*. As

---

[31] See Henry Mayhew, *London Labour and the London Poor* (Harmondsworth, 1985); Charles Booth, *Life and Labour of the People in London* (London, 1902).
[32] *MECW*, vol. 6, p. 494.

was so often the case, Engels was drawn back into print to denounce an act of philosophical deviation by an alternative power base. In this instance, the unhelpful prevalence of Proudhonist thought within French communist circles as well as the recent publication of Dr Emil Sax's *The Housing Conditions of the Working Classes and their Reform*, which had advocated a superficial, petit-bourgeois solution to the problem of working-class overcrowding in Continental cities. What is of interest to us is how Engels once again interrogates the issue of urban space and class power in the context of what he calls 'the spirit of Haussmann' and its effects on the morphology of the city. Christened in honour of Baron Eugène Haussmann, the *prefet* of the Seine *departement* who had despotically transformed Paris from a cobbled, decaying medieval city into an imperial metropolis worthy of Napoleon III, the term 'Haussmann' became a template for class-driven, inner-city regeneration. First of all, through economic forces. Just as the capitalist enriches himself from the industry of the proletarian by exploiting his labour power far above its exchange value, so when it comes to the property market if land values rise then old buildings are pulled down (with their working-class residents dispersed) and in their place shops, warehouses and public buildings are erected. And on demolition and construction sites across Manchester, Liverpool, Paris and Berlin, the bourgeoisie were exploiting the surplus value, the unearned increment, of land prices to reap huge profits at great human cost. 'The result is that the workers are forced out of the centre of the towns towards the outskirts; that workers' dwellings, and small dwellings in general, become rare and expensive and often altogether unobtainable.'[33]

However, the spirit of Haussmann could move in other ways. Under the guise of security, sanitation or gentrification, Engels detected a growing tendency on the part of city government to exert its spatial authority in order to dictate the urban form. 'By the term "Haussmann" I do not mean merely the specifically Bonapartist manner of the Parisian Haussmann', he explained, 'I mean the practice which has now become general of making breaches in the working-class quarters of our big towns, and particularly in those which are centrally situated, quite apart from whether this is done from considerations of public health and for beautifying the town, or owing to the demand for big centrally situated business premises, or owing to traffic requirements, such as the laying down of railways, streets, etc.' For no matter what the justification, the result was always the same: 'the scandalous alleys and lanes disappear to

---

[33] *MECW,* vol. 23, p. 319.

the accompaniment of lavish self-praise from the bourgeoisie on account of this tremendous success, but they appear again immediately somewhere else and often in the immediate neighborhood.' An obvious case in point was Manchester, where new railway lines, arterial roads and grand public buildings had seemed to camouflage the slums and rookeries which Engels had explored in the 1840s. Even Little Ireland – the most inhuman, bestial neighbourhood he had encountered – appeared to have been dispersed. 'The bourgeoisie pointed with pride to the happy and final abolition of Little Ireland as to a great triumph.' But when a flood inundated the area, it was suddenly revealed that, 'Little Ireland had not been abolished at all, but had simply been shifted from the south side of Oxford Road to the north side, and that it still continues to flourish'.[34]

London, of course, suffered equally heavily from such Haussmanesque interventions in the mid-Victorian years. *The Times* was convinced that 'as we cut roads through our forests, so it should be our policy to divide these thick jungles of crime and misery'.[35] And, again and again, it was the slumlands of St Giles (New Oxford Street), Whitechapel (Commercial Road), Pimlico (Victoria Street) and Clerkenwell (Farringdon Road) which suffered at the hands of the bourgeois city authorities. During Engels's years in the capital, it was the marshland rookeries of the East End – Stedman Jones's landscape of 'Outcast London' with its residuum of casual poor, Jewish migrants and 'the rough' – which attracted most attention.[36] With his 'slumming' days behind him, it is doubtful whether Engels himself (whom Henry Hyndman christened 'the Grand Llama of the Regent's Park Road') ever ventured amongst the backstreets of Hoxton and Bethnal Green, but he certainly got to know of them from Eleanor Marx's hands-on accounts of the radical clubs that she and Edward Aveling frequented, and the endless Yellow Press exposés of maiden tributes and Ripper-style criminality, as well as his own personal contacts with Will Thorne and John Burns, the dockers' leaders.

The common terminology of the time was of the East End as *terra incognita*: a 'dark continent' as foreign and unknown as the outer edges of the empire. Here lurked Other people and strange customs. 'May we not find a parallel at our own doors, and discover within a stone's throw of our cathedrals and palaces similar horrors to those which Stanley has found existing in the great Equatorial forest?', asked William Booth in his Salvation Army manifesto and riposte to H. M. Stanley, *In Darkest*

---

34 Ibid., pp. 365–366.   35 *The Times*, 2 March 1861.
36 Gareth Stedman Jones, *Outcast London* (Oxford, 1971).

England and the Way Out. 'Darkest England, like Darkest Africa, reeks with malaria. The foul and fetid breath of our slums is almost as poisonous as that of an African swamp ... A population sodden with drink, steeped in vice, eaten up by every social and physical malady, these are the denizens of Darkest England amidst whom my life has been spent.'[37] And the solution, as Engels had predicted, was further Haussmannisation with the latter decades of the nineteenth century becoming known as 'the time of tearing down' as new roads, railways, docks and Underground stations cleared away working-class districts. The dark East End was brought into the light.

Given how much official London liked to bask in its title as 'the heart of the Empire', what was so interesting about late-nineteenth-century urban analysis was the close proximity of thinking between metropole and colony. Foreign 'missions' to London's East End would often set up kindred institutions in the outer cities of other dark outposts of the British Empire. 'Settlement houses and district nursing programs in London and other "home" cities trained thousands of empire-bound women', explains Ellen Ross in her new history of slum travellers. 'The small hospital that the Canning Town Women's Settlement established in the 1890s to serve its local community soon became a way station for medical missionaries en route to other continents.'[38] Urban policy in the East End was a staging post for the colonial challenge of managing un-English metropolitan communities abroad.

If, in Jan Morris's idiom, urbanism was the most lasting of British imperial legacies, then similar notions of spatial authority evident in London and Manchester can be seen transplanted from West to East.[39] And, just as Engels recounted how social relations dictated the urban form of 1840s Manchester and 1870s Paris, in the imperial planning of cities such as Calcutta, Bombay, Cairo, Khartoum and, of course, New Delhi, one can exchange race for class to discover Engels's hypocritical forces at work. From the military cantonments to the bungalow compounds to the railway stations to the ornamental boulevards and slum-clearance projects, imperial hegemony stamped its authority just as savagely on the colonial city as on the outcast East End.[40] As in 1860s Paris or 1880s London, it was the premise of security or sanitation which often provided justification for the most brutal displays of 'improvement' towards the 'dark towns' of the indigenous inhabitants.

[37] General Booth, *In Darkest England and The Way Out* (London, 1890), pp. 11–15.
[38] Ellen Ross, *Slum Travellers* (California, 2007), p. 27.
[39] Jan Morris, *Stones of Empire* (London, 1994).
[40] See Jonathan Schneer, *London 1900* (London, 1999).

Under the 1864 Military Cantonments Act, the British in India
created a bureaucracy of Sanitary Commissions to protect the
Europeans from the Indian 'miasmas' and, in the process, throw up
walls, bulldoze markets, lay down esplanades and segregate the city
along aggressively racial lines (a practice which quickly embedded itself
in the colonial cities of South Africa). On his early twentieth-century
tour of India, the town planner Patrick Geddes was horrified at the
effects of the sanitary agenda on the civic fabric of Madras, with 'its
death dealing Haussmannising and its squalid industrial bye-laws'.[41]
But it had to wait until the mid-1970s work of Anthony King before
the totalising, ideological agenda of these colonial cities was fully realised. 'The physical and spatial arrangements characterizing urban development – indeed, the entire man-made environment – are the unique
products of a particular society and culture, operating within a given
distribution of power', he announced in the 'Preface' to his seminal
work, *Colonial Urban Development* (1976). 'From Rangoon to Cairo,
Luanda to Singapore, cities were laid out by the rulers not the ruled.
Here, juxtaposed in the environment of the colonised society, were the
urban forms of East and West, a unique type of social, physical and
spatial organization.'[42] In the wake of King's work, hundreds of books
have now approached the European colonial urban form – its domestic
and ceremonial architecture, streetscape, fortifications and civil society
of clubs, sports grounds and churches – in similar fashion. But very few
have done so with any recognition that powerful elements of this tradition of spatial analysis (whether oriented around class or race) can be
traced back to Engels's early critique of one of the central hubs of the
British Empire, Manchester. Do we not see in racial discussions of Raj
boulevards and bungalow compounds, the delineations of space and
power in the imperial city, clear resonances of Engels's class interpretation of the early Victorian city?

With typical *élan*, the California-based urban writer Mike Davis has
elucidated these connections and brought the critique up to date by
focusing on the morphology of the post-colonial city. In his 2006 essay,
Planet of Slums, he recounts with Engels-like vituperation the sanitary
state of the modern mass conurbation ('Today's poor megacities –
Nairobi, Lagos, Bombay, Dhaka, and so on – are stinking mountains
of shit that would appall even the most hardened Victorians'), but he
also points to the combination of race and class power relationships
which underpin the spatial inequality of the city. According to Davis,

[41] Quoted in Robert Home, *Of Planting and Planning* (London, 1997), at p. 148.
[42] Anthony D. King, *Colonial Urban Development* (London, 1976), p. xii.

the post-colonial city has reverted back from race to class as the primary determinant of spatial hegemony. 'Throughout the Third World, postcolonial elites have inherited and greedily reproduced the physical footprints of segregated colonial cities. Despite rhetorics of national liberation and social justice, they have aggressively adapted the racial zoning of the colonial period to defend their own class privileges and spatial exclusivity.'[43]

A chapter entitled 'Haussmann in the Tropics', investigating squatter and working-class clearances in contemporary Africa, China and central America, reads like pure Engels – not least the *Condition's* depiction of life in the great towns as 'the social war, the war of each against all'. 'Urban segregation is not a frozen status quo', Davis declaims, 'but rather a ceaseless social war in which the state intervenes regularly in the name of "progress," "beautification," and even "social justice for the poor" to redraw spatial boundaries to the advantage of landowners, foreign investors, elite homeowners, and middle-class commuters. As in 1860s Paris under the fanatical reign of Baron Haussmann, urban redevelopment still strives to simultaneously maximize private profit and social control.' In the sprawling slum and suburb conurbations of India, economic inequality now defines the nature of urban exclusion from Chenai to Mumbai. Behind this process of economic segregation, in Davis's sometimes crude template, are the forces of modern international capitalism – the IMF and the World Bank – determined to carve out islands of 'cyber-modernity' amidst unmet urban needs and general underdevelopment.[44] It is a criticism recently endorsed by the UN-Habitat State of the World Cities report (2008), which highlighted the extraordinary inequalities of cities in South Africa, Namibia, Kenya and Latin America. 'High levels of inequality can lead to negative social, economic and political consequences that have a destabilising effect on societies', said the report. '[They] create social and political fractures that can develop into social unrest and insecurity.'[45]

III

Apart from some obvious contemporaneous concerns over the brutality of capitalism, what has Engels to do with such urban developments today? Well, if one engages with the increasingly fashionable school of urban ethnography, there is a great deal that Engels has to answer for. According to the social historian Alan Mayne, it was the codification of the notion of a slum by social reformers and bourgeois critics (amongst whom Mayne

---

[43] Mike Davis, *Planet of Slums* (London, 2006), pp. 138 and 96.
[44] Ibid., pp. 96–99.
[45] 'Wealth gap creating a social time bomb', *The Guardian*, 23 October 2008.

curiously omits Engels) which helped to provide the political context for the urban clearances in the metropole and colony of the later nineteenth century. Building on the work of other scholars such as Jennifer Davis and Jerry White – who, respectively, have unpicked the mythology of the 'dangerous class' slumland encircling the Jennings' Buildings, Kensington and the notoriously rough Campbell Bunk, Islington – Mayne suggested in his provocative 1993 book *The Imagined Slum*, that 'Slums are myths. They are constructions of the imagination.' By which he did not mean that real people did not subsist in real and objectively wretched conditions, but 'to discuss slums is to deal with words, with discourse, with signs, and with the concepts they communicated, rather than with the social geography of the inner cities'.[46]

The slum was more of an idealised construct than codified material reality and Mayne suggests that the typology of slumland provided the intellectual kindling for just the sort of radical, surgical clearance – or 'improvement' or 'Haussmannisation' – which both Engels and Mike Davis condemn. In a study of late-Victorian slum-clearance projects Mayne argues that the dominant discourse of slumland (a description which working-class residents themselves rarely subscribed to) was an essential prerequisite to the regeneration projects. 'The imagined slum does therefore connect to spatial and social forms in so far as its stereotype fed into schemes of slum clearance and "city improvement", which in the nineteenth century began massively to intrude upon the actual conditions of working-class life in those inner-city communities to which the term *slum* was applied.'[47]

And surely this codification of slumland was exactly the strategy Engels was engaged with in *The Condition of the Working Class*? For his own ideological reasons – to prove the Feuerbachian case of dehumanisation – Engels created an idealised notion of depravity, amorality and sullen proletarian hopelessness in the dark heart of Manchester. His was not the late-nineteenth-century model of 'slumming', which was often as much about self-formation (or self-gratification) as class contact, but a codified, philosophical crafting of the urban environs.[48] Ignoring much of the differing spatial forms, economic stratification and social conditions within Cottonopolis, his was a city of the mind

---

[46] Alan Mayne, *The Imagined Slum* (Leicester, 1993), p. 1. See also Jennifer Davis, 'Jennings' buildings and the Royal Borough' in David Feldman and Gareth Stedman Jones (eds), *Metropolis – London: Histories and Representations since 1800* (London, 1989); Jerry White, *Campbell Bunk – The Worst Street in London Between the Wars* (London, 1986).

[47] Mayne, *Imagined Slum*, p. 4.

[48] See Seth Koven, *Slumming. Sexual and Social Politics in Victorian London* (Woodstock, 2004).

rather than matter. In a pitch-perfect description of Engels's own approach, Mayne describes the slumland stereotype as 'Universal in its application, it subsumed the innermost working-class districts of every city – notwithstanding their diversity of occupations, incomes, ethnic backgrounds and household arrangements; and the variations in age, size, and labour and housing markets amongst cities – into one all-embracing concept of an outcast society'.[49] Of course, neither Engels nor his discourse can accept any blame for the ensuing 'improvements' which scythed through Manchester, Glasgow, Birmingham and London in the 1870s and 1880s (about which he was, as a resident of the capital, surprisingly quiet), as *The Housing Question* was published to a small readership in Leipzig and the *Condition* didn't gain a British publisher until the 1890s. Nor was he responsible for the colonial civic projects of the 1900s. Nonetheless, his codification of the Victorian city, Mayne's work suggests, rather than providing an objective overview of Britain's 'great towns', was itself part of a class-based polemical literature which helped to distort understanding of nineteenth-century urban life with profound consequences for urban planning in Britain and around the world.

Intriguingly, in the light of Engels's self-proclaimed materialist ambitions, the response of Alan Mayne and a new generation of social geographers towards the nineteenth-century slumland stereotype is now to argue for a 'material turn' in approaching the Victorian city. By working with archaeologists uncovering the everyday artefacts of the urban poor, they seek to focus not on the idealised discourse of slums, rookeries and middens, but the actual lived experiences of nineteenth-century city dwellers as evinced through the remnants of their material goods. It is hoped that such an historical archaeology of slumland will provide an ethnography of place returning some form of human agency to the kind of voiceless, *lumpenproletariat* whom Engels encountered (or created) in the *Condition*. Indeed, in a specific study of 'the Crofts' district of Victorian Sheffield – which Engels, on the basis of various Royal Commission reports, airily dismissed as a sink of immorality – historian Paul Belford has sought to get beyond the caricature to reveal the differing communities, the economic resourcefulness and the carefully planned nature of the 'slum'.[50] 'To call life in these places "hell" makes impossibly remote the social contexts that shaped the data we study', Mayne concludes. 'It denies the individual and collective

[49] Mayne, *Imagined Slum*, pp. 1–2.
[50] See Paul Belford, 'Work, space and power in an English industrial slum: "the Crofts", Sheffield, 1750–1850' in Alan Mayne and Tim Murray (eds), *The Archaeology of Urban Landscapes* (Cambridge, 2001).

strategies by which neighbours and communities maximized circum-
scribed life chances, and pursued goals other than those legitimized by
hegemonic cultural determinants.'[51] As a card-carrying progressive,
Mayne likes to blame bourgeois reformers for this noxious process of
cultural condescension, but Engels the high-bourgeois millocrat might
seem equally to blame.

IV

Today, the forces of Haussmann grind on with remarkable similarity to
the mid-nineteenth century. Of course, the language has changed: policy-
makers talk now of 'sink estates' rather than 'slums', of 'worklessness' and
'the underclass' rather than 'the residuum', while the forces of progress
come in the form of New Deal for Communities, Neighbourhood
Renewal Strategies or Housing Market Renewal Funds. Does the Engels
template of spatial power relations provide any substantive critique of the
current transformation of the post-industrial city? Indeed it does, as the
analytical paradigm of choice for Anglo-American social geographers
today is the 'do(ugh)nut city', which typically also means different things
on different sides of the Atlantic. The American donut refers to the post-
industrial trend of a thinning out of the urban core to create a ring of high-
end suburban estates, out-of-town malls and freeway-dependent public
infrastructure which leaves a dangerous and deserted down-town increasingly inhabited by an often racially based, welfare-dependent populace.
By contrast, the British doughnut is all about jam in the middle: a publicly
funded process of city centre regeneration, often based around a mixed-
use economy of heritage, leisure, retail and high-end apartments ('loft
living'), which leaves an inner-suburban ring of usually council-based
housing estates disconnected from down-town gentrification.

So while city centre Manchester glistens amidst a revitalised historic
core, glitzy bars and restaurants, high-rise Hilton hotels and buy-to-let
penthouse investments, it is said that the communities of Moss Side and
Gorton have failed to benefit. The spatial form of the post-industrial
city, with an employment structure based around tourism, services,
retail and education, eerily begins to echo its industrial forebear. In the
judgement of Manchester sociologist Rosemary Mellor, 'This reclam-
ation of the city centre for a lifestyle whose motifs are boats (on
the Irwell), bars and bistros, supplemented by boutiques and balls (in
St. Ann's Square) is typical of city centres throughout the developed
economies ... The peculiarities of Manchester are the scale of the

---

[51] Mayne, *Imagined Slum*, p. 3.

poverty-belt enveloping the urban playground.'[52] There are still breezy heights for the bourgeoisie, there is still a shutting out of the thoroughfares, and there is still concealment. The same is true of Liverpool, where public resentment at the 'Gold Zone' regeneration of down-town Liverpool is palpable in the outlying communities of Croxteth and Norris Green and plans for the M62 'urban boulevard' into the city centre (involving the demolition of some 400 homes) comes complete with Haussmannesque indifference to local residents. While the historic core shimmers, the outer urban girdle experiences the familiar arrogance of civic aggrandisement.

And so too in London. The visible triumph of capitalism can rarely hide its ordure for long: alongside today's Canary Wharf of investment bankers and corporate lawyers, of City Airport shuttles and Olympic villages, there lurks the outcast London of Tower Hamlets and Whitechapel, child poverty and radical Islam. Reified and homogenised, improved and regenerated, the Victorian cityscape as economic entity and ideological construct lingers on. Yet amidst the heritage trails, cosy psycho-geography and the 2012 'World in One City' boosterism which suffuses the modern East End, no one has the power, incisiveness and passion (as Marx said of Engels) to take on the spatial hegemony of the 'money aristocracy'. In post-industrial Manchester and post-imperial London, the hypocritical gaze which, for all his simplifications, Friedrich Engels so brilliantly elucidated, still manages to codify, conceal and even dictate the urban edifice.

---

[52] Rosemary Mellor, 'Hypocritical city – cycles of urban exclusion', in Jamie Peck and Kevin Ward (eds), *City of Revolution: Restructuring Manchester* (Manchester, 2002), at p. 217.

7   The decline of institutional reform in nineteenth-century Britain

Jonathan Parry

If Richard Cobden, John Stuart Mill or any other rationally inclined mid-Victorian liberal writer were to inspect the state of England 150 years after their heyday, they would surely be surprised to find the country still in possession of a hereditary monarchy, an Established Church, and a socially well-entrenched army and diplomatic service. Surprised rather than astonished, since Cobden and Mill both lamented the continuation of *ancien régime* elements of English political practice into their own day, so could appreciate their tenacity. Nonetheless, Victorian radicals attached so much importance to the reform of the institutions of state, and could look back on a recent period of such significant activity in all these fields, that the rapid waning of emphasis on institutional reform would probably strike them as a major discontinuity.

The purpose of this chapter is to explain that declining emphasis, in the light of radicals' earlier focus on the subject. Quarrels about the power, accountability and cost of the Crown – that is, the monarch, the monarch's ministers, and the officers appointed by government, at home and in the diplomatic service – have long been recognised to be central to politics in the 'long eighteenth century', to 1832, and have been well covered by historians.[1] But their aftermath has been studied much less. Moreover, though there are useful treatments of particular episodes in the reform of the Crown, and the associated institutions of the army and the Church, during the post-1832 period, important connections between the several reform processes have not been made. This chapter argues that interest waned not because the institutions concerned were successfully reformed, but rather because a certain amount of superficial reform was accompanied by a much more

---

[1] P. Harling, *The Waning of 'Old Corruption': The Politics of Economical Reform in Britain, 1779–1846* (Oxford, 1996); J. R. Breihan, 'William Pitt and the commission on fees, 1785–1801', *Historical Journal*, 27, (1984), pp. 59–81; J. R. Dinwiddy, 'The "influence of the crown" in the early nineteenth century: a note on the opposition case', *Parliamentary History*, 4, (1985), pp. 189–200.

significant shift in perceptions of the legitimacy of the state. Between 1820 and 1870 the influence of vested interests in the state seemed to decline enormously. The key to understanding changing Victorian attitudes to the major national institutions lies not in the history of each of those institutions but in the evolution of views about the representativeness of the political regime as a whole. Much of the political controversy in this period arose on issues that involved the question of the fairness, accountability and inclusiveness of the British polity – something that Gareth Stedman Jones himself showed to be a Chartist preoccupation in his pioneering essay on the language of Chartism.[2] Institutional reform was important when it was a proxy for this discussion, but once radical indignation at the polity waned, the movement to tackle the remaining institutional shortcomings lost crucial momentum. In fact there was increasing political mileage instead in defending institutions and celebrating their representativeness. This process was part of a broader change in the tone of politics after 1867. The pursuit of disinterestedness and state neutrality increasingly gave way to a recognition of the legitimate role played by interests in the political process.

Party and the decline of 'Old Corruption', 1780–1850

Between 1780 and 1835, 'Old Corruption' was a major political issue because it touched on a question of the greatest significance: whether the executive could be trusted to act more or less disinterestedly on the nation's behalf, or whether it was a mere selfish collection of vested interests, of dubious legitimacy. In and outside Parliament there was enormous criticism of the extent of Crown patronage, which was allegedly being used to buy support at Westminster and keep corrupt and unpopular governments in power. After the Napoleonic Wars, opposition and independent MPs made it a priority to demand cuts in taxes and the reduction of the wartime bureaucracy. Extra-parliamentary radicals compiled lists of sinecures and other abuses, most famously John Wade's *Black Book* of 1820.[3] Cartoonists had a field day lampooning the extravagance and gluttony of George IV, as a symbol of the greed and selfishness of a monstrously overweight political regime.

From the days of Pitt the Younger, however, government had a retort to these criticisms. Pitt claimed to govern on behalf of the king but also the nation; that was why he deliberately eschewed party and

---

[2] G. S. Jones, *Languages of Class: Studies in English Working Class History, 1832–1982* (Cambridge, 1983), p. 178.
[3] On Wade, see Harling, *Waning*, pp. 143–148.

associated himself with the cause of economical reform, working to make the government fitter for purpose and less burdensome to taxpayers. In the 1780s he worked to balance budgets and tackled administrative inefficiency and sinecurism, though the needs of war later undid much of this work. Lord Liverpool continued this focus, and the central claim of the 'Liberal Tory' ministers of the 1820s was that they had demonstrated the unfairness of the 'Old Corruption' label by abolishing thousands of public offices, by abandoning the property tax in 1816 and patronage powers over customs posts in 1821, and by moving towards a tax burden that was fairer between different types of taxpayer and less unfavourable to commerce. Moreover, they suggested that they could govern the state more fairly and more efficiently than opposition MPs who talked about abstractions like liberty which were not in real danger in order to disguise their own vested interest, which was to shake up the system of representation in order to take power for themselves. After all, the opposition Whigs' embrace of the idea of party suggested that they were a faction seeking control of patronage for their own supporters, many of whom formed a close-knit aristocratic cousinhood. Significantly, the opposition charge about the excessive direct political power of the Crown was abandoned in the 1820s under this Liberal Tory onslaught. Dunning's famous motion of 1780, that the influence of the Crown was too great, had no outings in the Commons after 1822; it now looked too much like Whig hot air.[4] The break-up of the Tory regime in 1829–1830 and the establishment of a new 'Reform' coalition in November 1830 suggests that the question of Crown power was no longer potent enough to act as the dividing line between government and opposition.

Notwithstanding the Liberal Tory reforms, public determination to check official extravagance and other tax burdens flared up again at times of economic crisis. The depression of 1829–1830 prompted frequent calls for less government spending and for the purging of lazy officeholders – the latter mood reflecting also an evangelical anxiety for political purification, most evident in the increasing urgency of the lobby for the abolition of slavery in British colonies. The Reform government responded in dramatic style, changing the terms of political debate. Its coalition status transcended party and marginalised the Tories who opposed it. The 1832 Reform Act improved the accountability of government by its assault on the nomination boroughs and on electoral corruption; the abolition of slavery and the Irish reforms seemed to

---

[4] J. M. Bourne, *Patronage and Society in 19th Century England* (London, 1986), p. 21.

demonstrate a new responsiveness to public pressure; and there was renewed zeal for official economy. Diplomatic service spending, for example, was moved from the civil list and put under parliamentary control. In 1835 expenditure reached a low for the century, helped by a very cautious foreign policy. The 1834 Select Committee on sinecures could hardly find any remaining, while the 1834 Poor Law satisfied cheese-paring ratepayers and the 1835 Municipal Corporations Act was designed to establish ratepayer faith in the representativeness of urban local government.

The Whigs who led the Reform government also turned their attention to the army and the Church, which many saw as informally affiliated to the old Tory regime through family networks and self-interest. In the long-drawn-out Reform crisis of 1830–1832, there had been much radical criticism of the Tory leanings of the Church, manifest in the bishops' overwhelming opposition to the Reform Bill in the Lords, and evangelical attacks on its bloated and complacent internal state. The leading Whig ministers valued both institutions as agencies of social and moral order, but were conscious of their political bias and feared their power if not subordinated to the state. Therefore they asserted the control of the Reformed parliament over them, claiming that parliament now represented the national interest and should be able to redistribute the resources of these national institutions to national benefit. A Royal Commission of 1832 paved the way for a series of measures reducing inequalities in episcopal salaries, suppressing some offices and redistributing capitular property; tithes were commuted in 1836; then in 1839 the government asserted its intention to interfere in the Church's elementary schools. The greatest set-piece political battle of the 1830s was fought over the principle of parliamentary appropriation of the surplus revenues of the Church of Ireland. But these threats to the independence of the Church contributed to a large-scale Tory reaction, while their tendencies to Erastianism displeased religious radicals. Howick's proposed army reforms of 1837, centralising the army's civil administration under the control of a cabinet minister, were too contentious to implement: Wellington and other Tories charged that they increased Whig patronage powers to an unconstitutional degree.[5] Tories and radicals similarly defeated the government's attempt to give a generous annuity to the foreigner

---

[5] H. Strachan, *Wellington's Legacy: The Reform of the British Army 1830–1854* (Manchester, 1984), pp. 249–254; J. S. Omond, *Parliament and the Army, 1642–1904* (Cambridge, 1933), p. 77.

Prince Albert on his marriage to the partisan Queen Victoria at the depth of the economic depression in 1840.[6]

Meanwhile the Whigs' activist social policy required new forms of patronage: the Poor Law, prison, schools and factory reforms all involved the appointment of inspectors and other civil servants to ensure their implementation, and allowed opponents to paint the government as repressive of popular and local liberties.[7] Palmerston's liberal foreign policy was also increasingly ambitious and expensive. All in all, and particularly in the context of a severe economic depression after 1838, Whiggery failed to maintain the disinterested image that government had enjoyed in the early 1830s. This is not surprising, since though Whigs believed in public service, popular engagement and parliamentary scrutiny of institutions, they were never entirely comfortable with the rhetoric of disinterestedness. After all, the Reform Act itself was based on the representation of interests, while Whiggery was essentially a creed about virtuous and active leadership in state and Church. Whigs believed that party competition, targeted state expenditure and a civilised patronage culture were all important ways of ensuring good government by right-minded men.[8]

The fall of the Whigs in 1841 allowed Peel to continue the Liberal Tory strategy of the 1820s, demonstrating by rigour and efficiency in financial administration that the Conservatives understood the practical needs of taxpayers and of commercial interests. The Peelite approach focused on humdrum financial and administrative competence and on restricting expenditure, not least on foreign and defence policy. Peel believed that good government, avoiding Whig concessions to radical factions in parliament, and offering a hard-headed understanding of national economic needs based on official statistics and fair-minded common sense, would provide the best chance of rescuing the economy from depression. Furthermore, reductions in indirect taxes (tariffs, culminating in Corn Law repeal in 1846) and eventually in direct ones (income tax) would demonstrate the fairness of the state better than the Whigs' organic constitutional and institutional reforms. In the Liberal Tory tradition, party was merely to be

[6] R. Williams, *The Contentious Crown: Public Discussion of the British Monarchy in the Reign of Queen Victoria* (Aldershot, 1997), p. 91: they got it reduced from £50,000 p.a. to £30,000.

[7] Bourne, *Patronage*, pp. 25–26; Harling, *Waning*, pp. 208–216.

[8] For Russell's opposition to open competition in the civil service as 'republican', see J. Parry, 'Whig monarchy, Whig nation: Crown, politics and representativeness, 1800–2000' in A. Olechnowicz (ed.), *The Monarchy and the British Nation, 1780 to the Present* (Cambridge, 2007), at p. 54.

instrumental to the pursuit of good national government, rather than an end in itself – but this cavalier treatment of his party ended in Peel's fall from power.

In retrospect, these Liberal Tory and Whig strategies greatly improved the image of the state. However, it was still natural, at moments of economic crisis, for radical criticism to surface – aided by a continuing evangelical anxiety about political purification in the 'age of atonement'. Most radicals remained instinctively sympathetic to 'Old Corruption' rhetoric and suspicious of expenditure which seemed to threaten liberties or favour particular classes or interests. It was easy for them to charge that Tories were fundamentally defenders of the *ancien régime* and that Whigs remained an aristocratic faction interested only in creating jobs for their friends. Between 1847 and 1850, with the Continent in turmoil and both main parties in disarray at home, radical MPs launched a series of demands for institutional reform which at the time seemed as vehement as in the previous great political crisis of 1829–1831. Many northern nonconformists took up the cause of separation of Church and state, prompted by dislike of the Whigs' financial support for religion in Britain and Ireland. Parliament forced the Whigs to present several budgets in the crisis year of 1848; in the same year the Financial Reform Association was founded in Liverpool urging an end to all indirect taxes and attacking extravagance, the pension list, and army and aristocratic 'drones'.[9] In 1849 Cobden proposed a ten per cent cut in salaries of higher officials, and in 1850 he used the Select Committee on Official Salaries to propose sweeping reductions in diplomatic representation and remuneration, including the downgrading of Britain's two remaining embassies, at Paris and Constantinople, to the status of first-class missions. In May 1849 Osborne and Hume agitated for army reform, and a committee of 1850 urged the implementation of Howick's 1837 report to 'consolidate, economize, and simplify the Civil Administration of the Army'.[10] It was in this context that Charles Trevelyan, Secretary of the Treasury, began the investigations into civil service organisation that led to the Northcote–Trevelyan Report of 1854. He later admitted that 'the revolutionary period of 1848 gave us a shake, and created a disposition to put our house in order', while Gladstone, who as Chancellor commissioned

---

[9] W. N. Calkins, 'A Victorian free trade lobby', *Economic History Review*, 13, (1960), pp. 90–104.

[10] R. A. Jones, *The British Diplomatic Service 1815–1914* (Gerrards Cross, 1983), pp. 97–99; Strachan, *Wellington's Legacy*, pp. 255–257.

the report in 1853, saw it, in classic Peelite terms, as a superior alternative to parliamentary reform.[11]

However, as several scholars have suggested, the 1848–1851 period was a major watershed in British history, in which the 'Old Corruption' argument finally lost its potency. On the political stage, there was a cathartic and high-profile renunciation of both old Toryism and old Whiggery in favour of a more open style associated particularly with Palmerston. Thereafter, the combination of free trade, low taxes and the decline of the patronage culture meant that it was increasingly difficult to find examples of state economic bias as between classes or interests. The feebleness of the party system, the vigour of parliament and the populism of Palmerston's foreign policy all gave the lie to talk of an overpowering executive. Britain's escape from the revolutions that blighted the Continent in 1848 seemed to demonstrate the accountability of the system and the extent of popular confidence in it. Palmerston's system married attractive parts of the Liberal Tory and Whig traditions, helped by Gladstone's fiscal rigour as Chancellor and the introduction of limited competition in the civil service. This Liberal coalition was so broad and national that it hardly qualified as a party at all. 'Pressure from without' was now understood to be a legitimate tactic; it became a truism that Parliament would respond to any coherent and well-argued public campaign. This was all the easier to say because in the relative prosperity of the 1850s there was so little agitation. The maturity of 'public opinion' was a major theme of public discussion in that decade, underlined by the massive success of the Great Exhibition. Prosperity contributed to the waning of apocalyptic evangelical fervour for the immediate purification of national ills; ideas of smooth evolutionary progress increasingly dominated cultural discussion instead.[12] All this adds force to Gareth Stedman Jones's argument that the changing image of the state was responsible for the decline of Chartism, though preferably with a slight adjustment of time period to accommodate the continuing suspicion of the state (and the real vitality of Chartism)

---

[11] *Second Report of the Civil Service Inquiry Commission; with Appendix*, P.P. 1875, xxiii, 451, p. 100; J. Morley, *The Life of William Ewart Gladstone*, 3 vols, (London, 1903), I, pp. 511, 649–650.

[12] For the general point, see M. Daunton, *Trusting Leviathan: The Politics of Taxation in Britain 1799–1914* (Cambridge, 2001); Harling, *Waning*, pp. 255–266; M. Taylor, *The Decline of British Radicalism 1847–1860* (Oxford, 1995); and J. Parry, *The Politics of Patriotism: English Liberalism, National Identity and Europe, 1830–1886* (Cambridge, 2006). For specific arguments on the changing political image of the state, see Parry, pp. 59–73, 172–220; and for the administrative image, Parry, *The Rise and Fall of Liberal Government in Victorian Britain* (New Haven, 1993), pp. 181–183.

until the end of the 1840s.[13] Mismanagement during the Crimean War created a brief but fervent movement for administrative reform, but it is significant that its major parliamentary leaders, Layard, Goderich, Lowe and Bruce, were all in government by 1862 and able to make headway with modest schemes of army reform (Goderich) and education reform (Lowe).

Redefining institutional reform, 1850–1870

Despite this changed climate after 1851, institutional reform did not disappear as a theme, for two reasons. The first was that many aspects of it remained to be tackled. Nearly all the Pittite–Peelite reforms had concerned offices within the domestic administration directly paid for by taxation: here the executive and the taxpayer had a common interest in greater efficiency. There had been much less agreement on areas of state spending which might affect the power and prestige of the country, or other political interests. This was naturally true of the monarchy, a particularly sensitive issue given the official tie between the queen and her ministers. It was also true of the diplomatic service and defence spending. Palmerston in particular attached great importance to maintaining a powerful presence abroad. The government never

---

[13] 'Rethinking Chartism' (Jones, *Languages*, pp. 90–178) was written before recent work on the high politics of the late 1840s and 1850s, and as a result it was forced to pay too much attention to the political changes of earlier years, such as the 1839 Education Act, the 1842 Mines Act, the 1844 Bank Charter Act and the 1847 Ten Hours Act, as well as Corn Law repeal in 1846. Its claim that this legislation undermined Chartists' conviction of the malevolence of the state (pp. 175–178) appears to deny the strength of Chartism in 1848, as well as to exaggerate the importance and popularity of most of those bills. It thus makes the article's overall argument susceptible to attack by those who dispute its underlying rationale. For example, John Saville's *1848: The British State and the Chartist Movement* (Cambridge, 1987) effectively demonstrates the power of Chartism in that year. It is easy to overstate British complacency about political and economic conditions then – as, in my view, is done by L. Mitchell, 'Britain's reaction to the revolutions', in R. J. W. Evans and H. Pogge von Strandmann (eds), *The Revolutions in Europe 1848–1849: From Reform to Reaction* (Oxford, 2000). General confidence in British social stability only took effect slowly over the following couple of years; moreover, the survival and superiority of free trade was in question as late as 1849. An alternative argument would be that Chartism was undermined by growing confidence in free trade from 1850, the decline in the use of the workhouse as prosperity returned, and the Ten Hours Act of 1850 (more effective than that of 1847), as well as the publicity for British liberality vis-à-vis the Continent generated by Palmerston's foreign policy, the loyalty to the British regime manifest in the no-popery agitation of 1850–1851, and more institutional financial support for working men (most of it voluntary). To make such a case would broadly validate Stedman Jones's argument about Chartism as a political discourse, yet still acknowledge the intensity of radical animosity to the regime in 1848.

implemented the major recommendations of Cobden's 1850 Committee. Salary costs were only reduced cosmetically, by paying embassy expenses separately rather than through salaries. The embassies at Paris and Constantinople were not abolished, nor the German missions amalgamated; instead, Vienna, St Petersburg and Berlin were upgraded to embassy status in the early 1860s. A Select Committee report of 1861 led to an increase of expenditure on attachés in an attempt to deal with the problem of their career structure, and this threatened to push diplomatic service expenditure above the ceiling of £180,000 a year agreed in 1832. Palmerston presided over a major increase in defence spending, to pay for the Crimean War, for protection for commerce in Asia and for the cost of outbidding Napoleon's challenge to British naval supremacy in Europe. All this angered Cobden and Bright, who saw diplomatic activity and high defence spending as frauds on the public, giving an illusory sense of protection while increasing the risk of war. Cobdenite radicals continued to demand swingeing reductions in the cost of diplomacy, behind which lay their hope for a less active foreign policy, which seemed finally to be becoming a reality in the mid-1860s.

There was even less agreement on the reform of the army or the Church, because they were only semi-affiliated to the state and all discussions of change raised the awkward prospect that it might increase state power for ill. One key aim of army reformers was that military leaders should be accountable to the civil power, so as to ensure economical expenditure, but this meant boosting the state's patronage powers. Moreover, if the state had too much control of a large and dangerous institution like the army, this threatened liberties. Successive Commanders-in-Chief of the army had used this argument to defend their independence in making appointments and recommending honours. They were helped by their claim to act as the representative of the sovereign: George IV's brother the Duke of York, Commander-in-Chief from 1795 to 1827, had been particularly well placed to make that case, while the Commander-in-Chief from 1856 was Victoria's cousin the Duke of Cambridge. Despite the renewed efforts of radical MPs in 1849–1850, even the setbacks of the Crimean War only brought about minor changes in army administration. Similar tensions bedevilled Church reform. The bulk of Whigs and Liberals took a more or less Erastian view that the Church would be more useful, more tolerant, less unruly and less politically dangerous the more it was brought under the control of the state and made to act like a national body. This was in obvious tension with the views both of orthodox high church Anglicans, who believed that the Church was a distinctively doctrinal body whose traditions and independence must be defended from political meddling, and of Protestant nonconformists who rejected the idea of state Churches as socially divisive, potentially tyrannical, complacent and unchristian – but who also distrusted the catholicising tendencies of a Church dominated by the whims of high churchmen.[14]

Second, particularly given these ongoing problems, radicals would not abandon their familiar warnings against the influence of over-mighty vested interests. Their criticism of institutional inefficiency, bias and extravagance was ingrained, as the flurry of activity in 1855 over the Administrative Reform Association showed. Dickens's contribution to administrative reform, *Little Dorrit* (1856), created standard tropes – the Barnacles and the Circumlocution Office – for generations of satirists of civil service shortcomings.[15] Moreover, one reason for the attractiveness of the institutional reform cry was its class edge. Though couched mainly in constitutional and economical language, the 'Old Corruption' critique expressed anti-aristocratic sentiments that found new outlets in the 1850s and 1860s. By now, the most commonly cited model by radicals seeking institutional change was no longer France, as a result of its periodic instability and Napoleonic tendencies; it was the United States, and to some extent the settler colonies. Like Canada and Australia, the United States seemed to reap all the benefits of the 'English' aptitude for self-government while being more meritocratic and enterprising through lacking Britain's expensive and class-bound institutional and social traditions. It had no Church Establishment or monarchy, and a much smaller diplomatic service. To make Britain's major institutions cheaper and more open, serving national rather than elitist purposes, seemed the natural next step of the radical agenda. Enthusiasts for America such as Dilke, Chamberlain and Herbert were among those who took up the Republican cry in the late 1860s, while Cobden and his disciples held up the cheap, utilitarian American diplomatic service, and its modest entertaining, as a model for Britain.[16]

The Reform drama of the mid-1860s created great momentum behind these radical hopes. After the franchise was extended so dramatically in 1867, there was enormous radical optimism – and establishment alarm – that the reform of government, Church, army and even

---

[14] J. P. Parry, 'Liberalism and liberty' in P. Mandler (ed.), *Liberty and Authority in Victorian Britain* (Oxford, 2006), summarises my longer works on this theme.

[15] See, e.g., C. Marvin, *Our Public Offices* (London, 1879), p. 13 and passim.

[16] In 1850, Sir George Seymour, British minister at Lisbon, clashed swords with the Cobdenites when he told the Select Committee that 'giving dinners is an essential part of diplomacy'. Seymour had no time for American entertaining, complaining that at Lisbon he had only once been invited to the American residence there, 'to tea and to eat some pickled oysters lately arrived from New York': Jones, *Diplomatic Service*, p. 98.

monarchy would be a major theme in the new democratic era. At the
1868 election it was common to point to Cobden's plan of 1848 to
reduce central state expenditure by £10 million back to the 1835 level,
and to rue the fact that instead £10 million had been added since then,
to make £70 million in all. Harvey Lewis, for example, said that at least
£10 million might be taken off taxation 'without impairing the efficiency
of the public service one iota'. This would allow the 'free breakfast
table' – the abolition of the remaining duties on tea, coffee and sugar.
There was much radical talk about democracy and fairness as between
classes: Auberon Herbert claimed that 'the time had at length arrived
when an end must be put to those privileges and exclusions which still
existed as between different classes in this country'.[17] Peter Rylands
adopted the mantle of Cobden in urging expenditure reductions, particularly in the diplomatic service, and secured a Select Committee to
promote his Americanising agenda for it, which sat at length between
1870 and 1872. George Otto Trevelyan continued his father's battle for
administrative reform, launching complaints about army extravagance
and inefficiency, which he blamed largely on the obstructive royal influence of the Duke of Cambridge. Many Liberals felt that Victoria's
continuing behind-the-scenes influence in foreign as well as military
policy sat ill with the logic of 1867 that popularly elected institutions
should determine policy. A number of MPs criticised the cost and utility
of the monarchy, all the more so because of the queen's invisibility and
the Prince of Wales's involvement in the Mordaunt divorce case in
1869.[18] Radical candidates portrayed the Irish bishops and clergy as
overpaid and underworked, 'effete and unproductive', defrauding taxpayer and people and creating great resentment at the British state
among the Irish. Gladstone's attack on the Church Establishment in
Ireland was the main theme of the 1868 election, and many Liberal
candidates explicitly opposed all new endowments of religion, arguing
that it was an outdated and immoral policy to give taxpayers' money to
particular religious vested interests in order to pacify them. Liberals also
pointed to Canada, Australia, Scotland and Italy, where voluntary
churches were thriving. A number of candidates pledged to remove
Anglican bishops from the Lords as a first step towards disestablishment
in England.[19] The abolition of Church rates, the English Established
Church's last burden on the ratepayer, in the 1868 parliamentary session

---

[17] *The Times*, 6 November 1868, p. 7, 5 November 1868, p. 3.
[18] Parry, 'Whig monarchy', pp. 60–61.
[19] *The Times*, 2 November 1868, pp. 7–8 (Moffatt, Muntz), 6 November 1868, p. 7
(Potter) and others.

seemed a clear sign of the future. These developments alarmed Anglicans; the formation of the Charity Organisation Society, in 1869, was an attempt to provide an alternative structure for urban philanthropy in view of the apparently imminent attack on the Church of England.[20] Reformers also pressed for government to open up the historic Anglican educational institutions – the universities and the endowed schools – in order to ensure that their endowments were applied to national purposes rather than merely denominational or local ones. To this end, an Endowed Schools Commission was set up in 1869 and university religious tests were abolished in 1871.[21]

However, a different response was also possible to the far-reaching franchise extension of 1867 – one that ultimately predominated. The absorption of so many working men in the constitution, on top of free trade and low taxation on all classes, suggested that the victory had already been gained: the state was now in popular ownership. The radical tribune John Bright announced in 1868 that power 'has been given henceforth and for ever to the people . . . we have no longer charges to bring against a selfish oligarchy; . . . we no longer feel ourselves domineered over by a class . . . the responsibility of the future must rest with the great majority of the people'.[22] Similarly, Edward Baines and Edward Miall, the leaders of the long-standing nonconformist campaign against state involvement in elementary education, renounced their opposition in late 1867 on the grounds that the state had passed into popular hands.[23] Until the 1860s few government ministers had sat for popular constituencies and even fewer had held themselves to account annually in front of a large body of electors: when the radical Foreign Office minister Henry Layard did so with frank speeches at Southwark, from 1861, there was a good deal of approving press comment that it was now possible to be 'at once a placeman and a patriot'.[24] In 1868 Gladstone ascended to the premiership validated by a major speaking campaign. The phrase 'the people's William' began as a Tory sneer at his populism, around 1866, but within a few years became a badge of pride.[25] Gladstone's focus on Irish Church disestablishment at the 1868 election resonated with radicals because it seemed to

[20] M. J. D. Roberts, 'Charity disestablished? The origins of the Charity Organisation Society revisited, 1868–1871', *Journal of Ecclesiastical History*, 54, (2003), pp. 40–61.

[21] Parry, *Rise and Fall*, pp. 228, 264.   [22] *The Times*, 6 November 1868, p. 5.

[23] Parry, *Politics of Patriotism*, p. 118.

[24] *Daily Telegraph*, 5 December 1864, editorial; see Layard, *The Times*, 22 November 1861, p. 10.

[25] For Tory criticism see *Caledonian Mercury*, 6 July 1866, *Bristol Mercury*, 27 April 1867, *Manchester Times*, 27 April 1867, *North Wales Chronicle*, 4 May 1867.

recognise the importance of the majority will in Ireland and the need to counter the destructive consequences of state bias towards minority religious interests.

Gladstone in fact retained a Peelite determination to fight the battle against 'Old Corruption' by continually demonstrating the fairness and neutrality of the state. This was clear from his other major campaigning focus: the need for a purer and more economical approach to government spending than Disraeli and his sectional Conservatives had managed. Liberals claimed that there was a direct contrast between a popular government, resting on the strength of an electoral majority, and a minority one which, lacking that support, had necessarily to rest on the attachment of cliques and vested interests. Jobbery stemmed directly from lack of popular confidence; conversely mass involvement after 1867 would end reliance on a patronage system once and for all. 'Corruption on a grand scale ... was the only chance by which Mr Disraeli could keep in'.[26] The army and navy were singled out for criticism and Gladstone flagged up the need for major spending cuts on them. Defence expenditure fell from £27.1m to £21.1m between 1867/1868 and 1869/1870. Moreover, in 1870 Gladstone's government made two administrative changes which were designed to show that vested interest politics had ended. The introduction of competitive examinations across almost the whole civil service put the last nail in the coffin of 'Old Corruption' by removing the Treasury's vestigial remaining patronage powers. Meanwhile, the civil government definitively and boldly asserted its control over the military administration. The Horse Guards, the seat of the power of the royal Commander-in-Chief, were moved to Pall Mall and placed within the War Office bureaucracy, which was restructured into three large divisions. The large franchise extension of 1867, and the concern to control military spending, seemed finally to have overcome traditional radical hesitations about giving the state control over such a large military machine. But both changes reflected the concerns of Gladstone and like-minded ministers Lowe and Cardwell rather than any great popular pressure: both were effected by Orders in Council rather than legislation, in order to uphold the tradition that such matters were dealt with internally rather than through parliamentary lobbying. In fact Lowe's civil service reforms were designed to create a stronger, more efficient and disinterested service that would be more immune from sectional popular pressures, which he loathed.

[26] Labouchère, *The Times*, 3 November 1868, p. 5, Brodrick, *The Times*, 4 November 1868, p. 8, Miall, *The Times*, 5 November 1868, p. 3.

Moreover, it is striking that none of the energetic radical campaigns of 1867–1874 for more far-reaching institutional reform succeeded. Parliamentary motions for English Church disestablishment were introduced in 1871 and 1873, but not subsequently. Fractious army debates dominated the 1871 session, revealing dissatisfaction with the government's limited reforms for the appointment and promotion of officers, but no consensus on alternatives.[27] Rylands's assault on the diplomatic service was neutered by a Foreign Office rearguard defence, by Whig and Conservative opposition, and by the increasingly gloomy international situation. Extra-parliamentary republican agitation in 1871 was suffocated under the weight of a patriotic press and public reaction in favour of the monarchy, sparked off by the dangerous illness of the Prince of Wales and by alarm at the extent of political extremism on the Continent. None of these issues was ever so prominent in parliamentary debate again. What does this failure tell us about the altered expectations of politics after 1867?

1867 and the new politics

One major consequence of the changed political perspective was to popularise the view that the institutions of state were now clearly national bodies worthy of pride. This was partly because the language of 'Old Corruption' was unsuited to a more democratic era, and partly because of growing foreign rivalry after 1870. An early sign of both developments was the fate of Rylands's attack on the diplomatic service. In May 1871 he wrote a twenty-five-paragraph report for his Committee, based on Cobden's recommendations of 1850. It attacked 'family or political influence' and expenditure on 'receptions, balls, and dinner parties'; it proposed a halt to new attaché appointments for several years followed by the introduction of open examinations; it called for the downgrading of embassies to missions and the restriction of diplomatic salaries; it claimed that a new era of telegraphs, steamboats and railways would put an end to ambassadorial independence and the need for secret meddling diplomacy. But the Committee rejected his recommendations, arguing that the service offered good value for money already, that the international situation justified the present establishment and that the existing system of asking nominated candidates to pass an examination was more suited than open competition to a profession where confidentiality and status was important as well as

---

[27] Parry, *Politics of Patriotism*, pp. 289–291.

intelligence.[28] The row coincided with a defence panic and an awareness that the world was a more dangerous place than in the Cobdenite heyday of the early 1860s. The Franco–Prussian war, the Black Sea crisis and colonial tensions in West Africa led to a reversal of the defence spending cuts of 1868–1870. This made economy a divisive issue for the rest of the Gladstone government, and one on which the Prime Minister was no longer able to rally the party.[29] Cobdenism lost any traction that it possessed as a popular radical cry. When Rylands addressed his constituents at Warrington and boasted that during the Select Committee sittings he alone had asked over 3,000 questions, one heckler shouted 'What a bloody ignorant fellow you must be.'[30] Over time, most radicals also abandoned the Cobdenite cry that high foreign and defence policy expenditure was merely a way of subsidising lazy aristocrats. Instead, in the 1880s their new leaders Dilke and Chamberlain advocated a vigorous defence of British interests abroad, identifying the commercial benefits of this approach and complaining at the effeteness of the Foreign Office tradition for failing to adopt it.[31]

Frequent imperial wars and international disputes in the 1870s and 1880s also transformed the political standing of the army, particularly as a result of unprecedented, excited and patriotic newspaper coverage of the campaigns. They speeded up the change in the army's image that had been under way since the 1850s: much less was now heard of the old radical charge that it was an aristocratic bolt-hole and arm of domestic repression. Limited reforms – the abolition of purchase of commissions in 1871, followed by Childers's regimental territorialisation in the 1880s – probably contributed to this change, but tales of derring-do in far-flung parts of the empire contributed a lot more. Press interest in military vigour, and the difficulty of controlling overseas operations, also helped the army to resist cost-cutting pressure. Gladstone was furious at the drift into the Ashanti War in 1873 and the inability of the Prime Minister and Treasury to prevent it. This episode was also an early demonstration of the danger of the 1870 consolidation of the War Office into one large bureaucracy. The well-informed commentator Clode had

[28] *First Report from the Select Committee on Diplomatic and Consular Services*, P.P. 1871, VII, iii–xxiii.

[29] Parry, *Politics of Patriotism*, pp. 291–293. Note the disillusionment of C. E. Macqueen, Secretary of the Financial Reform Association, to Rylands, 3 May 1871: L. G. Rylands, *Correspondence and Speeches of Mr Peter Rylands, MP, with a Sketch of his Career*, 2 vols, (Manchester, 1890), I, p. 176.

[30] Handwritten memoir, Dilke papers, British Library Add MSS 43931, f.60; for the speech, see Rylands, *Rylands*, II, p. 271, 10 December 1870.

[31] Parry, *Politics of Patriotism*, pp. 365–368.

argued in his book of 1869 that the army would gain too much control over finance if the civil and military departments were united in this way. Would one civilian Cabinet minister be able to resist the influence of so many military men – especially when led by a Commander-in-Chief with such close royal connections? The answer was often 'no'. Trevelyan failed in his campaign to unseat Cambridge, and the queen was able to prevent Childers' reappointment to the War Office in 1886 after his earlier public criticism of the Commander-in-Chief. Even Disraeli felt that this royal axis had too much power over the army.[32]

It was Disraeli's Conservative opposition that gained most from this transformation in perception of the monarchy, army and Church. His high-profile attack on the Gladstone government in 1872 was founded on the claim that an unpatriotic Liberal radicalism was 'assail[ing] or menac[ing] every institution and every interest': the Crown, the Church, the army, the Lords. By-election returns showed that the nation agreed with the Conservatives 'that it is the first duty of England to maintain its institutions, because to them we principally ascribe the power and prosperity of the country'.[33] This argument chimed with growing middle-class anxiety about the defence of traditional social and moral values in the face of what appeared to be the increasing power of democracy at home. The meddling of the Endowed Schools Commission with established local and religious middle-class educational interests was a significant factor in the Conservative revival in London in 1874, and one of Disraeli's first acts, significantly, was to abolish the Commission.[34] Radical nonconformist opposition to the official teaching of religion in state elementary schools, on the grounds of bias and state neutrality, alarmed many centrist Anglicans. At the general elections of 1874 and 1885 the Conservatives were the beneficiaries – and stokers – of a 'Church in danger' furore. Nonconformists, in fact,

---

[32] Ibid., pp. 292–294; C. M. Clode, *The Military Forces of the Crown: Their Administration and Government* (London, 1869); Ponsonby to the queen, 3 February 1886, in G. E. Buckle (ed.), *Letters of Queen Victoria: Third Series . . . between the Years 1886 and 1901*, 3 vols, (London, 1930–1932), I, at p. 42; W. F. Monypenny and G. E. Buckle, *The Life of Benjamin Disraeli Earl of Beaconsfield*, 6 vols, (London, 1910–1920), VI, pp. 473–474.

[33] *Speech of the Right Hon. B. Disraeli MP at the Free Trade Hall, Manchester, April 3, 1872* (London, 1872), pp. 4, 6–7, 21; *Speech of the Right Hon. B. Disraeli MP at the Banquet of the National Union of Conservative and Constitutional Associations, at the Crystal Palace, on Monday, June 24, 1872* (London, 1872), pp. 4–5, 7.

[34] J. P. Parry, *Democracy and Religion: Gladstone and the Liberal party, 1867–1875* (Cambridge, 1986), pp. 311, 380; L. Goldman, 'The defection of the middle class: the Endowed Schools Act, the Liberal Party, and the 1874 election' in P. Ghosh and L. Goldman (eds), *Politics and Culture in Victorian Britain: Essays in Memory of Colin Matthew* (Oxford, 2006).

moderated their calls for disestablishment, while naturally continuing to believe in the spiritual benefits of free churches. Those who had urged a political campaign for it since the 1840s had done so as part of a broader attack on vested interest and patronage politics. From the mid-1870s they had less reason to be suspicious about the religious conduct of the state, for several reasons: elected local authorities now determined the parameters of religious teaching in schools; Conservatives did not play into their opponents' hands by overtly favouring Anglicanism in national policy; and Church patronage was exercised in a way that did not excite party animosity.[35]

The changed political atmosphere not only bolstered the institutions of state; it also altered attitudes to the role of interests in politics. Completely disinterested government of the sort that Gladstone had identified with was soon recognised to be a fiction. Thus, to his obvious surprise, his attempt to rally the electorate in 1874 with the promise of income tax repeal failed in the face of a general understanding that abolition would merely mean imposing taxes on something else, or weakening national defence. Even his attempt to distance himself from patronage politics became problematic. His Chief Whip, George Glyn, complained bitterly about the reduction of Treasury influence over the civil service, mainly because the change removed his daily correspondence with MPs. He (probably unjustifiably) blamed the catastrophic breakdown in party discipline in 1871 on the loss of this influence, while one reason for the establishment of a separate Home Rule party in Ireland in 1870 was the perception that an overly pure British government was no longer paying enough attention to Irish patronage issues.[36] After 1874 Disraeli quixotically reverted to an active personal patronage policy in senior civil service appointments, though this was a demonstration of how old-fashioned he was; most Conservatives had since the 1860s accepted the principle that civil and diplomatic service appointments should be non-partisan.[37] But his successor Salisbury discovered

---

[35] For the complexity of issues bearing on Church appointments, and the constraints on politicians, see D. W. R. Bahlman, 'Politics and Church patronage in the Victorian age', *Victorian Studies*, 22, (1979), pp. 253–296.

[36] E. Hughes, 'Postscript to the Civil Service reforms of 1855', *Public Administration*, 33, (1955), pp. 305–306; H. J. Hanham, 'Political patronage at the Treasury, 1870–1912', *Historical Journal*, 3, (1960), 75–84; Parry, *Politics of Patriotism*, p. 266.

[37] Whereas the minority Conservative governments of 1852 and 1858–1859 had both increased spending on patronage in order to satisfy supporters after the long drought while in opposition, there was a new mood in 1866. This was particularly evident in diplomatic appointments: Stanley, the Foreign Secretary, an advocate of a professional diplomatic service, was the first of his party not to remove any ambassadors on party grounds: Jones, *Diplomatic Service*, pp. 46–48, 147.

a much better way of using patronage to get party political support: the extensive use of the honours system. Under his governments, creations of peerages, baronetcies and knighthoods nearly tripled, and the cash-strapped Liberals quickly adopted the same habits, even selling two peerages for money in 1891.[38] By 1900, the fiction of the patronage-free state had been abandoned.

More generally, now that the state seemed open to so many political pressures from all classes, the activities of special lobby groups did not seem so threatening. A vigorous competition between them was now assumed. The (Birmingham) National Education League battled with the Church's National Education Union for sway over education policy, while the railway interest and chambers of commerce became active influences on commercial policy in the 1880s, often able to modify bills because of their superior grasp of policy details.[39] The ignorance of most civilian MPs about internal army matters dashed hopes that Parliament could effectively decide army policy. This became painfully apparent during high-profile and interminable debates on military flogging in 1879, which Chamberlain had hoped to use to attack aristocratic inhumanity, but which descended into absurdity as most MPs felt the need to defer to military opinion on the topic.[40]

By the 1880s, as its organisation became more democratic, the Liberal Party itself was often seen as a coalition of special interest factions and sections, each with particular policy desires rather than one agreed philosophy.[41] Formalised organisation increased the influence of constituency activists who desired specific changes and who pressed them on MPs and on the National Liberal Federation (NLF). This growth of grass-roots interest in the policy agenda culminated in the controversial Newcastle Programme of 1891, an omnibus package approved by that year's NLF conference, incorporating Irish Home Rule, disestablishment in Wales and Scotland, the local veto on alcohol sales, employers' liability legislation, the establishment of parish and district councils, the abolition of plural voting and other constitutional changes, few of which were desired by a majority of Liberals, let alone a majority of voters.

---

[38] The Conservatives started the practice of promising future honours to rich men who agreed to do political favours for the party when they were in opposition in the early 1880s. See H. J. Hanham, 'The sale of honours in late Victorian England', *Victorian Studies*, 3, (1960), pp. 277–289, including pp. 278–279n for figures on creations.

[39] G. Alderman, *The Railway Interest* (Leicester, 1973); W. G. Hynes, *The Economics of Empire: Britain, Africa and the New Imperialism 1870–1895* (London, 1979).

[40] *The Annual Register: A Review of Public Events at Home and Abroad, for the Year 1879* (London, 1880), pp. 53–65.

[41] D. A. Hamer, *Liberal Politics in the Age of Gladstone and Rosebery: A Study in Leadership and Policy* (Oxford, 1972), ch. 1.

This process allowed Conservatives to charge that they were now the 'national' party and the Liberals a mere gaggle of cliques, beholden to Irish and other agitators. This was a return to the politics of the 1830s, and a reversal of the general perception in the Liberals' mid-Victorian heyday, which probably contributed significantly to the Conservatives' increasing ability to capture former Liberal votes. And ultimately Liberal sectionalism spawned the most significant political interest group of all, the labour movement.

Notwithstanding this suspicion of the *extent* of Liberal factionalism, the most important political development in the post-1867 period was the growing acceptance on both sides of the benefits of party organisation. In the 1870s particularly, some old Liberals and radicals still expressed animosity to the party machine in general, and specific elements of it such as the caucus, which they said undermined the virtuous independence of both the MP and the voter, but these arguments became increasingly rare.[42] From the mid-1880s there was a dramatic increase in the willingness of MPs to support a party line regularly throughout the parliamentary session.[43] Party seemed a necessary element in politicising and disciplining the vast new democracy, but it also allowed discussion of religious and constitutional issues to be conducted in a more orderly way. Nonconformists satisfied their religious tribalism by voting against Tory churchmen and for Liberal candidates who made bland declarations in favour of the principle of disestablishment while knowing that it was not a party priority. Participation in a voting ritual of this sort seemed virtuous in itself; so it was now the election of a Liberal government, and no longer the disestablishment of the Church, that would demonstrate the purity of the political process. Meanwhile, discussions about further parliamentary reform after 1867 were brought within the ambit of the party structures and were increasingly considered in terms of party advantage. In the first half of the century the debates about reform were tense affairs involving serious popular scrutiny of the legitimacy of the state and potentially violent extra-parliamentary agitation, but from the 1860s they were mostly conducted within the expanded party organisations themselves and on a more technical basis – at least until the arrival of the suffragettes. In other words, the battles to purify both the religious and political aspects of the constitution, that for so much of the century had been battles over the basis of the state itself,

---

[42] A. Beattie (ed.), *English Party Politics*, 2 vols, (London, 1970), I, pp. 161–177; Parry, *Rise and Fall*, p. 271.

[43] Hugh Berrington, 'Partisanship and dissidence in the 19th century House of Commons', *Parliamentary Affairs*, 21, (1968), pp. 340–344.

were now fought as tamer struggles for supremacy within the party system. Party, no longer a mere aristocratic faction, now channelled and softened opposing popular opinions, laying the ground for workable compromises between them.

Conclusion

Of course pressure for institutional reform did not disappear completely. Between 1874 and 1880 the Liberals turned the issue of Crown power into the overarching interpretative explanation of what was at fault with the Disraeli government and why it must be removed. They attacked increased defence expenditure and government patronage policy. They made various more or less veiled criticisms of the Queen for her political partisanship and her interference in foreign policy. They claimed that Disraeli had abused executive prerogatives and reverted to an unconstitutional form of government, by his behaviour over the Suez Canal shares, the movement of Indian troops to Malta in 1878, controversial agreements with Turkey and Russia, and the Afghan war. Many Liberal MPs who distrusted the ethos of Disraeli's Foreign Office demanded that parliament should have the right to ratify treaties – as the American Senate did.[44] It was the ability to create a narrative about Disraeli's consistent abuse of Crown power that did most to unite the party while in opposition. But it also followed that the destruction of Beaconsfieldism in 1880 marked a return to normalcy. It was a key element in Gladstone's self-presentation that his government exemplified virtuous constitutional and fiscal practice; further institutional reform hardly seemed a priority. Still, many radicals continued to be vigilant for manifestations of elitist privilege; but it was now an effort, rather than a knee-jerk response, to make a major issue out of them. Rosebery's campaign against the Lords in 1894 should be seen as an attempt by a peer enthusiastic about the moral power of the American democracy to revive the great tradition of Liberal institutional reformism – though it attracted much less party support than he anticipated, and it took massive Conservative provocation before Asquith's Liberal government seriously addressed the issue in 1910–1911. The institutional conservatism of the twentieth-century Labour Party has often been noted, but it is idealistic to think that the transition from Liberal to Labour was responsible for the decline of

---

[44] Parry, *Politics of Patriotism*, pp. 336–339. For Rylands, for example, parliamentary power over treaty-making was logical since 'the sovereign power now rests with the three estates of the realm': Rylands, *Rylands*, II, p. 8.

this style of radicalism, rather than the earlier shifts in priorities and perceptions discussed in this essay.[45]

It has been claimed here that the modest reforms that took place after 1850 were not sufficient to explain the changed image of the major institutions of state. Many traditional practices and biases survived. Competitive examinations gave the public schools and universities a stranglehold over the upper echelons of the civil service, and did not alter the general perception that the service was overstaffed and unimaginative. Queen Victoria and the Duke of Cambridge continued to influence foreign and military policy. Continuing Treasury accusations of army jobbery reflected its inability to rein in the military men.[46] In general Treasury 'control' was a misnomer; civil service departments remained kingdoms unto themselves, and the Treasury's preferred mode of operation was to seek compromise with their powerful ministers.[47] Overall expenditure in 1885 was 32 per cent higher than in 1867, after two full terms of Gladstonian Liberal government; income tax was 8*d* in 1885 against the 6*d* bequeathed by Disraeli in 1880. The Foreign Office continued to evade pressure for cuts in the diplomatic service, while from the 1870s governments began to hold back more information about foreign policy from Parliament. Salisbury as Foreign Secretary and later Prime Minister was the worst offender, but Gladstone himself used pleas of confidentiality more because the world was a more dangerous place and because he wanted to be considerate to foreign powers. As Temperley and Penson pointed out long ago, 'it is literally true to say that as Parliament became more democratic its control over foreign policy declined'.[48] Gladstone, who had a high notion of executive power, was opposed to Parliament's right to ratify treaties and did not grant it after 1880. As for disestablishment, by 1885 it was a second-order issue for radicals. The *Radical Programme* gestured unenthusiastically towards it as a sop to Birmingham nonconformists, but generally downplayed institutional reform, arguing that the Lords, the monarchy and the Church were harmless institutions unless they actually made a nuisance of themselves, and that radicals have 'something else to do than to break butterflies on wheels'. Indeed the

---

[45] B. Jones and M. Keating, *Labour and the British State* (Oxford, 1985); J. R. Vincent, *Pollbooks: How Victorians Voted* (Cambridge, 1967), pp. 49–50.

[46] See Goschen's remarks in 1887: Sir Horace Hamilton, 'Treasury control in the eighties', *Public Administration*, 33, (1955), p. 15.

[47] Maurice Wright, *Treasury Control of the Civil Service, 1854–1874* (Oxford, 1969), ch. 15.

[48] H. W. V. Temperley and L. M. Penson (eds), *A Century of Diplomatic Blue Books, 1814–1914* (Cambridge, 1938), p. ix; H. W. V. Temperley, 'British secret diplomacy from Canning to Grey', *Cambridge Historical Journal*, 6, (1938), p. 1.

Radical Programme even suggestively recognised the validity of the basic Whig argument against disestablishment, that the Church would be a more threatening and politically dangerous corporation if left unchecked by a national parliament.[49] Disestablishment only occurred, belatedly, in Wales, where it was as much a nationalist as a religious concern. By the 1880s, economy was out of fashion, as Rylands and his friends lamented. As early as December 1872 T. B. Potter, another of Cobden's disciples, advised Rylands to drop his attempts at cost-cutting which would 'lead to no great success in political life' and instead take up Cobden's other theme, of the land, a much better way of attacking aristocratic dominance.[50] In 1883 Chamberlain declared that 'social politics' – a politics that involved a much more positive role for the state – was the future.[51]

The main reason for the waning of interest in institutional reform was, rather, the growing acceptance of the notion that politics itself was no longer controlled by an unrepresentative elite, but was open to popular influence. In the first half of the century, suspicion of the elites in control of the state supplied radicalism with a master narrative which could make many individual grievances appear significant and breathe political life into issues which were not always of first-rate importance in themselves. After 1850, and particularly after 1867, that master narrative was no longer available, as attitudes to the state became more complex. Between 1820 and 1870, two elite strategies reformed the image of the polity sufficiently to neuter the radical challenge. The Whig–Liberal tradition of measured constitutional reform did a good deal to improve the representativeness, reputation and remit of Parliament and strengthen popular confidence in the state, while the Liberal Tory tradition succeeded in making the conduct of government efficient and economical enough to appease taxpayers and to encourage the notion that policy was essentially disinterested as between classes and interest groups. These strategies are clearer in retrospect than they were at the time: the actual process of change was usually hesitant, muddled and contested. Nonetheless, the fact that so many politicians identified at some level with these broad approaches to government, and that after 1846 they effectively merged in a broad Liberal coalition, helped to ensure British political stability whenever it was under threat. By the

[49] J. Chamberlain and others, *The Radical Programme* [1885], ed. D. A. Hamer (Brighton, 1971), pp. 39–46, 169.
[50] Rylands, *Rylands*, I, pp. 214, 334.
[51] To Sir Edward Russell, J. L. Garvin, *The Life of Joseph Chamberlain: I: 1836–1885* (London, 1932), p. 384.

late 1860s, British politics seemed so open, and so secure from the pressure of powerful vested interests, that in fact the activities of interest groups and parties, contending in the political market place, became less contentious. Most of all, the process of parliamentary reform strengthened authority. Each of the three big Reform Acts was at some level a response to popular pressure, but each ended by giving government more legitimacy to do what it wanted. The movement to strip the executive of excessive influence was ultimately undone by the passage of the Reform Acts – as most Whigs and Peelites had always wanted. Among the pillars of authority that Whig and Peelite reformism succeeded in strengthening were a constitutional monarchy, an Established Church and the other institutions of state. The survival and increasing popularity of these institutions was due to these political changes much more than to their own behaviour. Within a few years of 1867 those radicals who continued to criticise them appeared no longer patriotic, but rather sectional, selfish or out of touch. This was part of the process whereby the Conservative Party came to steal the patriotic mantle, which did so much to spruce up its fusty undergarments of institutional defence.

British women and cultures of
       internationalism, *c.*1815–1914

Anne Summers

Writing on British women's international interests in the nineteenth century has tended to focus on three areas: pacifism;[1] links between national feminist movements;[2] and the relationship between feminists and women subjects of the British empire, particularly India.[3] Relatively little attention has been paid to women's involvement in the shaping of national foreign policy, where they are usually depicted as either following male politicians and activists or being cultivated (or manipulated) as a particular 'emotional' constituency.[4] This chapter – while not suggesting that male and female internationalisms were at all times separate and distinct – argues that the growth of a movement for sexual equality in this period led many women to develop their own criteria for judging the international issues of the day. Three main case-studies are chosen to explore the development of female internationalism: the Italian unification movement, conflicts between the Ottoman empire and its Christian subjects, and the Boer War of 1899–1902. However, it is also necessary to examine campaigns which might at first sight appear to have little international relevance, and above all to explore

---

[1] See, e.g., Anne Wiltsher, *Most Dangerous Women: Feminist Peace Campaigners of the Great War* (London, 1985); Jill Liddington, *The Road to Greenham Common: Feminism and Anti-Militarism in Britain since 1820* (London, 1989; Syracuse, 1991); Sybil Oldfield, *Women Against the Iron Fist: Alternatives to Militarism 1900–1989* (Oxford, 1989); Jo Vellacott, *Pacifists, Patriots and the Vote: The Erosion of Democratic Suffragism in Britain during the First World War* (Basingstoke, 2007).
[2] See, e.g., Leila J. Rupp, *Worlds of Women: The Making of an International Women's Movement* (Princeton, NJ, 1997); Margaret H. McFadden, *Golden Cables of Sympathy: The Transatlantic Sources of Nineteenth-century Feminism* (Lexington, KY, 1999); Bonnie S. Anderson, *Joyous Greetings: The First International Women's Movement, 1830–1860* (Oxford, 2000).
[3] Antoinette Burton, *Burdens of History: British Feminists, Indian Women and Imperial Culture 1865–1915* (Chapel Hill, 1994).
[4] E. Biagini, *British Democracy and Irish Nationalism* (Cambridge, 2008), ch. 2, extending A. J. P. Taylor's concept of the 'politics of emotionalism', describes this strategy as the 'feminization of Gladstonianism'. See Taylor, *The Troublemakers: Dissent over Foreign Policy 1792–1939* (London, 1957), p. 75.

the religious roots of women's public interventions, in order to understand how their networks of international activism came into being.

If the growth of a movement for female emancipation influenced women's perception of international issues, scandals and controversies in the international arena in their turn inflected the development of a feminist movement. The connections between these currents pose a complex set of questions. Did foreign causes expose the weakness and corruption of male political domination, and suggest ideal or alternative ways of organising society? Did either a Christian formation, or a stress on a maternal and nurturing female identity, predispose women to pacifism? Did a sense of superiority to sisters in foreign climes vitiate a rhetoric of gender equality? The view that the development of the British feminist movement was dependent on the construction of an inferior and colonised female 'Other', bolstering the metropolitan woman's sense of vocation and entitlement to equal citizenship, is currently something of an academic orthodoxy.[5] However, this post-colonial critique risks ignoring the broad spectrum of causes taken up at home and abroad, of which the condition of colonised women was only one,[6] leaving out of account British women's capacity and sense of obligation to identify with suffering womanhood worldwide. It also simplifies the world in which they had to exercise their sympathies and judgement.

Religion and a wider world

At the beginning of our period, Christianity, or more precisely Protestantism, gave most activist British women their perspective on the world. A sense of the urgent duty to proselytise, particularly throughout the empire, linked distant peoples in a network of faith, commitment and often consanguinity. Belief in the Gospels shaped the interpretation of

---

[5] This view, expounded by Burton, has been widely endorsed: see, e.g., Mrinalini Sinha, *Colonial Masculinity: The 'Manly Englishman' and the 'Effeminate Bengali' in the Late Nineteenth Century* (Manchester, 1995), p. 60; Inderpal Grewal, *Home and Harem: Nation, Gender, Empire and the Cultures of Travel* (London, 1996), pp. 60–61; Indira Ghose, *Women Travellers in Colonial India: The Power of the Female Gaze* (Delhi, Oxford, 1998), p. 61; Mrinalini Sinha, Donna Guy and Angela Woollacott (eds), *Feminisms and Internationalism* (Oxford, 1999), p. 11; Ian Christopher Fletcher, Laura E. Nym Mayhall and Phillipa Levine (eds), *Women's Suffrage in the British Empire: Citizenship, Nation and Race* (London, 2000), pp. 18–19; Philippa Levine, *Prostitution, Race, and Politics: Policing Venereal Disease in the British Empire* (New York/London, 2003), p. 194; Christine Bolt, *Sisterhood Questioned? Race, Class and Internationalism in the American and British Women's Movements, c.1880s–1970s* (London, 2004), p. 14.

[6] Arabella Shore, for example, a feminist whose concerns over 'the Eastern question' are noted later, deplored her compatriots' indifference to Indian affairs: *Journal of the National India Association*, September 1882, pp. 506–515.

news from afar and made it intelligible to contemporaries – frequently in ways which the present-day reader may find hard to understand or take seriously. What happened on the other side of the world was of absorbing interest in Britain, not just as a matter of current affairs, but as a portent of the world to come.

Christianity was also women's main vehicle for activity outside the private realm. The home was idealised as the arena for moral and religious exercises;[7] however, where the Church could supply a platform for public life, and religion provide its justification, domestic virtues could be taken out of doors with relatively little difficulty. While the leading roles of Quaker and Unitarian women are reminders that the term 'church' can be applied very broadly, the form of Protestantism embodied by the Church of England constituted the established national church; its parishes were both pastoral and secular units of administration. This gave the public actions and utterances of its women members particular validation. Thus the celebrated evangelical writer and educationist Hannah More 'took that lively interest in the public secular affairs of her country that Jeremiah and Ezekiel did of old, and on the same plain ground that where the state professes to be modelled and the executive to act on principles of God's instilling . . . nothing done by the state can be indifferent to the church or unworthy the anxious watchful regard of Christians'[8]. The statement was as applicable to events overseas as to those nearer the parish pump.

From the late 1780s to the late 1830s, the chief cause challenging British Christians to claim the oppressed Other as their fellow was the abolition of slavery, in the first instance in the plantations of the Caribbean. The echoes of this campaign, in which Quaker women played a particularly prominent role, resonated through nineteenth-century reforming projects and liberal communities: in the movement for prison reform; in the response to the outbreak of Civil War in the United States; above all, in the campaign for the repeal of the Contagious Diseases Acts. Abolitionism introduced British women to their first international organisation other than a religious community – albeit

---

[7] Within an immense literature, see Martha Vicinus (ed.), *Suffer and be Still: Women in the Victorian Age* (Bloomington, IN, 1972), and *A Widening Sphere: Changing Roles of Victorian Women* (Bloomington, IN, 1977); Leonore Davidoff and Catherine Hall, *Family Fortunes: Men and Women of the English Middle Class 1780–1850* (London, 1987); Anne Summers, *Female Lives, Moral States: Women, Religion and Public Life in Britain, 1800–1930* (Newbury, 2000), ch. 1, reviews discussion up to publication date.

[8] *Personal Recollections By Charlotte Elizabeth* [Charlotte Elizabeth Phelan, afterwards Tonna (1790–1846)] (London, 1841), p. 211; for the latest scholarship on More (1745–1833), see the *Oxford Dictionary of National Biography* (henceforth *ODNB*).

one based on religious principles.[9] A celebrated feminist turning-point was reached in London in 1840, when seven American women delegates to the World Anti-Slavery Convention were barred from taking their seats. This galvanised the women concerned into agitating for the equal rights of American women, and radicalised British women such as the Quaker Anne Knight.[10]

However, a feminist critique was always inherent in the abolitionist cause, even though, as Clare Midgley has shown, women's anti-slavery propaganda contained elements of condescension and 'maternalism'.[11] Protestant opposition to slavery was based on the concept that the individual soul must be free to seek its own salvation and reconciliation with God. This was impossible where the body was so restrained that the individual could take no responsibility for her or his actions. Women brought to this critique a particular emphasis on the sexual abuse of female slaves or prisoners, who were liable to be forced into a state of sexual immorality. Historians of feminist thought have noted the influence of John Stuart Mill's *On the Subjection of Women*, which linked the institutions of slavery and marriage;[12] but – not least because many leading emancipationists were married – this linkage was to be much less powerfully internalised than that between slavery and prostitution.

In the campaigns of the feminist and Christian Josephine Butler against the state registration of prostitutes, a measure presaged by the Contagious Diseases Acts, this critique received its most explicit and feminist formulation. Under this legislation, women were 'continually passing from the state of freemen into the state of slavery'.[13] In speaking for prostitute women, Butler intended to demonstrate that all women were implicated in the dynamic of sexual oppression: 'the slave now speaks. The enslaved women have found a voice in one of themselves.'[14]

---

[9] See essays in Parts One and Three of Christine Bolt and Seymour Drescher, (eds), *Anti-Slavery, Religion and Reform* (Folkestone, 1980).

[10] Christine Bolt, *The Women's Movements in the United States and Britain from the 1790s to the 1920s* (Hemel Hempstead, 1993), p. 68; Bonnie Anderson, *Joyous Greetings*, p. 13; Jill Liddington, *Road to Greenham* (Syracuse, 1991), p. 16.

[11] Clare Midgley, *Women against Slavery: the British Campaigns 1780–1870* (London/New York, 1992).

[12] Laura E. N. Mayhall, 'The rhetorics of slavery and citizenship: suffragist discourse and canonical texts in Britain, 1880–1914', *Gender & History*, 13(3), (2001), pp. 481–497, at p. 486. See also S. Pedersen, 'The maternalist moment in British colonial policy; the controversy over "child slavery" in Hong Kong 1917–1941', *Past & Present*, 171, (2001), pp. 161–202, at p. 181.

[13] Josephine Butler, *The Constitution Violated* (Edinburgh, 1871), p. 10.

[14] G. and L. Johnson (eds), *An Autobiographical Memoir of Josephine Butler* (Bristol, 1928), p. 113, quoting Butler's letter to Aimé Humbert of 1875. On the anti-Contagious Diseases Acts campaign, see Judith R. Walkowitz, *Prostitution and Victorian Society:*

Significantly, when she took her campaign against registration to Europe in 1875, many of her supporters came from Protestant and anti-slavery networks.[15] As we shall see, this perception of women as the particular targets of abuse found its way into more than one campaign against injustices overseas; and it maintained its power to create and mobilise feminists to the end of the century and beyond.

There were, moreover, other strands in Christian thinking which coloured women's perspectives on world affairs. Believers who linked the second coming of Christ to the conversion of the Jews and their resettlement in Palestine identified the Ottoman caliphate as the chief obstacle to the messianic age. British policy in the East, which for most of the century propped up Turkey, 'the sick man of Europe', against the encroachments of Christian Russia, was therefore to be deplored and opposed. Exceptionally, at the battle of Navarino of October 1827, Russian, British and French fleets combined to defeat Ibrahim Pasha and thereby liberate Greece. Traditionalists wary of Czarist expansionism were alarmed, but the evangelical writer Charlotte Elizabeth Tonna rejoiced:

Greece was struggling for freedom and the Mahommedan despot was crushing her deeper into the dust beneath his merciless hand ... unsent, unauthorized, and acting under an impulse that could not be accounted for, England and France went into action side by side with Russia ... I resolved, if this blow was not followed up by sudden ruin ... I would proceed on my new assumption of prophetic meanings as established.[16]

Millennialism, unlike the movement to abolish state regulation of vice, did not supply a specifically female critique of world affairs. Nor was it the mainstream conviction within British Protestantism.[17] But views closely akin to Tonna's on 'prophetic meanings' were entertained by many influential reformers, such as Lord Shaftesbury and Josephine Butler. In discussing the later history of popular British protests concerning Turkey, it is well to bear Tonna's apocalyptic reactions in mind. Her world view also embraced a passionate anti-Catholicism, which was even more widely shared. Just as Tonna saw the independence of Greece

Women, Class and the State (Cambridge, 1980); Jane Jordan, *Josephine Butler* (London, 2001).

[15] Bolt and Drescher, *Anti-Slavery*, Part One; *The New Abolitionists: A Narrative of a Year's Work* [by Josephine Butler] (London, 1876).

[16] *Personal Recollections by Charlotte Elizabeth*, p. 233. Her theology and advocacy are also set out in *The Christian Lady's Magazine*, which she edited from 1834.

[17] However, Kathryn Gleadle argues for it as the majority Evangelical position in 'Charlotte Elizabeth Tonna and the mobilization of Tory women in early Victorian England', *Historical Journal*, 50(1), (2007), pp. 97–117, at p. 99.

as a religious rather than a liberal project, so too the British minister in Berne, granting a visa to the Italian insurrectionary Mazzini in 1836, reportedly urged that he 'give our cause a religious character and propagate the Bible amongst the people'.[18] In 1851, even the liberal Friends of Italy insisted that the failed revolution of 1848, when the Roman people separated the Pope's temporal and spiritual powers, produced 'a great Reformation, such as we Englishmen were supposed to have been praying for and longing for'.[19]

Anti-Catholicism had considerable staying power among liberal women. In 1860, Josephine Butler's sister, domiciled in Naples, helped to bring Italian Bibles to wounded Garibaldini, hoping for a Protestant harvest;[20] and as late as 1882, the liberal and feminist *Englishwoman's Review* sounded a faint echo of the old refrain in an obituary of the Italian patriot Sarah Nathan: 'her house was ever open to the faithful workers against Austrian and Papal tyranny'.[21] Nathan was a Protestant convert of Jewish parentage; and the anti-clericalism of many of her fellow patriots, together with their hostility to the Pope's temporal powers, could be said to have bestowed on them an aura of 'virtual Protestantism'. The nature of female support for Italian unification throws into sharp relief the religious content of what is often characterised as one of nineteenth-century Britain's quintessentially liberal enthusiasms.

Italy and the female imagination

In 1832, European discontent with the post-Napoleonic political settlement acquired new momentum when Giuseppe Mazzini founded the organisation 'Young Italy', which spread to Germany, France, Switzerland, Poland and Austria. 'Young Europe', as it became, failed in its ambition to fuse Rousseau-esque ideals of moral regeneration, individual liberty and social progress with armed insurrection, principally against the Hapsburg empire; Mazzini, its prophet, was forced to flee to London in 1837, spending the rest of his life either in exile in Britain or in clandestine escapades in Italy. Yet Mazzinism and the Italian cause had the most profound impact on British public opinion, and on women in particular. While Polish and Hungarian independence movements aroused public sympathy, it was Italy which held the imagination and

---

[18] E. E. Y. Hales, *Mazzini and the Secret Societies: The Making of a Myth* (London, 1956), p. 196.
[19] *Address of the Society of the Friends of Italy* (London, 1851), p. 9.
[20] Josephine Butler, *In Memoriam Harriet Meuricoffre* (London, 1901), pp. 72–74.
[21] *Englishwoman's Review*, 15 March 1882, pp. 138–139.

sustained the engagement of British men and women over the decades. The cause survived changes in the British political climate, the disappointments of the European revolutionary year of 1848 and the abortive insurrectionary expeditions of the 1850s. The effusions of poets, the scholarly projects of historians and a vast output of published letters and memoirs all bear witness to the importance of the 'Risorgimento' in British cultural life.[22]

It has been suggested that much romantic and Risorgimento rhetoric presented Italy as a powerless female, reinforcing women's identification with 'her' struggle against Austrian domination;[23] but the masculine aura of the movement should not be understated. Britain was a favoured haven for Continental exiles in the nineteenth century, most of them men. One notable way in which women showed their commitment to Italian unification was to marry into the cause. The roll-call of wives includes Emilie Ashurst Venturi, Jessie White Mario, Georgina Craufurd Saffi, as well as the American Margaret Fuller Ossoli,[24] women who campaigned in print and in public meetings,[25] travelled to Italy and willingly put themselves in danger there. Their sisters and female relatives were often equally devoted to the movement. Emilie Ashurst's sisters – Elizabeth Ann Ashurst Bardonneau, Caroline (who married the radical MP James Stansfeld) and Matilda Ashurst Biggs, all of whom moved seamlessly from the anti-slavery campaign into Mazzinism – are a particularly well-known sibling network devoted to radical and progressive causes; but their so-called 'Muswell Hill Brigade' also had kinship links to conservative and religious networks sharing their enthusiasm for Italy.[26]

A wide circle of women idolised the prophetic and austere Mazzini and the dashing military leader Guiseppe Garibaldi; and they contemplated the destruction of Hapsburg regiments with as much complacency as

---

[22] Maura O'Connor, *The Romance of Italy and the English Imagination* (London, 1998). The poets included Swinburne and the Brownings; among the historians were Thomas Hodgkin, Bolton King and G. M. Trevelyan.

[23] O'Connor, *Romance*, pp. 109, 113.

[24] The Ashurst family are well served by *ODNB*; for Jessie White Mario, see the latter and Elizabeth A. Daniels, *Jessie White Mario: Risorgimento Revolutionary* (Athens, OH, 1972).

[25] The lecture circuit of Jessie White (see O'Connor, *Romance*, ch. 4), and the later activism of Fanny Albert (see the section below on 'The Eastern question') contradict Biagini's suggestion that women did not address secular public meetings before the Home Rule agitation of the 1880s: *British Democracy and Irish Nationalism*, p. 90. See also Jordan, *Josephine Butler*.

[26] For example, the freethinking Emily Winkworth, married to the radical William Shaen, could assume the support of her Anglican sisters Susanna and Catherine, known for their translations, especially of hymns, from the German: *Memorials of Two Sisters: Susanna and Catherine Winkworth, edited by their niece Margaret J. Shaen* (London, 1908), pp. 195–196.

Charlotte Elizabeth Tonna did the crushing of the Ottoman fleet. Garibaldi was a military hero in an almost operatic mould,[27] whose appeal is not hard to discern even at a century and a half's distance; his personality had much to do with women's enthusiasm for joining the armed wing of the Risorgimento as nurses. Mazzini's was a more complex charisma. To some, he was a virtual messiah. Harriet Baillie Hamilton longed to emulate Jessie White, to nurse Garibaldi's soldiers and 'offer relief and consolation to the Martyrs of the Holy War'. She also addressed Mazzini as 'You, crowned and anointed one of God' in 1863, using similar terms throughout their friendship without, apparently, provoking rebuke or demur.[28] Mathilde Blind, brought up without religion by parents intimate with radical exiles such as Karl Marx and Louis Blanc, also responded to Mazzini as 'a guarantee of the sacredness of life. ... The materialist school of thought, which recognised force and matter as the only factors in the world ... left a void which it required Mazzini's essentially spiritual doctrine to bridge over'.[29]

Mazzini's philosophy, as set out in *I doveri delluomo* [*The Duties of Man*] (1860), saw human existence consecrated to the struggle for moral progress, and his idealist theory of evolution was reinforced by a personal life of genuine austerity. His concept of the moral regeneration of society, through the combined efforts of both sexes, resonated with female advocates of 'Woman's Mission', who were moved more by a sense of religious and social obligation than by the demand for equal rights. Mazzini himself squared the circle adroitly, writing 'We have no rights: we have only duties; when bent on fulfilling them, we have a right to not be prevented or checked: thence liberty, thence equality, thence association.'[30] *Duties*, published in Emilie Venturi's English translation in 1862, thus appealed to women with divergent views of emancipation and the development of new social roles.

The argument that Mazzini contributed to forming a rhetoric of sexual emancipation, and that *Duties* profoundly influenced the women's movement,[31] overlooks the fact that British women embraced his teachings

---

[27] Marjan Schwegman, 'In love with Garibaldi: romancing the Italian risorgimento', *European Review of History*, 12(2), (2005), pp. 383–401.

[28] Mrs [Harriet Eleanor Baillie] Hamilton King, *Letters and Recollections of Mazzini*, ed. G. M. Trevelyan, (London, 1912), pp. 11, 26, 31–32.

[29] Mathilde Blind, 'Personal recollections of Mazzini', *Fortnightly Review*, 49, (May, 1891), pp. 702–712, at pp. 702–703.

[30] Ibid., p. 709.

[31] Mayhall, 'Rhetorics of slavery', pp. 481–485, 490–491; Jane Rendall, 'Citizenship, culture and civilisation: the languages of British suffragists, 1866–1874' in C. Daley and M. Nolan (eds), *Suffrage and Beyond: International Feminist Perspectives* (Auckland, 1994).

because these resonated with ideas they had already developed. Women were in many cases members of radical or liberal families and networks before they encountered Mazzini, either in the word or the flesh. Their previous involvement in the anti-slavery movement had confirmed their conviction that moral purpose justified and indeed demanded political activity; had sharpened their perceptions of the dynamics of state power; and had alerted them to the particular subjection of the female sex. Those who launched the campaign against state-regulated prostitution in 1869 did not do so because they were Mazzinians; but it is no coincidence that the group of women at the forefront of that campaign – Josephine Butler, Emilie Ashurst Venturi, Emily Winkworth Shaen – also endorsed Mazzini's vision of a moral society. In the same way, women would support W. E. Gladstone's later stand on the 'Bulgarian horrors' because this was consonant with their own principles and experience.

The Eastern question

Women's responses to the 'East' – the Balkan areas under the Ottoman caliphate which included substantial Orthodox Christian communities – have been described in the context of their pacifist initiatives.[32] They have also been interpreted as a form of orientalism, with the iniquities of the 'harem' being deployed as tropes to bolster the social status of British feminists.[33] Neither perception does justice to women's concerns over the Balkan Christian women with whom they identified. However, women certainly used 'the East' to illustrate the need for both sexes to play an equally valued part in a re-moralised British society.

When the Serbs spearheaded a revolt in 1875, which spread to the Bulgarians of Eastern Rumelia in the spring of 1876, Turkish irregular troops, the so-called bashi-bazouks, repressed the revolt with great ferocity. Current scholarship suggests that between four and fifteen thousand men, women and children were murdered.[34] Horrifying reports from foreign correspondents aroused public outrage in Britain. The origins of the atrocity agitation as a mass movement are largely attributable to W. T. Stead, editor of the *Northern Echo*, whose 'reports of the kidnap of Christian women into Turkish harems, which evoked fears of a white slave trade and prefigured his own investigation of child abuse

---

[32] Liddington, *Road to Greenham*, ch. 2.
[33] Antoinette Burton, *Burdens of History* (Chapel Hill and London, 1994), ch. 3, where tropes relating to Turkish and Indian Islam are conflated.
[34] Ann Pottinger Saab, *Reluctant Icon: Gladstone, Bulgaria and the Working Classes, 1856–1878* (Cambridge, MA, 1991), p. 24; R. T. Shannon, *Gladstone and the Bulgarian Agitation 1876* (London, 1963), p. 22.

in the "Maiden Tribute of Modern Babylon", were designed to at once horrify and titillate the reader'.[35] In the summer of 1876, Stead's articles prompted public meetings throughout the north-east, which denounced the Conservative government's traditional support for Turkey against Russia. The mood of the working and middle classes was reinforced by the statements of Church dignitaries and an influential group of academics, writers and artists.[36] By late August Gladstone, who had retired from the Liberal leadership after the 1874 election, had been moved to write *The Bulgarian Horrors and the Question of the East*, demanding the Turks' withdrawal from Bulgaria.[37] Political opposition, often personalised in attacks on the prime minister, Disraeli,[38] ran parallel with the creation of a plethora of relief schemes, accelerated when Russia declared war on Turkey in April 1877.

Women played an important role in this agitation. As might be expected of persons schooled in philanthropic organisation, they raised funds, collected clothing and materials for bandaging, and travelled to the affected regions as nurses and relief workers. While women worked to support male-dominated organisations such as the National Society for Aid to the Sick and Wounded in War, they also mounted independent initiatives. Travellers included Emma Pearson and Louisa MacLaughlin, by now veterans of ambulance work in wartime,[39] and Emily Anne Beaufort Smythe, Lady Strangford, whose studies of the Middle East and of nursing prompted her to set up and manage her own relief projects in Bulgaria in 1876, and in Adrianople, Sofia and Scutari in 1877. Fundraisers and relief organisers at home included Baroness Burdett-Coutts, the historian E. A. Freeman's daughter Margaret, as well as two of Josephine Butler's closest campaigning colleagues, Elizabeth Malleson and Sarah Sheldon Amos.[40]

---

[35] Rebecca Gill, 'Calculating compassion in war: the "New Humanitarian" ethos in Britain 1870–1918', unpublished DPhil thesis, University of Manchester (2005), p. 80.

[36] Gill, 'Calculating compassion', pp. 79–84; Taylor, *Troublemakers* pp. 70–71: 'the only occasion in our history when the majority of the leaders of the Established Church were against the government'; E. P. Thompson, *William Morris: Romantic to Revolutionary* (London, 1977), p. 207.

[37] Roy Jenkins, *Gladstone* (London, 1996), p. 400.

[38] Thompson, *William Morris*, p. 215; Rebecca Gill, '"A very Moses in the House of Lords": Disraeli, nationality and the "Bulgarian atrocities" agitation, 1876–78', in Jean-François Moisan (ed), *Parcours judaïques*, VIII. Actes du colloque international Disraeli et l'Europe, l'homme d'état et l'homme de lettres, 18 juin 2004 (Nanterre, 2004).

[39] Emma Pearson and Louisa MacLaughlin, *Our Adventures during the War of 1870–1* (London, 1871).

[40] On this episode in general, see Dorothy Anderson, *The Balkan Volunteers* (London, 1968), and A. Summers, *Angels and Citizens: British Women as Military Nurses 1854–1914* (London, 1988 and Newbury, 2000), ch. 5.

Although the route to the East in some ways recalled the nursing mission of Florence Nightingale in Turkey and the Crimea two decades earlier, for most women the Balkan Christians were an unfamiliar cause. However, they could look for enlightenment to women pioneers, particularly Paulina Irby, who had been undertaking charitable and educational work in the Balkans from the late 1850s, first with Georgina Muir Mackenzie and, after 1871, with Priscilla Johnston. Although none married into the cause, they were as much in love with Christian Serbia, Bosnia and Bulgaria as any Ashurst with Italy. Following the 1875–1876 revolts, Irby devoted herself and her associates to a threefold programme of fundraising for refugees, overseeing relief projects and publishing general information on the area.[41] Gladstone considered her and Mackenzie's book *Travels in the Slavonic provinces of Turkey-in-Europe* (1867) 'by far the best English book I have seen on Eastern matters'[42] and contributed the preface to a new edition in 1877.

While Gladstone, doubtless with Indian Muslim subjects of the Empire in mind, had insisted that to criticise Turkey was not to denigrate Islam,[43] British public opinion was less tolerant or politic. In 1876, Lady Strangford was publicly accused of 'Turkish proclivities' by E. A. Freeman, and forced to declare her exclusive concern for Christians.[44] Baroness Burdett-Coutts incurred considerable criticism for launching a 'Turkish Compassionate Fund' in 1877, which was initially destined for Muslim sufferers.[45] The Balkan Christians took on something of the 'Honorary Protestant' aura of Italian revolutionaries: indeed, there was little support for the de facto annexation of Bosnia by Christian – but Catholic – Austria in 1878. Irby and Mackenzie emphasised the Slavonic Christians' struggle for independence from the encroachments of Greek and Russian orthodoxy on the one side and 'Jesuits' on the other;[46] their staunch ally, the archaeologist Arthur G. Evans (who later married Margaret Freeman) deprecated the 'Jesuit intrigues' of Austria and Catholic Croatia.[47]

---

[41] Dorothy Anderson, *Miss Irby and her Friends* (London, 1966).

[42] W. T. Stead, *The M. P. For Russia: Reminiscences and Correspondence of Mme Olga Novikoff* (London, 1909), vol. 1, pp. 317–318.

[43] W. E. Gladstone, *The Bulgarian Horrors and the Question of the East* (London, 1876), pp. 14, 15, 61.

[44] Gill, 'Calculating compassion', p. 74.

[45] Anderson, *Balkan Volunteers*, pp. 173–176.

[46] Paulina Irby and Georgina Muir Mackenzie, *Travels in the Slavonic Provinces of Turkey-in-Europe; the Turks, the Greeks and the Slavons* (London, 1877), vol. 2, p. 15. Some enthusiasts went so far as to claim affinities between Slavonic Christianity and Anglicanism: see John Macray to W. E. Gladstone, 1876, BL. Add. Ms Add. 44451 f. 234.

[47] Arthur J. Evans, 'The Austrians in Bosnia', *Macmillan's Magazine*, 38, (October, 1878), pp. 495–504, at pp. 501 and 504.

Within this sectarian and political maelstrom, it was nevertheless possible to articulate a specifically female point of view. While doubtless influenced by the outpourings of W. T. Stead (who became a supporter of Josephine Butler, and whose 'Maiden Tribute' scoop of 1885 was a collaboration with her), it expressed a somewhat more temperate critique of Turkey, and insisted on foregrounding the impact of war on women. By 1876, British women had demonstrably more experience of specifically feminist organisation than at the start of the pro-Risorgimento movement. From the late 1850s they had organised to change laws on married women's property rights and the electoral franchise, and to promote opportunities for employment and education. From 1869, opposition to the Contagious Diseases Acts not only produced a major critique of patriarchy, but breached taboos on women's public discussion of sexuality. Some traces of these decades of activism are discernible in the history of the Women's Memorial, a petition sent to Queen Victoria in early October 1876, to which 43,845 women's signatures were attached in the space of three weeks.[48]

The prime mover of the Memorial was Frances [Fanny] Ellen Albert. She spoke out at a public protest meeting at the Cannon Street Hotel, London, and was said to have spent five years in Constantinople as governess and 'lady of honour ... to the niece of the present viceroy of Egypt' and subsequently to have taken up an appointment in India in 'a Government school for girls'.[49] Between September 1876 and March 1877 she published three articles 'On Turkish Ways and Women' in *Cornhill Magazine*. These demonstrated a commitment to female emancipation, without crude anti-Turkish or anti-Muslim prejudice – 'Turkish women have assured me that the Koran itself never imposed seclusion on women' – while setting up an opposition between British hearth and Turkish harem which others were to echo: 'Mussulmans will have to ... understand the value of our Western home life, with its simplicity, its moral restrictions, and yet free choice of action ... [and] ... principles of action which are safer guards than veils, barred windows, and sentinelled doors.'[50]

Albert assembled a very mixed group of women to work on the Memorial, including the novelist, translator and Catholic convert Frances Cashel

---

[48] *Englishwoman's Review*, October 1876, pp. 453–455; *Northern Echo*, 2 October 1876; *Daily News*, 7 October 1876.

[49] *Englishwoman's Review*, October 1876, p. 453.

[50] F. E. Albert, 'On Turkish ways and women', *Cornhill Magazine*, 34, (September, 1876), p. 293.

Hoey, Caroline Ashurst Biggs, editor of the *Englishwoman's Review* between 1871 and 1889, and Arabella Shore, who with her sister Louisa was an active suffragist writer and lecturer.[51] They gathered in the Kensington girls' school of which Fanny Aikin Kortright was headmistress. Kortright, a churchwoman, was much exercised by fears of the rise of modern sexual immorality, which she visualised in terms of the 'East' as well as slavery: 'With the overthrow of the altar, [the British woman] must lose her hearth and sink back into slavery, or at the best, into a harem life!' Although a busy single woman, teacher and novelist, she extolled domesticity, opposed female suffrage and was by no means using the Memorial to advance legislative equality.[52]

The group's objective was thus that of securing justice for a specific community of Christian women, rather than denigrating the 'East' for the benefit of the domestic feminist movement; and it attracted support across the female political spectrum. Distinguished figures such as Mary Carpenter, Florence Nightingale, Millicent Garrett Fawcett, Frances Power Cobbe, Octavia Hill, Lydia Becker and Dr Elizabeth Garrett Anderson, and unknown signatories all over the country, especially the north, wrote of their 'relief at being able to turn to her Majesty at once as a Queen and as a woman whose sympathy and compassion for every form of suffering have endeared her to all classes of her subjects'.[53]

The text of the Memorial was relatively terse: the petitioners, 'having heard with horror and indignation of the atrocities committed and still continuing to be perpetrated in Bulgaria and other provinces subject or tributary to Turkey, earnestly beg your Majesty to use your Royal prerogative in directing your Majesty's Government to adopt measures, in concert with the other Powers of Europe, to provide effectually against the continuance and recurrence of such atrocities'.[54] The *Daily News* reported on 26 October that the Queen had been 'graciously pleased' to receive the Memorial, and reproduced a fulsome tribute, by two 'Bulgarian delegates', Zankof and Balabanow, to Englishwomen and to human civilisation of which they were the foundation except where – as in Turkey – they were reduced to the status of slaves.[55]

---

[51] On the Shore sisters, see *ODNB*; Elizabeth Crawford, *The Women's Suffrage Movement, A Reference Guide 1866–1928* (London, 1999), pp. 635–636; and footnote 6 above.

[52] Fanny Aikin Kortright, *A Little Lower than the Angels* (London, 1874); *Pro Aris et Focis* (London, 1869), pp. 4–5, 12.

[53] *Daily News*, 7 October 1876, p. 2.

[54] *Englishwoman's Review*, October 1876, pp. 452–454.

[55] *Daily News*, 26 October 1876, p. 3.

The Memorial had not been a pacifist project as such. It did indeed insist that conflict with other powers was to be discouraged by the positive approach of framing a new policy in conjunction with them; but its main thrust was that war was a women's issue. In its direct address to the Queen and through amassing female signatures only, it highlighted the fact that the bulk of suffering had been inflicted on women. Women pacifists were certainly active at this time, though few in number.[56] In 1878, when anti-Russian war fever produced the frenzy of British bravado ever since known as 'jingoism', support for pacifist petitions also increased. Several thousand female signatures were again sent to the Queen, including that of Arabella Shore; ironically, two decades earlier she had, with her sister, published lyrics in ecstatic praise of the noble British soldier of the Crimean War.[57]

Feminism – or at the least, female self-assertion – rather than pacifism, was the main driving force behind this movement. The *Englishwoman's Review*'s reference to a conflict 'in which women are, more even than in civilised wars, the chief sufferers'[58] was not a convincing denunciation of militarism; and most signatures undoubtedly expressed emotions and convictions other than straightforward revulsion against war. Primarily, the Memorial expressed solidarity with women who were fellow-Christians. But it had a subtext: not so much the superiority of Western women to their Eastern sisters as the frustration of those who, unlike the Queen, were powerless to intervene in any way sanctioned by the constitution. Philanthropy was not enough: many of those who threw themselves into a frenzy of fundraising and bandage-rolling were aware that relief measures were only palliative. They wanted to see a long-term solution to the Eastern question in the emancipation of the Balkan nationalities, in the same way that so many had longed for the emancipation of Italy from the Hapsburgs.

The *Englishwoman's Review* drew the moral that only the recognition of women's right to equal partnership with men in political life could mitigate the horrors of war.[59] Millicent Fawcett extended the discussion, describing the subjection of Balkan women in 'normal' circumstances: 'The oppression which the Bosnians and Herzegovinians most deeply and bitterly resent, is the forcible carrying off of girls and women to the Turkish harems.'[60] Fawcett did not expatiate on the opposition of

---

[56] Liddington, *Road to Greenham*, p. 25.
[57] *Englishwoman's Review*, May 1878, pp. 225–226; *War Lyrics, By A. and L.*, (London, 1855).
[58] *Englishwoman's Review*, October 1876, p. 452.
[59] Ibid., September 1876, p. 411.
[60] *Papers on the Eastern Question, No. 11. The Martyrs of Turkish Misrule*, by M. G. Fawcett [with supplement by Paulina Irby] (London, 1877), p. 10.

hearth and harem, or the outrages committed against Christian women, but she had touched on the key issue. Even those feminists avoiding close association with Butler's controversial campaigns had been influenced by her arguments: political subjection, legal inequality and sexual abuse went hand in hand. Just as it is unsurprising to find Butler's lieutenants Elizabeth Malleson and Sarah Sheldon Amos heavily involved in Bulgarian relief committees,[61] so it was not an eccentric change of direction for Fanny Albert to turn away from Balkan affairs in favour of involvement with the Social Purity Alliance, and founding membership of the Moral Reform Union (MRU).[62]

A similar constellation of sympathies and convictions, and many familiar figures from these networks, resurfaced in the early 1890s, when the cause of Armenian Christian women under Ottoman rule was taken up by much of the British women's movement. The feminist and temperance campaigner Lady Henry Somerset played a particularly prominent role.[63] In 1895, at the first mass meeting of the Armenian campaign (held at St James's Hall, Piccadilly, scene of a famous protest on behalf of the Bulgarians in 1876), she spoke of the love of Christian women 'for their sisters yonder in the clutch of the harem-despot of Constantinople', and claimed that 'the martyrdoms of the first century in Jerusalem have been suffered again at Sasun. The hills and valleys of Judea are hardly more sacred than the blood-saturated hills and valleys of Armenia.'[64]

Lady Henry's journal, the *Woman's Signal*, provided her with an expansive platform for fundraising and canvassing political support, but other female initiatives included the Women's Liberal Federation's Armenia Bureau, women's relief funds in centres such as Birmingham and Edinburgh, and committees established by the Quaker community.[65] There were many continuities with the Bulgarian campaigners: relief work among Armenian refugees was undertaken by, among others, Sarah Sheldon Amos, and also by Laura Ormiston Chant, now a colleague of Fanny Albert's within the Moral Reform Union. Another of Albert's MRU colleagues, Florence Balgarnie, was also active in the

---

[61] *Elizabeth Malleson 1828–1916: Autobiographical Notes and Letters with a Memoir by Hope Malleson* (London, 1926), pp. 123, 126, 132–134, 219–220.

[62] Biographical information from Moral Reform Union, *Reports*, and catalogue of The Women's Library.

[63] Jeremy Salt, *Imperialism, Evangelism and the Ottoman Armenians, 1878–1896* (London/ Portland, OR, 1993); Olwen Claire Niessen, *Aristocracy, Temperance and Social Reform: The Life of Lady Henry Somerset* (London, 2007).

[64] Salt, *Imperialism*, p. 127, quoting *The Times*.

[65] *Woman's Signal*, 19 March 1896, p. 189; 1 October 1896, p. 222.

cause, having called in 1894 for the 'united action of Europe' against 'the monstrous tyranny of the cruel Turk'.[66]

In June 1895, as agitation gathered steam, a Conservative government came to power. Liberal opinion was, as in 1876, free to denounce inactivity without taking responsibility for provoking a war. Once again the perpetuation of outrages against women overseas was linked to the political powerlessness of women at home. Lady Henry thundered, and readers of the *Woman's Signal* agreed:

The manhood of the world has witnessed the spectacle of four hundred Christian women shut up in a church and undergoing a night of outrage, ending in murder, the streams of blood flowing out under the church doors. And yet knowing these things men have passively awaited the decision of a Mohammedan despot . . . Women who look on and have no power to act, must, if they think at all, say to themselves sometimes, 'Could women have governed worse?'[67]

She was speaking to a newer generation of women gaining a sharper focus on national party politics. The Women's Liberal Federation and its Conservative counterpart, the Primrose League, established in 1886 and 1883 respectively, provided indispensable electoral muscle by canvassing in local and national elections: both could consider strategies beyond protest, fundraising and relief measures.[68] Opportunities, however, were productive of dilemmas. One woman asked *Woman's Signal* readers if they should withhold support from a parliamentary candidate who did not favour women's suffrage, but did propose to do something to help the Armenians: 'could we have balanced our own enfranchisement, even though the "our" included all the women of England, against the liberties of a nation, the lives of its people, the honour of its women?'[69] The strategy of making difficulties for parliamentary candidates, pioneered by Josephine Butler, was to reach its apogee with Christabel Pankhurst; but it caused apprehension among feminists who were also organised as Liberals. The potential conflict between the goals of British feminism, political Liberalism and the championing

---

[66] Quotation from the *Woman's Signal*, 27 December 1894, pp. 416–417; *Reports* of the Moral Reform Union.

[67] *Woman's Signal*, 5 September 1895, p. 152.

[68] Janet Henderson Robb, *The Primrose League 1883–1906* (New York, 1942); Martin Pugh, *The Tories and the People 1880–1935* (Oxford, 1985); Claire Hirshfield, 'Fractured faith: Liberal Party women and the suffrage issue in Britain, 1892–1914', *Gender & History*, 2, (1990), pp. 173–197; and 'Liberal women's organisations and the war against the Boers, 1899–1902', *Albion*, 14, (1982), pp. 27–49.

[69] Letter of 'H. M. S.', – answered firmly in the affirmative by the Secretary, Union of Practical Suffragists (Women's Liberal Federation), *Woman's Signal*, 17 June 1897 p. 383; see also Bolt, *The Women's Movements*, p. 184.

of oppressed womanhood overseas was soon to come to a head with the outbreak of the Boer War in 1899.

A transitional moment? Opposition to war 1899–1902

The invasion of the independent Dutch-speaking republics of South Africa in 1899, in defence of the legal rights of British 'Outlanders', provoked the formation of organisations at home such as the 'Stop The War' committee, and the less radical South Africa Conciliation Committee. The revelations in 1900 of the official military strategy of burning farmsteads and forcing the families of guerrilla fighters into concentration camps scandalised British women into public intervention at the highest level. Never before had so many reformers plainly accused their own government of deceit, folly and downright barbarity; and the violence shown to 'pro-Boers', male and female, was directly proportionate to the enthusiastic 'mafficking' of patriotic crowds.[70] Where previously the government had been urged to act in support of an oppressed group, even if this meant expanding its sphere of influence and risking war, now it was denounced as the oppressor, and urged to make peace without annexations. Nevertheless, there were continuities between this and previous episodes of passionate protest and solidarity with peoples overseas; and many of the same principles and personalities were involved.

In February 1901 the 'Stop The War' committee, led by W. T. Stead, denounced conditions in the camps as atrocities which 'can only be paralleled in our time by the operations of the Turks in Armenia and Bulgaria',[71] and it is unsurprising to find James and Elizabeth Bryce, of the Anglo-Armenian Association, involved with the South Africa Conciliation Committee.[72] Nor was it anomalous for a scion of a Liberal dynasty such as Emily Hobhouse to organise a meeting in June 1900 whose participants, including Elizabeth Bryce, Henrietta Barnett, Kate Courtney and Catherine Booth, endorsed a resolution which 'desires to express its sympathy with the women of the Transvaal and Orange Free State and begs them to remember that thousands of English women are filled with profound sorrow at the thought of their sufferings'. The objects of their sympathy were, after all, not only women but European women, and not only Christian but Protestant.[73]

---

[70] See, among many others, Thomas Pakenham, *The Boer War* (London, 1979); Stephen E. Koss (ed.), *The Pro-Boers. The Anatomy of an Anti-war Movement* (Chicago, 1973).
[71] J. O. H. Fisher, *That Miss Hobhouse* (London, 1971), pp. 143–144.
[72] Gill, 'Calculating compassion', p. 109.
[73] Jennifer Hobhouse Balme, *To Love One's Enemies: The Work and Life of Emily Hobhouse* (Cobble Hill, BC, 1994), p. 41.

Hobhouse's initiative in setting up the South African Women and Children Distress Fund recalled many previous enterprises by British philanthropic women,[74] but was distinguished from them in two significant respects. Its agenda was overtly anti-government – so much so that the Victoria League subsequently took on the role of 'non-partisan' war relief work;[75] and it ignored the hardships of the indigenous African populations.[76] Hobhouse expressed strong views on the dangers to white women represented by 'the Kaffir';[77] less well known was her concern with a feminist preoccupation of longer standing: the moral threat to white women from white men. She wrote: 'I intend going out … mainly with a view of rescuing the women and girls driven to sell themselves for bread and shelter. With timely aid they may be saved.'[78]

As with the Bulgarian and Armenian agitations, feminist women drew their own political conclusions from the conduct of the war. Hobhouse's main audience at the meeting of June 1900 had been supplied by the Women's Liberal Federation, which had worked to prevent the outbreak of war in autumn 1899. Members were swift to point out that while the Colonial Secretary Joseph Chamberlain had denounced the disenfranchisement of Transvaal 'Outlanders', he 'had never taken a single step to give the Suffrage to the mothers, wives and daughters of England'.[79] The war's end was marked by the Federation's 'Cambridge Resolution' to refuse electioneering services to Liberal parliamentary candidates who would not declare support for female suffrage.[80] They could be forgiven for thinking that their moment had come: between 1899 and 1902 they had witnessed the most remarkable acknowledgement of women's power to influence political events.

In 1901, the publication of Emily Hobhouse's reports on the appalling sickness, malnutrition, starvation and death rates among the non-combatant inmates of the concentration camps had aroused a national

---

[74] Liddington, *Road to Greenham*, p. 48.

[75] Women of the Asquith and Lyttelton families chose this vehicle for their charitable efforts: S. B. Spies, 'Women and the War' in Peter Warwick (ed.), *The South African War: The Anglo-Boer War 1899–1902* (Harlow, 1980), at p. 181.

[76] However, Harriette Colenso, daughter of the Bishop of Natal, drew their situation to the notice of the Aborigines Protection Society, which set up a Zulu Relief Fund; Spies, 'Women and the War', p. 182.

[77] Paula M. Krebs, '"The last of the gentlemen's wars": women in the Boer War concentration camp controversy', *History Workshop Journal*, 33, (1992), pp. 38–56, at p. 45.

[78] Balme, *To Love One's Enemies*, pp. 52–53, quoting a letter to Leonard Hobhouse of 2 November 1900.

[79] Hirshfield, 'Liberal women's organisations', pp. 28, 36.

[80] Ibid., pp. 29, 47; the resolution applied only to the central WLF organisation, not to local branches.

furore which forced the government to act – choosing to meet the testimony of one woman with the commission given to a group of women, headed by Millicent Fawcett, to investigate camp conditions. Fawcett was known as a staunch opponent of Home Rule for Ireland, unlikely to be sympathetic to Boer nationalism. At the time and subsequently, her commission's report was condemned as 'whitewash', accepting official statements of good intentions and raisons de guerre at face value, and attributing much of the morbidity and mortality among Boer children to their mothers' ignorance. But the facts emerging even from this sanitised narrative reflected credit on neither the government nor army command, and Fawcett called for much the same reforms in the camps as had Hobhouse. Camp death rates began to drop towards the end of 1901, and the government survived the threat to its moral standing, but the crisis in public relations had been a severe one.[81] Peace returned with women on all sides, from anti-war liberals to patriotic nursing sisters, feeling they had proved their importance to the body politic at national and imperial level.[82]

Internationalisms and their limitations

By the start of the twentieth century, British women's growing sense of confidence in their claims to citizenship was reinforced by their leading role in international women's organisations: the International Council of Women (ICW), which facilitated communication between nations and continents, enhanced the status and encouraged the expansion of women's public initiatives, without advocating the suffrage; and the International Woman Suffrage Alliance (IWSA), which from 1904 organised separately to support campaigns for the vote.[83] If suffrage itself was divisive, it was hardly to be expected that either organisation would take a stand on national or international controversies. In 1906, the ICW constitution was revised to exclude 'political and religious questions of a controversial nature affecting the inter-relationship of two or more countries'.[84] Despite this studied neutrality, perhaps unhelpful to a generation of women determined to enter the political arena on the same terms as men, some feminist preoccupations retained their power to mobilise

---

[81] Krebs, 'Gentlemen's wars', p. 51.
[82] Summers, *Angels and Citizens*, chs 7 and 8.
[83] International Council of Women, *Women in a Changing World: The Dynamic Story of the International Council of Women since 1888* (London, 1966); Liddington, *Road to Greenham*, p. 63.
[84] Liddington, *Road to Greenham*, p. 63; *Women in a Changing World*, p. 29. This followed the break-up of the Union of Norway and Sweden.

enthusiasm across national frontiers: the IWSA continued to advocate women's suffrage as a means of combating male militarism,[85] and considered the proposal to investigate the 'white slave' traffic as one of the most important achievements of its 1913 Congress.[86]

The decade preceding World War I saw the increasing collaboration and dominance of the Anglo-American sections of the movement. Earlier Continental initiatives had suffered the backlash from the failed revolutionary year of 1848, and the later growth of French and German socialist movements divided socialist from 'bourgeois' feminists.[87] The first IWSA president, from 1906 to 1916, was the American Carrie Chapman Catt, with Millicent Fawcett as her vice-president; shortly before World War I, the Association's headquarters moved from Amsterdam to London. The first ICW President from 1893 to 1899, Ishbel Countess of Aberdeen, was succeeded by the American May Wright Sewall between 1899 and 1904, but resumed the Presidency from 1904 to 1920 and from 1922 to 1936.[88] British suffragism's longevity, and British women's achievements in working alongside men, promoting social reforms and widening educational access for their sex, distinguished them from their European neighbours;[89] after 1905 the sensational militant tactics of the Women's Social and Political Union, while officially rejected as a model of activism, nevertheless made a profound impression on feminists elsewhere.[90]

Many were to experience the most bitter disappointment in the years before the war. Arguably, however, the sense of betrayal experienced by suffragists, as session after parliamentary session denied them the vote, was as nothing compared to the despair of pacifist women in 1914. As Emily Hobhouse's brother recalled, her South African exploits had raised false hopes: 'When the Great War broke out she no doubt had in mind from the beginning that a personal intervention might win a similar success.'[91] But now there was far less scope for British women to suggest that their own country might be in the wrong. The trope of the 'rape of

---

[85] Liddington, *Road to Greenham*, p. 64.

[86] Subsequently both the ICW and the IWSA changed this terminology to 'traffic in women': Rupp, *Worlds of Women*, p. 151.

[87] See Karen M. Offen, *European Feminisms 1700–1950* (Stanford, CA, 2000); Rita Huber-Sperl (ed.), *Organisiert und Engagiert: Vereinskultur bürgerliche Frauen im 19. Jahrhundert in Westeuropa und den USA* (Königstein/Taunus, 2002).

[88] *Women in a Changing World*, p. 125; Liddington, *Road to Greenham*, p. 63.

[89] Anne Summers, 'Which women? What Europe? Josephine Butler and the International Abolitionist Federation', *History Workshop Journal*, 62, (2006), pp. 214–231, at pp. 220, 223.

[90] Bolt, *The Women's Movements*, p. 201.   [91] Balme, *To Love One's Enemies*, p. 303.

Belgium' and the uproar over Nurse Edith Cavell's execution have been portrayed as manipulative propaganda, designed to subvert a female critique of militarism;[92] but again the record of women's own campaigns suggests a different interpretation. By denouncing abuses perpetrated by men against women, women had placed a critique of patriarchy in the public domain. While male exploitation of reports of women's sufferings may have been cynical or titillatory, it may also have been a genuine response to the challenges of Butler, Somerset and Hobhouse. It was no accident that the official report on Belgian atrocities was commissioned from one of the principals in the campaigns over Armenia and the Boer camps.[93] It may be argued that this propaganda turned women's own weapons against the feminist movement, but it is no less plausible to argue that it represented an acknowledgement of women's concerns and agendas.

Edwardian women activists' sense of being in the social and political vanguard both domestically and internationally may have blinded them to the growing danger of war in Europe. ('I wonder why they all talk so much about war', a British delegate allegedly said at the 1913 IWSA Congress in Budapest, 'There will never be another European war.'[94]) This unconcern might also support the contention that British women considered the bulk of the world's political surface to consist of their own empire, with their most important international role being the 'white woman's burden'. Certainly, against the anti-suffragists who conceded that women could exercise responsibility at local government level, but were unfit to govern a national state which was also an imperial one, both legal and militant suffragists stressed their right and duty to work on behalf of imperial female subjects. However, as the developments outlined in this chapter indicate, to infer from this that British feminism was predicated on the construct of the colonised Other offers a limited and not wholly plausible model for understanding women's social action.

★★★★

The historiography of British womens' internationalism has for some time been limited by a tendency to read the dramatic developments of World War I back into the nineteenth century; and in the last decade it has been dominated by a focus on relations between empire and metropole. The fact that the suffrage movement suffered a dramatic split between supporters and opponents of war in 1914 has understandably

---

[92] Nicoletta Gullace, *The Blood of Our Sons: Men, Women, and the Renegotiation of British Citizenship during the Great War* (Basingstoke, 2002), ch. 1.

[93] James Bryce: the connection is overlooked in the above work.

[94] Liddington, *Road to Greenham*, p. 74, quoting Helena Swanwick.

led to a concentration on those activists who mounted earlier critiques of militarism, and sometimes to a suggestion of a natural or essential affinity between women and movements for peace. The fact that the growth of the women's movement coincided with the period of Britain's greatest expansion of imperial rule has encouraged a school of writing which insists on linking all women's initiatives to the perpetuation of imperialism. Both these approaches are one-dimensional, and flatten the contours of a variegated landscape. They underplay women's capacity for identification with the female Other, and the extent to which they were moved by narratives of sexual abuse and corruption; most importantly, they underestimate the power of the Christian concept of spiritual freedom, and obscure the range of ways in which this concept influenced political practice.

The phenomenon of identification is of course not unproblematic. There was more sympathy felt for Bulgarian and Armenian victims of Turkish atrocities than was felt for Jewish victims of Russian pogroms; more sympathy for Boer women and children than for the indigenous black communities of South Africa. Hostility to the Ottoman and Hapsburg empires was in few instances matched by any desire to see the dismantling of British imperial rule.[95] Empires as well as communities were ranked, without discomfort, in moral hierarchies. Moreover, sympathies based on similarly liberal and Christian impulses could be in conflict. Emily Hobhouse's liberal background predisposed her to oppose the war and to champion incarcerated Boer women and children. The equally liberal Josephine Butler broadly supported the war, not as a militarist or an imperialist, but because she considered the Boers as essentially slaveowners.[96] And members of the Women's Liberal Federation who supported Hobhouse's campaign nevertheless distanced themselves from her idealisation of the Boers and feared the possible mistreatment of native Africans under autonomous Boer rule.[97]

Difficulties also arose through the limitations of knowledge, even where, as we have seen, women had first-hand experience of the circumstances of the peoples they championed. Even in the Internet age, sources of information are biased, filtered by government agency or

---

[95] The principal exception is, of course, Annie Besant's work for the Indian National Congress. This to some extent subordinated feminist to nationalist imperatives: Anne Taylor, *Annie Besant* (Oxford, 1992); N. L. Paxton, 'Complicity and resistance in the writings of Flora Annie Steel and Annie Besant' in N. Chaudhuri and M. Strobel (eds), *Western Women and Imperialism: Complicity and Resistance* (Bloomington, IN, 1992), at pp. 173–174.

[96] Jordan, *Josephine Butler*, p. 283.

[97] Hirshfield, 'Liberal women's organisations', pp. 37–39.

personal prejudice. The nineteenth century was equally hampered, though not necessarily more so. No cause can be defended without privileging one version of events over another; the empowerment of one group often entails another's disempowerment. British champions of the Risorgimento had little inkling of popular resentment in Naples and Sicily.[98] The British Positivists, possibly the sole supporters of the Zulu nation against British imperialist aggression, were oblivious to the plight of Sotho victims of Zulu expansionism.[99] The post-colonial critique implies that Victorian and Edwardian women and men should have helped more Others achieve their own liberation; but this ignores the dilemmas posed by competing claims, and simplifies the contexts in which nineteenth-century women chose to act.[100]

The Christian concept of spiritual freedom, the belief that an individual's control over her own actions was the indispensable condition for salvation, identified a slave as an individual denied this control in respect of either labouring or sexual activity. This spiritual concept had to be realised in material situations of great complexity, and interventions could be self-defeating or contradictory. Nevertheless, there was considerable consistency in British women's campaigns throughout the century. The same activists might condemn state-registered prostitution in Europe, the practice of suttee in India and the customs of the harem in Turkey. They did not do so in the belief that they were racially superior to Italian, Indian or Turkish women (though they were not at all times innocent of such beliefs). They took up these causes because they considered themselves as enjoying – and demanding – rights which should be extended to all. They were also convinced that their principles should inform the policies of their own government, and should lead to collaborative action at an international level; and for most women, this did not exclude the possibility of meeting force with force. Only through examining women's cultures of internationalism through this lens of religious and moral imperatives is it possible to analyse their engagements with any clarity. In doing so, we can perhaps hope to gain a clearer view of the factors moving peoples to bellicosity and reconciliation.

---

[98] John A. Davis, *Conflict and Control: Law and Order in Nineteenth-century Italy* (Basingstoke, 1988).

[99] F. Harrison, *The Present and the Future. A Positivist Address* (London, 1880), pp. 22–23, 25–26.

[100] On the dilemmas of assistance and control with reference to the inter-war period, see Susan Pedersen, 'Metaphors of the schoolroom: women working the mandates system of the League of Nations', *History Workshop Journal*, 66, (2008), pp. 108–207; and on the dilemmas of contemporary anti-imperialist agitation, see Nadje Al-Ali and Nicola Pratt, *What Kind of Liberation? Women and the Occupation of Iraq* (Berkeley, 2009).

9 Psychoanalysis, history and national culture

Daniel Pick

Why have so few historians in twentieth-century Britain engaged with psychoanalytic theories of the mind? More particularly, why have our most celebrated Marxist historians paid so little attention to Freud? In various contexts psychoanalysis and historiography have been pulled together in significant, if necessarily contentious, ways.[1] Leftist politics, historical analysis and Freudian thought have been made to join forces, for better or for worse, in other times and places.[2] In some European countries, noted historians expressed firm reservations about the presuppositions of 'psycho-history', but there were nonetheless significant forays into psychoanalytic terrain.[3] But in England, neither the illustrious Communist Party Historians Group (CPHG) nor any other substantial historical movement or 'school' was much troubled by Freud's account of the unconscious. While a number of anthropologists, philosophers and art critics sought to challenge or qualify psychoanalytic

---

[1] Influential claims for the significance of 'Freud for historians' were made in 1950s America (the heyday for psychoanalytic fortunes in the US in general) via Erik Erikson, Norman O. Brown, William Langer and others. More recently, Peter Gay, Dominick LaCapra, Lynn Hunt and Peter Loewenberg (to name a few) illustrate the diversity of historical dialogues with Freud. For the broader evolution of American historiography, see Peter Novick, *That Noble Dream: The 'Objectivity Question' and the American Historical Profession* (Cambridge, 1988), and Anthony Molho and Gordon S. Wood (eds), *Imagined Histories: American Historians Interpret the Past* (Princeton, 1998).

[2] See Russell Jacoby, *Repression of Psychoanalysis: Otto Fenichel and the Political Freudians* (New York, 1983); Elizabeth Ann Danto, *Freud's Free Clinics: Psychoanalysis and Social Justice, 1918–1938* (New York, 2005).

[3] See Solange Leibovici, 'Dutch history and depth psychology', *The Psychohistory Review*, 27, (1999), pp. 49–58; Jacques Maître, 'Psychological history in France: 1968–1997', *The Psychohistory Review*, 27, (1999), pp. 23–48; Hedwig Röckelein, 'Psychological history in Germany', *The Psychohistory Review*, 27, (1999), pp. 3–22. For an example of critical engagement, see Carlo Ginzburg, 'Freud, the wolf man, and the werewolves' in his *Myths, Emblems, Clues*, trans. J. and A. Tedeschi, (London, 1990). See also Peter Burke, 'Freud and cultural history', *Psychonalysis and History*, 9, (2007), pp. 5–15.

postulates, historians generally seem to have concluded that the 'talking cure' was irrelevant, hardly worth the trouble of detailed critique.

Despite this apparent lacuna, the problems and topics that have been addressed by historians and psychoanalysts in post-war Britain have important affinities. For example 'images of power' and 'the popular mentalities of subordination', to borrow phrases from E. P. Thompson, preoccupied many historians (Marxist or otherwise) in the later decades of the century.[4] In psychoanalysis, the potentially crippling effects of 'the superego' within the psychic and social order had proved ever more central concerns since the 1920s. 'The superego' was seen as an extremely fruitful 'applied' concept elsewhere (for instance in the work of the Frankfurt School intellectuals who studied the politics of authoritarianism, the attractions of consumer capitalism, the lure of fascism or the modern resurgence of anti-Semitism), but among historians, at least in Britain, this was not so.

In a fleeting reference to the question of the unconscious in the late 1970s (an 'aside' within a larger discussion of *Annales*), Eric Hobsbawm illustrated the distance between the disciplines of history and psychoanalysis, and reaffirmed the case for keeping them firmly apart: Freud was a 'bad historian' and the post-war French rediscovery of the Viennese professor's ideas was to be deplored in so far as it 'diverts attention into the unconscious or deep structures from, I won't say conscious, but anyway logical cohesion. It neglects system.'[5] Historians, it seems, are well advised to steer clear lest they end up in ahistorical abstractions or in viewing the past as but an expression of psychic life. Hobsbawm was not, as he had suggested at the time, particularly 'heterodox' in this disparaging view, at least amongst fellow professionals, although his claim to have 'no opinion' about Freudian psychology itself was more unusual.[6]

Other instances can easily be found of this swift intellectual rejection. The decidedly anti-Marxist Tudor specialist Geoffrey Elton, for example, took a dim view of Freud and concluded that his psychology was worthless in its own right. In his inaugural professorial lecture in Cambridge in

---

[4] E. P. Thompson, *Whigs and Hunters*, quoted in Geoff Eley, 'Edward Thompson, social history and political culture: the making of a working-class public' in Harvey J. Kaye and Keith McClelland (eds), *E. P. Thompson: Critical Perspectives* (Cambridge 1990), at p. 16. Cf. Thompson's observation in *The Making of the English Working Class* (London, [1963] 1980), p. 8: 'I do not see class as a "structure" nor even as a "category", but as something which in fact happens (and can be shown to have happened) in *human relationships*' [emphasis added].

[5] Hobsbawm, 'British history and the *Annales*: a note' [1978], reprinted in *On History* (London, 1997), at p. 184.

[6] Ibid., p. 244.

the late 1960s, Elton dismissed Freudian views as dated before likening the appeal of psychoanalysis, alongside Marxism, to psychedelic drugs.[7]

What cultural and historiographical significance can be attached to such critical observations and generalisations? Is historical practice necessarily as remote from a psychoanalytic vision of mind as these brusque accounts suggest? And how should we explain the muted response to Freud that has characterised historiography in Britain?

I

One might first imagine that the answer lies with the peculiarities of the 'national culture', as anatomised by the *New Left Review* (*NLR*) in the 1960s. Here, it was claimed that lack of contact with the classical sociological tradition and other advanced forms of Continental knowledge vitiated and impoverished English intellectual life, rendering it 'immune' to challenging and revolutionary thought. Particularly influential in this regard was Perry Anderson's essay 'Components of the National Culture' (1968). It surveyed, in memorably caustic prose, a range of academic disciplines and cultural practices that, so it was claimed, not only failed to produce their own revolutionary thinkers, but also eschewed meaningful engagement with powerful foreign theories. (I am not concerned here to explore the general merits, context or shortcomings of such an approach, which have been widely rehearsed elsewhere, but rather with its particular implications for an argument about the reception of psychoanalysis in historiography.)[8]

Anderson invites the reader to picture an England that had produced 'a culture in its own image: mediocre and inert'. This could, he proposes, be traced back to a nineteenth-century bourgeoisie that had no need to overthrow the *ancien régime* because it had already made an accommodation with it in the seventeenth century; in the ultimate economic sense the rising class felt no need finally to overthrow traditional values.[9] In the first half of the twentieth century, the fundamental cleavage between English and Continental social, political and

---

[7] *The Future of the Past: An Inaugural Lecture* [1968] (Cambridge, 1969), p. 19.

[8] For a critical reflection on the intellectual and political context of these debates, see Gareth Stedman Jones, 'History and theory: an English story', *Historein*, (Athens), 3, (2001), pp. 103–124; also Stefan Collini, *Absent Minds: Intellectuals in Britain* (Oxford, 2006). E. P. Thompson famously criticised the 'inverted podsnappery' of the *NLR* under Anderson and Tom Nairn in 'The peculiarity of the English' [1965] in *The Poverty of Theory* (London, 1978). For Anderson's later reflections, see *English Questions* (London, 1992).

[9] Anderson, 'Components of the national culture', *New Left Review* [henceforth *NLR*], 50, (1968), pp. 3–58, reprinted in Robin Blackburn and Alexander Cockburn (eds), *Student Power* (London, 1969) (references are to this edition).

intellectual life deepened: whilst the mainland knew the transformative effects of occupation, civil war or revolution virtually everywhere, this island suffered neither invasion nor the overthrow of its political system. Marxism and 'bourgeois' Continental sociology had only limited impact. (The devastating human consequences of that modern, Continental history seemed of rather less concern within this argument than its supposedly galvanising intellectual effect.) Marx may have found a less persecuting base in London than anywhere on the Continent, but his work remained, in its fine texture, obscure to English or English-based intellectuals, even those on the left, at least until the 1930s. In this barren national landscape, Anderson sees two oases of outstandingly innovative thought: anthropology and psychoanalysis. But these, he argues, never provided the basis for a wider transformation. Symptomatically, psychoanalytic ideas were confined to a 'technical enclave', as though exclusively the concern of clinicians, not of intellectuals at large, unlike in France, Germany and the United States.[10]

The first half of the twentieth century brought a wave of major Continental talents to these shores, but their effect was – so this account continues – to be less genuinely disruptive than appeared: those who prospered were closest to the conservatism and empiricism of their new home (witness the remarks of the émigré Elton above), and most hostile to what they had witnessed abroad.[11] 'Established English culture naturally welcomed these unexpected allies. Every insular reflex and prejudice was powerfully flattered and enlarged in the magnifying mirror they presented to it.'[12] English culture, according to this damning collective portrait, was repeatedly drawn to a static vision and appealed to a timeless 'mind'. The universalising pretensions of certain forms of psychology (albeit not derived from a psychoanalytic body of thought) were particularly congenial to the intellectuals who found most favour in England. The problem of any psychologism, Anderson argues, is to account for historical change, since the initial assumption is a self-contained, universal psyche. He criticises Ernst Gombrich for just this reason. Although he does not spell this out, there is an implied difference between the 'psychologism' he deplores and the psychoanalysis that he applauds. Anderson laments the fact that it took so long for Freud's work to reach a wide public in Britain (he was, according to this view, one of

[10] Anderson, 'Components', p. 259.
[11] Anderson lists leading figures as: Wittgenstein (philosophy); Malinowski (anthropology); Namier (history); Popper (social theory); Berlin (political theory); Gombrich (aesthetics); Eysenck (psychology); Klein (psychoanalysis); Deutscher (Marxism).
[12] Anderson, 'Components', p. 232.

the émigré intellectuals who did not 'fit in' with English homespun wisdom, and thus was marginalised). Anderson is appropriately critical of the anti-Freudian psychologist and publicist Hans Eysenck (doyen of IQ testing and consistent positivist opponent of psychoanalysis), whose work was widely feted. Freud's marginalisation, according to this line of thought, would only change much later in the century. It was facilitated, for instance, by the appearance of a relatively cheap paperback abridgement of Ernest Jones's biography of Freud in the 1960s and the paperback 'Pelican Freud' (including the major case histories) in the 1970s. Even then, Freud's position arguably remained more tenuous and marginal than in some other Western countries.

II

But Anderson stretched this point too far. True, Britain produced no precise equivalents to Freudian-influenced thinkers such as Parsons, Jakobsen, Adorno, Lévi-Strauss and Althusser, but it does not follow that 'There is no Western country where the presence of psychoanalysis in general culture is so vestigial'.[13] Certainly psychoanalysis was always controversial. Some early English audiences greeted the mere discussion of psychoanalysis in hostile silence, even in professional circles.[14] But if moral disgust was apparent enough, in mapping cultural responses to Freud we also need to consider the variety of popularisations and adaptations in the inter-war years, as well as the critical engagement of many major intellectual figures, from Malinowski to Wittgenstein. An important example (and a notable exception to my general argument about the dearth of interest in Freud within English historiography) is R. G. Collingwood. This Oxford philosopher and historian was to be a key proponent of an historical approach to psychology. Despite Collingwood's scepticism about modern psychologies at large, he took a very close personal and professional interest in psychoanalysis and expressed considerable admiration for Freud, despite some substantial misgivings, especially about the latter's more speculative 'anthropological' assumptions.[15] If Collingwood was, arguably, something of a lone voice within 'History' itself, his more than passing interest in psychoanalysis

---

[13] Ibid., p. 259.

[14] See Malcolm Pines, 'A history of psychodynamic psychiatry in Britain' in Jeremy Holmes (ed.), *Textbook of Psychotherapy in Psychiatric Practice* (Edinburgh, 1991), ch. 2, at p. 31; Isabel Hutton, *Memories of a Doctor in War and Peace* (London, 1960), pp. 128, 241–246.

[15] See James Connelly and Alan Costall, 'R. G. Collingwood and the idea of a historical psychology', *Theory and Psychology*, 10, (2000), pp. 147–170; David Boucher, *The Social and Political Thought of R. G. Collingwood* (Cambridge, 1989), p. 203.

was matched by that of other leading English academic and literary figures. Discussion of 'the talking cure' by a number of Bloomsbury and Cambridge luminaries needs to be part of the reckoning.[16] Keynes's extraordinarily prescient book, *The Economic Consequences of the Peace* (1919), for instance, paid more than mere lip-service to psychoanalysis. Extended discussion of psychoanalysis and the unconscious occurred in English art criticism, from Fry to Stokes, and beyond.[17] As to novelists (admittedly beyond Anderson's stated scope), where to begin? 'And so, who could remain unmoved when Freud seemed suddenly to plunge towards the origins?'[18] The answer to D. H. Lawrence's question was evidently meant to be 'nobody'. His own brooding discussions of history as well as sexuality sought to give due weight, albeit often in more mystical terms than Freud's, to the subterranean depths of human motivation. A different response was provided by Aldous Huxley in his inter-war satirical visions of a 'brave new world' of supposedly free but actually compulsory sexual promiscuity, devoid of love, loyalty or guilt. Huxley is ambivalent about Freud's disenchanting insights into the psyche, but in his dystopian account the psychoanalyst, scarcely less than the psychologist Ivan Pavlov or the industrialist Henry Ford, is cast as an agent of modern alienation.

Lawrence's writings on psychoanalysis, or for that matter Huxley's stories and letters,[19] turned between awe and derision. But whatever the tone, these were responses that indicated Freud's complex and important *presence*. Many would have accepted Lawrence's characterisation of the moving effect of reading Freud, even if they reached quite different conclusions. Freud's ideas, if often relayed inaccurately and 'second-hand', were increasingly widely discussed. With the establishment of a British Psychoanalytical Society after World War I, the movement had a focal point and, in the controversial person of Ernest Jones, an indefatigable ambassador, with a hot line to Freud himself.[20] Jones's own prolific published work, speeches and lectures over more than half a century did

---

[16] See Eli Zaretsky, *Secrets of the Soul: A Social and Cultural History of Psychoanalysis* (New York, 2004).

[17] See, for instance, Roger Fry, *The Artist and Psycho-Analysis* (London, 1924); Adrian Stokes, 'Painting and the inner world' [1963], in *The Critical Writings of Adrian Stokes* (London, 1967), vol. 3.

[18] D. H. Lawrence, *Psychoanalysis and the Unconscious* (London, 1923), p. 14.

[19] Aldous Huxley, *Letters*, ed. Grover Smith, (London, 1969).

[20] For Freud's influence on other psychotherapeutic organisations, see Henry Dicks, *Fifty Years of the Tavistock Clinic* (London, 1970); Pines 'A History'; Suzanne Raitt, 'Early British psychoanalysis and the medico-psychological clinic', *History Workshop Journal* [*HWJ*], 58, (2004), pp. 63–85; cf. Matthew Thomson, *Psychological Subjects: Identity, Culture, and Health in Twentieth-Century Britain* (Oxford, 2006).

much to bring psychoanalysis to wider public attention and scientific respectability. In 1921, the author of a popular primer on the subject observed that 'This country was very slow to receive the Freudian theories', although it was noted how the value of psychoanalysis was now being recognised. The ultimate 'rock of offence' here was said to be Freud's sexual theory.[21] Such books were a striking testimony to the growing reach of Freud's ideas in the 1920s. No small number of artists, actors and writers found Freud's insistence on the centrality of the Oedipus complex illuminating, even compelling. Thus by the 1930s, Laurence Oliver chose to pay close attention to Jones's distinct perspective on *Hamlet* (as well as *Othello*): indeed, the actor consulted the psychoanalyst in person, and at some length, before beginning rehearsals.[22]

III

It would thus be simplistic to treat the scepticism of so many professional historians as a by-product of a supposedly century-old 'native' English indifference or hostility to psychoanalysis. One could equally well provide instances of critical Continental reviewers as well as dissatisfied erstwhile followers.[23] Moreover, when one turns more specifically to the historians' prolonged neglect of Freud one encounters a further problem with Anderson's cultural diagnosis. It may explain some historians' reluctance to 'cross intellectual borders', but by no means all. Despite his deep scepticism about borrowing from psychoanalysis, Hobsbawm, for example, was never an intellectual 'little Englander'. On the contrary, he was in all senses 'well travelled', at ease in many parts of the world and open to many subjects beyond his own; his published work provides copious evidence of a richly cosmopolitan approach to the past and his Marxism, although a continuing and important feature, was often put 'in dialogue' with other approaches or concerns. There is no necessary reason to believe Hobsbawm's intellectual scepticism to be mere squeamishness about the complex theoretical or, for that matter, the intimate sexual, terrain that Freud explored (unlike some earlier radical-liberal historians who did view open discussion of such matters as plain revolting).[24] Personal predilections and

---

[21] Robert Hingley, *Psycho-Analysis* (London, 1921), p. 21.

[22] Brenda Maddox, *Freud's Wizard: The Enigma of Ernest Jones* (London, 2006), p. 257.

[23] George Makari, *Revolution in Mind: The Creation of Psychoanalysis* (New York, 2008).

[24] Prominent liberals, including the historians Barbara and Lawrence Hammond, believed not only that a general assault upon civilisation had begun in 1914, but also that modernism was an invitation to chaos. Freud's work was seen as part of this affront to

first-hand knowledge (or lack of it) may play their part, but here our knowledge is often scanty (this is true even for Lewis Namier, who we know had some experience of psychoanalysis in Vienna).[25] In any event, we will refrain from the risky business of second-guessing, case by case, the extent of exposure to psychoanalysis. Nor will we pursue 'wild analysis' of 'resistance' in the historical 'objectors', but will rather adopt the principle that their intellectual critique be taken on its own terms. Hobsbawm's, as noted, turned upon the risk that a psychoanalytically informed historiography would use 'the unconscious' to by-pass 'logical cohesion' and 'system'.

To understand Hobsbawm's distaste for Freud in historiography we also need to consider the power of the historians' *professional* identity. After 1945, the CPHG pitted itself *against* the conservative supposedly apolitical or non-committed approach of 'establishment historians'. The CPHG historians had usually trained in the same Oxbridge world as their liberal and conservative colleagues, even if they later chose, or were obliged, to move to less cloistered university settings (Christopher Hill was an exception here in remaining an Oxford don). Their professional ethos often trumped Party demands for rote interpretations. They remained committed to the view that historical analysis must flow from the records, close immersion in the archives and the factual evidence: history was a *craft*, with its own specific protocols and conventions, not simply an instrument in the service of a predefined political or philosophical interpretation of the world.[26] Thompson's later diatribes against Althusser, for instance, reflected a mistrust of abstract theory that was strongly shared within the historical profession at large, although in his case it may also have stemmed from another early influence upon him: F. R. Leavis. Not that Thompson, any more than the other leading figures of the CPHG, could be said to be averse to 'theory' per se.[27] Marxism had importantly shaped his intellectual career, even if he strongly repudiated any vestiges of Stalinism and extolled the virtues of an indigenous, less abstract, radical English tradition. But the sense of the self-conscious and practical *craft* of

common decency. In 1918 Barbara Hammond wrote to her husband: 'Lord, how I do loathe the psych.ans. Can disgustingness or folly go further or be more far-fetched?'; quoted in Peter Clark, *Liberals and Social Democrats* (Cambridge, 1978), at p. 207.

[25] Linda Colley, *Namier* (London, 1989), p. 27.

[26] See the interviews with Hobsbawm and Thompson in MARHO [Mid-Atlantic Radical Historians Organization], *Visions of History* (Manchester, 1983), [eds Henry Abelove, Betsy Blackmar, Peter Dimock and Jonathan Schneer].

[27] On Thompson's relationship to Leavis and to Raymond Williams (also no enthusiast for psychoanalysis), see Stedman Jones, 'History'; cf. Williams, *Politics and Letters: Interviews with New Left Review* (London, 1979).

the historian did present an additional hurdle to be crossed in the face of certain forms of theory, notably psychoanalysis.

IV

Psychoanalysis, of course, has a diverse history; thus, for its serious critics it represents something of a moving target. As is well known, the social, political, cultural and psychological convulsions of World War I and its aftermath coincided with and, in part, stimulated the expanding theoretical and clinical vocabulary of the Freudian movement. That would in turn be put back to work in interpreting the catastrophes of contemporary European history. 'The shadow of the object' fell upon psychoanalysis with a tremendous force, in a path-breaking publication 'Mourning and Melancholia'. The 'death drive' emerged in *Beyond the Pleasure Principle*. By 1923, the 'structural model', involving the agencies of 'ego', 'id' and 'superego', provided in effect a new account of the mind. Inter-war Freudian thought was superimposed upon earlier psychoanalytic ideas. One might then go back to those beginnings, re-read them afresh, in the light of what had been postulated since, not only by Freud himself, but also by talented followers, such as Abraham, Ferenczi or Klein. Freud famously drew an analogy between the human mind and the strata of Roman remains, but he might equally have applied this to the dense 'laying down' of psychoanalytic theories. Still to come from Freud, after 1923 and before his death in London in 1939, were (amongst other works) *Civilization and its Discontents*, the *New Introductory Lectures on Psycho-Analysis* and *Moses and Monotheism*. None, as far as I am aware, caused any detectable intellectual problem or aroused any methodological interest amongst English historians, radical or otherwise. But if there was a rich variety of different psychoanalytic approaches or directions to choose from by the 1920s and 1930s, historians tended to regard the field as a monolith, without its own history.[28]

The new modernist experimentalism in conceptualising the mind and the interactions of minds had been stimulated by Darwin's evolutionary theory, Nietzsche's critique of Western morality and, of course, by Freud's insistence that the ego is not master in its own house. These and other major intellectual developments threw up new *potential*

---

[28] It was not uncommon in this period more generally to conflate 'Freudian', 'Jungian' and 'Adlerian', long after the individuals in question had parted company. See Thomson, *Psychological Subjects*.

challenges to conventional historical understanding.[29] If psychoanalysis was felt to be dissonant with and disturbing to 'Victorian' ideals of behaviour or morals, 'modernists' often regarded this as a point in its favour. As Graham Richards puts it:

While the radical, even bizarre nature of psychoanalytic doctrines had, by 1918, become evident, this was not necessarily a handicap ... for had not the world itself become bafflingly bizarre? Besides the war itself, aircraft, radio, the Russian Revolution, the influenza epidemic, Picasso, X-rays and Einstein (to cite but a selection) had, in under two decades, overthrown all previous assumptions about the world – from what was beautiful to what was common sense, from the essentially civilized character of Europeans to the nature of the universe.[30]

'Modernists' characteristically perceived 'Victorianism' to have been marked by its over-complacent certainties about representation and identity. Think here, for instance, of Virginia Woolf's famous accounts of a previous literary generation's false certainties (she had Wells, Bennett and Galsworthy in her sights), their supposed vision of life as a series of gig-lamps symmetrically arranged. Earlier shibboleths about self and other depended, it was now said, upon the arbitrary and ultimately unsustainable exclusion of whole areas of psychic life. The idea of biography took on a very different hue in the work not only of Freud (whose *Interpretation of Dreams* might be seen as a new way into the writing of a life) but also in the novels of Joyce or Proust. Yet the professional historians continued to offer individual or collective chronicles without much reference to this presumed crisis of narrative style or authorial identity.[31]

V

By 'History', I intend here a restricted sense of the term: the largely university-led academic field that was organised around groupings of professional teachers, researchers and students, consciously presented as a single subject. Its emergence, in this sense, had been signalled in the last four decades of the nineteenth century, in England and elsewhere, by a variety of new societies and periodicals, as well as increasing numbers of university posts. There had been one or two dedicated

---

[29] Dorothy Ross (ed.), *Modernist Impulses in the Human Sciences, 1870–1930* (Baltimore, 1994), p. 1.

[30] Graham Richards, 'Putting Britain on the couch: the popularisation of psychoanalysis in Britain 1918–1940', *Science in Context*, 13, (2000), pp. 183–230, at p. 188.

[31] Frank Manuel, *Freedom from History and Other Untimely Essays* (New York, 1972), p. 48, describes the 1930s edition of the *Cambridge Modern History* as 'that grand masterpiece of provincialism', concluding 'you could read chapter after chapter without even suspecting the existence of these transformations'.

professorial chairs in the subject earlier than 1870, but it was across the following sixty years that 'History' fully emerged as an autonomous university discipline.[32] In England, the Royal Historical Society had been founded in 1868; Oxford and Cambridge both established History as a distinct field of study in the 1870s.[33] The *English Historical Review* appeared in 1886. Throughout the Victorian period, there had, of course, been many different accounts of the purposes of historical understanding, but when it crystallised as a formal university enterprise, it was a particular version of the 'outward' not 'inward' life that was, overwhelmingly, to be studied. Increasingly, the professional skills and moral balance of the trained historian were emphasised.

Serious history was insistently cordoned off from antiquarian enthusiasm, political advocacy, a passion for collecting or mere armchair speculating. According to the influential champion of the subject in Oxford, William Stubbs, the historian should be the patient learner, *not* the theorist; he rejected the requirement of an explicit philosophy of history.[34] History, declared Seeley, on succeeding Kingsley as Regius Professor of History at Cambridge in 1869, is the school of statesmanship ... the school of public feeling and patriotism'.[35] The Oxbridge historians were to develop as close-knit 'fraternities' – a 'little band of friends' as one commentator has put it.[36] The study of History at university was very frequently to serve as a stepping-stone to careers in the domestic civil service or in the administration of the empire.[37] Herbert Butterfield, writing many years later, nicely captured this ethos: 'We teach and write the kind of history which is appropriate to our organization, congenial to the climate of our part of the world. We can

---

[32] Phillipa Levine, *The Amateur and the Professional: Antiquarians, Historians and Archaeologists in Victorian England, 1838–1886* (Cambridge, 1986), p. 165. See also Alon Kadish, *Historians, Economists and Economic History* (London, 1989); Reba Soffer, *Discipline and Power: The University, History and the Making of an English Elite, 1870–1930* (Stanford, 1994).

[33] In Cambridge, the Natural Sciences Tripos and the Moral Sciences Tripos were introduced in 1848. The latter Tripos included political economy, jurisprudence, English law, modern history and moral philosophy. A Law and History Tripos was established in 1870, with a separate History Tripos in place by 1873. In Oxford, a separate School of History was established in 1871.

[34] Quoted in Levine, *The Amateur*, at p. 76.

[35] Quoted in T. W. Heyck, *The Transformation of Intellectual Life in Victorian England* (London 1982), at p. 140.

[36] G. P. Gooch, referring to Stubbs and the other prominent historians in late-nineteenth-century Oxford; *The Transformation*, p. 140.

[37] On this point, see Gareth Stedman Jones, 'The pathology of English history', *NLR*, 46, (1967), pp. 29–43, at p. 29.

scarcely help it if this kind of history is at the same time the one most adapted to the preservation of the existing regime.'[38]

Early twentieth-century History was not fertile soil for psychoanalysis. Among the published surveys of the early reception of Freud in this country, none identifies History as even a minor 'port of entry' for his work.[39] Nor did academic History appear much affected by the avant-garde spirit so evident in art, literature and certain areas of science.[40] Where these major bodies of thought had been glimpsed at all, it was often enough through 'the blurred light of caricature and vulgarization'.[41] The modernist challenge to represent the past anew was more strongly and widely taken up outside of university History departments than within it. The wave of German-speaking historians who fled Nazi persecution in the 1930s and found a new home in Britain did not alter this basic trend in relation to psychoanalysis and the modernist ferment of which it was a part.[42] Admittedly, there are limits to the regular pattern described here. There are, for instance, arguably some psychoanalytic resonances in Lytton Strachey's biographical portraits, but Strachey was anything but a conventional professional historian. Traces of Freud's influence can also be detected in the work of Namier, although perhaps less so than Nietzsche's.[43] Namier aside, none of the

---

[38] Herbert Butterfield, *The Englishman and his History* [1944] (London, 1970), pp. 1, 11, where Butterfield praised the English achievement of maturely resisting wild Continental aberrations.

[39] See, for example, Robert Hinshelwood, 'Psychoanalysis in Britain: points of cultural access, 1893–1918', *International Journal of Psycho-Analysis*, 76, (1995), pp. 135–151; Dean Rapp, 'The reception of Freud by the British press: general interest and literary magazines, 1920–1925', *Journal of the History of the Behavioural Sciences*, 24, (1988), pp. 191–201; Richards, 'Britain'; Stuart Raymond Samuels, 'Marx, Freud and English intellectuals: a study of the dissemination and reconciliation of ideas', unpublished PhD thesis, Stanford University (1971).

[40] In *That Noble Dream*, Novick discusses how early twentieth-century historians, on both sides of the Atlantic, largely by-passed the challenges of modernism. For the wider modernist challenge and its relationship to Freudian thought, see Peter Collier and Judy Davies (eds), *Modernism and the European Unconscious* (Cambridge, 1990).

[41] Stedman Jones, 'The pathology', p. 29.

[42] Significant émigré historians in Britain are listed in Peter Alter (ed.), *Out of the Third Reich: Refugee Historians in Post-War Britain* (London, 1998). Hans Israel Bach's (1902–1977) interest in Jung makes him an exception, see C. Hoffmann, 'The contribution of German-speaking Jewish immigrants to British historiography' (Appendix), in *Second Chance: Two Centuries of German-Speaking Jews in the United Kingdom* (Tübingen, 1991).

[43] Strachey's biographical portraits, though richly evocative, could not be claimed to apply psychoanalysis in any sustained way. Namier's Freudianism, it has been argued, is also limited. On this point, see Stedman Jones, 'The pathology', p. 46; cf. Anderson, 'Components', p. 245. But on Namier's interest in Marx and Freud, see Julia Namier, *Louis Namier: A Biography* (London, 1971), p. 318. The historian's (embarrassing) enthusiasm for Marx and Freud was always 'airbrushed' in retrospective accounts by historians who were, in other respects, his admirers; Colley, *Namier*, p. 31.

most important university historians who grew up during Freud's lifetime seem to have expressed much interest in his theory of the unconscious.[44] It seemed easier for those outside the formal profession to make imaginative and critical use of Freud in writing of the past. In this respect, Elias (*The Civilizing Process*), Dodds (*The Greeks and the Irrational*) and Cohn (*Europe's Inner Demons*) are exemplary of this tendency both before and after 1945.

VI

In the decades after World War II no major British historian declared psychoanalysis to be 'the new frontier' (William Langer's controversial description, when president of the American Historical Association in the late 1950s). Like T. S. Eliot's mystery cat, psychoanalysis continued to be routinely absent from the scene or, if it did make an appearance, was soon 'shooed away'. A. J. P. Taylor, like Hobsbawm, was briskly dismissive.[45] Lawrence Stone referred to Erik Erikson and the American tradition before suggesting that the whole subject was out of reach: 'The Freudian psychologists who followed the Social Darwinists pointed to an area that historians couldn't follow – the bedroom, the bathroom, the nursery. Even Eriksonian psychology with its stress on character formation through childhood and adolescence, to later identity crises has opened new possibilities but been little followed up.'[46] This fell somewhere between description and prescription. Stone was right to say that Freud was 'little followed up' although, strikingly, many of the most discussed historical works of the post-war period, including his own, were indeed venturing into the bedroom, the bathroom and the nursery, even if not in Freudian terms. Historical works on sex, marriage, death and divorce, magic and religion, the history of crowds

---

[44] Influential contributors to English historical writing, who came to maturity between the 1920s and the 1940s, when Freud's work was widely discussed in the arts and humanities, included Postan (born 1898), Cole (1889), Collingwood (1889), Power (1889), Toynbee (1889), Carr (1892), Butterfield (1900), Needham (1900), Cobban (1901), Runciman (1903), Boxer (1904), Taylor (1906), Plumb (1911), Hill (1912), Trevor Roper (1914), Chadwick (1916), Hilton (1916), Hobsbawm (1917), Mack Smith (1920), Briggs (1921), Elton (1921) and Thompson (1924). For the broad development of the field, see Christopher Parker, *The English Idea of History from Coleridge to Collingwood* (Aldershot, 1988), and *The English Historical Tradition Since 1850* (Edinburgh, 1990).

[45] See, for instance, A. J. P. Taylor, 'The historian as biographer' [1979], reprinted in his *From Napoleon to the Second International* (London 1993): 'If this sounds like nonsense, I can only plead that it represents my view of psychoanalysis as a biographical weapon' (p. 28).

[46] Lawrence Stone, 'Prosopography' [1971], in *The Past and the Present* (London, 1981).

and riots owed more to cultural anthropology than psychoanalysis, but this is not to say there were no hidden affinities. There are again exceptions to this generalised picture: for instance, the historiography of fascism has sometimes referred explicitly (critically or otherwise) to Freud, Wilhelm Reich or American 'psycho-historians'. Yet overall the disconnection remains striking in comparison with cognate fields: thus it is still quite possible in many universities to complete a history degree and never be expected to read a word of Freud.

Although Freud may be summarily repudiated, as Peter Gay observed, most history writing involves an implicit model of the inner working of the human mind.[47] In other words, eschewing Freud's versions of the unconscious, historians do not necessarily avoid their own psychological speculation into the unspoken motives of their dead characters. It is unwise to exaggerate the uniformity of the psychology that is routinely deployed in modern historical narratives, but often 'mind' appears through the lens of traditional utilitarianism (with the focus exclusively upon the conscious calculus of pains and pleasures driving 'purposive actions'). In some work, we may detect the remnants of nineteenth-century biologism and instinct theories (without their subsequent Freudian reworking into the psychosomatic borderline of 'drives', still less their Kleinian transformation into psychic 'positions'), perhaps also echoes of behaviourism, or rational choice theory.[48] Key figures from the CPHG, intent on debunking the snobbery of traditional accounts about the 'mindset' of the poor and lowly, characteristically endeavoured to show how a subject's action (within the historical constraints and available languages of the period) could be seen as reasonable, the choices made rational, in relation to 'interest', defined in terms of collectively comprehensible, overt goals. Evidently, such suppositions as to the 'legibility' of the actions of the dead are important, indeed required in any serious historical reconstruction of the past, but what is often elided entirely in such accounts is the possibility of an unconscious dimension to decision-making and action.

The historians' endeavour to take stated utterances seriously, to reconstruct intentions, or the 'method' in the apparent madness of the past is, in one sense, congruent with a psychoanalytic no less than an anthropological stance: the patient's communications after all are, ideally, to be listened to as sensitively and carefully as possible, without an attempt to judge, impose or smooth over. But the psychoanalytic

---

[47] Peter Gay, *Freud for Historians* (New York, 1985).
[48] See Colin Elman and Miriam Fendius Elman (eds), *Bridges and Boundaries: Historians, Political Scientists, and the Study of International Relations* (Cambridge, MA, 2001).

attention also presupposes precisely an unconscious communication, a world of unconscious fantasy, in operation throughout. For the 'Freudian' historical biographer or prosopographer there is, of course, always a methodological difficulty, and this cannot be gainsaid. Unlike the psychoanalyst, the historian usually has no direct interlocutor (oral history is a special case here, of course); certainly, historical study is not analogous to the psychoanalytic situation, 'here and now', and involving unconscious transference (other, that is, than of the researcher to the material or period itself). Lack of evidence may mean that the unspoken motivations of the characters remain necessarily obscure to us, but recognition of potential unconscious intra-psychic and interpersonal complexities could at least be acknowledged as a 'known unknown'. To do so might usefully serve to check overconfident assertions about the motives that drove people in the past to act or speak as they did.

To return to our opening question about Hobsbawm and company, it was perhaps significant that those who had found an intellectual base in the CPHG strove to match or even to 'out-professional' the professionals.[49] *Past & Present*, something of a CPHG flagship, was to offer impeccably researched articles. A series of groundbreaking studies appeared, offering, among other important things, substantial new work on working-class life, labour and struggle. The CPHG had pioneered a new version of 'social history', in conscious rejection both of the legal, diplomatic, high-political or ecclesiastical history that had previously dominated the field, and of overtly romantic celebrations of 'the English people'. They also fostered a new, more complex, understanding of the dynamic relationship between socio-economic and cultural forces. In the process they challenged the view that it was possible mechanically to understand writing, still less feelings, attitudes or group identities by routinely attributing them to the subject's economic location.[50]

---

[49] For the background to the CPHG, see Bill Schwarz, '"The people" in history: the Communist Party Historians' Group, 1946–56' in Richard Johnson (ed.), *Making Histories: Studies in History-Writing and Politics* (London, 1982). Thompson felt that he was increasingly required to work in 'minute brush stokes', to 'sharpen my scholarly equipment', to 'Namierize', i.e. 'to examine in minute detail', whilst 'watched by this largely conservative profession'; see Abelove *et al.* (eds), *Visions of History*, p. 7.

[50] Thus Hilton declared in the first issue of *Past & Present*: 'it is not enough to study capital, wage labour and units of production in their economic aspects alone. The historian intent on discovering the political and social consciousness of a given class must also study religion, art, law and politics. Consciousness is not a direct reflection of the economic activity of a class.' 'Capitalism – what's in a name?', *Past & Present*, 1, (1952), pp. 32–43, at p. 42. On this point, see also Christopher Hill, 'Puritans and the poor', *Past & Present*, 2, (1952), pp. 32–50; E. P. Thompson, *Customs in Common* (London, 1991), p. 187; Eric Hobsbawm, *Interesting Times: A Twentieth-Century Life* (London, 2002), p. 97.

These writers were concerned with economic factors, of course, but their achievement was to demonstrate, again and again, the impossibility of making simple assumptions about the relationship of 'superstructure' and 'base'. Here 'culture', not 'psyche', was the fly in the ointment of an older 'economism', but a *potential* space was nonetheless opened up to consider seriously the place of unconscious fantasy and identification in the making of social positions.

Another way to look at this conundrum is in relation to 'identity'. Those who emerged from the CPHG do not appear to have concerned themselves with Freud's demonstrations of the split nature of identity, yet the question of splits and reconciliations, conflicts and cohesion within and between groups was of major concern in other ways, perhaps in part because they had themselves struggled to stay together (and indeed ultimately broke apart) in the face of their divergent views of the Soviet Union in the Cold War, above all in relation to the crisis of Hungary in 1956. E. P. Thompson's work in general, it has been argued, derived from and in turn contributed to 'socialist humanism'.[51] His great book, *The Making of The English Working Class* (1963), draws upon Fromm's socialist–humanist arguments about the 'fear of freedom',[52] but Freud is not directly addressed. According to Anthony Easthope, the 'humanist' Thompson fails to see that an unconscious process might also be at work, troubling and dislocating any notion of 'wholeness' of identity or of identification, cutting across our conscious allegiances.[53] Yet some parts of the book come close to suggesting exactly that. The central thesis is that 'In the years between 1780 and 1832 most English working people came to feel an identity of interests between themselves and as against their rulers and employers'. But various forces subvert or at least complicate this straightforward worldly 'us' and 'them'. One thorny question in Thompson's story is the power and attraction of Methodism in the popular imagination. Thompson does not want to conceptualise this terrain in an old Marxist (for Thompson 'Stalinist') language of 'false consciousness'. The reasons *why* it proved so enticing, even thrilling, to many, remain somewhat elusive here, but what is vividly described is the sheer intensity of the emotions at stake. Methodism is presented as a series of 'psychological atrocities committed upon children', but nonetheless a social

---

[51] On the diverse influences at work here, see Kate Soper, 'Socialist humanism', in Kaye and McClelland (eds), *E. P. Thompson*, at p. 206.

[52] In relation to the process of turning the labourer into 'his own slave-driver', *The Making*, p. 393.

[53] See Anthony Easthope, *The Unconscious* (London, 1999), p. 155.

force that evidently also channelled and played upon human desire and passion. This was a collective phenomenon with complex psychic causes and consequences. As he develops his account, Thompson describes the repressed sexual wishes and fears that he suspects run through this religious movement.

Here, in the presentation of the excesses of evangelical religion at the turn of the nineteenth century, there is an endeavour to give unconscious fantasies some real weight in the historical analysis of a mass phenomenon, even if, as Barbara Taylor has shown, such 'irrational' features are also implicitly linked with femininity and described with a kind of moral disgust.[54] The iconography of Methodism, its focus on sin, its obsessive horror at the body, appears open to psychological, perhaps even psychoanalytical, investigation. Thompson notes the layers of conflicting symbolism in the representation of Christian Wesleyan hymns. He refers to the maternal, Oedipal, sexual and sado-masochistic tendencies that emerged. The utility of Methodism as a work discipline is evident to him, but why working people would internalise it, why, as it were, they would choose their own 'psychic exploitation' remains an open question.[55] Thompson's discussion of 'The Transforming Power of the Cross' can be read as a form of 'psycho-history'. He refers to mass hysteria as a 'component of the psychic processes of counter-revolution', but in ways that appear to leave other forms of *political* identification untouched.

In the case of 'the crowd in history', as developed by Thompson and Hobsbawm, as well as by George Rudé (another to have joined the Communist Party in the 1930s), the aim was to uncover the variety and continuity of indigenous national protest against authority. In terms of psychology, the bone of contention was not Freud's writings on groups (nowhere discussed), but a preceding, hostile, approach to 'the masses' exemplified, above all, by Gustave Le Bon in the late nineteenth century, and echoed in New Liberal works such as J. A. Hobson's *The Psychology of Jingoism* (1901). Riot, argued Thompson, was not, as earlier crowd theorists had suggested, just some kind of instinctual 'spasm' or feral relapse. Instead, he found in almost every eighteenth-century crowd action that he studied, a 'legitimating notion'.[56] What crowds rioted *against*, time and again, was a perceived outrage to moral assumptions, as much as 'actual deprivation'.[57]

---

[54] Barbara Taylor, 'Religion, radicalism and fantasy', *HWJ*, 39, (1995), pp. 102–112.
[55] *The Making*, pp. 407–414.
[56] E. P. Thompson, 'The moral economy of the crowd in the eighteenth century', in *Customs*.
[57] Ibid., p. 188.

Thompson later insisted on the centrality of 'the moral economy of the crowd' for the entire body of his work.[58] Hobsbawm had also followed this line when, in the opening number of *Past & Present*, he had repudiated an earlier claim that Luddism was but 'pointless, frenzied, industrial *Jacquerie*'.[59] Instead, the machine breakers were engaged in straightforwardly intelligible 'direct action'. This was part of an established pattern of advancing shared social goals, during the early historical phase of industrial conflict, and it took the form of 'collective bargaining by riot'.[60] According to Hobsbawm, in none of the instances he encountered 'was there any question of hostility to machines as such'; it was 'simply a technique of trade unionism in the period before, and during the early phases of, the Industrial Revolution'.[61] But how can we be sure that it was 'simply' (Hobsbawm's word) an expression of a rational and easily comprehensible public purpose? This is too strong a claim. For how are we to know that no hostility to the machine was involved? Might attacks on machines not be considered (after Freud) as, at least potentially, 'over-determined'?

This insistence on viewing eighteenth- or early nineteenth-century mass violence as merely (conscious) politics by other means was, of course, an understandable reaction to the rhetorical violence and class prejudices of European crowd psychology, to say nothing of the brute force that had so often greeted the radical protest movements of modern European history. (In similar vein, Raymond Williams wrote in *Keywords* that there is no such thing as a mob, only ways of describing people thus.) Yet there is a problem here: in the (benign) rehabilitation of the crowd with its 'moral economy', other collective or individual 'purposes' are not considered; the possibility that, say, sadism, cruelty, envy, hatred, idealisation (as well as love, appreciation or gratitude) may warrant consideration as potent collective 'political' forces. Later, in *Interesting Times*, Hobsbawm claimed that in his own experience, participation in crowds might in fact also usefully be likened to sexual enjoyment: 'Next to sex, the activity combining bodily experience and intense emotion to the highest degree is the participation in a mass demonstration at a time of great public

---

[58] 'The moral economy revisited', in *Customs*, at p. 260.

[59] Hobsbawm was referring here to J. H. Plumb's account in *England in the Eighteenth Century* (London, 1950).

[60] Hobsbawm, 'The machine breakers' [1952], reprinted in *Labouring Men: Studies in the History of Labour* [1964] (London, 1968), p. 7; and Hobsbawm, *Primitive Rebels* (Manchester, 1959), p. 111: 'The classical mob did not merely riot as a protest, but because it expected to achieve something by its riot.'

[61] Hobsbawm, *Labouring Men*, p. 8.

exaltation.'[62] One can only imagine what Hobsbawm's accounts of banditry, riots and working-class protest movements might have looked like had he pursued this observation further.

The historians who had emerged from the CPHG explored group phenomena in ways that provided, *inter alia*, a more illuminating collective portrait of previously ignored working people, especially 'labouring men', but not in the same close dialogue with social psychology as some early pioneers of *Annales*, nor with Freud's distinct arguments on the subject of mass psychology, let alone with later psychoanalytic contributions to the study of the group, such as those of Wilfred Bion. Particularly intriguing in respect to presuppositions about reason and passion was Hobsbawm and Rudé's *Captain Swing* (1968). Here emotions were acknowledged, but firmly demarcated. The Swing rioters of 1830 sought, albeit often inchoately, to resist the wider havoc of social, industrial and economic transformation in rural England. But a different kind of moral or emotional scrutiny is also implied. We are told that it is probable that only some of them 'carried their hate into practice' and these individuals could be identified as a particular sub-group within the various villages studied:

> Hatred and revenge were universally felt . . . Yet it is also probable that those who carried their hate into practice were a special section of the village; the wild, independent, savage marginal men – poachers, shepherds and the like – and the youths (or those most likely to be inspired by their actions). Such men had no doubt been active in 1830 . . . Yet the core of the movement was in the respectable, peaceful labourers, its leadership lay among them and among village artisans, and nothing is more impressive than the absence of violence. Even the collective revenge on overseers of the poor, whose oppressions might well have released reactions of blind fury, never seems to have exceeded the conventional limits of fights at fairs . . . the limits of violence were known and not overstepped.[63]

Hobsbawm and Rudé allow for hatred and fury. Such factors become the particular signature note, however, of one sub-group, the so-called savage men (just as in Thompson's work, hysterical traits particularly mark one religious movement, Methodism), whilst others are seen to know the limits of violence, internally to master their passion, manage hatred and thereafter to operate according to the principle of 'peaceful assertion'. The broader narrative describes psychic states (a raging desire for revenge, for instance, presumed to be 'universally felt') and actions, but the movement's core members appear to have pacified

---

[62] Hobsbawm, *Interesting Times*, p. 73.
[63] Hobsbawm and Rudé, *Captain Swing* (London, 1969), pp. 287–288.

themselves within. Is this to assume that their less violent behaviour can be directly mapped onto a less violent psychic state? The text is ambiguous here. As well as the obvious gender bias toward the study of men (a tendency later vigorously challenged by a number of feminist historians), what goes unremarked is that this description tends towards *psychological* speculation about the sometimes unspoken feelings of the characters in *Captain Swing*. The absence or presence of violent *behaviour* is of course a central issue in the analysis and argument, but what is interesting in relation to my discussion here is the way this account edges towards a different kind of claim about the psychic work that underpins that behaviour. How can we know for sure what was 'experienced' from such a distance as this, and how can we claim certain 'feelings' to have been either universal or confined to the 'wild' group?

My point here is not to reverse this account, i.e. to propose a different distribution of feelings among the Swing Rioters, nor to criticise the historians' endeavour to empathise with, or at least to imagine, those protestors' states of mind, but simply to notice, in the face of the objections Hobsbawm raised to psychoanalysis in historiography, the unacknowledged operation of a certain 'psychologism' here. We cannot know for certain as much as this account implies about the 'feelings' of those involved, nor about their limits. The problem here is not in fact that too little is imputed to the actors' internal world, as perhaps some psycho-historians might argue, but, arguably, rather too much. Psychoanalysis might cause the historian to hesitate more, not less, before claiming to discriminate definitively between the groups, or to demarcate what was really, or even most probably, going on inside their minds, and, conversely, what was not.

Be that as it may, the broader achievement of Thompson, Hobsbawm and other contributors to this historical literature on crowds, protest and working-class life was to show that the relationship of economic conditions to cultural production, social action and literary form could not be assumed in advance.[64] They needed to be researched, case by case. There was growing interest amongst historians in the late twentieth century in exploring how culture fashioned the meanings of social, economic or political processes. Anthropology (notably the 'thick

---

[64] Perry Anderson, *Considerations on Western Marxism* (London, 1976). Hobsbawm observes that English communists did not encounter the Frankfurt School approach and the work of Lukács and Korsch until the 1950s; see his *Interesting Times*, p. 97. Thompson would later criticise the Frankfurt School (alongside the much longer diatribe against Althusser) in *The Poverty of Theory* (p. 377) because it left too little room for free will, underestimating the real difference that could be made by popular, radical dissent and mass protest.

descriptions' of local customs, beliefs and ways of life, memorably provided by Clifford Geertz) was influential. Stimulated by Foucault and other post-structuralist thinkers, 'discourse' also became, for some, a key term, used in order to show how we are positioned as subjects within an available, historically constituted (and constraining) horizon of meanings and connections. Some of this had already been influentially elaborated, albeit in very different terms, by Foucault's one-time teacher, Althusser. In the Althusserian account, the individual was called into being, interpellated through language.[65] Foucault did not share Althusser's desire to amalgamate psychoanalysis and Marxism, but in his work subjectivity was made equally if not more contingent – 'man' but a figure drawn in the sand: life, death, sex, the self could not be assumed as 'givens' – all were produced, at least in their modern senses, within particular historical moments of epistemic rupture: washed in and thus potentially washed out by the discursive tide.

Competing theoretical accounts of subjectivity, language and discourse developed in the last three decades of the twentieth century. As Raphael Samuel pointed out, historians were now required to be close readers of signs.[66] It was the myths, metaphors and models through which individuals and groups come to know themselves as subjects (or as races, classes or nations) that required close historical investigation. 'Class' could not be taken as some given analytic category that simply preceded its discursive construction, as Gareth Stedman Jones showed in an influential book, *Languages of Class* (1983). Studies of the 'forging', 'constituting', 'shaping' or 'fabricating' of this or that social identity proliferated. The tendency also aroused disquiet and calls for a reinstatement of older verities, as was made clear by some contributors to a set of debates in the journal *Social History* in the 1990s. Yet the assumed framework on either side was largely consistent with the trend identified here: despite discussing subjectivity and agency, and referring

---

[65] For Thompson's bitter critique of Althusser's 'interpellation' as a 'common terminus of unfreedom', see *The Poverty*, pp. 340, 344–345, 357, 395 n. 148. Thompson seemed to leave a chink open for Freud here: 'it was the oldest error of rationalism to suppose that by defining the non-rational out of its vocabulary it had in some way defined it out of life' (p. 369), but Freud remains invisible. Althusser's own tendentious reading of Lacan was one problem; another was Thompson's apparent misconstructions of Althusser; see Anderson, *Arguments within English Marxism* (London, 1980). The Althusserian version of Freud (and Lacan) was no doubt uncongenial to Thompson, but this is not addressed directly in *The Poverty*. Even when Thompson referred, elsewhere, to how 'alternating identities' might exist in the same individual (thus the same person could be deferential at one point, rebellious at another), he turned to Gramsci rather than to Freud or the idea of the unconscious: *Customs*, p. 10.

[66] Samuel, 'Reading the signs', *HWJ*, 32, (1991), pp. 88–109.

to French post-structuralist thought within which Freud had indeed been an important reference point, the historians concerned in this *Social History* polemic scarcely mentioned psychoanalysis.[67]

The mixed signals about the relevance of psychoanalysis can be gleaned from many other landmark historical works since the 1960s. In Keith Thomas's influential *Religion and the Decline of Magic* (1971) we are told that it is not necessary 'to look for a psychological or psychoanalytical explanation of the fact that the majority of accused witches were women'. Thomas points instead (and as though this might be sufficient) to their socio-economic situation as the most dependent members of the community. Yet, on the very next page, he declares: 'Undoubtedly there is still much about the fantasy side of witchcraft which cries out for explanation.'[68] The 'Cambridge School' of intellectual history provides another influential example. In Quentin Skinner's classic work, for example, psychoanalysis is not an important reference point; the significant connections are with analytic philosophy and cultural anthropology. Nonetheless, there are some striking parallels between Skinner's use of speech-act theory and recent psychoanalytic approaches to 'enactment'.[69] The virtual invisibility of psychoanalysis in the intellectual landscape of many historians is also well illustrated in Stefan Collini's stimulating study *Absent Minds* (2008). This otherwise far-reaching account of the concept, role and influence of intellectuals in modern Britain makes no reference at all to Freud or other psychoanalysts.[70]

Anderson, as we have seen, did protest against Freud's cultural and academic marginalisation in the UK and appeared to suggest that some methodological reckoning was required with psychoanalysis, but his own historical work does not develop this. Indeed, it seems to

---

[67] See, for instance, David Mayfield and Susan Thorne, 'Reply to "The poverty of protest" and "The imaginary discontents"', *Social History*, 18, (1993), pp. 219–233, at p. 223; Patrick Joyce, 'The end of social history', *Social History*, 20, (1995), pp. 73–91, at pp. 82–84.

[68] Keith Thomas, *Religion and the Decline of Magic: Studies in Popular Beliefs in Sixteenth- and Seventeenth-Century England* [1971] (Harmondsworth, 1980), pp. 678–679.

[69] See Daniel Pick and Michael Rustin, 'Introduction to Quentin Skinner', *International Journal of Psychoanalysis*, 89, (2008), pp. 637–645. In *Philosophy in History* (Cambridge, 1984), co-edited by Skinner, Freud is considered only once, by American philosopher Richard Rorty. Intriguingly, there is more attention to Freud and psychoanalysis in some later additions made to the seminal essays republished in Skinner's *Visions of Politics* (Cambridge, 2002), vol. 1. The marginal place of psychoanalysis overall in this approach is partly accounted for by the central methodological aims: the close exploration and precise historical contextualisation of the *conscious* intentions of authors.

[70] Despite its sustained engagement with Anderson's thesis, this wide-ranging work omits all reference to the *intellectual* presence of Strachey (that is to say James, not Lytton), Jones, Anna Freud, Riviere, Klein, Rickman, Money-Kyrle, Winnicott, Bowlby or Bion (to name but a few).

have little if any connection with Freudian thought: his highly erudite, but rather abstract, studies of feudalism and the absolutist state, for instance, eschew discussion of psychic processes, unconscious fantasy or affects. Not even the more abstract Althusserian perspective on Freud that shadows 'Components' is evident. Tantalisingly, Anderson insisted in 'Components' that the psychoanalytic account of the mind had to be taken seriously; yet the conundrum of how it could be taken seriously by Anderson himself, or at least how it would inform his methodology, was never explained. Be that as it may, the neglect of Freud by English intellectuals was interpreted, as we noted earlier, as evidence of a wider failure to engage with any revolutionary thought from across the Channel. Such positive exceptions as anthropology and psychoanalysis aside, the crucial components of Anderson's national culture in fact turn out to be those that are missing. The key explanatory terms are to do with absence and lack. What characterises English culture, he muses, is an *absent centre*, namely a proper relation to theory: 'The whole configuration of its culture has been determined – and dislocated – by this void at its centre.' In addition to the consideration of this absence, Anderson suggests that at the heart of the English experience lay a trauma: an industrial bourgeoisie horrified by a French Revolution it could neither emulate nor forget.

The language here sounds vaguely Freudian, as though Althusser's work, relied upon elsewhere in the essay, leads unwittingly to the adoption of psychoanalytic metaphors in the characterisation of English peculiarity. One could hardly call it an exercise in psycho-history, yet it is intriguing how ideas of trauma, of defensive organisation, of repression and an unconscious sense of lack are suggested, colouring somewhat, in the process, the Marxist political and cultural analysis. English philosophers are said here, for instance, to have 'repressed' all consciousness of Freud's work. In another sentence Anderson refers to how the idea of 'the totality' had to be 'repressed' by the bourgeoisie, since the bourgeoisie sought – and achieved – integration into the existing ruling order, not the overthrow of that order: 'Forgotten one moment, it was repressed the next.' The idea of the 'absent centre' used here to encapsulate English cultural peculiarity reappears later to describe the fundamental truth about human subjectivity that Freud had revealed:

Freud has shown us in his turn that the real subject, the individual in his singular essence, does not have the form of an I centred on the 'ego', 'consciousness' or 'existence' – that the human subject is decentered, constituted by a structure which itself has no centre.

The unconscious, Anderson insists, cannot be fitted into the language of a secure self-present 'I' that thinks – as in the Cartesian 'cogito'. Yet this conclusion does not appear to have much purchase on, or for, the narrative voice in this essay, despite Anderson's claim that Freud is unavoidably troubling, and his criticisms of philosophers who have failed to enter into dialogue with psychoanalysis: 'Taken seriously, psychoanalysis strikes at the very basis of linguistic philosophy'.[71]

VII

To recap: the aim here is not to argue that historical analysis necessarily benefits from psychoanalytic ideas (that must depend on the question at issue), but rather to consider the striking pattern wherein these are nonchalantly dismissed or occluded. It goes without saying that Freudian ideas have indeed on occasion been misused in order to give implausibly 'omniscient' explanations of the actions and motives of the dead. But this is not a sufficient *historical* explanation of the phenomenon at issue here. Psychoanalysis can equally well be used to enrich, or to cast doubt upon, the often unacknowledged 'psychologistic' explanations that historians routinely provide in writing about individuals and groups.[72]

Psychoanalysis has had, as Anderson acutely observed, important and original things to say. It transforms our way of conceptualising psychic organisation, as well as its relationship to social systems and the unconscious 'logic' that informs and skews political choices and allegiances. But whilst psychoanalysis enquired into the agencies of the mind, and the interaction of minds, our sense of time, and, unconsciously, of timelessness, fantasies in, and of, group psychology, or our struggles to live with and rework the past in the present, it did so by and large without reaching the ears of the historians, or at least with little by way of answering response.

[71] All quotations from Anderson, 'Components', pp. 225, 226, 260, 261.
[72] See Stephen Greenblatt, *Renaissance Self Fashioning: From More to Shakespeare* (Chicago 1980), esp. p. 85; Jacques Barzun, *Clio and the Doctors: Psycho-History, Quanto-History and History* (Chicago, 1974); Saul Friedlander, *Histoire et psychanalyse: Essai sur les possibilités et les limites de la psychohistoire* (Paris, 1975); Gay, *Freud for Historians*; Hans-Ulrich Wehler, 'Psychoanalysis and history', *Social Research*, 47, (1980), pp. 519–536; T. G. Ashplant, 'Fantasy, narrative, event: psychoanalysis and history', *HWJ*, 23, (1987), pp. 165–173; Ashplant, 'Psychoanalysis in historical writing', *HWJ*, 26, (1988), pp. 102–119. For an inquiry into the problem of psychobiography, see Pick, *Rome or Death: The Obsessions of General Garibaldi* (London, 2005). For a withering assessment of past attempts, see David E. Stannard, *Shrinking History: On Freud and the Failure of Psychohistory* (New York, 1980).

I have sought to identify a pattern, but also exceptions to it. In recent decades historians have increasingly questioned the characteristic account of 'mind' sketched above. Strikingly, for instance, in *History Workshop Journal* (*HWJ*; a product of the 1970s) these questions were increasingly taken up.[73] The emergence of *HWJ* and its associated public engagements and events were in part a reflection of the original editors' dissatisfaction with the restrictions of the 'academic', 'professional' establishment history described earlier. It was also, particularly in its early days, a reflection of their interests in or commitment to socialism and/or feminism. It spoke, as one of its founding editors, Raphael Samuel, put it in 'many voices' and concerned itself with forms of history that tended to disappear from view in more conventional academic work. Perhaps not by chance this journal was also to provide considerable attention to the history of psychoanalysis as well as the problem of its application to the past. Amongst the catalysts for this particular development was a reappraisal of the significance of Freud for feminism, notably through Juliet Mitchell's influential book, *Psychoanalysis and Feminism* in 1974. There was no consensus on this thorny set of issues within the *HWJ* collective, or even on the desirability of engaging with them, but nor was the debate foreclosed. The problem of unconscious processes, or psychosocial questions of sexual difference, ought not to be simply 'jettisoned', as one of the editors, Sally Alexander, put it.[74] Other journals have emerged since (notably *Psychoanalysis and History* in the 1990s) that accommodate various aspects of this field more systematically, but *HWJ* was in this sense something of a pioneer. An exploratory seminar series on psychoanalysis and history that has run for the best part of two decades at the Institute of Historical Research was the creation of Alexander and Barbara Taylor. In a series of innovative studies, Lyndal Roper showed how Kleinian psychoanalytic concepts might be usefully brought to bear in the consideration of witchcraft, but also how misleading any such applications could be when not tempered by the most meticulous historical attention.[75]

What can we conclude? At least this: the particular 'dog that didn't bark' story that we have traced here has complex historical roots. The present account suggests that an explanation of my opening

---

[73] References are too numerous to cite individually; relevant material can be found, for example, in issues 9, 21, 23, 26, 32, 45, 48, 49, 50, 57 and 61.

[74] See Sally Alexander, *Becoming a Woman and Other Essays in Nineteenth and Twentieth-Century Feminist History* (London, 1994).

[75] See, particularly, Lyndal Roper, *Oedipus and the Devil: Witchcraft, Sexuality and Religion in Early Modern Europe* (London, 1994).

questions may require that one return to the Victorian origins of the formal subject of history as well as its subsequent development. It has sketched some important trajectories of historical thought before and after the war and noted how a lack of attention to psychoanalysis might be related to Britain's limited historiographical encounter with modernism. (This is not to say that historians have been uninterested in charting modernism, but to suggest that the key debates about how to *do* history have not primarily been influenced, let alone transformed, by it.) It has also dwelt on some of the most prominent and groundbreaking work in post-war historiography, and it has noted how, for better or for worse, psychoanalysis played virtually no direct part in these crucial developments. And yet it has also acknowledged certain potential affinities, or at least space for dialogue across the disciplinary boundaries.

Historians, it is sometimes argued, are peculiarly impervious to high theoretical speculation.[76] But this also needs qualification: the nature of the theoretical speculation and its context make a difference. The claim is sometimes made that psychoanalytic thought did not flourish here because of the strength of native empiricism; alternatively, that Freudian discoveries were ignored because (to borrow Orwell's famous quip), the English are not sufficiently interested in intellectual matters to be intolerant about them. But the argument, in the present case, needs more focus. If 'national culture' is not a sufficiently convincing answer, nor will it do to explain the absence of historiographical engagement by appealing to the admittedly sometimes forbidding and excluding aura of the psychoanalytic institution itself or the sometimes narrow furrow ploughed by clinicians in their writing or public engagements. Many links and connections were made with other disciplines in the inter-war period, and beyond. Whatever the blind spots, uncertainties and rancour that accompanied it, and the shrill invective of some, if not all, of its critics, psychoanalysis has constituted a 'revolution in mind'.[77] Indeed, it has sometimes been suggested that psychoanalytic images and models have become our native 'common sense'. While that is an exaggeration, certainly, during the first half of the twentieth century, elements of psychoanalytic terminology became relatively common parlance, even if not always finding shared acceptance. In his essay 'Britain on the Couch', Graham Richards notes how terms such as 'Oedipus complex', 'phallic symbol', 'the Censor', 'projection' or 'defence mechanism' were recycled in an extensive popular literature. 'To be able to speak

---

[76] See, for instance, Tony Judt, *Postwar: A History of Europe since 1945* (London, 2005), p. 399.

[77] Makari, *Revolution in Mind.*

Freudish', he suggests, 'marked one as modern in the same way as being able to refer to electrons, endocrines or the "fourth dimension".'[78]

W. H. Auden famously wrote upon Freud's death in 1939, 'To us he is no more a person/Now but a whole climate of opinion'. But not so for the historical profession in England. The history of the discipline, not 'the national culture' at large, is where we need to start, if we are to understand why Freud was to be made marginal even among most radically minded, self-consciously heterodox historians: either an unwarranted diversion or an occasional oblique presence.

---

[78] Richards, 'Britain', pp. 199–202. D. H. Lawrence remarked in 1923 that the Oedipus complex was now 'a household word', and 'amateur analysis became the vogue': *Psychoanalysis and the Unconscious*, p. 10.

10   Labour and the politics of class, 1900–1940

Jon Lawrence

Class feeling in Britain

Class feeling was written deep into the fabric of pre-1914 British society and culture. Stephen Reynolds, an Edwardian writer who 'threw up' middle-class society to live with a Devon fishing family, wrote that 'there are two high walls between us and them; theirs and ours; and theirs is the higher and stronger. It's strange how undemocratic they are; how they look on "the gen'leman" as another species of animal.'[1] Similarly, in his memoir of growing up in an Edwardian 'classic slum', Robert Roberts recalled that 'the real social divide existed between those who, in earning daily bread, dirtied hands and face, and those who did not' – although he was equally clear that, internally, slum society represented a finely graded 'social pyramid' of class distinctions.[2] As this suggests, there was no consensus about exactly where the lines of class were drawn, but few doubted that Britain was a society structured around deep, even impenetrable, class distinctions.

As Bernard Waites has argued, down to World War I it remained common to view this class-bound society through an essentially Tory lens: that is, as a 'natural' and immutable social hierarchy dictated by the rules of God and/or the market.[3] But this perspective, long challenged by radicals and socialists, began to crumble under the strains of wartime mass mobilisation. The state was obliged to arbitrate between the competing interests of different social groups, which in turn came to see their own 'sacrifices' as disproportionate and unjust. Workers railed against

I would like to thank Jane Elliott, David Feldman, Helen McCarthy, Ross McKibbin, Mike Savage, David Thackeray and Geraint Thomas for their helpful comments on earlier drafts of this chapter.

[1]   Harold Wright (ed.), *Letters of Stephen Reynolds* (London, 1923), pp. x, 41 (to Garnett, 28 September 1906); Stephen Reynolds, *A Poor Man's House* (1908: London, 1911), p. 81, reworks the idea of the 'two high walls'.

[2]   Robert Roberts, *The Classic Slum: Salford Life in the First Quarter of the Century* (Manchester, 1971), pp. 1–16, quotations at pp. 6, 8.

[3]   Bernard Waites, *A Class Society at War: England, 1914–18* (Leamington Spa, 1987), pp. 41–47.

the imposition of 'leaving certificates' and compulsory arbitration, land-lords bemoaned controls on rents, and from 1916 almost everybody came to believe that others were more favoured by the implementation of military conscription.[4] For sure, the state had already begun to act as an arbitrator between competing market interests before the war, notably in the so-called sweated trades and, perhaps more surprisingly, on the coalfields, where the Liberals had legislated on miners' hours and wages. But such interventions tended to represent finely balanced compromises between the competing claims of different interests. By contrast, wartime interventions were ad hoc and apparently arbitrary responses to short-term crises. For instance, the government's decision to peg 'working-class rents' to their August 1914 level to quell protest strikes among war workers, meant that by 1918 many urban landlords had seen their income more than halved in real terms.[5]

If anything, class feeling intensified amidst the social and industrial turmoil of the immediate post-war years. Though not immediately. Labour and the unions initially proved relatively successful at defusing hostility to industrial militancy. The eight-hour day, won across much of British industry during the first half of 1919, was portrayed as one of the 'fruits of victory' necessary to build a better world after the horrors of war. Labour and the unions also won the publicity battle with govern-ment over the national rail strike of September 1919, portraying the dispute as the last resort of hard-pressed men desperate not to return to starvation wages.[6] But the national coal disputes of 1920 and 1921 appear to have marked a turning-point. Miners' leaders cared less about the battle for public opinion than the railwaymen's leader Jimmy Thomas, but the main difference was that the economic and political climate had turned much colder by late 1920. Government-induced deflation was undermining hopes for a better post-war world, and as the economy contracted and unemployment rose, the clamour of the radical right against 'waste' and 'socialism' became more insistent. Letters to the press complained that 'the miners think themselves able to hold the country to ransom', while an Independent Labour

[4] Adrian Gregory, *The Last Great War: British Society and the First World War* (Cambridge, 2008).

[5] Jon Lawrence, 'Material pressures on the middle classes' in Jay Winter and Jean-Louis Robert (eds), *Capital Cities at War: London, Paris, Berlin, 1914–1919* (Cambridge, 1997), Table 8.6.

[6] Hugh Armstrong Clegg, *A History of British Trade Unions since 1889: volume II, 1911–1933* (Oxford, 1985), pp. 252–255, 290; Laura Beers, 'Is this man an anarchist? Industrial action, publicity and public opinion in interwar Britain', *Journal of Modern History*, 82, (2010), pp. 30–60.

Party (ILP) pamphlet depicted an Ilford commuter lambasting the miners for having 'no consideration whatever for the Public' and declaring 'the working class will have to be taught a lesson'.[7] It was not without reason that, returning to the east Midlands during the prolonged miners' strike of 1926, D. H. Lawrence wrote, 'I am afraid of the class hatred which is the quiet volcano over which the English life is built'.[8]

This story of class polarisation represents one of the linchpins of standard accounts of the growth of Labour politics between 1900 and 1922. Some historians would argue that the process was already well advanced before 1914, and that only the distortions of the pre-war franchise frustrated its expression in politics, but they too portray the war and its aftermath as accentuating class polarisation, thereby helping Labour to consolidate its hold over new industrial heartlands.[9] Nor do I wish to suggest that this view is fundamentally mistaken. On the contrary, across much of Britain it was precisely the politicisation of class feeling that accounted both for Labour's dramatic post-war breakthrough, and for the remarkable durability of its core support in the face of anti-socialist scares in the 1920s, and economic and political crisis in 1931. Rather, I want to explain why most inter-war Labour leaders continued to see class feeling as a problem to overcome, not as an opportunity to exploit – why they distanced themselves from vernacular languages of class rooted in the supposed opposition between manual and non-manual labour, preferring instead to construct an alternative, more inclusive politics intended to transcend the visceral tensions of class feeling; and why, crucially, this was vital to the Party's decisive breakthrough in 1940.

This is not a simple story of radical continuity. For one thing, in Labour's industrial and urban heartlands not only was class feeling integral to the Party's advance, but this, in turn, was more about defending concrete, material gains wrung from a reluctant state (rent control, the dole, subsidised housing and the regulation of wages and hours) than about constructing a new politics structured around a radical vision of political change. In addition, Labour's national leaders broke with many of the discursive traditions of Victorian and Edwardian Liberalism. In particular, they pared down the old radical language of

---

[7] Clegg, *History of Trade Unions*, II, pp. 295–302; *The Times*, 7 May 1921, p. 6; A. Ernest Mander, *Mr Wilkins: The Story of a 'Middle Class' Man* (London, 1921); also C. L. Mowat, *Britain Between the Wars 1918–1940* (London, 1955), p. 122.

[8] James T. Boulton (ed.), *The Selected Letters of D. H. Lawrence* (Cambridge, 1997), p. 320 (to Else Jaffe, 26 August 1926).

[9] Ross McKibbin, *The Evolution of the Labour Party, 1910–1924* (Oxford, 1974), pp. 236–47, and H. C. G. Matthew, R. I. McKibbin and J. A. Kay, 'The franchise factor in the rise of the Labour Party', *English Historical Review*, 91, (1976), pp. 723–752.

'producers' versus 'idlers', which had bracketed employers and workers together as the 'industrious classes', so that only those who lived by selling their labour were now recognised as truly useful to the community. Labour often sought to mobilise anti-employer feeling. Even in 1929, at the height of Ramsay MacDonald's moderate, progressivist strategy, the Party issued a leaflet called 'Tory money-bags' that began by reminding potential voters that 'the Tory Party is the Employers' party'.[10]

Labour explicitly based its arguments for a 'better life for the workers' on the claim that 'the workers "make" the wealth which is the food, clothing, houses, railways, motors and banks of the country'.[11] Here, Labour leaders were drawing on alternative, non-liberal nineteenth-century discursive traditions. Arguments that stressed labour as the source of all wealth had retained an enduring subterranean popularity among radical artisans since the 1820s, even when the trades unions came under the sway of liberal doctrines stressing the potential harmony of capital and labour. These economistic arguments remained central to demotic socialism, despite the theoretical objections of most radical and socialist intellectuals.[12] But no less important were romantic eulogies to the 'nobility' and 'dignity' of labour. In 1906, humanist writers such as Burns, Carlyle, Ruskin and Dickens, who frequently stressed the inherently communal character of wealth production, featured prominently among the most popular authors for the first generation of Labour MPs.[13]

It was precisely because its political language retained strong 'workerist' elements that Labour was able to hold its own in industrial communities embittered by the struggles of 1915–1926, as well as reach out to Britons much less profoundly alienated from the status quo. It was what enabled Labour to marry anger and aspiration, in the process marginalising radical left voices keen to accentuate, rather than dampen, class feeling. Crucially, it was also what allowed Labour to counter

---

[10] Labour, 'Tory money-bags' (no. 229, 1929). Labour publications were consulted at the Labour History Archive and Study Centre (Manchester), the British Library, the British Library of Political and Economic Science and Cambridge University Library.

[11] Labour Party, *The New Power in Politics* (London, nd [1936]), pp. 6–7.

[12] Ross McKibbin, *Classes and Cultures: England, 1918–1951* (Oxford, 1998), pp. 139–40; Ben Jackson, *Equality and the British Left: A Study in Progressive Political Thought, 1900–64* (Manchester, 2007), pp. 38–53.

[13] W. T. Stead, 'The Labour Party and the books that helped to make it', *Review of Reviews* (June, 1906), pp. 568–582; Jonathan Rose, *The Intellectual History of the British Working Classes* (New Haven and London, 2001), pp. 40–42, 48–53; Jose Harris, 'Labour's political and social thought' in Duncan Tanner, Pat Thane and Nick Tiratsoo (eds), *Labour's First Century* (Cambridge, 2000), at pp. 19–21.

Conservative claims to embody the 'public' interest.[14] In opposition to the Conservatives' vision of a public that was quiet, private and more than a little genteel, Labour advanced a rival, more communal, vision of the public which valorised 'the workers' as the backbone of the nation. To Labour's great advantage, it was a vision that would finally come into its own during the 'people's war'.

Rejecting class politics

The new Party constitution of 1918, with its commitment to managerial state socialism, individual Party membership, and promoting the interests of 'producers by hand or brain' is sometimes portrayed as a decisive break with Labour's earlier sectional, 'workerist' tendencies, and sometimes as a skilful smokescreen for the consolidation of trade union power.[15] But it is important to remember that the Party's decisive rejection of class politics came much earlier. The conference called to establish the Labour Representation Committee in 1900 had explicitly rejected both the Marxist Social Democratic Federation's call for recognition of the 'class war' and Lib–Lab attempts to confine the new party's independent role to issues directly touching the 'labour interest'.[16] Indeed, the constitution's strained formula that it represented all workers 'by hand or brain', with its roots in pre-modern conceptions of society as a living body with workers as its 'hands', was already a standard trope of Labour politics before the war.[17] What was new, and at first deeply controversial, was the decision to open the Party to individual as well as affiliated members. Many pro-war trade unionists saw this as a plot to swamp the Party with intellectuals and pacifist former Liberals. In the summer of 1918, the Gas, Municipal and General Workers' leader Eldred Hallas, who had links to the ultra-right British Workers League, denounced 'the free-trade, liberal, middle-class pacifists who are to fight under the Labour party banner', and backed calls from right-wing union leaders for an alternative 'Trade Union

[14] Ross McKibbin, 'Class and conventional wisdom: the Conservative Party and the "public" in inter-war Britain' in McKibbin, *Ideologies of Class: Social Relations in Britain, 1880–1950* (Oxford, 1990). Also Alison Light, *Forever England: Femininity, Literature and Conservatism between the Wars* (London, 1991).

[15] Waites, *Class Society*, pp. 60–61, 259; McKibbin, *Evolution*, pp. 91–106.

[16] Labour Party, *The Labour Party Foundation Conference and Annual Conference Reports 1900–1905* (London, 1967), pp. 11–13; Frank Bealey and Henry Pelling, *Labour and Politics, 1900–1906: A History of the Labour Representation Committee* (London, 1958), pp. 25–31.

[17] Jon Lawrence, *Speaking for the People: Party, Language and Popular Politics in England, 1867–1914* (Cambridge, 1998), pp. 143–146.

Labour Party', with membership confined to bona fide trade unionists.[18] Similarly, George Milligan of the Dockers' Union declared that 'They did not want middle-class or higher-class ladies to come and tell them what to do, or theorists like Mr H.G. Wells or Mr Bernard Shaw'.[19]

Such arguments ran directly counter to the thinking of Arthur Henderson and Sidney Webb, the architects of the new constitution, who wanted to 'bring in the intellectuals'.[20] According to Webb, the Party had been 'publicly thrown open to all workers "by hand or by brain"' in order 'to attract many men and women of the shopkeeping, manufacturing and professional classes ... dissatisfied with the old parties'.[21] Writing in November 1918, fellow Fabian Joseph Baptista claimed that individual membership meant the 'breaking down of class barriers', and predicted 'the days of the class war are numbered ... men and women of all classes are determined to remove the causes which produce class distinctions and the class war'.[22] As a semi-official Party history put it in 1925, whereas in the past brainworkers 'were merely "tolerated," it was now provided that they should be welcomed on terms of equality ... The effect of this change was to abolish any class distinction ... It meant the definite and deliberate transforming of the Labour Party from a sectional party to a national party.'[23]

Labour leaders held up their vision of a new, more communitarian politics as the antithesis of the strikes and class enmity of the post-war era. In doing so they were motivated by more than a desire to appease middle-class voters. For one thing, they recognised that class feeling was as likely to divide as unite Britain's workers. On issues such as dilution, 'badging' (exemption from military service) and pay differentials, the politicised war economy had destabilised established hierarchies between workers in different occupational and skill categories, creating shop-floor tensions which often spilled over into strike action and other forms of industrial militancy.[24] If anything, things deteriorated after

---

[18] *Monthly Journal of the Amalgamated Society of Gas, Municipal and General Workers*, July 1918 and September 1918; McKibbin, *Evolution*, pp. 100–104.

[19] Waites, *Class Society*, p. 61.

[20] McKibbin, *Evolution*, pp. 93–95.

[21] Sidney Webb, 'The new constitution of the Labour Party: a party of handworkers and brainworkers' (London, 1918), pp. 2–3.

[22] *Herald*, 30 November 1918.

[23] Herbert Tracey (ed.), *The Book of the Labour Party: Its History, Growth, Policy and Leaders*, 3 vols (London, 1925), I, p. 18. But significantly, Henderson's idea of renaming Labour the 'People's Party' was not pursued: McKibbin, *Evolution*, pp. 93–94.

[24] Gerry R. Rubin, *War, Law and Labour: The Munitions Acts, State Regulation and the Unions, 1915–1921* (Oxford, 1987); A. Reid, 'The impact of the First World War on British workers' in R. Wall and J. Winter (eds), *The Upheaval of War: Family, Work and Welfare in Europe, 1914–1918* (Cambridge, 1986).

the Armistice. The implementation of the Restoration of Pre-War Practices Act in 1919 generated some of the sharpest intra-class struggles. For instance, in the Midlands moulders belonging to Henderson's union, the Ironfounders' Society, fought a long and bitter dispute to exclude members of general unions from their trade. At a protest meeting in West Bromwich, John Beard, the Workers' Union leader, declared that 'he didn't want any more humbug about this solidarity of labour. There was none.' Beard called on Labour 'to raise itself above the narrow outlook of craft unionism' whose message to the labourer appeared to be 'Get back to your place, dog'.[25] In such disputes, class feeling was manifestly a corrosive force, which, if not contained, threatened to destroy independent Labour politics at birth. Labour's answer was to distance itself as much as possible, not only from inter-union politics, but from strikes and industrial unrest in general. A *Labour Leader* editorial from 1919 epitomised this attitude, pitying the striker who 'has to embarrass the community, dislocate industry ... bring suffering ... upon himself and those nearest him in order to secure a comparatively infinitesimal increase in his very small share of that wealth which is the fruit of his labour'.[26]

Socialism, by contrast, would restore social harmony by ensuring that all workers, skilled or unskilled, received the 'full value' of their labour. It was an argument that also lay at the heart of the Party's post-war appeal to non-manual workers. In the 1920s, Labour propaganda made much of the Party's constitutional commitment 'to obtain for the workers whether by hand or by brain the full fruits of their industry', though it was much less clear about exactly how these fruits would be divided up between the competing fractions of the working (and non-working) population.[27] The Party's national leaders were determined to resist their opponents' accusation that Labour was a 'class party'. In 1922, Philip Snowden rejected Liberal charges along these lines by declaring 'The Labour party is the very opposite of a Class Party. It has come into politics to abolish class government and class control'.[28] As MacDonald consistently argued, class struggle was pathological – the result of the 'unnatural' competitive system – and as such had no

---

[25] *Midland Chronicle* (West Bromwich), 12 December 1919; *Workers' Union Record*, October 1919.

[26] *Labour Leader*, 30 January 1919 (editorial); see also Bernard Barker (ed.), *Ramsay MacDonald's Political Writings* (London, 1972), p. 47.

[27] Labour Party, 'Why brain workers should vote Labour' (no. 2, 1922); for a discussion of the intellectual debate on this problem, see Jackson, *Equality and the British Left*, pp. 47–53.

[28] Philip Snowden, 'What is the Labour Party?', *Labour Magazine*, 1, (June 1922), p. 76.

part to play in the building of socialism. On the contrary, socialism was a communitarian creed, focused on a co-operative effort to build a 'New Jerusalem' where both insecurity and competition would be vanquished by a benign, mediating state dedicated to ending the war of all against all.[29]

To understand this attitude we need to recognise that Labour politicians were reacting against the persistence of a powerfully hierarchical and paternalist social and political order, which sustained deeply engrained assumptions about the inferiority, even depravity, of most Britons (the so-called 'lower orders'). This *ancien régime* of privilege and class prejudice bred a democratic politics in which the left sought to overthrow (not establish) class politics and class rule. In turn, the right sought to disguise its defence of privilege in languages of 'common sense' and 'national interest'. In short, class was evacuated from politics precisely because it saturated everyday life. The very power of 'class' as a pejorative political term spoke to its centrality to Britons' understanding of themselves and their society in the first half of the twentieth century. When Conservatives spoke of the dangers of selfish 'class politics', they consciously played on deep-rooted fears about a largely unknown urban 'working class'. When Labour did the same they exploited deep-rooted hostility towards the power and privileges of a largely unknown wealthy elite.

But in the early years, class, though rarely spoken, was physically embodied in the person of many Labour leaders – not least in the way that their very presence on the hustings, and at Westminster, destabilised the traditional assumption that politics was a 'gentleman's game'. MacDonald and Snowden, in particular, were celebrated for their humble origins and their triumph over personal and class disadvantage. For sure, these were stories about their journeys *away* from the people they claimed to represent, but one should not underestimate the vicarious satisfaction encoded in contemporary accounts of the first 'working men' to occupy the highest offices of state.[30]

However, the Labour leaders of the 1920s were the product of a very distinct socio-cultural milieu. Most were autodidact working men from the class borderlands of artisanry and clerkdom. Allied with politicised trade unionists like Henderson and Bevin, they sought to construct a political movement capable of harnessing the aspirations of 'respectable'

[29] Barker (ed.), *MacDonald's Writings*, pp. 47–48, 162.

[30] Iconoclast [Mary Agnes Hamilton], *The Man of Tomorrow: J. Ramsay MacDonald* (London, 1924), esp. pp. 61–70; *Railway Service Journal* (December, 1929), p. 480; Tracey (ed.), *Book of the Labour Party*, III, pp. 126–127, 167–168.

manual and non-manual workers for a better, more secure life, to a broader politics of social reform aimed at eradicating the evils of poverty, unemployment and the slums. This politics could not have grown organically out of working-class life, because, as many social historians have shown us, that life was too diverse, too localised and too riven by internal tensions and conflict.[31] Instead, it had to be made by activists who first sought to capture organisations such as trades unions and co-operative societies for their new politics, and later sought to proselytise their vision as an answer to the myriad dissatisfactions of workers' everyday lives.[32]

But the downside to this story of the making of a new politics was that Labour's autodidact leaders always struggled not to look down upon those who fell short of their own exacting standards of respectability, rationalism and purpose. Chris Waters suggests that socialists had shed many of these attitudes by the eve of World War I, embracing a more pragmatic, realist approach to politics that saw them prepared to reach out to workers on the latter's terms.[33] But work on later periods would suggest that this is an overly optimistic interpretation.[34] Labour leaders' urge to remake 'the people' in their own image did not die so easily, even if there was always a minority strain – part 'Tory-socialist', part 'workerist' – that was more willing to embrace the people, warts and all.[35]

---

[31] McKibbin, *Classes and Cultures*; Trevor Griffiths, *The Lancashire Working Classes, c. 1880–1930* (Oxford, 2001); Marc Brodie, *The Politics of the Poor: The East End of London, 1885–1914* (Oxford, 2004).

[32] Alastair Reid, 'Politics and economics in the formation of the British working class: a response to H. F. Moorhouse', *Social History*, 3, (1978), pp. 347–361; also Huw Beynon and Terry Austrin, *Masters and Servants: Class and Patronage in the Making of the Labour Organisation. The Durham Miners and the English Political Tradition* (London, 1994); Raphael Samuel and Gareth Stedman Jones, 'The Labour Party and social democracy' in Samuel and Jones (eds), *Culture, Ideology and Politics: Essays for Eric Hobsbawm* (London, 1982), at pp. 325–327.

[33] Chris Waters, *British Socialists and the Politics of Popular Culture, 1884–1914* (Manchester, 1990).

[34] Stuart MacIntyre, 'British Labour, Marxism and working-class apathy in the nineteen twenties', *Historical Journal*, 20, (1977), pp. 479–496; Jeremy Nuttall, *Psychological Socialism: The Labour Party and Qualities of Mind and Character, 1931 to the Present* (Manchester, 2006), esp. pp. 52–58; Lawrence Black, *The Political Culture of the Left in Affluent Britain, 1951–1964: Old Labour, New Britain?* (Basingstoke, 2003).

[35] Jon Lawrence, 'Labour – the myths it has lived by' in Tanner *et al.* (eds), *Labour's First Century*; David Howell, *British Workers and the Independent Labour Party, 1888–1906* (Manchester, 1983), pp. 373–388; Martin Pugh, 'The Rise of Labour and the political culture of Conservatism 1890–1945', *History*, 87, (October, 2002), pp. 514–537.

Labour's heartlands

But before exploring in greater detail Labour's attempts to construct a new politics capable of transcending the class feeling that so often divided workers against each other, we need first to look at the rather different, more overtly materialist politics that thrived in Labour's post-war 'heartlands'. After 1918, Labour did best in areas of heavy industry, urban poverty and of course on the coalfields, while their opponents did best in the suburbs, the counties and in the surviving citadels of urban privilege such as Clifton (Bristol), Edgbaston (Birmingham) and London's West End – although crucially, until 1945, they could also hold their own across much of urban, industrial Britain. At least at this level, social class was manifestly not irrelevant to voting – but nor, crucially, was it the magic key to political power that the Labour left sometimes implied.[36]

Labour's success on the coalfields and in the inner cities pointed to an important lesson for the Party – the social and political solidarities they sought to weave seemed most plausible when they were rooted in concrete interests, such as nationalisation or doles, strongly identified with specific localities and their sense of themselves as communities under attack.[37] Labour's problem was that, outside its heartlands, place and occupation translated less easily into a new language that could elide social and political identities. In most of Britain, social space was more complicated and heterogeneous, intra-class relations more fractious and vernacular understandings of social difference more difficult to mobilise behind a unifying politics. Worse, the issues and language that flourished in Labour's heartlands played directly into its opponents' hands elsewhere. As McKibbin and Jarvis have demonstrated, Conservatives learnt to appeal to urban, industrial workers by arguing that Labour was a sectional, special-interest party – governing in the interests of miners, the poor and the unemployed – and thereby *against* the interests of the ordinary 'public' – i.e. all those (the vast majority) who were not poor, not unemployed and not miners.[38]

---

[36] Kenneth Wald, *Crosses on the Ballot: Patterns of British Voter Alignment since 1885* (New Jersey, 1983); W. L. Miller, *Electoral Dynamics in Britain since 1918* (London, 1977). The classic leftist argument is Ralph Miliband, *Parliamentary Socialism: A Study in the Politics of Labour* (London, 1961).

[37] Duncan Tanner, 'The Labour Party and electoral politics in the coalfields, 1910–1947' in Alan Campbell, Nina Fishman and David Howell (eds), *Miners, Unions and Politics* (Aldershot, 1996); John Marriott, *The Culture of Labourism: The East End Between the Wars* (Edinburgh, 1991), pp. 58–66.

[38] McKibbin, 'Class and conventional wisdom'; David Jarvis, 'British Conservatism and class politics in the 1920s', *English Historical Review*, 111, (1996), pp. 59–84. The thesis was first advanced by John Bonham in *The Middle Class Vote* (London, 1954), p. 20.

Labour sought hard to neutralise such arguments through both word and deed. Much was made of the achievements of Labour's minority governments in 1924 and 1929–1931, particularly in the fields of housing, tenants' rights, food taxes and foreign policy,[39] but it was at the local level that Labour had the greatest opportunity to counter its opponents' arguments by pioneering concrete social improvements. In many parts of Britain, Labour sought to construct a broad popular alliance based on citizens' shared interests as consumers, rather than on their more heterogeneous and antagonistic interests as producers.[40] Egon Wertheimer, the London correspondent for the German Social Democrat newspaper *Vorwärts*, felt British Labour politicians to be uniquely indifferent to the politics of production (which, in truth, most saw as the special preserve of the unions).[41] However, he had little to say about that bulwark of Labour's politics of consumption, the co-operative movement, which drew closer to Labour and the unions in the aftermath of World War I, becoming in many towns and cities a vital channel through which Labour extended its appeal beyond organised male workers.[42] But nonetheless, Labour leaders sometimes misjudged things – embracing policies that accentuated rather than transcended local social tensions. At Leeds in the mid-1930s, the city's Labour council implemented an ambitious programme of slum clearance underpinned by a radically redistributive rent rebate policy. This involved better-off municipal tenants cross-subsidising the poor, so that some tenants saw their rents fall to zero, while others faced significant increases. Labour had overestimated the reserves of social solidarity among their supporters. By 1935 the Conservatives had ousted them from power.[43]

---

[39] For instance, see the 1924 Labour leaflets 'Food prices down!' (no. 97), 'Houses by the million' (no. 125), 'Labour stops evictions' (no. 129) and 'The Prime Minister's appeal' (no. 131). Labour also sought to neutralise attacks on 'Poplarism'; see Labour, 'The truth about Poplar' (no. 95, 1924?).

[40] Becky Taylor, John Stewart and Martin Powell, 'Central and local government and the provision of municipal medicine, 1919–39', *English Historical Review*, 122, (2007), pp. 397–426.

[41] Egon Wertheimer, *Portrait of the Labour Party* (London, 1929), pp. 88–89.

[42] Paddy Maguire, 'Co-operation and crisis: Government, co-operation and politics, 1917–22' in Stephen Yeo (ed.), *New Views of Co-operation* (London, 1988); Nicole Robertson, 'The political dividend: co-operative parties in the Midlands, 1917–39' in Matthew Worley (ed.), *Labour's Grass Roots: Essays on the Activities and Experiences of Local Labour Parties and Members, 1918–1945* (Aldershot, 2005).

[43] Robert Finnigan, 'Council housing in Leeds, 1919–39: social policy and urban change' in Martin Daunton (ed.), *Councillors and Tenants: Local Authority Housing in English Cities, 1919–1939* (Leicester, 1984), at pp. 110–118; Geraint Thomas, 'Conservatism and the political culture of "National" government between the wars', unpublished PhD thesis, University of Cambridge (forthcoming), ch. 3.

The language of Labour politics

It is with good reason that historians have devoted much attention to understanding the dynamics of local Labour politics between the wars. It was here that Labour established the political power base that allowed it to recover quickly from the debacle of 1931. But it was not by a series of incremental local advances that Labour ultimately secured power at the national level. Despite the revival of middle-class radicalism in the later 1930s, Labour's progress in both municipal and parliamentary contests remained limited. Indeed, work on borough elections suggests that Labour was losing ground across much of England in 1937–1938, while early opinion polls by Gallup in October 1937 and February 1939 put support for Labour between 30 and 32 per cent (compared with 38 per cent at the 1935 general election).[44] Rather, Labour's breakthrough came suddenly, in the summer of 1940, as a result of a sea change in public opinion following the collapse of the anti-Labour 'National Government', and the Party's inclusion in Churchill's *genuinely* national wartime Coalition. As McKibbin rightly argues, Labour's entry into government managed 'at a stroke to undo twenty years' work' in which Conservatives had portrayed Labour as a sectional, unpatriotic and incompetent party unfit for office.[45] But this could only happen because, throughout those twenty years, Labour leaders had consistently rejected their opponents' caricatures of their party, insisting instead that it stood for national against class interests, and that socialism meant the resolution of class tensions through enlightened state action (among European socialist parties, Labour's confidence in the neutrality and malleability of the central state was at least as unusual as its attitudes to class). It was at the national level that this vital battle over Labour's place within polity and nation was waged. And though Labour was consistently on the back foot in the discursive battles of the 1920s and 1930s, that is no reason for paying their arguments less attention than those of their Conservative adversaries.

The historiography of inter-war Conservatism has recently taken a dramatic 'linguistic turn', with the discursive strategies of the Party's

---

[44] Sam Davies and Bob Morley, *County Borough Elections in England and Wales, 1919–1938: A Comparative Analysis*, 3 vols (Aldershot, 1999–2007), vol. 3, pp. 642–643; Anthony King (ed.), *British Political Opinion, 1937–2000: The Gallup Polls* (London, 2001), p. 1; George H. Gallup (ed.), *The Gallup International Public Opinion Polls: Great Britain, 1937–1975*, 2 vols (New York, 1976), vol. 1, p. 14.

[45] Ross McKibbin, 'Classes and cultures: a postscript', *Mitteilungsblatt des Instituts für Soziale Bewegungen*, 27, (2002), pp. 153–166, an argument further developed in his *Parties and People: England, 1914–1951* (Oxford, 2010); also Paul Addison, *The Road to 1945: British Politics and the Second World War* (London, 1975), pp. 102–127.

national leaders now widely argued to hold the key to its ability to contain the twin challenges of democracy and Labour after 1918 (with, conversely, little interest shown in either grass-roots Conservatism or the policies of Conservative governments).[46] By contrast, Labour historiography remains strongly stamped by the impress of older, Whiggish narratives about the 'rise of class' and the 'forward march of labour'. In consequence, the analysis of Labour's national political language takes a back seat to studies of the Party's grass roots, and its ideological battles between left and right. The historiographies of the two parties are therefore currently arguing past each other; and while each has its exclusions and weaknesses, the failure to take seriously what Labour leaders said to the public (compared even with what they said to each other or to the party faithful) represents a serious omission. Of course there are exceptions,[47] but the dominant approach still tends to portray Labour politicians as corks bobbing on a rising tide of class feeling, rather than as the creative architects of a new politics intended to transcend the internecine tensions that threatened to dissolve Labour's constituency into warring factions.

Labour's propaganda efforts between the wars were no less centralised and 'national' than their opponents'. Besides the leaders' national radio broadcasts, their widely reported platform speeches and their occasional newsreel appeals, Labour also reached a broad national audience through its in-house publishing activity. Like its rivals, Labour printed leaflets and pamphlets by the million between the wars, but it also pioneered the integration of national and local propaganda through its so-called 'election news-sheets', which combined general Party propaganda, often extensively illustrated, with local news and features.[48] Significantly, Labour's in-house publications consistently sought to appeal to those groups, such as women, farm-workers, small property owners and the elderly, most assiduously cultivated

---

[46] Bill Schwarz, 'The language of constitutionalism: Baldwinite Conservatism' in Formations Editorial Collective, *Formations 7: Formations of Nation and People* (London, 1984); McKibbin, 'Class and conventional wisdom'; Philip Williamson, *Stanley Baldwin: Conservative Leadership and National Values* (Cambridge, 1999); Jarvis, 'British Conservatism'.

[47] For instance, Duncan Tanner, 'Class voting and radical politics: the Liberal and Labour parties, 1910–31' in Jon Lawrence and Miles Taylor (eds), *Party, State and Society: Electoral Behaviour in Britain since 1820* (Aldershot, 1997); Maurice Cowling, *The Impact of Labour: 1920–1924: The Beginning of Modern British Politics* (Cambridge, 1971), pp. 359–367.

[48] *Labour Organiser*, February 1922, p. 5 and September 1924, pp. 14–15. For an example, see *The Pioneer* (East Woolwich), 8 (November 1922), LP/ELEC/1922/1, LHASC, Manchester; also Laura DuMond Beers, '"Selling socialism": Labour, democracy and the mass media, 1900–1939', unpublished PhD thesis, Harvard University (2007).

by their opponents as core members of the supposedly common-sensical, anti-socialist 'public'.[49]

But Labour also went on the offensive; insisting that, despite their claims to embody patriotism and the national interest, it was Labour's opponents who constituted the real 'class parties' in British politics. Fighting Romford in 1922, the writer and businessman Emil Davies argued that Labour 'stands for every section of the community, and aims at the building up of a nation enjoying security in all its sections. It is the other parties which are "class" parties and frame their policy to suit the interests of a narrow class, composed for the greater part of Super-tax payers.'[50] Nationally, Labour consistently used this argument to discredit opposition to its controversial proposal for a capital levy to reduce the nation's war debt. Indeed, it claimed that Liberals had only dropped their own plans for a levy at the dictation of the party's rich backers.[51] In 1925, Winston Churchill's first budget as Conservative Chancellor was denounced as 'class warfare with a vengeance!' and the public was called on to 'Stop this class legislation and vote Labour'.[52] Similarly, in his 1929 election broadcast, MacDonald alleged that the Conservative government was 'deeply stamped' by 'class and sectional interests', and proclaimed 'I detest class politics and want to end them in real national unity'.[53] But of course when he took this literally, by allying with the Conservatives to form a coalition government, Labour consistently challenged the 'national' pretensions of his new administration. Not only was the word 'National' always placed within inverted commas, but Labour insisted it, not the government, was truly representative of Britain. In 1931, a Labour leaflet entitled 'Who are the patriots?' insisted that 'the Labour Party, comprised as it is of all grades of society, of persons who dwell in baronial halls and persons who live in the humblest homes in the land, is far more national than their party'.[54]

---

[49] For example, see the following leaflets from 1929: '67,525 old people refused pensions' (no. 174), 'What the farm worker wants' (no. 185), 'Women voters know your friends!' (no. 208), 'Penalising the householder and shopkeeper' (no. 224) and 'The Tories refuse to lighten the ratepayers' burden' (no. 228). See also Laura Beers, 'Counter-toryism: Labour's response to anti-socialist propaganda, 1918–39' in Matthew Worley (ed.), *The Foundations of the British Labour Party: Identities, Cultures and Perspectives, 1900–39* (Farnham, 2009); Clare V. J. Griffiths, *Labour and the Countryside: The Politics of Rural Britain* (Oxford, 2007).

[50] A. Emil Davies, *His Election Book: General Election 1922, Romford* (Barking, 1922), p. 22.

[51] Labour Party, 'Liberals and the capital levy' (no. 79, 1923).

[52] Labour Party, 'The rich man's budget' (no. 167) and 'Mr Baldwin does not know how the poor live' (no. 170), both 1925.

[53] *The Times*, 29 May 1929, p. 9.

[54] Labour Party, 'Who are the patriots? Vote for Labour and the nation' (no. 321, 1931) and, from 1935, 'End the financiers' dictatorship' (no. 41); see also J. R. Clynes's 1931

Often such arguments would be expressed through overtly non-class languages that appealed to traditions of communitarianism, left patriotism, Christian socialism, humanitarianism and, of course, popular radicalism (Labour frequently sought to rework the old Gladstonian opposition between 'the masses' and 'the classes'). Labour's patriotism was generally articulated through ideas about the need to place collective, communal interests above those of class (and self) interest. For instance, in 1929 Jim Simmons echoed the Party's national programme for government, 'Labour and the nation', by telling his Erdington electors that 'Labour is the real national party – its policy is designed to serve the whole community and not a class'.[55]

By contrast, humanitarian arguments tended to assume a stratified public, and could adopt a distinctly patrician tone. In his personal appeal as prime minister in 1924, MacDonald declared 'we are fighting for the common folk so that their burdens may be lightened'. At St Pancras North in 1929, James Marley put humanitarianism at the centre of his appeal, declaring 'We place humanity before property'.[56] Such sentiments often shaded into explicitly Christian appeals presenting Labour as the political embodiment of universal brotherhood and fellowship. Fighting affluent Sheffield Hallam in 1923, Arnold Freeman declared: 'I care only that the Will of Christ should prevail in human affairs', adding he had only entered politics so that the city's poor 'may have in their hearts laughter instead of despair'. Similarly, in 1922 Emil Davies told Romford's electors: 'I believe in the divine spirit in man.' Nationally the Party published leaflets with titles such as 'Religion and Labour' and 'A call to Christians', which sought not simply to neutralise charges of socialist irreligiosity, but to demonstrate that the Party was the natural home for all socially concerned Christians.[57] But then the revivalist spirit ran deep in British Labour politics. In 1918, Lansbury's *Herald* ran a story about a dumb, shell-shocked soldier 'so keenly . . . touched' by

broadcast, *The Listener*, 21 October 1931, p. 676; and Paul Ward, 'Preparing for the People's War: Labour and patriotism in the 1930s', *Labour History Review*, 67, (2002), pp. 171–185, at 178–179.

[55] C. J. Simmons election address, 1929, LP/ELEC/1929/1, 'Boroughs' file, LHASC; Labour Party, *Labour and the Nation*, 2nd edn (London, 1928): 'the treasures of civilisation shall be, not the monopoly of a class, but the heritage of the nation', p. 46. See Paul Ward, *Red Flag and Union Jack: Patriotism and the British left, 1881–1924* (Woodbridge, 1998), esp. ch. 8.

[56] Labour Party, 'The Prime Minister's appeal' (no. 131, 1924); James Marley election address 1929, LP/ELEC/1929/1, 'Boroughs' file.

[57] Arnold Freeman election address, 1923, LP/ELEC/1923/1, 'Boroughs', LHASC; Davies, *Election Book*, p. 19; Labour Party, 'Religion and Labour' (no. 58, 1923) and 'A call to Christians' (no. 252, 1929); see Robert Pope, *Building Jerusalem: Nonconformity, Labour and the Social Question in Wales, 1906–1939* (Cardiff, 1998).

hearing Ethel Snowden preach socialism that 'he felt he must shout', and miraculously found his speech restored.[58]

But it was the tropes of popular radicalism that featured most consistently in Labour discourse. Here Labour was building on a long tradition of radical hostility to the privileges of birth and wealth – a tradition that Lloyd George's belligerent platform style had brought to new prominence in the decade before the war. Indeed, Labour often explicitly echoed the populist language of pre-war Liberal causes such as free trade, Lords reform and the land crusade. During the 1923 election on protectionism, Labour issued leaflets with slogans such as: 'taxes on the workers' food but NO TAX ON THE RICH MAN'S LUXURIES', and MacDonald spoke of his Party's special concerns for the 'industrious masses'. More generally, Labour portrayed itself as the party 'of equality against the privileges of wealth and place'. In a leaflet attacking the 'millionaire's press' in 1922, Labour played on simple stereotypes of the idle rich, declaring: 'To return the Rolls-Royce Parties is to permit the rich to levy their own taxes.'[59] This was the populist politics of the classes against the masses, of 'the rich versus the rest', rather than the politics of rich versus poor that one might hear in Labour's heartlands. A 1929 election leaflet nicely captured this vulgar populism in the slogan 'The Labour Party stands for the millions not the millionaires'.[60]

But in Labour's hands, populism often veered into workerism; indeed Labour politicians frequently deployed the language of 'the people' and 'the workers' interchangeably.[61] One early Labour leaflet ended with the slogan, 'The Labour Party is the People's Party! Workers, vote solid for Labour'. At Carlisle in 1924, George Middleton deployed classic anti-aristocratic radical language by attacking the Conservatives for packing their last government with twenty-nine peers and near-relations of peers. But his arguments emphasised the misrepresentation, not of 'the people', but of 'the workers': 'These are the people who claim to represent the workers of the country. Do they represent YOU?'[62] It was a good example of how the tone of Labour's radicalism often leant more towards workerism than populism, and

---

[58] *Herald*, 7 December 1918; see Stephen Yeo, 'A new life: the religion of socialism in Britain, 1883–1896', *History Workshop Journal*, 4, (1977), pp. 5–56.

[59] Labour Party, 'Your food will cost you more' (no. 23, 1923); 'Why women should join the Labour Party' (no. 1, 1918); 'The millionaire press' (no. 38, 1922); *The Times*, 30 July 1923, p. 12 (MacDonald).

[60] Labour Party, 'Ten reasons' (no. 236, 1929); much the same slogan appeared in Labour's pre-election newsletter *The Citizen*, 8, (November, 1928), p. 4.

[61] Lawrence, *Speaking*, pp. 144–148.

[62] Labour Party, 'The Labour party and its work' (no. 37, 1909); Middleton leaflet, 'Tories against workers', LP/ELEC/1924/1, 'Boroughs', LHASC.

how the valorisation of work continued to give the Party's message a distinctly class-inflected dimension.

Labour, the middle class and 'the workers'

But if Labour stood for the interests of workers against employers, it remained adamant that there was no place for customary distinctions between workers 'by hand or brain'. Labour's consistent message was that 'all who work are on the right path, that all labour is ... honourable'.[63] Labour argued that 'in alliance with the manual workers', Britain's 'brainworkers' would be able 'to insist on their proper share in the government of the country', sweeping away 'monopoly and privilege and the whole system of the government by the few over the many'.[64] But, Labour did not shirk from the need to confront head-on the misconceptions and class prejudices which frequently soured relations across the manual/non-manual divide. In 1923, Frank Smith warned Labour speakers not to 'denounce as parasites all who do not happen to be manual workers', pointing out that 'the idea that those who don the black coat and high collar are "snobs" is a mistake. To be well dressed, is, to one class of the community, as essential as the bag of tools and the overall to another.' At the same time, Labour admonished shopkeepers and clerks whose 'false class outlook' led them to avoid elementary schools and panel doctors. Holding out the prospect of improved state services for all, Labour implored 'black-coated workers' to 'discard the social prejudices which for generations have separated man from man'.[65]

But why, one might ask, did Labour go to such lengths to challenge vernacular understandings of social difference that stressed a manual/non-manual divide? One reason was that many Labour leaders were themselves non-manual workers who strongly identified with the workers' cause. Some, like Margaret Bondfield and Alexander Walkden, had been pioneers of trade unionism among non-manual workers, while others, such as MacDonald and Snowden, had long lived by speaking and writing, even if their origins were poor. It is also important to remember that, thanks to the ravages of unemployment, trade union density in the early 1930s was broadly comparable among non-manual

---

[63] Tracey (ed.), *Book of the Labour Party*, vol. 1, p. 17. By contrast, the language of 'workers' and 'working class' is elided in Bernard Barker, 'The anatomy of reformism: the social and political ideas of the Labour leadership in Yorkshire', *International Review of Social History*, 18, (1977), pp. 1–27, at 23–27.

[64] Labour Party, 'Why brain-workers should join the Labour party' (no. 2, nd [1918?]).

[65] Frank Smith, 'About propaganda', *Labour Organiser* (March, 1923), p. 2; Labour Party, 'Socialism and the black-coated worker' (no. 23, nd [1933?]).

and manual workers.[66] At the same time, clerical unions such as the Railway Clerks Association (RCA) were fervently committed to Labour politics. Not only was the RCA one of the first unions to establish a political fund under the Trade Union Act of 1913, but it recorded the strongest support of any union: 92 per cent approval on an 88 per cent turn-out. By contrast, 43 per cent of miners and 44 per cent of weavers voted against establishing a political fund in ballots with broadly comparable turn-outs.[67] It is noticeable that groups such as the railway clerks and post office workers often explicitly identified themselves as part of the 'working classes', but they nonetheless remained conscious of the distinctions between manual and non-manual, waged and salaried. For instance, in 1921 one finds postal workers anxious that the popular press might turn 'public opinion, working-class opinion, schooled in the field of humility and semi-starvation . . . against us'.[68] Similar anxieties may explain why the railway clerks' journal published a harsh satire on the snobbish attitudes of the non-union clerk who 'knows that there is something about himself, a certain something that marks him off from the common herd'.[69]

Labour's inclusive strategy had appeared to meet with remarkable success during the economic upswing of 1919. After advancing on a broad front in the November municipal elections, in December 1919 the party came within 713 votes of capturing St Albans in Hertfordshire, and a week later polled 47.5 per cent in a straight fight with the Conservatives at suburban Bromley in Kent. But thereafter the tide began to turn against Labour, especially in the suburbs. 'Anti-waste' and 'anti-socialist' cries gathered momentum, and Labour's high expectations for a rapid and decisive breakthrough had to be recalibrated.[70] Even in 1929, when Labour made significant gains outside its heartlands, the party came a poor third at Bromley and trailed the Conservatives by 8,737 votes at St Albans.

---

[66] W. G. Runciman, *A Treatise on Social Theory, III: Applied Social Theory* (Cambridge, 1997), p. 75n.

[67] Registrar of Friendly Societies, *Annual Report, 1912*, pp. 91–92; also Duncan Tanner, *Political Change and the Labour Party, 1900–1918* (Cambridge, 1990), pp. 322–323.

[68] *The Fellowship*, December 1921, although earlier the journal had been clear that the union's members were part of 'the working classes': *The Fellowship*, November 1921; see also Waites, *Class Society*, pp. 242–264.

[69] *Railway Service Journal*, March 1927, p. 85.

[70] Christopher Howard, 'Expectations born to death: local Labour Party expansion in the 1920s' in Jay Winter (ed.), *The Working Class in Modern British History: Essays in Honour of Henry Pelling* (Cambridge, 1983); Davies and Morley, *County Borough Elections*, 3, pp. 639–640.

But Labour continued to fight for the votes of middle-class workers throughout the inter-war period. According to Nick Tiratsoo, in the early 1920s, party strategists concluded that 'support among the urban working classes ... would never be enough to ensure majority government', and that therefore the Party had to redouble its efforts 'to make inroads where it was presently weak, in rural areas and middle-class suburbs'.[71] Sidney Webb first outlined his arguments for 'stratified electioneering' (tailoring political messages to specific electoral sub-groups) in 1922, the same year that Herbert Morrison argued that Labour could only win London by deliberately targeting the middle-class vote.[72] But if seats like St Albans and Bromley were not to come into Labour's sights again between the wars, the party did begin to make progress in many socially mixed urban areas. Morrison's London Labour Party famously captured control of London government in 1934, and in 1929 Labour fended off the challenge of a revitalised Liberal party to capture seats such as Acton, Brigg, Leyton West, Romford, Southampton and Sowerby for the first time.[73]

But how did Labour go about promoting its socially inclusive brand of workerist politics? First, unlike many in the wider movement, national leaders rarely spoke of 'the working class', preferring softer-edged formulations such as 'the workers' or 'the working classes' when they were not deploying the old radical language of 'the people' or 'the masses' against 'vested interests'.[74] Occasionally, Labour addressed propaganda directly at 'wage earners', but this was usually within 'stratified' campaigns, as in 1929 when the Party used the term in election posters targeted at agricultural workers and trade unionists.[75] Second, it sought to demonstrate that salaried and professional workers had good, substantive reasons to make common cause with manual workers. Besides arguing that they would receive the 'full fruits' of their labour and a larger say in the affairs of state, Labour's appeal focused on two classic Liberal causes during the 1920s: international peace and, perhaps more surprisingly, lower taxes. The 1922 leaflet 'Why brainworkers should

---

[71] Nick Tiratsoo, 'Labour and the electorate' in Tanner et al. (eds), Labour's First Century, at pp. 295–296.
[72] Sidney Webb, 'Stratified electioneering', Labour Organiser (November, 1922), p. 6; Herbert Morrison, 'Can Labour win London without the middle classes?' Labour Organiser (October, 1923), p. 19 (reprinted from the London Labour Chronicle); Beers, 'Counter-toryism'; Tom Jeffery, 'The suburban nation: politics and class in Lewisham' in David Feldman and Gareth Stedman Jones (eds), Metropolis – London: Histories and Representations since 1800 (London, 1989).
[73] Jeffery, 'Suburban nation'; Tanner, 'Class voting', pp. 120–122.
[74] The Listener, 17 April 1929, p. 528 (Henderson).
[75] Labour Party, 1929 election posters 'A' & 'B', LP/ELEC/1929/1, 'Boroughs', LHASC.

vote Labour' promised that 'steeper graduation' would reduce the tax burden on ordinary salary earners, while in 1929 Labour called on hard-pressed consumers to 'Vote Labour and end the Tory Tax mania!' In the same year it also made a strong appeal to shopkeepers and other rate-payers allegedly penalised by Churchill's de-rating proposals.[76] Such arguments were classic examples of MacDonald's 'progressivist' strategy aimed at consolidating Labour's position on the left by squeezing the Liberal vote.

In 1929, this approach helped Labour come close to forming a majority government, but in the wake of the 1931 debacle Labour leaders reconfigured their appeal to the middle-class worker along more explicitly socialist lines. One of the more extended elaborations of the Party's new thinking on class and politics was the 1936 pamphlet, 'The New Power in Politics', which started from the premise that Britain was 'a nation of workers' where the owners had all the power.[77] Readers were told that barely one in a thousand Britons lived solely off the work of others, that only four in a hundred were employers, farmers or professional men, and that 'so far as numbers go, therefore, the "nation" is overwhelmingly a nation of wage-earners and salary-earners'. Together, these two groups, representing at least 90 per cent of the population, were said to constitute the 'working classes', and the pamphlet triumphantly declared 'the nation is kept alive by their work and they are the nation'.[78] Here Labour was explicitly challenging Conservative conceptions of 'the public' that marginalised workers, especially organised workers, and in doing so was preparing the discursive ground on which the rhetoric of a 'people's war' (and peace) would later be constructed.

But perhaps the key theme that Labour stressed to try and bind wage and salary earners together was that of security. In the 1921 ILP pamphlet 'Mr Wilkins', the eponymous 'hero' is an Ilford clerk thrown into worklessness, and ultimately despair and ruin, by a prolonged illness. Even before he loses his job we are told that Wilkins 'would lie awake uneasily thinking of old age, sickness or some other disaster', acknowledging that life was 'unfair' and even that the working classes were probably right to take whatever they could get. But such thoughts would evaporate the next day 'when he took his daily dope' (his newspaper).

---

[76] Labour Party, 'Why brainworkers should vote Labour' (1922), 'Vote Labour and end the Tory tax mania!' (no. 219, 1929), 'What the Conservatives have done' (1929), 'Tories hand out gifts' (no. 223, 1929), 'Penalising the householder and shopkeeper' (no. 224, 1929); also *The Listener*, 8 May 1929, pp. 656–658 (Snowden).

[77] Labour Party, *New Power*; also *Why a Labour Party?* (London, 1932).

[78] Labour Party, *New Power*, p. 1.

Finally, broken by poverty, he stumbles on a crowd cheering the anti-union rhetoric of a speaker from the Middle Classes Union. But Wilkins, we are told, now 'knew that they lived on the brink of the abyss. He understood how blind they were, how ignorant of the precarious nature of their hold on "respectability".'[79]

This was a message that Labour echoed repeatedly between the wars: that all those obliged to work for their living were vulnerable, and that personal savings alone could never ensure security. Only genuine *social* security could guarantee safety from the abyss of poverty and despair. In the 1930s, as Labour sought to develop a more concrete policy programme, the concept of 'security' became central to Party propaganda. Appeals to salaried workers talked of their lives being 'continually haunted by the fear of insecurity'. In a tortured piece on the middle class and socialism, Stafford Cripps wrote that Labour 'must make clear that their interests lie with us', and acknowledged that 'security' was the key to this since it was 'the aim of everyone who lived by hand or brain power'.[80] Perhaps most strikingly, in his 1935 election broadcast, Clement Attlee began and ended his talk by playing on the double meaning of 'collective security' which, he argued, represented the only solution to Britain's problems both at home and abroad. The politician's first 'duty', Attlee insisted, must be 'to give security to the citizens, and to banish fear from their minds'.[81]

However, in the 1930s the theme of 'security' was placed as much in an economic as a social context. Greater attention was now paid to the mechanics of the transition from capitalist to socialist production, and hence to the roles that different strata of workers would play in the coming socialist economic and social order.[82] At the 1935 election Labour published 'What socialism will really mean to you', a lavishly illustrated, large-format brochure, which predicted 'a life of all-round general abundance' within ten years of socialist government. Unlike in earlier formulations, no attempt was now made to elide the interests of manual and non-manual workers under socialism. Manual workers were still told that receiving 'the full values they produce by their work' would mean 'wealth unparalleled', but the appeal to

---

[79] Mander, *Mr Wilkins*, pp. 4, 8.
[80] Labour Party, 'Socialism and the black-coated worker'; Stafford Cripps, *Are You a Worker? Where the Middle-Class Stands* (London, 1934), pp. 5, 7. See also Labour Party, 'Socialism is the means to security', 'The right to security', and 'Citizens can rule themselves' (all 1933).
[81] *The Listener*, 6 November 1935, pp. 820–821.
[82] Richard Toye, *The Labour Party and the Planned Economy, 1931–1951* (Woodbridge, 2003), chs 1–3.

non-manual workers now stressed not rewards, but rather 'service'. Socialism, they were assured, would develop to an unparalleled degree 'the social and civilising services' that it was their 'particular function' to provide. These arguments were developed at length in a Labour pamphlet aimed specifically at 'the middle-class worker'. In leaden language that epitomised the new vogue for 'planning', Labour promised that 'all professional workers, who are doing, or will be willing to do, work of a socially useful nature will be recognised as valuable and socially necessary parts of civilised organisation and will be guaranteed security of their civilised positions in the transition to Socialism'.[83]

Where once Labour's emphasis had been on wage and salary earners' shared interest in a fairer distribution of rewards, now it was on the different roles each would play in building a socialist society. Not only would the two blocks of Labour's imagined constituency – its workers by hand and brain – perform different functions within the new order, crucially, they were now appealed to through different idioms: economic/materialist for 'hand' workers, but social/idealist for the 'brain' workers of the new middle class.[84] Paradoxically, thinking more deeply about the socialist future appears to have undermined Labour leaders' confidence in a universalist appeal structured around security and a 'fair' wage or salary. Labour continued to believe in the resolution of class antagonism through a benign, interventionist state, but it now conceded that class difference would prove more intractable. Crucially, however, in the field of social security Labour continued to preach universalism, and, as Peter Baldwin has shown, in power after 1945 it proved decidedly generous in its treatment of salaried and self-employed groups brought within the expanded state insurance system.[85] If actions speak louder than words, Labour's encoding of its rhetoric of 'producers by hand or brain' into the fabric of the new welfare state must be judged the most significant long-term consequence of these earlier discursive battles.

[83] Lawrence Benjamin, *The Position of the Middle-class Worker in the Transition to Socialism* (London, 1935), pp. 17–18.

[84] Labour Party, *What Socialism Will Really Mean to You* (London, 1935), pp. 6, 15–16, and *New Power*, pp. 2, 7; Benjamin, *Middle-class Worker*, pp. 16–19. See Robert Skidelsky, 'The Labour Party and Keynes' in Skidelsky, *Interests and Obsessions: Selected Essays* (London, 1993), and Toye, *Planned Economy*, pp. 1–4, 13–16, 28, 34–64.

[85] Peter Baldwin, *The Politics of Social Solidarity: Class Bases of the European Welfare State, 1875–1975* (Cambridge, 1990), pp. 116–134.

Conclusion

By falling in with the construction of a 'National' Government in 1931, Baldwin and his allies sought to underscore Labour's identity as 'un-National'. But Labour did more than simply contest such arguments, it actively struggled to rework radical languages of 'nation' and 'people' so that they came to be founded unambiguously on the workers whose labour supposedly created the nation's wealth and power. Labour leaders consistently argued that most Britons were 'workers' in this sense, indeed they were usually careful to insist that housewives were no less 'workers', just because their work went unpaid (though some studies might suggest otherwise, Labour was intensely conscious of the dangers of appearing to valorise only male, manual labour).[86] But elections do not lie. In a nation where more than three-quarters of voters were manual workers, or their dependants, and where, by its own estimation, approximately 90 per cent belonged to the 'working classes', the Party failed to poll above 38 per cent before 1945. Most obviously, Labour did not succeed in winning the new, technological and managerial middle classes to socialism, despite the growth of progressive, anti-government feeling among such groups in the later 1930s (perhaps being 'necessary parts of civilised organisation' proved less appealing than they hoped).[87]

But if Conservatism remained dominant in 1930s Britain, Labour's discursive project to valorise a broadly defined understanding of 'the workers', and to insist on its salience to political life, nonetheless had long-term implications. Most obviously, it reworked older traditions of anti-aristocratic radical politics into a powerful critique of class privilege more broadly. In the process it placed 'the workers' at the heart of conceptions of 'public' and 'nation' in ways that proved difficult to resist under the new democratic franchise of 1918 (this was why inter-war Conservative rhetoric was never explicitly exclusionary or anti-worker, it could not afford to be).

But it was in 1939–1940 that Labour's discursive project truly came into its own. In the crisis days of 1939 and 1940, few doubted either the Party's national credentials or its instinctive patriotism. Only a minority of Labour politicians may have been strong advocates of rearmament,

---

[86] See Labour Party, 'Home is the housewife's workshop' (no. 21, nd [1933?]), and 'Labour's work for women' (no. 109, 1924).

[87] McKibbin, *Classes and Cultures*, pp. 49, 62–69, 90–98, and 'Classes and cultures: a postscript'; James Hinton, 'The "class" complex: Mass-Observation and cultural distinction in pre-war Britain', *Past & Present*, 199, (2008), pp. 207–236; Benjamin, *Middle-class Worker*, pp. 17–18.

but almost all had consistently embraced the socially inclusive discourse analysed in this chapter.[88] As Britain drifted once again to war, even Labour's fiercest critics rushed to acknowledge the Party's claim to be a full and indispensable part of the nation. Conservative newspapers lauded Arthur Greenwood, the acting Labour leader, for rising to Amery's challenge to 'Speak for England' (or rather 'Britain' – as Labour MPs properly insisted) in the fevered parliamentary debates of 2 September 1939. Ignoring counter-calls to 'speak for the working classes' (possibly from John McGovern of the Glasgow ILP), Greenwood skilfully used the first person plural to ally Labour with the national cause. He declared his hope that 'we shall march in complete unity', and his belief that 'We shall not, we cannot, be beaten'.[89] The following day, with war declared, Greenwood was offering 'whole-hearted support to the measures necessary to equip the State', and insisting, 'we shall make our full contribution to the national cause'.[90]

Over subsequent days the *Daily Mail* ran patriotic headlines lifted directly from Greenwood's speech, and even the *Daily Telegraph* rejoiced that 'organised labour should have thrown itself so whole-heartedly into the national effort', observing: 'their instant reaction to the challenge does honour to themselves and to the nation that bred them; and it strengthens immeasurably both the confidence of the forces of democracy and the resources on which they rely.'[91] In fact, Labour, like the Liberals, remained outside the government – insisting that it could do most good by offering 'loyal opposition'. When, during spring 1940, Chamberlain's stock collapsed in the country (and the House), it was this independence that allowed Labour to play a decisive role in the political manoeuvrings that brought Churchill to power as the leader of a genuinely 'national' government. Labour had not only been recognised as a vital part of the nation, it had played its part in shaping that nation's destiny.[92] Crucially, it had also consistently championed the ideals and aspirations that now resonated through propagandist talk about fighting a 'people's war', and building a 'people's peace'.

---

[88] Ward, 'People's war'.
[89] L. S. Amery, *My Political Life: vol. 3, The Unforgiving Years, 1929–1940* (London, 1955), p. 324; Hugh Dalton, *The Fateful Years: Memoirs, 1931–1945* (London, 1957), pp. 264–265; *The Times*, 4 September 1939, p. 3; Ward, 'People's war', p. 180; *Parl. Debates*, 5th ser., 351, HofC, cols 282–283 (2 September 1939).
[90] *Daily Chronicle*, 4 September 1939, p. 11.
[91] *Daily Mail*, 4 September 1939, p. 6; *Daily Telegraph*, 5 September 1939, p. 6.
[92] Addison, *Road to 1945*, pp. 96–102, 112.

11 The dialectics of liberation: the old left, the new left and the counter-culture

Alastair J. Reid

> Our play's chief aim has been to take to bits
> great propositions and their opposites
> see how they work then let them fight it out ...
>
> Peter Weiss, *Marat/Sade* (1965)

I

In applying this pronouncement from *Marat/Sade* to the historical context of its first English-language production in London in the mid-1960s, the first 'great proposition' to consider is that of the old left. This is understood here as referring to a range of views, shaped by the Bolshevik revolution and the inter-war economic crisis, broadly in favour of organised labour pressing for a centrally planned economy and state-administered social provision. There may have been disagreements about how quickly this could be achieved, the role of vanguards and mass parties in bringing it about, and the degree of egalitarianism in the outcome. However, all those who subscribed to this proposition stressed the same notions of the main agent and the main direction of change, rooted in nineteenth-century materialism of either the Marxist or the Revisionist variety.[1]

The parliamentary old left was widely seen as confronting a serious crisis of social change and political realignment as a result of the affluence associated with the long period of economic growth after 1945. Full employment, a shift from manual to non-manual occupations, new residential patterns and increasing access to consumer goods were

For their supportive and challenging comments I would like to thank: Kevin Borman, Rychard Carrington, Margaret Dyson, David Goodway, Ian Patterson, Troy Roberts, Richard Taylor and, last but by no means least, the editors of this collection.

[1] For stimulating surveys of the issues discussed in this section, see J. Seed, 'Hegemony postponed: the unravelling of the culture of consensus in Britain in the 1960s', in B. Moore-Gilbert and J. Seed (eds), *Cultural Revolution? The Challenge of the Arts in the 1960s* (London, 1992); G. Andrews, 'The three New Lefts and their legacies', in G. Andrews, Richard Cockett, Alan Hooper and Michael Williams (eds), *New Left, New Right and Beyond. Taking the Sixties Seriously* (Houndmills, 1999).

thought to be undermining older habits and loyalties, contributing to the Labour Party's defeat in three successive general elections during the 1950s. The key intellectual response came from a prominent Labour politician, Anthony Crosland, who argued that prosperity had combined with an effectively mixed economy and the increasing separation of management from ownership in the private sector to reduce the intensity of economic conflict and the urgency of further rounds of public ownership. The emphasis of progressive reforms should therefore shift to greater social equality and freedom: focusing on education, industrial democracy and more diversity of lifestyles.[2] This systematic revisionism contributed to a long-lasting polarisation within the party, with the 'Labour Left' becoming increasingly marginalised by its heavy reliance on traditional formulas and loyalties.

Meanwhile the extra-parliamentary old left was undergoing a parallel crisis, seen as linked to the same processes of domestic social and political change but also in this case intensified by international issues.[3] For, initially squeezed to the margins of public life by the polarisation of the Cold War, it was rocked to its foundations in 1956 by the public acknowledgement of Stalin's excesses closely followed by the Soviet suppression of an uprising in Hungary. A group of communist dissidents formed around the key figures of John Saville and Edward Thompson, then merged with a wider network of younger Oxford intellectuals who had initially been provoked into activism by the government's intervention in Suez, also in 1956, to establish the journal *New Left Review* in 1960. This was partly the result of an intense period of joint activity around the Campaign for Nuclear Disarmament (CND) in 1959–1961, calling for a 'third way' of 'positive neutrality' from both East and West along with unilateral nuclear disarmament, and seeming at first to be having an impact on Labour Party policy.[4] Coming out of a particularly rigid economic-determinist background, this self-declared 'New Left' spent a good deal of time struggling with notions of 'agency' and 'morality', particularly marked in the lively and influential essays of Edward Thompson, as well as beginning to explore

[2] A. Crosland, *The Future of Socialism* (London, 1956). For the wider context of Labour Party thinking in the period, see L. Black, *The Political Culture of the Left in Affluent Britain, 1951–64* (Houndmills, 2003).

[3] For detailed accounts of the developments outlined in the following paragraphs, see L. Chun, *The British New Left* (Edinburgh, 1993), esp. pp. 1–59; M. Kenny, *The First New Left. British Intellectuals after Stalin* (London, 1995). For retrospective commentaries by some of those involved, see Oxford Socialist Discussion Group, *Out of Apathy. Voices of the New Left Thirty Years on* (London, 1989).

[4] R. Taylor, *Against the Bomb. The British Peace Movement, 1958–1965* (Oxford, 1988).

the previously largely excluded field of 'culture', particularly marked in the pioneering surveys of Raymond Williams.[5]

However, its overall position was in the end not dissimilar to that of the revisionists within the parliamentary old left: for in both milieus it became common to argue for the rethinking of conventional economic definitions of class, the development of new concepts to grasp the shaping of political identities in advanced democracies and the granting of a higher priority to issues of participation and personal fulfilment. In retrospect, it is possible to see this broadly humanising renewal of British socialism in the late 1950s as an instinctive reaching back beyond a narrowly functional focus on the public ownership of the means of production to a broader set of ambitions, sometimes consciously remembered in the form of the ethical outlook of Britain's early socialist sects with their deep roots in romantic social criticism and religious nonconformity.[6] This certainly had the potential to provide the left with a distinctive identity in opposition to the then-predominant Conservatism, which remained paternalistic, backward-looking and conformist. Indeed, some of this renewed left programme was enacted by Harold Wilson's Labour governments of the mid- to late 1960s. Wilson was only temporarily able to reunite his own party around what soon proved to be a rather empty rhetoric of industrial modernisation but, often through the acceptance of a wave of Labour backbench and Liberal Party bills, his governments did enact significant reforms in the areas of education, family life and sexual rights.[7]

However, apart from growing economic difficulties in these years there was, almost inevitably, a failure to keep up with a revolution of rising social expectations. For there were new sorts of community politics focusing on the inadequacies of central-state social provision, with campaigns around homelessness and claimants' rights. There were also new sorts of demands from those within the rapidly expanding higher-education sector, for both new relationships between teachers and learners and new contents for courses. And there was even a widening disagreement between the Labour government and its closest

[5] E. P. Thompson (ed.), *Out of Apathy* (London, 1960); R. Williams, *The Long Revolution* (London, 1961).

[6] Naturally, the historians involved were most aware of this: for the parliamentary old left see H. Pelling, *The Origins of the Labour Party, 1880–1900* (London, 1954) and H. Pelling (ed.), *The Challenge of Socialism* (London, 1954); for the extra-parliamentary old left see E. P. Thompson, *William Morris. Romantic to Revolutionary* (London, 1955) and E. P. Thompson, *The Making of the English Working Class* (London, 1963). For one historically minded literary critic who was trying at this point to bridge both positions, see R. Williams, *Culture and Society, 1780–1950* (London, 1958).

[7] Seed, 'Hegemony postponed', pp. 29–35.

traditional allies, with the national leaderships of some of the biggest unions openly campaigning against relatively modest proposals for reform of industrial-relations law. These protests increasingly involved dramatically visible forms of direct action in public spaces: squatting in empty council properties, occupying university buildings, continuing to work in firms abandoned by management.[8] The social-democratic state, it seemed, was being torn apart from within by its own beneficiaries, something which the old left, even in its renewed version, could not really understand, for its thinking was still rooted in nineteenth-century assumptions about the inevitability of social progress. Thus, reviewing the successes and failures of their period in office, the Labour revisionists looked mainly for further rounds of central-state spending and more efficient social and economic planning.[9] Meanwhile, a significant regrouping of the extra-parliamentary old left worked hard to distance itself from the limitations of Wilson's leadership, but still envisaged the alternative as a more committed socialist government implementing a distinctive national economic strategy.[10]

While the old left seemed incapable of moving on from the reshuffling of familiar ideas, the whole framework of corporatist economic management and liberalising social reform which it took for granted, even when criticising its limitations, was being fundamentally challenged by a renewal on the right. For the 1960s were also seeing the emergence of extremist pressure groups, often around rather bizarre fringe figures: the Institute for Economic Affairs, the National Viewers' and Listeners' Association (around Mary Whitehouse), and the Black Papers on Education (around Rhodes Boyson). However, this potent combination of economic neo-liberalism with self-consciously backward-looking morality soon found charismatic champions within parliamentary Conservatism, first Enoch Powell then second, and much more successfully, Margaret Thatcher.[11] As the extent and permanence of the Thatcherite counter-revolution began to sink in during the 1980s, there was another widespread round of rethinking on the old left, once again with clear parallels between its extra-parliamentary and its parliamentary wings. On the one hand were the trends in a group which formed around the Eurocommunist journal *Marxism Today*, most notably a veteran of the younger Oxford group within the 'first New Left', Stuart Hall, who reworked the issues of 'agency' and 'culture' in urging a definitive reconciliation with new forms of mass subjectivity

[8] Ibid., pp. 36–39.   [9] A. Crosland, *Socialism Now and Other Essays* (London, 1974).
[10] R. Williams (ed.), *May Day Manifesto 1968* (Harmondsworth, 1968).
[11] Seed, 'Hegemony postponed', pp. 40–41.

produced by improving living standards and increasing consumer choice.[12] On the other hand were the successive steps in the 'modernisation' of the Labour Party's policy commitments and internal constitutional arrangements, culminating in the removal of the Clause Four commitment to public ownership, the displacement of collective by individual membership and finally the presentational change of name to 'New Labour' under Tony Blair.[13] These shifts clearly drew on important aspects of the revisionism of the 1950s, but fundamentally reshaped them in the context of a demoralised acceptance of what was seen by the late 1980s as the worldwide dominance of right-wing, neo-liberal political and social assumptions.

II

The second great proposition to consider is that of the new left, understood here as referring to a range of views considering organised labour as having become too incorporated to remain a progressive force and looking instead to new, largely youthful and largely middle-class, movements to bring about a liberation of social institutions from traditional authoritarian and alienated forms. There may have been disagreements about how explicitly this should be linked to public ownership of economic resources and whether organised labour in the developed core could still be stimulated into some sort of revival, or alliances should instead be built mainly with revolts at the underdeveloped periphery. However, all those who subscribed to this proposition stressed the same notion of the main agent and the main direction of change, rooted in nineteenth-century idealism of a predominantly Hegelian type, albeit initially mediated by the writings of the young Marx.[14]

The student movement of the late 1960s was the key seedbed for other new social movements, asking radical questions about post-war affluence, demanding a greater role in self-government than established institutions were accustomed to allowing and exploring new forms of more or less spontaneous protest. The first signs of this in Britain were at

---

[12] S. Hall, *The Hard Road to Renewal. Thatcherism and the Crisis of the Left* (London, 1988).

[13] P. Mandelson and R. Liddle, *The Blair Revolution. Can New Labour Deliver?* (London, 1996).

[14] For a combination of reasons, including the larger populations of students and young blacks, as well as the more immediate impact of the Vietnam War, the new left was a much stronger presence in north America: for stimulating definitions from this perspective see M. Teodori (ed.), *The New Left. A Documentary History* (Indianapolis, 1969), pp. 34–37, 72–83; G. Katsiaficas, *The Imagination of the New Left. A Global Analysis of 1968* (Boston MA, 1987), pp. 17–27, 198–204.

the London School of Economics in 1966–1967, when resistance to the appointment of a new head from Rhodesia led to some of the first boycotts of lectures and occupations of university buildings. Revived Trotskyite sects, especially the International Marxist Group, were very involved, and there were also close links with the Vietnam Solidarity Campaign: three major demonstrations outside the US embassy in Grosvenor Square in 1967–1968 involved some spectacularly repressive policing and mini riots. The student movement then escalated further after the events of May 1968 in Paris provoked self-conscious emulations, especially at Hornsey School of Art where a three-month occupation began over a dispute about student-union funds but moved on to challenge the whole notion of a fixed curriculum and formal assessment.[15] These types of struggle for increasing resources, equal opportunities and more democratic participation could be seen not only as liberating in themselves but also as opening up the possibility of a wider undermining of the dominant ideology in the reproduction of which universities were key institutions.

One of the most important outgrowths of the student movement was what is often referred to as 'second-wave feminism', initially focused on the women's liberation movement which was reacting, at least in part, against the male domination of other protest groups. Launched in 1970, its initial demands still focused on national legislation for equal rights but it also gave rise to hundreds of local self-help groups and newsletters, co-ordinated to some degree by the publication of *Spare Rib* from 1972. On this basis there then emerged a number of parallel, and lasting, national networks: especially women's refuges from domestic violence, rape-counselling centres and preventative-health clinics.[16] Another important offshoot was what might be called 'second-wave environmentalism', turning traditional concerns about nature conservation into a radical ecological critique of economic growth and political centralisation. Friends of the Earth arrived in Britain from North America in 1970, turning from the protection of areas of outstanding beauty to publicising more widespread threats from industrial pollution and nuclear power, and challenging both 'big business' and 'big government'. This provided the background for a widening range of even more daring and

[15] C. Crouch, *The Student Revolt* (London, 1970); J. Callaghan, *British Trotskyism. Theory and Practice* (Oxford, 1984), pp. 128–130.

[16] P. Byrne, *Social Movements in Britain* (London, 1997), pp. 109–113; M. Pugh, *Women and the Women's Movement in Britain, 1914–1999*, 2nd edn, (Houndmills, 2000), pp. 312–330.

dramatic direct-action groups spearheaded by Greenpeace, which arrived in Britain from North America in 1978.[17]

Within the loose network around *New Left Review* the younger generation had already begun to explore more specifically new-left positions from the late 1950s.[18] When it became clear that the wave of protest around CND had run into the ground these tendencies came into the open in 1962 in the form of a new editorial board around the 24-year-old Perry Anderson, who went on to argue that the failure of the 'first New Left' had been the result of the complete inadequacy of all aspects of British public life. In a country which had even failed to produce a systematic 'bourgeois social science' it was quite unrealistic to expect the cultural resources among the masses, or even among those intellectuals closest to them, to yield any strategic grasp of the overall situation and how to change it. What was needed was a comprehensive conceptual framework rather than piecemeal insights, and this would require the importation of totalising visions from elsewhere in Europe to clear away the narrow-minded, conservative empiricism which was fogging up England.[19] Drawing especially on the Italian Antonio Gramsci's suggestions about the role of 'hegemonic' world views in shaping the outcomes of political struggles, these young intellectuals began to consider themselves almost as another new social movement: for the spreading of revolutionary ideas through their own writing and publication would be the key to wider social transformation.

There was, however, an underlying ambiguity in this project, as it was still felt necessary to ground it in a long-run view of the 'origins of the present crisis'. The arguments about Britain's intellectual backwardness were therefore based on a schematic account of its unusual capitalist development, including the distorting effects of its possession of a vast maritime empire, accompanied by the assumption that the Marxist model of historical stages had still been occurring as predicted elsewhere in Europe. That the younger generation at *New Left Review* was only breaking partially from the old left was also evident in its approach to the student movement. On the one hand, some prominent members of

---

[17] Byrne, *Social Movements*, pp. 128–132, 138–139. For an exploration of some of the intellectual influences on the new environmentalism, see M. Veldman, *Fantasy, the Bomb and the Greening of Britain. Romantic Protest, 1945–1980* (Cambridge, 1994), pp. 205–302.

[18] For the existence of this current before the open break in 1962, see Kenny, *First New Left*, esp. pp. 54–118; for a detailed account of subsequent developments see Chun, *British New Left*, esp. pp. 60–117.

[19] See esp. P. Anderson, 'Origins of the present crisis', *New Left Review*, 23, (1964), pp. 26–53. This led to a bitter inter-generational conflict which rumbled on for a decade and more, recorded in E. P. Thompson, *The Poverty of Theory* (London, 1978) and P. Anderson, *Arguments Within English Marxism* (London, 1980).

the group took part in the Vietnam Solidarity Campaign and in protests at London colleges; on the other hand, even at the time of their most ambitious formulation of 'red bases', largely sympathetic commentators such as the postgraduate historian Gareth Stedman Jones still saw the student protest as only a first step towards the necessary reawakening of organised labour.[20] Then, as the strength of the establishment's reaction became more evident, this ambiguity was resolved in favour of a return to a more traditional emphasis on armed class struggle against the coercive power of the state. Anderson himself highlighted the fragmented and pessimistic nature of Gramsci's thinking, simultaneously in effect dismissing much of his own intellectual effort throughout the 1960s as typical of idealist distortions in 'Western Marxism'.[21] This renunciation of what had been a genuine attempt at intellectual innovation only confirmed its own initial diagnosis of the irremediable conservatism of British public life: the expansive diversity of *New Left Review* in the 1960s had resolved itself into little more than narrow Trotskyism by the late 1970s.

Meanwhile, others among those inspired by the initial project of theoretical innovation resisted this re-imposition of revolutionary materialism and struggled to work out different implications of the various theories exploding from Paris in the aftermath of 1968. The joint influence of the rather tortuous structuralist philosophy of Louis Althusser and the highly idiosyncratic psychoanalytic theory of Jacques Lacan eventually produced a specifically British form of post-structuralism, more solemn and more politically engaged than its largely playful and literary counterpart in North American deconstruction, but equally focused on prioritising the sphere of 'discourse'. As a result, its influence was largely restricted to the close reading of texts in a handful of new academic disciplines, most notably film theory, cultural studies and literary theory, along with distinctive interventions in some more established fields, such as the application of 'the linguistic turn' to social history.[22] Unwilling to take the step of reconciling itself to the increasing domination of right-wing neo-liberalism, the new left was only able to maintain something of its initial momentum within the

---

[20] G. Stedman Jones, 'The meaning of the student revolt', in A. Cockburn and R. Blackburn (eds), *Student Power. Problems, Diagnosis, Action* (Harmondsworth, 1969).

[21] P. Anderson, 'The antinomies of Antonio Gramsci', *New Left Review*, 100, (1976), pp. 5–78; P. Anderson, *Considerations on Western Marxism* (London, 1976). See also G. Stedman Jones, 'The Marxism of the early Lukacs: an evaluation', *New Left Review*, 70, (1971), pp. 27–64.

[22] A. Easthope, *British Post-Structuralism since 1968* (London, 1988); G. Stedman Jones, *Languages of Class* (Cambridge, 1983).

realm of scholarly speculation, at times even seeming to revel in its increasing detachment from social reality.

However, the new social movements carried on, becoming more ambitious and more influential. The women's movement went beyond its initial emphasis on equal opportunities to develop new struggles for recognition of the value of women's differences and for politicisation of what had previously been regarded as the private sphere of the family and sexuality: even though activism has since declined, this has had an enormous long-term impact on intellectual and cultural assumptions throughout the country. Moreover, the environmental movement increased its membership dramatically from the late 1980s and broadened its tactical repertoire from direct action to encompass traditional lobbying methods and advising on environmental audits and ethical consumerism: this has had a considerable impact on public attitudes and private habits, leading most recently to a foothold for the Green Party in the House of Commons, in some local authorities and to mainstream acceptance of the reality of the threat of 'global warming'. Even CND underwent a marked revival in the 1980s, becoming part of a wider peace movement and developing expertise in the use of the media and conventional political lobbying channels: though its success was limited to a marginal impact on the removal of Cruise missiles, it helped to lay the basis for massive popular demonstrations against the invasion of Iraq in 2003. Although support for these movements appears to be strongest among a generation which is ageing, it has opened the door for successive cohorts to launch new campaigns: against road building and airport expansion, for animal rights and civil liberties.[23] Single-issue protest campaigns and broader social movements among well-educated young people disillusioned with mainstream parties have become a permanent part of the British political landscape.

III

The third great proposition to consider is that of the counter-culture, understood here as referring to a range of views considering all forms of conventional politics as too limited and goal-oriented to promote real freedom, and looking instead for long-term social benefits from participation in immediate artistic experience to bring about an expansion, or even transcendence, of ordinary consciousness. There may have been

[23] Byrne, *Social Movements*, pp. 91–108, 114–127, 134–157; G. McKay, *Senseless Acts of Beauty. Cultures of Resistance since the Sixties* (London, 1996); Pugh, *Women*, pp. 330–353.

disagreements about whether this should involve the use of mind-altering drugs, whether it would be productive to engage with Eastern spiritual traditions and whether it might be compatible with more playful forms of politics. However, all those who subscribed to this proposition stressed the same movement away from formal schemes for the reorganisation of society towards an informal exploration of 'inner space', rooted in the avant-garde experiments of early-twentieth-century modernism, above all Dadaism and Surrealism.[24]

The urgent requirements of World War II and post-war reconstruction had pushed literary and artistic experimentation to the fringes of public life, but modernist avant-gardes were reviving, especially among self-exiled writers in post-war Paris, and made a wider public impact when the 'Theatre of the Absurd' began to appear in London from 1955. This work, above all by Samuel Beckett, Eugene Ionesco and Harold Pinter, pointed towards irreducible features of the human condition beyond the confines of language and outside the control of governments; a theme taken even further by the shift towards immersion in noise, movement and colour in the 'Theatre of Cruelty', intended by Antonin Artaud as a direct exposure to the necessary pain of being in the world and an appeal to the deeper understanding of the senses and instincts. This had a high-profile influence on the experimental work of Peter Brook at the Royal Shakespeare Company, most notably his 1964 production of Peter Weiss's *Marat/Sade*, further intensifying debates between straightforward storytelling and discordant perspectives on the same events; between the will to improve society and despair about human powerlessness.[25] Behind all this, informing both the work of the playwrights and the responses of their audiences, was the growing realisation of the full extent of the Nazi attempt to exterminate European Jewry towards the end of World War II, which only really began to enter wider public awareness throughout the world following the Israeli government's kidnapping and high-profile public trial of Adolf Eichmann in 1960.[26]

---

[24] For stimulating surveys of the issues discussed in this section, see R. Hewison, *Too Much. Art and Society in the Sixties, 1960–75* (London, 1986); P. Waugh, *Harvest of the Sixties. English Literature and its Background, 1960–1990* (Oxford, 1995). For acute insights into the importance of Dadaism and Surrealism for the events of May 1968 in France, see A. Willener, *The Action-Image of Society. On Cultural Politicization* (London, 1970), esp. pp. 193–229.

[25] M. Esslin, *The Theatre of the Absurd* (London, 1962); A. Artaud, *The Theatre and Its Double* (London, 1970); P. Brook, *The Empty Space* (London, 1968).

[26] P. Novick, *The Holocaust in American Life* (Boston, 1999).

This work in the theatre was paralleled by the emergence of a radical critique of conventional psychiatry, centred on the charismatic figure of R. D. Laing, who rejected scientific and institutional approaches in favour of direct personal engagement with the mentally ill and a more relaxed, phenomenological, approach to their personal worlds. What began as a distinctive practice within hospital wards was then generalised into a critique of the society which was unable to cope with mental illness except through incarceration: calling for a general turning away from the pursuit of material progress towards a mystical, and perhaps even drug-enhanced, exploration of inner space.[27] Meanwhile, blueprints for a distinctive 'cultural revolution' were being circulated informally by the experimental novelist Alexander Trocchi under the overall heading of the *Sigma Portfolio*: running from 1963 to 1967, this eventually consisted of twenty-eight pamphlets and manifestos by many of the leading names in the international avant-garde, including Laing, William Burroughs, Timothy Leary, the French Situationists and, of course, Trocchi himself. In fact what was being advocated was not so much a 'revolution' as a 'revelation', not political struggle but personal transformation through spontaneous art, not the mind-numbing consumption of yet another object but a continuous remaking of all the participants as the only valid outcome.[28]

This burgeoning cultural movement had an appeal to many of those who had been involved in CND, for it built directly on the experience of the Aldermaston marches as an alternative way of life and offered another outlet for anti-war impulses following the failure of more orthodox pressure-group activity. What was coming to be known as the 'Underground' then emerged from a lively network of little presses and local performances to break cover at the iconic 'International Poetry Incarnation' at the Royal Albert Hall in the summer of 1965, inspired by Michael Horowitz's earlier series of 'Live New Departures' jazz-poetry celebrations, and with Trocchi in the chair. It went on to produce an intense set of drug-fuelled multi-media 'happenings' over the next couple of years focused around the London Free School,

---

[27] R. D. Laing, *The Divided Self. An Existential Study in Sanity and Madness* (London, 1960); R. D. Laing, *The Politics of Experience and the Bird of Paradise* (Harmondsworth, 1967). For a renewal of serious interest in his contribution, see N. Crossley, *Contesting Psychiatry. Social Movements in Mental Health* (London, 2006), esp. pp. 99–125.

[28] A. Trocchi, 'The invisible insurrection of a million minds' (1962) and 'Sigma: a tactical blueprint' (1962), both reprinted in A. M. Scott (ed.), *Invisible Insurrection of a Million Minds. A Trocchi Reader* (Edinburgh, 1991). For a renewal of serious interest in his contribution, see G. Bowd, *'The Outsiders': Alexander Trocchi and Kenneth White* (Kirkaldy, 1998).

IT (*International Times*) and their fundraising events, featuring the first 'psychedelic' bands, Pink Floyd and Soft Machine, soon joined by Jimi Hendrix. Laing was usually present, often accompanied by some of his clients from the experimental psychiatric community he had just set up with some younger colleagues at Kingsley Hall, which went on to become the organising group for the climax of this brief explosion in the two-week-long 'Dialectics of Liberation Congress' in 1967, an ambitious attempt to position the counter-culture at the centre of the country's intellectual life.[29]

Most of the new social movements discussed alongside the new left in the previous section also manifested profound counter-cultural influences. Thus the student movement was just as much about the adoption of a new lifestyle as it was about a set of specific demands: participants enjoyed intense moments of catharsis and euphoria in mass sit-ins and demonstrations, accompanied by distinctively counter-cultural elements such as street-theatre and music, and they tended to prefer informal, inclusive discussions to formally structured meetings. Similarly, the women's movement was as much about consciousness-raising and reshaping identities as it was about public action: prominent cultural figures such as Doris Lessing tried to keep their distance from political feminism, and even those who did pursue legislative changes tended to remain in networks of local groups opposed to hierarchical and bureaucratic forms of organisation. And, of course, the environmental movement posed a fundamental challenge to the anthropocentric and materialistic underpinnings of all conventional ways of life: from the outset it aimed to 'be the change it wished to see', emphasising participatory democracy, decentralisation and 'green' personal practices of transport and recycling in everyday life.[30]

Within the immediate experience of the generation born around 1940 the various great propositions were indeed so intertwined that some sort of vaguely defined 'New Left' was widely considered as the political expression of the counter-culture.[31] However, a more appropriate candidate for this role would be a less widely noted movement which

---

[29] For more detailed accounts, see J. Green, *All Dressed Up. The Sixties and the Counterculture* (London, 1998); A. Wilson, 'Spontaneous Underground: an introduction to London psychedelic scenes, 1965–68' in C. Grunenberg and J. Harris (eds), *Summer of Love. Psychedelic Art, Social Crisis and Counterculture in the 1960s* (Liverpool, 2005). For a rich collection of interview material from participants, see J. Green, *Days in the Life. Voices from the English Underground, 1961–71* (London, 1988).

[30] Byrne, *Social Movements*, pp. 32–33, 125–126, 133–134, 137–138, 175–177.

[31] For an early example of a now standard type of lively but insufficiently discriminating discussion, see I. MacDonald, *Revolution in the Head. The Beatles' Records and the Sixties* (London, 1994), pp. 1–34.

might be called 'revisionist anarchism', the main proponent of which in Britain was Colin Ward, tireless editor of the small-circulation monthly *Anarchy* throughout the 1960s and subsequently a regular columnist in the more widely read weekly *New Society*. Although closely involved with the more orthodox 'Freedom Press Group', Ward developed a particular emphasis on not waiting for a revolution in the future but rather enhancing already-existing practical forms of self-organisation, with a special focus on his own areas of expertise in housing, town planning and progressive education. This was an anarchism emphasising the ways in which people were naturally co-operative when left to their own devices; that 'mutual aid through direct action' was already widely practised and was only in need of further cultivation for a new order to emerge gradually out of the old; and that imagination and inventiveness in choosing libertarian solutions to immediate problems were therefore crucial to wider processes of social change.[32]

However the political establishments of both right and left had no intention of leaving people to their own devices. Indeed, the first signs of reaction against the expansion of 'the sixties' were focused particularly against the counter-culture. The Dangerous Drugs Act (1964) was regularly augmented to include new substances and new offences culminating in the comprehensive Misuse of Drugs Act (1970), and in the meantime criminal prosecutions were targeted specifically against key individuals around *IT*. The Obscene Publications Acts (1959 and 1964) were used to tighten up controls on free expression, with raids and legal actions against *IT*, for conspiring to corrupt public morals by carrying homosexual advertising, and its friendly rival *Oz*, for conspiring to corrupt young children and various obscenity offences in its *School Kids' Issue*.[33] These warning shots helped to drive the more challenging elements of the avant-garde back into exile on the fringes of public life, turning the Underground from a provocation to the whole of society into an alternative lifestyle choice for those who were interested. But if the continuously increasing popularity of, for example, recreational drug use, complementary medicine and East-Asian spiritual practice is anything to go by, there is still a lot of it going on in private, even in conservative Britain.[34]

---

[32] C. Ward, *Anarchy in Action* (London, 1973). For a pioneering discussion of this revisionism within a broader movement of anarchist literature, see D. Goodway, *Anarchist Seeds Beneath the Snow. Left-Libertarian Thought and British Writers from William Morris to Colin Ward* (Liverpool, 2006), pp. 309–325.

[33] Hewison, *Too Much*, pp. 129–133, 170–177.

[34] C. Partridge, *The Re-Enchantment of the West. Alternative Spiritualities, Sacralization, Popular Culture and Occulture*, 2 vols (London, 2004–2005).

IV

Having considered each of the great propositions in circulation among those pressing for social changes beyond those achieved by the Labour Party's post-1945 reconstruction, it may now be possible to investigate the ways in which they 'fought it out' when they came into contact with each other. A major occasion on which this happened was at one genuinely remarkable event in London during the so-called 'Summer of Love' in 1967, when for two weeks in July the Roundhouse in Camden was effectively occupied by the 'Dialectics of Liberation Congress'. Organised by the rather grandly titled Institute of Phenomenological Studies, a temporary offshoot of R. D. Laing's Philadelphia Association, there were public lectures by prominent intellectuals in the mornings; discussion groups in the afternoons; poetry readings, music, plays and films in the evenings; and a general spontaneous 'happening' the rest of time.[35]

International spokesmen of all three of the great propositions outlined above were invited. However, while a number of prominent European Marxists are reported as having been present, the old-left speeches on record came from social scientists based in universities in the United States: Jules Henry, John Gerassi and Paul Sweezy. They were prepared to talk confidently about how the whole world economy worked, about the material interests of any given state or class, about the collective social perceptions which served those interests, and about the way all of that placed systemic constraints on individual choices. In this vision what mattered was that the coercive power of the state would be used against any real threat to the capitalist-imperialist system.[36] Also taking this

---

[35] The Congress was recorded in a variety of formats. A series of twenty-one twelve-inch vinyl discs was issued by the organisers as Liberation Records, available in the British Library Sound Archive. Then they went on to publish two collections of more or less revised transcripts: *The Dialectics of Liberation* (Harmondsworth, 1968), a widely distributed paperback edited by David Cooper with a Constructivist cover design giving a distinctly 'New Left' impression; and *Counter Culture* (London, 1969), a small-press hardback edited by Joseph Berke, more adventurous graphically and typographically giving a distinctly 'Underground' impression. Film footage of the Congress is also available in R. Klinkert and I. Sinclair (dirs), *Ah! Sunflower* (The Picture Press, 2007), along with a vivid memoir of events around the production in I. Sinclair, *The Kodak Mantra Diaries. October 1966 to June 1971* (London, 1971, reprinted in a special issue of *Beat Scene*, December 2006). For a pioneering account of the event in its wider context, see R. Carrington, 'Cultural and ideological challenges of the London Underground movement, 1965–1971', unpublished PhD thesis, Anglia Ruskin University (2002), pp. 279–325.

[36] J. Henry, 'Social and psychological preparation for war', J. Gerassi, 'Imperialism and revolution in America' and P. Sweezy, 'The future of capitalism', all in Cooper (ed.), *Dialectics*. For a historical account from a similar point of view, dismissing the new left for its lack of discipline and the counter-culture for its self-indulgence, see T. Judt, *Postwar. A History of Europe since 1945* (London, 2005), pp. 390–421.

broad position was the charismatic black activist Stokely Carmichael, whose heavy involvement in the new social movement of civil rights had left him with a more sceptical view of the traditional role of organised labour, but whose shift towards black separatism was leading to a convergence with old-left attitudes. For him the Third World had become the proletariat with the whole of white Western society as the bourgeoisie, but he still saw the process of change as one of violent struggle between large masses and the imperialist state over quite straightforward and transparent interests.[37] Meanwhile, his revolt against cultural imposition led him to make some extraordinarily fierce attacks on the white majority in his audience, and in particular to be more explicitly dismissive of the organisers of the conference than any of the more orthodox old-left speakers: 'I'm not a psychologist or a psychiatrist, I'm a political activist and I don't deal with the individual. I think it's a cop out when people talk about the individual.'[38]

In some contrast, Gerassi gave a less structural, more historical, analysis and was more interested than the others on the old left in engaging with the new social attitudes and movements. He was prepared to welcome dropping out and drug taking because they disrupted the system, but he neutralised the distinctiveness of the counter-cultural position by presenting it merely as an account of the psychological aspects of oppression which complemented the old left's account of the physical ones.[39] Moreover, he argued that counter-cultural activities were only tolerated because they involved a tiny minority of the population, and if they were to become more numerous and more threatening they too would be dealt with by organised violence. He was therefore more welcoming to the political direct action of the new left, but argued that this would have to be organised on a nationwide basis to become really effective:

Yesterday in a seminar here, everybody was asking, 'How do you fight this corporation-elite, how do you destroy this structure?' And no one had any sure overall answer. Yet there were all sorts of detail-type answers . . . One can blow up

[37] S. Carmichael, 'Black power', in Cooper (ed.), *Dialectics*.

[38] Carmichael, 'Black power', p. 150; some of the more extraordinary attacks on the white audience are to be found in S. Carmichael, 'You had better come on home', in Berke (ed.), *Counter Culture*.

[39] This line of thought was more informally celebrated in J. Gerassi, 'Revolution by life style', in Berke (ed.), *Counter Culture*. Interestingly enough, the editor of this more 'Underground' collection developed a similar position for, though closely associated with the radical psychiatrists and though giving a central role to the dynamic contribution of counter-cultural experiments, he located them within a largely old-left framework; see J. Berke, 'The creation of an alternative society', in Berke (ed.), *Counter Culture*.

trains, blow up factories, one can infiltrate a draft board and burn its records. One can launch picket lines against banks and industries instead of government agencies . . . But what good would all these courageous acts achieve unless there is an organisational structure behind them, a programme?[40]

He did acknowledge new-left critiques of the authoritarian leadership of most existing socialist societies and revolutionary parties, but argued that this could be overcome: in his account it already had been in Cuba, where the arming of the people had ensured government by consent and with active participation.

The main new-left speeches on record came from émigré scholars from central Europe who had settled in universities in France and the United States: Lucien Goldmann and Herbert Marcuse. Their references to the more hard-edged issues of the economy and material interests were restricted to the background, for in their view advanced industrial society's combination of unprecedented affluence and social alienation was bringing questions of subjectivity centre-stage. However, they were just as prepared to make confident statements about the overall dialectics of social consciousness as the old left was about those of the capitalist economy. In this vision what mattered was the intelligentsia's fostering of the historically necessary new values, needs and aspirations in order to ensure that political revolutions did not just replace one system of domination with another.[41] Thus, in contrast to the old left, Marcuse was much more enthusiastic about the relatively spontaneous protests and direct actions of the new social movements, as they were challenges to established consciousness: 'a demonstration of an aggressive non-aggressiveness which achieves, at least potentially, the demonstration of qualitatively different values, a transformation of values.'[42]

However, in relation to the counter-culture Marcuse, like the old left, could go no further than a condescending indulgence: 'much of it is mere masquerade and clownery on the private level, and therefore indeed, as Gerassi suggested, completely harmless, very nice and charming in many cases, but that is all there is to it.'[43] Similarly, the new-left speakers had a rather ambiguous attitude towards the activities of the conference's organisers. For, while they were clearly prepared to acknowledge that

---

[40] Gerassi, 'Imperialism and revolution', p. 92. For a historical account from a similar point of view, urging that the old left absorb the new left and the counter-culture, see G. Eley, *Forging Democracy. The History of the Left in Europe, 1850–2000* (Oxford, 2002), esp. pp. 355–357, 366–383, 472–490.

[41] L. Goldmann, 'Criticism and dogmatism in literature', and H. Marcuse, 'Liberation from the affluent society', both in Cooper (ed.), *Dialectics*.

[42] Marcuse, 'Liberation', p. 190.   [43] Ibid.

subjectivity was a valid area for theoretical and practical work, they criticised psychoanalysis and psychiatry for paying too much attention to the individual and too little to social classes. From this point of view these disciplines became something of an irrelevance: they were unable to produce really satisfying accounts of public intellectual and artistic creation, and they were unable to contribute much of substance to the liberation of the imagination, not as a private individual matter, but as a transformation of public social planning. Among the radical psychiatrists, David Cooper was already moving in this direction, seeing the work of progressive professionals within their own field as potentially part of a new movement towards national and international revolutionary consciousness:

We have one advantage over our rulers – we have a consciousness, although only marginal at times, of what is going on in the world; we see through their mystifications – the mystifications that mystify the mystifiers but need no longer mystify us. By a transactional network of expertise we can transform each institution – family, school, university, mental hospital, factory – each art form, into a revolutionary centre for a transforming consciousness.[44]

There were colourful interventions from a number of poets and artists present, including Julian Beck, Allen Ginsberg and Simon Vinkenoog.[45] However, the more systematic counter-cultural speeches on record came from the other figures among the group of radical psychiatrists which had been gathering around R. D. Laing in the immediately preceding years: Laing himself, Gregory Bateson and Ross Speck. Their outlook was distinguished from both the old and new lefts by being considerably more sceptical and pessimistic: they questioned the grandiosity of the revolutionaries, saw the overall social system as more complex and interactive, assumed there would always be a plurality of views and refused to take sides in violent political conflicts. Very close in his analysis was the US 'revisionist anarchist' writer who had played a part in the development of Gestalt psychotherapy, Paul Goodman, the only morning lecturer to express serious concerns about the imminent threat of nuclear war, the longer-term threat of environmental disaster and the likelihood that Third World attempts to 'catch up' would only exacerbate both of them. In this vision, what mattered was the fostering of all-round creativity and genuine respect for others in small-scale,

---

[44] D. Cooper, 'Beyond words' in Cooper (ed.), *Dialectics*, at p. 197.
[45] J. Beck 'Seminar' on recordings DL15 and DL19; A. Ginsberg, 'Consciousness and practical action', in Berke (ed.), *Counter Culture*; S. Vinkenoog, 'Revolution in consciousness' on recording DL19.

face-to-face human groups.[46] Laing in particular questioned the sweeping analyses from the left, arguing that all anybody had to go on was the limited inputs from their own senses plus hearsay evidence based on the equally limited fields of observation of others. As a result:

There are those who know they don't know, those who don't know they don't know, and legions of those who find denser and denser realms of darkness in which to veil their own ignorance from themselves. And there are those who, no matter what they think they know or don't know to any metalevel, will *just do what they are told* when it comes to the bit. Those that are left, who know they don't know and who will not necessarily do what they are told – it is to them that this speech is addressed, which I hope may be of some service, if only as a joke, to the last surviving *human beings* on the planet.[47]

He went on to develop his concern about the very deep-rooted nature of obedience to authority through extended reference to the remarkable results of Stanley Milgram's Yale experiments, which had been inspired in part by growing awareness of the full extent of the Holocaust. Laing concluded, 'we have all a "reflex" towards believing and doing what we are told', and used this as a warning to be more sceptical about all forms of political and intellectual authority.[48] This was warmly endorsed by Goodman, who argued that Marxist analysis of economic exploitation missed the greater importance of the impulse to domination: contemporary imperialism was tending to revert to genocide, while domestically governments in the developed world were increasingly concerned about conformity and control. The dispersed counter-cultural experiments in lifestyle therefore had a similar salience for him as the direct action of the new social movements had for the new left:

When John Gerassi said that the State can tolerate the Hippies because they are no threat to the structure, he was misinformed. Proportionate to its numbers, this group is by far the most harassed, beat up, and jailed by the police. Negroes go scot free in comparison. The social response to the demonstrating Negroes is, primarily, 'Why don't they go away?' It is at the point of riot that anxiety begins to be aroused. But with the Hippies there is a gut reaction from the beginning – they are dirty, indecent, shiftless; they threaten the self-justification of the system.[49]

---

[46] R. D. Laing, 'The obvious', G. Bateson, 'Conscious purpose versus nature' and P. Goodman, 'Objective values', all in Cooper (ed.), *Dialectics*; R. V. Speck, 'The politics and psychotherapy of mini and micro groups' on recording DL5. For a first-hand account of the experimental community at Kingsley Hall, see M. Schatzman, 'Madness and morals', in Berke (ed.), *Counter Culture*.
[47] Laing, 'The obvious', p. 26.   [48] Ibid., p. 32.
[49] Goodman, 'Objective values', pp. 122–123.

Clearly, then, the three great propositions considered in a British context in the first sections of this essay were part of broader international movements of ideas. Bringing them together under one roof and within the covers of two collections was an ambitious and generous project, with other sources indicating that it provoked interesting discussions among those sharing the same basic outlook. For example, the Trotskyite activist Tariq Ali politely reminded Stokely Carmichael that 'Lenin, Trotsky and the other Bolsheviks were white'; while Paul Goodman gently chided Allen Ginsberg for being 'afraid of being serious'.[50] However, since each of these great propositions was based on such fundamentally different assumptions, they could at best only co-exist as examples of the excited mood of the time without much meaningful dialogue between them. Indeed, in some cases the Congress led to a clarification of differences and thus to growing rifts between participants who had until then been close colleagues. This was especially marked among the radical psychiatrists who organised the event, with R. D. Laing breaking off his working relationships with both Joseph Berke and David Cooper as he realised the full extent of their political commitments. Indeed Laing's disillusionment with the predominance of rigid left-wing thinking eventually contributed to his withdrawal from the London scene altogether for a year's retreat in Buddhist meditation centres in Ceylon (now Sri Lanka) and India.[51]

V

For many of those who took part, the Dialectics of Liberation Congress had a paradoxical outcome: what had been intended as a critical inquiry into the social and psychological roots of violence had turned into a celebration of the use of violent means in pursuit of progressive ends. The launching of counter-cultural ideas from a national platform had turned out to be premature, or perhaps these ideas were intrinsically unsuited to exposure in such a high-profile public role. At first it seemed that it was new-left ideas which had been triumphant, dramatically underlined by a particular interpretation of the explosive events of May '68 in France. However, in the longer run the new left turned out to be relatively weak as a political force in Britain: limited to a small number of charismatic intellectuals influenced by central-European

---

[50] T. Ali, 'Demystifying Mr Carmichael', *New Statesman*, 28 July 1967, p. 108; Sinclair, *Kodak Mantra Diaries* (2006 reprint), p. 44.

[51] B. Mullan, *Mad to be Normal. Conversations with R. D. Laing* (London, 1995), pp. 218–219, 235–236.

idealist traditions, and soon largely swallowed up again by more orthodox socialist analysis. Thus the old left remained remarkably dominant in public life, with much of what was called 'New Left' at the time being a product of people holding old-left ideas but emphasising direct action or opting for some aspects of counter-cultural lifestyles. In the absence of a fully developed new-left position, each of the new social movements was still able to keep reinventing itself at the grass roots without ever becoming effectively integrated into wider political alliances. Similarly, the possibilities of bridge-building between the left and the counter-culture were reduced, with the latter going off on its own way as a largely non-political exploration of personal lifestyles. But perhaps the intellectual gulf between the left and the counter-culture was unbridgeable anyway, as a result of the latter's deep scepticism about the possibility of controlling large-scale political and social change.

Indeed, with the benefit of hindsight and contrary to much of the common rhetoric of the time, it is the left of these years which now seems naive and over-optimistic. For John Gerassi was not alone in anticipating a worldwide transformation in human nature variously perceived as already underway in Cuba, Vietnam or China:

... for those who suffer from lack of necessities, liberation is to fight; while for those who have the necessities and more, liberation is to break the restrictions and establish a new society that will allow all men to talk about their souls. But that new society cannot exist unless it fights and destroys individual greed. Therefore we who wish to liberate our souls must first establish Socialist Man.[52]

On the other hand, in so far as the counter-culture was romantic at all, it was in a deeply ironic way. Thus Ginsberg emphasised that what was being called 'Flower Power' was not about love but about self-awareness, not about struggling against negative emotions but about accepting and containing them, that this could only be done on a small scale and that he for one had no illusions about the long-term prospects: 'it's the one thing that they arrived at which makes a possible beautiful moment, then, for history – or maybe the last moment, of recognition, before the giant comedy ends with an explosion.'[53]

---

[52] Gerassi, 'Imperialism and revolution', p. 94.
[53] Ginsberg, 'Consciousness and practical action', p. 174.

12 Why the English like turbans: multicultural politics in British history

David Feldman

Exclusion

One day in June 1967, Tarsem Sandhu, a 23-year-old Sikh living in Wolverhampton, turned up for work as a corporation bus driver. He had been at home unwell for the previous three weeks and during that period he had decided to dedicate himself more determinedly to Sikhism. *Kesh* – uncut and knotted hair – is one of the five symbols of Sikh identity introduced by Guru Gobind at the end of the seventeenth century. Accordingly, Sandhu now refrained from shaving and from cutting his hair. By the time he returned to work he was wearing both a turban and a beard. Although Sandhu's appearance conformed to Sikh prescription, his turban departed from the regulation uniform prescribed for bus drivers by the Wolverhampton Transport Committee and his beard transgressed an informal agreement between the local branch of the Transport and General Workers Union and the Committee that employees should be clean-shaven. Sandhu's manager immediately suspended him from work without pay.[1]

The ban on Wolverhampton bus crews wearing beards and turbans initiated a two-year-long dispute that reverberated far beyond the town itself, both in Britain and India.[2] The Sikhs' repertoire of protest involved lobbying and letter-writing as well as public demonstrations. The visible high point of their campaign occurred in March 1968 when 4,000 Sikhs marched silently through Wolverhampton.[3] They were opposed by Wolverhampton Corporation and by its transport committee

---

[1] David Beetham, *Transport and Turbans* (Oxford, 1970) pp. 37, 39. Guru Gobind did not prescribe wearing turbans to cover uncut hair, however. On the emergence of customary Sikh costume, see Bernard S. Cohn, *Colonialism and its Forms of Knowledge* (Princeton, NJ, 1996), pp. 109–110.

[2] National Archive, UK (hereafter, NA), HO 376/151/34, W. K. Slatcher to T. D. O'Leary, 14 May 1968 reports protests in India.

[3] See the materials in NA, CK3/20 esp. J. Peyton to Joginder Singh Sandu, 19 April 1973; Meeting of Sikh Leaders and the Community Relations Council Chairman, 23 April 1973; *The Times*, 5 February 1967, p. 2.

in particular, by managers in the corporation's transport department, as well as by the local leadership of the Transport and General Workers Union. In January 1969, after months of fruitless opposition and lobbying, one of the leaders of the protest movement, Sohan Singh Jolly, dramatically raised the stakes. He announced, 'I shall burn myself to death just as the Buddhist monks did in Saigon two years ago'. The Wolverhampton transport committee was apparently unmoved and refused to back down in the face of Jolly's threatened self-immolation. The Labour government took a different view: concerned that martyrdom would inflame race relations, it despatched a junior minister to the town who successfully pressured the corporation's transport committee to back down.[4]

Jolly was exultant. 'This is not a victory for myself', he announced, 'but a victory for the whole Sikh community. It has proved that the British people have very strong sentiments for Sikhs generally.'[5] He made a good point. The outcome in Wolverhampton was not an isolated moment but one episode in a larger story. A range of similar issues arose in the 1960s, the 1970s and the 1980s with regard to Sikh men and, specifically, whether – in various contexts – they were permitted to wear turbans. What is striking is that in all cases the issue was decided in their favour. Disputes concerning bus drivers' uniform in other towns were all resolved in the same way, albeit after a long battle in some cases. In the law courts it was established that a Sikh barrister could appear before a judge wearing his turban in place of a wig. The Home Secretary decided that Sikh policemen, special constables and traffic wardens could wear turbans rather than caps or helmets. In 1976 – after three years of campaigning – turban-wearing Sikhs won an exemption from the law that required motorcycle riders to wear a crash helmet and in 1989 they received a similar freedom from the legal requirement to wear safety helmets on building sites. In 1983, following a long legal struggle, the House of Lords established the right of Sikh pupils to wear a turban at school. It is in the light of these consistent outcomes that we can ask why it is that the English like turbans.[6]

---

[4] *The Times*, 9 March 1968, p. 8; 7 January 1969, p. 3; 10 April 1969, p. 1; Beetham, *Transport and Turbans*, pp. 41–45.

[5] *The Times*, 10 April 1969, p. 1.

[6] This formulation owes much to John Bowen, *Why the French Don't Wear Headscarves* (Princeton, NJ, 2006). For the Sikh victories listed, see Gurharpal Singh and Darshan Singh Tatla, *Sikhs in Britain. The Making of a Community* (London, 2006), pp. 126–315; Sebastian Poulter, *Ethnicity, Law and Human Rights: The English Experience* (Oxford, 1998), pp. 49–50, 307–308, 314–355; *The Times*, 5 October 1967, p. 2.

Despite their common resolution, the legal and political implications of these cases altered according to the context in which Sikhs asserted their right to wear a turban. In the instance of a bus driver, for example, the question simply was whether workplace discipline and the agreements reached by collective bargaining between management and trade unions could accommodate Sikhs' demands to modify their apparel and appearance.[7] Very similar problems were raised by the clash between customary Sikh dress and school uniform. However, in the case of policemen, special constables and traffic wardens the issue acquired an additional dimension. Here the question did not merely involve the dress of an employee or pupil but whether the authority of the state and the law could be represented by a man wearing headgear which followed the conventions of his own religion. As we shall see, the case of crash and safety helmets forced ministers and others to adjudicate between their duty to safeguard the health of the population, to prevent needless loss of life and serious injury, on one side, and the demands of religious toleration, on the other. In these different ways, the question of where and under what circumstances it has been permissible to wear a turban reflects on the extent to which British culture, as well as the British state and its practices of governance, have been able to accommodate cultural diversity. This chapter takes debates on turbans as a starting point from which to examine British responses to the dilemmas of a multicultural society.[8]

The Sikhs' victories in the 1960s and 1970s signal a history of pluralism that formed part of the British reaction to immigration in these years. This is especially notable because these episodes do not fit with our predominant view of how Britain responded to immigrants from South Asia and the Caribbean. Most analyses emphasise how immigration from colonies and former colonies provoked a vision of the nation as an exclusive and white community. Both among political elites and in popular culture, we find the idea that the presence in London and other cities of dark-skinned immigrants was a threatening inversion of the natural order of things.[9]

---

[7] HO 376/151/27c, clipping from *Daily Telegraph*, 31 August 1964, and Maidstone and District Motor Services Ltd to A. J. Murray, 28 July 1965.

[8] It will be helpful if we, like many others, distinguish between a multicultural society and multiculturalism. A multicultural society is one in which different cultural communities live together. Multiculturalism, however, seeks self-consciously to promote a common life within these societies but, crucially, also seeks to preserve the identities of its several communities. See, for example, Bikhu Parekh, *Rethinking Muliculttturalism*, 2nd edn, (London, 2006), pp. 2–9.

[9] This view is expressed aphoristically in the title as well in the substance of Paul Gilroy's book, *There Ain't No Black in the Union Jack* (London, 1987). See, too, for example, Wendy Webster, 'Immigration and Racism' in Paul Addison and Harriett Jones (eds),

This theme of inversion and the idea that Britain was a white man's country was crystallised and galvanised by Enoch Powell's 'rivers of blood' speech, delivered in Birmingham on 20 April 1968. Here Powell conjured an image of black men having the 'whip hand' over England's white inhabitants: a metropolitan reversal of the legacy of slavery and colonial governance. The Sikhs' dispute in Wolverhampton was contemporaneous with Powell's speech and formed a part of its context. Powell was Member of Parliament for one of the three Wolverhampton constituencies. It was on the basis of local knowledge that he asserted 'large numbers of Sikhs who have been serving the Wolverhampton Corporation voluntarily and contentedly have found themselves against their will made the material for communal agitation'. And communalism, he explained, 'has been the curse of India'.[10] The Sikhs' public campaign was a vivid demonstration of the changing demography of post-imperial England. It seemed, moreover, to bring a form of political practice and identification – communalism – formerly assigned to the empire into the heart of the English West Midlands.

Six years later the same idea of inversion was used by men and women who wrote to the Race Relations Board in the name of the nation's white majority, to voice their disgust at the Sikhs' exemption from wearing helmets on motorcycles. The letter sent by Mrs E. M. Treacher from Wells was characteristic. She objected to the way the new law discriminated against Englishmen 'whose country this is' and who were now 'suffering' an 'invasion by hundreds of thousands of coloured foreigners'. Neglected by their leaders, she felt that the National Front was now 'the only party which cares what happens to English men and women in their own country'.[11] Yet the cause of the white majority did find a champion. In 1978, in the course of a television interview, Margaret Thatcher expressed her sympathy with British people who feared they were being swamped by immigrants with a different culture. She received 10,000 letters thanking her for speaking out, as well as a commendation from Enoch Powell.[12] The next year she became prime minister.

The Conservative triumph in 1979, it is sometimes said, signalled the triumph of a malign construction of the nation as an exclusively white community. It follows that multiculturalism emerged in the 1970s and

A Companion to Contemporary Britain (Oxford, 2005); On the idea of inversion, see B. Schwarz, '"The only white man in there": the re-racialization of Britain, 1956–68', *Race and Class*, 38, (1996), pp. 65–78.

[10] www.telegraph.co.uk/comment/3643823/Enoch-Powells-Rivers-of-Blood-speech.html.

[11] NA, CK2/277 E. M. Treacher to Race Relations Board, 13 July 1976.

[12] J. Campbell, *Margaret Thatcher*, vol. 1, (London, 2000), pp. 399–400.

developed in the 1980s as a reforming and oppositional movement.[13] This narrative is less wrong than it is incomplete. The disputes over turbans should alert us to this because their outcomes appear so anomalous. These clashes were fought out in the 1960s and 1970s, for the most part, before the victories of multiculturalists and anti-racists in education policy and local government. These were the years when Britain, we are told, was imagined as a white, homogenous nation. Yet time and again the Sikhs won concessions. Their success suggests the need for a different narrative; one that takes into account a history of pluralism.

Assimilation

The idea that people of colour were out of place in Britain was neither the only nor the most significant obstacle to pluralist policies in post-war Britain. It was the goal of assimilating the immigrants that shaped the perspective of most politicians and policy-makers in the 1960s and which provided a formidable obstacle to pluralism. 'Assimilation' provided the language with which ministers in both Conservative and Labour governments justified new immigration controls. The controls themselves were predicated upon an acute colour consciousness. The civil servants charged with formulating a practical scheme understood very well the 'real (though not the professed) aim . . . which was to cut down coloured immigration while allowing white immigrants to come in much as before'.[14] But the laws introduced were intended to regulate not terminate immigration by people of colour. Ministers conceived the conflicts associated with immigration as problems of 'race relations'. It followed that the difficulty they faced was how to manage the co-existence of different races as they came together in British cities in unprecedented ways. Within this framework it was easy for them to argue that there was a limit to the numbers the country could absorb. Immigration policy was also assimilation policy.[15]

---

[13] For this characterisation of Conservatism in the 1980s, see, for example, Stuart Hall, 'Ethnicity, identity and difference' in Geoff Eley and Ronald Grigor Suny (eds), *Becoming National* (Oxford, 1996), at p. 346, and M. Keith, *Race, Riots and Policing: Lore and Disorder in a Multi-racist Society* (London, 1993), pp. 236–237; on the emergence of multiculturalism, see Tariq Modood, 'British Muslims and multiculturalism' in Tariq Modood, Anna Triandafyllidou and Ricard Zapata-Barrero (eds), *Multiculturalism, Muslims, and Citizenship* (London, 2006), at pp. 39–42; Avtar Brah, *Cartographies of Diaspora* (London, 1996), pp. 229–230.

[14] NA, DO 175/54, CWP (fifth meeting) 14 July 1961, p. 4.

[15] See, for example, the Home Secretary, R. A. Butler, speaking on the second reading of the 1962 Commonwealth Immigrants Bill, *Parliamentary Debates*, 16 November 1962, p. 694, and compare to the view of his Labour Party successor, Frank Soskice, in

Labour and Conservative governments pursued the goal of assimilation for most of the 1960s and 1970s. At the same time, they devolved responsibility for particular policies to local government. They prescribed bussing in education and promoted dispersal policies in housing.[16] The practice of bussing originated in Southall, just to the west of London, in 1963 and was later endorsed first by the Conservative Secretary of State for Education, Sir Edward Boyle, and then by his Labour successor, Anthony Crosland. The Department of Education advised local authorities to disperse immigrant children so they would not form more than 30 per cent of the pupils in any one school. The policy was, in part, an attempt to appease white parents who protested against the presence of immigrant children but it was also justified as a measure that would assist integration. Only a few authorities ever implemented the policy but assimilation remained the goal for the Department of Education and for local education authorities, with an emphasis on the need for instruction in English by specially trained teachers.[17]

'Assimilation', moreover, was congenial to two powerful currents in the Labour party in the post-war decades: the culture of trade unionism and the commitment of social democrats to universalism. Both tendencies were evident as the Labour Party responded to Sikh demands in the 1960s and 1970s, and beyond. At a national level the Transport and General Workers Union repudiated racial discrimination in principle but its General Secretary, Frank Cousins, refused to intervene when his Manchester branch resisted the introduction of turbans on the buses in that city. In a number of towns, Wolverhampton among them, union branches tried to resist the recruitment of immigrant workers.[18] Trade unions generated a procedure-bound culture based on conformity, collective action and the absolute rule of the majority. Concern for 'our people' and established union practice could easily lead to

---

HO345/181, Integration of the immigrant population. Memorandum by the Secretary of State for the Home Department, March 1965; also Edward Heath, *The Course of My Life* (London, 1979), p. 455. Assimilation, of course, was normative and white. For a stimulating discussion of the role of 'race' in policy formation in these years, see Ali Rattansi, 'The uses of racialization: the time-spaces and subject-objects of the raced body' in Karim Murji and John Solomos (eds), *Racialization: Studies in Theory and Practice* (Oxford, 2005).

[16] On housing policy and the assimilationist assumptions of local government, see Graham Thomas, 'The integration of immigrants: a note on the views of some local government officials', *Race*, 9, (1967–1968), pp. 239–248.

[17] Eliot Rose, *Colour and Citizenship: A Report on British Race Relations* (Oxford, 1969), pp. 264–295; D. L. Kirp, *Doing Good by Doing Little* (Berkely, CA, 1979).

[18] Beetham, *Transport and Turbans*, pp. 14, 28; Robert Miles and Annie Phizacklea, *Labour and Racism* (London, 1980), pp. 92–93; Alastair Reid, *United We Stand: A History of British Trade Unions* (London, 2004), 343–344.

indifference to the particular claims of immigrant minorities.[19] At Wolverhampton, the Transport and General Workers Union district secretary took the view that in their refusal to allow turbans to be worn the town's transport department 'was doing no more than enforce well established and clearly understood regulations'.[20] As late as 1989, one representative of this culture, Lord Houghton of Sowerby, the former General Secretary of the Inland Revenue Staff Federation and Chairman of the Parliamentary Labour Party between 1967 and 1974 insisted, in the name of the majority, that Sikhs on building sites should have to wear safety helmets: 'we should question the concessions sought by those who come here or are born here and who adopt [sic] religions which require them to depart from laws imposed on Christians, agnostics and atheists.'[21]

The Sikh campaigns of the 1960s and 1970s also encountered opposition from social reformers and socialists who could not reconcile their support for universalism with Sikh demands for particular exemptions. Indeed, universalism was at the heart of Labour's opposition to racialism. In 1959 Hugh Gaitskell had written into the Party's constitution an explicit commitment to 'the brotherhood of man' which rejected 'discrimination on grounds of race, colour and creed'.[22] It followed, however, that special treatment for particular groups was also offensive. Shirley Williams, for example, wrote to John Lyttle, Chief Officer at the Race Relations Board, 'I intend to be horrid to Sikhs on motorbikes. But – how about turbans *on top* of their helmets – a kind of crash turban. Though heaven knows where they stick the pins.'[23]

It was a universalist vision of laws being made for the general good that led both Conservative and Labour Ministers of Transport, the Community Relations Commission and then the Race Relations Board to oppose Sikh requests for exemption from the requirement to wear a motorcycle helmet. Fred Mulley, when Minister of Transport, wrote to Singh Bindar of the Save the Turban Action Committee, 'fairness requires that everyone is treated alike'.[24] The law had been passed to save life and prevent injury and an exemption would make Sikhs privileged members of the community: an unacceptable outcome. In September 1973 the Community Relations Commission issued a statement declaring 'We think that in general the law of the land should

---

[19] Alfred Sherman, 'Deptford' in Nicholas Deakin (ed.), *Colour and the British Electorate 1964* (London, 1965), at p. 111.

[20] NA, HO 376/151 /34, K. Smith to J. T. A Howard Drake, 18 August 1967.

[21] *Parliamentary Debates, Lords*, 511, 16 October 1989, p. 740.

[22] S. Fielding, 'Brotherhood and the brothers: responses to "coloured" immigration in the British Labour Party c. 1951–65', *Journal of Political Ideologies*, 3(1), (1998), pp. 79–97, at p. 87.

[23] NA, CK2/277, Shirley Williams to John Lyttle, 3 April 1973.

[24] NA, CK 2/277, Fred Mulley to M. Singh Bindar, 3 May 1974.

apply to all groups without exception, unless very special circumstances apply'.[25] One size of safety helmet would fit all.

In so far as Labour governments did make special provision for immigrants before the mid-1970s it was either with the aim of promoting assimilation or disguised heavily as universal provision. The most important example of the former sort of intervention was Section 11 of the 1966 Local Government Act which allowed local authorities to recoup 50 per cent of the cost for staff expenses incurred educating or providing services for Commonwealth immigrants whose language or culture was different from the rest of the community. This helped to fund public health inspectors and English-language teaching in schools.[26] The latter case was exemplified by the Urban Programme, constructed in the wake of Powell's 'rivers of blood' speech. This targeted areas of general social need and, at times, it was used to channel funds to areas of immigrant concentration. However, as the authors of an evaluation of the programme point out, 'great care was taken in the drafting of any public statement to avoid the association between immigrants and deprivation'.[27]

Conservative pluralism

The ministerial consensus in favour of policies promoting assimilation leaves the Sikh victories in the 1960s and 1970s standing all the more in need of explanation. A part of the answer must lie in the actions of the Sikhs themselves. They engaged in a programme of public protest. They demanded and won meetings with government ministers and representatives of the Race Relations Board whom they berated both in person and by post.[28] Not least among their successes was that campaign leaders managed to present the Sikhs as a united and pious community despite denominational diversity, factional rivalries and the fissiparous influences of sect, caste, class and politics. Above all, they managed to obscure the fact that very many Sikhs had chosen to discard beards and turbans as they made their way in English society.[29]

---

[25] NA, CK3/20, Press statement, 14 September 1973.

[26] Rose, *Colour and Citizenship*, pp. 346–347.

[27] J. Edwards and R. Batley, *The Politics of Positive Discrimination: An Evaluation of the Urban Programme 1967–77* (London, 1978), p. 140.

[28] See for example NA, MT 92/657, Notes on a meeting of ministers with the Turban Action Committee on 29 January 1976.

[29] Beetham, *Transport and Turbans*, pp. 37–40. A. W. Helweg, *Sikhs in England* (Delhi, 1986), pp. 5, 86–87; D. K. Takhar, *Sikh Identity: An Exploration of Groups Among Sikhs* (Aldershot, 2005); Singh and Tatla, *Sikhs in Britain*, pp. 54, 72–74, 82–83.

From a tactical standpoint, civil disobedience was crucial. Jolly's threat to set himself alight catapulted the Wolverhampton campaign to a successful conclusion. Eight years on, Baldev Singh Chahal – the leader of the Turban Action Committee – amassed at least forty-two convictions for riding without a helmet within two years of the new law coming into force. Chahal refused to pay his fines and by the autumn of 1976 it appeared likely that his contempt of court would land him in prison. Government ministers feared incarcerating Sikhs would heighten tension and this contributed to their decision to amend the law.[30]

Yet repeated disregard for the law and threats of self-harm have not always won concessions from the British state; certainly not concessions enshrined in Acts of Parliament. The Sikhs' cause, however, was not only pressed forcefully but also carried a degree of legitimacy with politicians of all parties, with large sections of the public and, ultimately, with ministers. In order to understand why this was the case we should discard the idea that multicultural societies are a new phenomenon. Of course, the term 'multicultural' as a way of describing ethnic and religious diversity is a neologism. However, the problem of governing and making law for a society in which two or more cultural communities live together is not a new one for the British state.[31]

Most fundamentally, perhaps, the United Kingdom is a multinational kingdom whose politicians have long faced the problem of containing English, Welsh, Scottish and Irish nationalities within the polity. The predominant tendency here has been for England, the dominant power, to insist on the sovereignty of Westminster but at the same time to acknowledge and incorporate subordinate nationalities without erasing them. After the Union of 1707, for example, the English rejected federal forms of union. Scottish MPs sat in the Westminster parliament but, at the same time, Scotland retained its own ecclesiastical, legal and educational systems. In the nineteenth and twentieth centuries Unionists were happy to allow special treatment and particular status to Scotland. It was a Unionist government which created the post of Secretary of State for Scotland in 1885 and in 1932 a Conservative-dominated National Government transferred the Scottish Office from London to Edinburgh.

---

[30] *The Times*, 22 September 1975, p. 2; NA, MT92/657, memorandum by John Gilbert, Sikhs and Safety Helmets, May 1976; *Daily Telegraph*, 18 June 1976, clipping in MT 92/657.

[31] The earliest usages cited in the *Oxford English Dictionary* and which refer to British society date from 1970 and 1973. For a different attempt to connect the present with some of the history discussed in this chapter, see Mary Hickman, 'Ruling an empire, governing a multinational state: the impact of Britain's historical legacy on the ethno-racial regime' in Glenn Loury, Tariq Modood and Steven Teles (eds), *Ethnicity, Social Mobility and Public Policy: Comparing the USA and UK* (Cambridge, 2005).

The terms of Scotland's incorporation was the ground for conflict and argument. Nevertheless, for most of this period, Scottish nationalism did not present a fundamental challenge to the Union. Until 1942, when the Scottish Nationalist Party distanced itself from the Unionist tradition, nationalists tried to reconcile their beliefs with the sovereignty of the British state.[32]

In the case of Ireland the policy of Home Rule was a central feature of British politics between 1886 and the bloody sequel to the Easter Rising. The defining feature of Home Rule was that it strove to align Irish nationalism with the sovereignty of Westminster. The Liberal Party won elections with Home Rule as a part of its platform and secured majorities for the policy in the House of Commons in 1894 and 1914. Although Home Rule ultimately was thwarted by the House of Lords and by the power of Unionism in Ulster, its centrality within Liberal politics highlights the popular appeal of a pluralist answer to the question of how to integrate Ireland within the Union. Indeed, institutional pluralism was not only a Liberal enthusiasm but became convenient for Conservatives too following partition. Home Rule achieved a long afterlife in Ulster through the devolved administration at Stormont, and was further reinvented in the 1998 Belfast Agreement.[33]

At first sight, Wales presents a counter-example. Conquered by Edward I and incorporated into the structures of English governance in the sixteenth century by Henry VIII, Wales's independent political, legal and ecclesiastical institutions were eviscerated. Yet from the late nineteenth century onwards Wales's relationship to the United Kingdom has become more like the relationship of the other component nations. Governments created specifically Welsh institutions and promoted Welsh culture. In 1893 the nation's university colleges were united in a federal structure to create a national university and a national library at Aberystwyth was sanctioned by a Unionist government in 1905. Welsh was recognised as a subject in elementary schools eligible for financial assistance under the Board of Education code and in 1907 the teaching of the Welsh language and literature received a further boost when the Liberal government created a separate Welsh department within the Board of Education.[34]

From the middle decades of the nineteenth century, pluralism also became the predominant political response to religious diversity. The

---

[32] Keith Robbins, *Great Britain. Identities, Institutions and the Idea of Britain* (London, 1998), pp. 263–272; Richard Finlay, *A Partnership for Good: Scottish Politics and the Union since 1880* (Edinburgh, 1997), pp. 9–31; Colin Kidd, *Unions and Unionism: Political Thought in Scotland, 1500–2000* (Cambridge, 2008), pp. 257–300.

[33] Alvin Jackson, *Home Rule: An Irish History 1800–2000* (London, 2003).

[34] Keith Morgan, *Rebirth of a Nation. Wales 1880–1980* (Oxford, 1982), pp. 106–112.

battle for uniformity within the Union was fought and lost by Anglicans in the first four decades of the nineteenth century. As population growth outstripped Church building, as large numbers of Christians affiliated themselves to non-Anglican denominations, and as growing numbers appeared indifferent to formal Christian observances, Anglicans preserved the privileges of the established Church by extending state support not only to Protestants beyond the Church of England but to Catholics and Jews as well. The crucial decisions were taken in the 1830s when Parliament determined that the Church would have to rely on its own efforts and funds and no longer on parliamentary grants and subsidies.[35] Thenceforth, a sort of pluralism was the guiding principle. This went beyond removing the religious disabilities which prevented individual Catholics or Jews from participating as equals within the polity. It extended to acknowledging those religions in law and administrative practice and offering them financial support for some of their activities. The state began to promote education after 1833. Within twenty years these funds were used not only to support Anglican schools but Catholic, Wesleyan and Jewish schools as well. This policy reached its apotheosis in the 1902 and 1903 Education Acts. By this time, Anglican voluntary schools were in profound financial difficulty. Their future was secured by the Conservative Party when it legislated that secular education in these schools should be funded from the rates. However, the same support was also extended to Catholic and Jewish Schools.[36] The state's preparedness to tolerate non-Anglican, indeed, non-Christian, practices extended to a wide range of activities. There were extraordinary arrangements enabling observant Jews to take civil service exams on days other than the Jewish Sabbath, for Jewish prisoners and workhouse inmates to receive kosher foods and to exempt Jews from laws prohibiting certain sorts of work on Sunday if they kept their own Sabbath.[37] So here too a sort of pluralism was embedded within state institutions.

In this way, the state not only acknowledged religious minorities, it also supported the authority claims of particular groups and institutions to represent those minorities. The Marriage Registration Act of 1836 was one expression of the religious pluralism practised by the state in the

---

[35] Stewart Brown, *The National Churches of England, Ireland and Scotland, 1801–1846* (Oxford, 2001), p. 405.

[36] George Bernstein, *Liberalism and Liberal Politics in Edwardian England* (London, 1986), pp. 50–52; Eugene Black, *The Social Politics of Anglo-Jewry 1880–1920* (Oxford, 1988), p. 105.

[37] David Feldman, 'Jews and the state in Britain' in M. Brenner, R. Liedtke and D. Rechter (eds), *British and German Jews in Comparative Perspective* (Tubingen, 1999), at pp. 149–152.

nineteenth century. This Act recognised the Board of Deputies of British Jews and, by extension, the Chief Rabbi, as the body competent to record Jewish marriages and to ensure they were performed 'according to the usages of the Jews'. This was a convenience for the state but had a huge impact on the Jewish community. The power invested in the Board and the Chief Rabbinate enabled both to discipline and exert sanctions on those congregations – both reform-minded and strictly observant – which challenged the writ of the Chief Rabbi, and they did so repeatedly and ruthlessly. In 1842, for example, the Chief Rabbi was able not only to excommunicate the reform-minded West London Synagogue of British Jews but also to refuse it a licence to perform marriages according to the usages of the Jews. By choosing one body to represent Jewish interests, the state bolstered the claim of one part of the Jewish population to speak in the name of the whole, even as this claim was contested.[38]

Government in the colonies was conducted on lines divorced from the practices of representative government and parliamentary sovereignty within which conservative pluralism developed in the United Kingdom but here too a form of pluralism developed as British rulers made an accommodation with what they thought to be traditional institutions. 'One of the principal axioms of British policy in Asia and Africa alike', wrote Margery Perham in 1930 in *The Times*, had been 'to conserve the authority of traditional and established rulers wherever possible.'[39] On the ground, Perham's maxim was applied inconsistently. In the case of Tanganyika, however, Orders in Council issued in 1920 did determine that in all civil and criminal cases to which natives were parties every court should be guided by native law, so long as it was not repugnant to morality or justice. These were broad limits. Accordingly, slavery was outlawed as was witchcraft, but within these limits British colonial policy judged the validity of local customs by standards considered appropriate to the situation at hand. As the Governor of Tanganyika, Sir Donald Cameron observed, the aim was not to turn Africans into Europeans but to encourage them to become better Africans. Indirect rule was a policy underpinned by the belief that each people had its own traditions and character and that these should be reflected in its institutions.[40]

---

[38] David Feldman, *Englishmen and Jews: Social Relations and British Culture, 1840–1914* (London, 1994), pp. 66–69.

[39] Cited in Anthony Kirk-Greene, 'Margery Perham and colonial administration: a direct influence on indirect rule' in Frederick Madden and David Fieldhouse (eds), *Oxford and the Idea of Commonwealth* (London, 1982), at p. 124.

[40] John Iliffe, *A Modern History of Tanganyika* (Cambridge, 1979), p. 321; Poulter, *Ethnicity, Law and Human Rights*, p. 41; R. Cranford Pratt and D. Anthony Low, *Buganda and British Overrule 1900–55* (Oxford, 1960), pp. 167–168.

This had important consequences for the subject peoples themselves. The British empire offered strength to the institutions it endorsed. It entrenched the cultural distinctions and identities that those institutions and leaders perpetuated. Where indirect rule was put into practice it was likely to mould rather than reflect African behaviour. John Iliffe observes, 'the British wrongly believed the Tanganyikans belonged to tribes; Tanganyikans created tribes to function within the Imperial framework'.[41] Something similar was evident in the case of the Sikhs. Following the assistance of Sikh soldiers in defeating the Indian Mutiny, the army recruited Sikhs in large numbers. By the start of the twentieth century Sikhs provided 25 per cent of the manpower of the Indian army where they were formed into separate Sikh regiments and companies. The British army designated the Sikhs 'a martial race'. It insisted Sikh recruits wear the full regalia of the orthodox Khalsa. Whereas once the dividing line between Sikh and Hindu had been indistinct, British policy in the Punjab worked to consolidate the diverse practices of the different groups calling themselves Sikhs in the middle of the nineteenth century, in the process helping to create an orthodox and martial Sikh identity.[42]

In all these spheres – within the multinational Kingdom, in the relationship between the state and Catholics, Jews and nonconformists, and in the empire – governments of all political parties developed pluralist solutions. There were, we should acknowledge, countervailing policies and strategies. We can point to militant opposition to Irish Home Rule, for example, to Anglican aspirations in the early nineteenth century to overcome the resistance of Catholics and Dissenters and to convert the Jews, and to the contingent and controversial status of the policy of indirect rule. At the very least, however, we should recognise the striking recurrence in British history of pluralist solutions to multicultural dilemmas. Moreover, in each case, we should note, these solutions were part of a strategy of incorporation and governance; designed to preserve English dominance within the United Kingdom, to govern subject peoples within the empire, and to preserve the privileges of the established Church. In this perspective we can see that the policies were, in a structural sense, conservative. They were meant to reform but also to preserve vestiges of the English *ancien régime* at home and to sustain British rule overseas.

---

[41] Iliffe, *A Modern History of Tanganyika*, p. 318.
[42] Richard Fox, *Lions of the Punjab* (Berkeley, 1985), pp. 140–159.

Multiculturalism

If we look at the arguments used by the Sikhs' supporters we can see that they drew on these older traditions of conservative pluralism. Repeatedly, the imperial legacy was brought to bear. Speakers and letter-writers pointed out that Sikhs had served the British army with distinction – in India, at Gallipoli and in Europe in World War II. They always made the same point: Sikhs had never been made to wear regulation helmets in the British army but had been allowed to keep their turbans in place, often with a regimental insignia on the front. If Sikhs wearing turbans had been prepared to die for Britain – and Britain had been happy to accept their sacrifice – then it was only right that Sikhs should be allowed to ride motorcycles and work on building sites similarly wearing their turban.[43] This argument was made by figures from across the political spectrum but not least by Conservative Members of Parliament whose patriotism was shaped by the disorientation that attended decolonisation and immigration. John Biggs Davison, for example, combined support for the Sikhs with admiration for Enoch Powell. He derided 'socialists' for asking Sikhs to do something never demanded when they were serving in the armed forces – to forgo beards and turbans. More generally, he argued that 'every group must be allowed its cultural identity and this is one reason why the "house full" sign must now go up'. Regard for the integrity of cultural identities, both Sikh and British, led Biggs Davison both to support the Sikhs' right to wear a turban as part of their uniform on public transport and to call for a stop to immigration.[44] This was a multiculturalism of the right.

Many Anglicans supported the Sikhs. In particular, churchmen involved in local Community Relations Councils pleaded the Sikhs' cause in the interests of religious toleration.[45] Others drew a parallel in the press and in the House of Commons between the concessions the Sikhs were claiming and those allowed in 1878 to Jews to open their workshops on Sundays if they had been closed on the Jewish Sabbath.[46]

The idea of religious toleration was crucial in 1976 when the Labour government gave way over the issue of motorcycle helmets and surreptitiously assisted Sidney Bidwell to draft a bill to exempt Sikhs from

[43] *The Times*, 21 September 1967, p. 11; 14 January 1969, p. 2; 17 January 1969, p. 9; *Parliamentary Debates, Lords*, 374, 4 October 1976, pp. 1060–1062.
[44] *The Times*, 3 January 1969, p. 7.
[45] NA, CK3/20 The British Council of Churches Community and Race Relations Unit, *Sikh Turban Problem in Relation to the Wearing of Crash Helmets* (nd).
[46] *The Times*, 5 January 1967, p. 9; NA, MT 92/658, clipping from *Parliamentary Debates*, 23 June 1976.

wearing crash helmets on motorcycles. The intervention of John Gilbert, the new Minister of Transport, was vital. Gilbert feared the consequences of imprisoning Sikhs and creating 'martyrs' even more than he feared a 'backlash against the Sikhs themselves'. However, he allied pragmatism to principle when he pointed out to the Cabinet that 'we risk appearing intransigent in defence of a rule which has proved to be at variance with our traditional social and religious tolerance'. In the House of Commons, Bidwell, who had a large Sikh population in his West London constituency of Southall, also based his case on 'a long historic tradition of toleration in this matter'.[47]

But it was a particular sort of toleration invoked in these debates. It was different from the idea expressed in the campaigns for Catholic and Jewish emancipation which had focused on the removal of disabilities. In this case, toleration required the state not merely to remove a disqualification but to make positive provision for the religion and customs of minorities. This was a second model of toleration that had developed through the nineteenth century as governments extended allowances and financial support to religious minorities, and as it developed in the empire in the face of customary laws, practices and beliefs. At the very least, in circumstances in which the government found it expedient to concede to the Sikhs, these traditions of conservative pluralism provided a set of precedents and parallels that led some to support the Sikhs' cause enthusiastically and, for others, made it appear unreasonable to say 'no' to turbans.

The outcomes of the Sikhs' campaigns demonstrate that policies which sanctioned cultural pluralism predate the drive to multiculturalism in the 1980s. But it is clear that the pace quickened in that decade. In the field of education, from the late 1960s a growing number of professionals were advocating a multicultural curriculum, but it was not until 1977 and 1980 that the Inner London Education Authority and Manchester became the first two education authorities to adopt formal statements on multicultural education. In the early 1980s these policies were more widely adopted as one response to the disadvantage evidenced by rising unemployment among black school-leavers and the unsettling disaffection highlighted by urban riots in 1980 and 1981. By 1982 a further thirty-six local education authorities (LEAs) had introduced a policy. Multicultural education was variously seen as a practice that would promote educational achievement among ethnic

---

[47] NA, MT 92/657 Cabinet Ministerial Committee on Home Affairs. Sikhs and Motor Cycle Helmets. Memorandum by the Minister for Transport, nd; *Parliamentary Debates*, Commons, 885, 28 January 1975, p. 224.

minorities and as a project that would reduce prejudice and discrimination.[48] In 1985 the report issued from the Committee of Inquiry into the Education of Children from Ethnic Minority Groups – the Swann report – explained that multiculturalism expressed a vision for modern Britain as well as for its educational system.

We consider that a multi-racial society such as ours would in fact function most effectively and harmoniously on the basis of pluralism, which enables, expects and encourages members of all ethnic groups, both minority and majority, to participate fully in shaping the society as a whole within a framework of commonly accepted values, practices and procedures whilst also allowing, and where necessary assisting, the ethnic minority communities in maintaining their distinct ethnic identities within this common framework.[49]

In the 1980s there was also a new direction to policy. In some cities and boroughs, not least in London, policies extended beyond culture and the school curriculum to address employment and economic disadvantage.[50] Many local authorities developed 'race units', employed 'race advisors', and adopted ethnic monitoring and positive action in their employment policies. In the London borough of Hackney the ethnic minority share of council staff rose from 11.5 per cent to 34 per cent between 1980 and 1988. The number of staff employed at the Greater London Council and classified as 'black' trebled between 1981 and 1985.[51] This activity was promoted by and identified with Labour local authorities, particularly those with large ethnic minority populations, and with resistance to the Conservative government and policy at a national level.

This combination of innovation and resistance has helped shape the view that the Conservative governments of these years promoted the views and preferences of the country's white majority at the expense of its minority communities.[52] In fact, Conservative government policy and

---

[48] Sally Tomlinson, 'Political dilemmas in multicultural education' in Zig Layton Henry, *Race and Government in Britain*, (London, 1986), at pp. 192–193; Hazel Carby, *Cultures in Babylon: Black Britain and African America* (London, 1999), pp. 200–201; Barry Troyna and Wendy Ball, *Views from the Chalkface: School Responses to a LEA's policy on Multicultural Education*, Policy Papers in Ethnic Relations No. 1, University of Warwick, 1985; Wendy Ball, *Policy Innovation on Multicultural Education in 'Eastshire'*, Policy Papers in Ethnic Relations No. 4, University of Warwick, 1986.

[49] Cited in Flora Anthias and Nira Yuval-Davis, *Race, Nation, Gender, Colour and Class and the Anti-Racist Struggle* (London, 1992), at p. 159.

[50] These policies ran alongside a continuing concern with culture. In the borough of Camden the grants channelled to ethnic minority groups rose by 350 percent in just five years in the mid-1980s: C. Joppke, *Immigration and the Nation State* (Oxford, 1989), p. 241.

[51] Herman Ouseley, 'Resisting institutional change' in Wendy Ball and John Solomos (eds), *Race and Local Politics* (1990), at p. 142.

[52] For example, Wendy Ball and John Solomos, 'Racial Equality and Local Politics' in Ball and Solomos (eds), *Race and Local Politics* (London, 1990), at p. 15.

practice as it responded to unemployment, riot and overwhelming evidence of 'racial disadvantage' was contradictory. In the aftermath of the Brixton riots the Conservative government increased funding to local authorities with large ethnic populations – albeit through universalist schemes such as the Urban Fund – but equally important – it instructed 'local authorities . . . to consult their local immigrant communities before applying for this grant aid'. Michael Heseltine, Secretary of State for the Environment, went further and promoted ethnic monitoring.[53]

There were majoritarian initiatives in the Thatcher years but their success was qualified by the persistence of pluralism. The 1988 Education Act specified that a majority of acts of collective worship in state-run schools were to be 'wholly or mainly of a Christian character'. This was the outcome of successful lobbying by a group of Conservative Anglicans in the House of Lords. However, the intentions of the majoritarians were subverted by the Education Secretary, Kenneth Baker, and the Bishop of London, Graham Leonard, who ensured that the Act also provided for the establishment of local Standing Advisory Councils for Religious Education which would consist of representatives of several faiths. This body, together with the LEA, would draw up guidelines to ensure practices took account of the composition of particular schools.[54] The head teacher of a predominantly Muslim primary school in Birmingham described the situation there in these terms: 'By law, the daily assembly must be of broadly Christian character. I think we, as most schools, get round this by focussing on the moral aspect that is shared among religions.'[55] At the Department of Education, through the Thatcher years, much to the prime minister's frustration and dismay, cultural diversity became entrenched in the state education system and was reproduced within the national curriculum. Guidance issued by the National Curriculum Council in 1990 emphasised that 'cultural diversity' should be 'actively promoted' and that teachers should prepare their pupils for 'adult life in a multicultural, multilingual Europe'.[56]

---

[53] Timothy Raison, 'The view from the government' in J. Benyon (ed.), *Scarman and After* (Oxford, 1984), at pp. 253–255; other sources of central government funding for 'community' groups were the Department of Education and the Department of Industry: Anthias and Yuval-Davis, *Race, Nation*, p. 169; Michael Heseltine, *Where There's a Will* (London, 1987), pp. 185–186.

[54] Kenneth Baker, *The Turbulent Years. My Life in Politics* (London, 1993), pp. 207–209.

[55] Joel Fetzer and J. Christopher Soper, *Muslims and the State in Britain, France and Germany*, (Cambridge 2005), pp. 39–40.

[56] Cited in Poulter, *Ethnicity, Law and Human Rights*, at pp. 57–58; on this theme more generally, see Abby Waldman, 'The politics of history teaching in England and France during the 1980s', *History Workshop Journal*, 68, (2009), pp. 197–221.

Why then was assimilation abandoned from the late 1970s and why did one or other form of pluralism become the dominant mode through which politicians and policy-makers thought about how to address the different cultural communities living in Britain? Some of the particular obstacles to pluralism within the Labour Party – trade unionism and universalism – lost potency in these years. In the 1980s and 1990s, the membership and influence of trade unions declined precipitously. In this context of defeat and disorganisation, a number of Labour local authorities used the issue of equal opportunities as a mechanism for widening their basis of support among ethnic minorities.[57] The decline of universalism can also be traced back to the 1976 Race Relations Act. This Act did not in general allow affirmative action but it placed on local authorities a statutory duty to promote equal opportunities between people of different 'racial groups'.[58] In this way it created space for claims to be made on behalf of ethnic groups. As we have seen, some local authorities energetically developed this opportunity. Interestingly, the Race Relations Act can be seen as one of the unintended consequences of feminism and the 1975 Sex Discrimination Act in particular. The 1976 Act was in many respects modelled on the powers given to the Equal Opportunities Commission a year earlier. Feminism, moreover, promoted the concept that there should be statistical parity in employment, an idea that was adapted and applied in relation to ethnic employment. The advance of multiculturalism, therefore, was closely connected with the waning power of what had been the organisational basis of the Labour Party – trade unionism – and its ideological motor – universalism, as both had taken shape in the decades after 1945.[59]

The reassertion of pluralism extended beyond the Labour Party, however. Here we need to take account of the growing perception that the problems once associated with immigrants now arose in relation to *British-born* members of ethnic minorities. The idea that these difficulties could be solved by assimilation (or for Powellites, by repatriation) of foreign-born subjects began to look unpromising. By the mid-1970s we see the development in the civil service of ideas about 'ethnicity' and 'racial disadvantage' to account for the persistence of cultural difference, high rates of poverty, unemployment and low educational attainment. In 1978 the Labour Home Secretary Merlyn Rees acknowledged that there were 'special problems of racial disadvantage arising particularly

---

[57] Ball and Solomos, 'Racial equality and local politics', p. 10.
[58] Ken Young, 'Approaches to development in the field of equal opportunities' in Ball and Solomos, *Race and Local Politics*, p. 26.
[59] Joppke, *Imigration and the Nation* State, pp. 229–230.

from colour and cultural background'.[60] This perception was shared across political parties. As early as 1976 an internal Conservative Party document made the same point more decisively.

> We are not facing tiresome problems caused by 'immigrants' who got here because defective immigration laws let them in but indigenous minority groups which because of racial discrimination and cumulative disadvantage are in some danger of being trapped in a situation of permanent minority.[61]

It is easy enough to uncover quotations from Conservative politicians, usually backbenchers, crudely advocating assimilation.[62] Nevertheless, in the face of urban crisis, deprivation and unemployment all heavily connected with the nation's ethnic minorities, pluralist tendencies generally were uppermost. This can be seen in the way that both William Whitelaw and Michael Heseltine repudiated Powellism in the aftermath of the Brixton riots; the former in the House of Commons, the latter to huge applause at the Conservative Party conference. If neither assimilation nor repatriation were plausible options then there was nothing left but to try to inculcate civility and celebrate difference. Whitelaw's condemnation of the rioters as 'disgraceful' and 'shameful' was yoked to recognition that there was, indeed, black in the Union Jack, and that a wholly punitive response to the riots would not secure the future of 'a free democratic society'. The language of Michael Heseltine's prescription for multicultural Britain went further and echoed the pluralism of indirect rule in the empire: 'This is what we seek: not conformity from our ethnic minorities, not white people with black faces, but a society in which the variety of our people enriches our country.'[63]

Conclusion

Multiculturalism is a cause associated with liberals, radicals and the left. This view certainly points to the political forces that drove multiculturalism forwards in the 1970s and 1980s but it also leaves much out of the account. As we have seen it captures neither the antecedents nor the structural features of multiculturalism. The antecedents lie in a long history of pluralist solutions to the problem of reconciling different

---

[60] HO 378/227, Proposals for a new form of CF Grant Aid to assist local authorities in meeting the special needs of ethnic minorities.
[61] Nicholas Crowson, 'Conservative Party activists and immigration policy from the late 1940s to the mid-1970s' in Stuart Ball and Ian Holliday (eds), *Mass Conservatism: The Conservatives and the Public since 1880* (London, 2002), at p. 179.
[62] For a selection, see Poulter, *Ethnicity, Law and Human Rights*, p. 220.
[63] William Whitelaw, *The Whitelaw Memoirs* (London, 1989), pp. 191–195; Michael Heseltine, *Where There's a Will*, p. 194.

cultural communities within a single polity. They connect to the more recent history of multicultural politics not least because they feature in public debate as justifications for pluralism in the present. It will require more research and further reflection before we can specify more extensively the mechanisms and linkages – in personnel, ideas and processes – that tie the striking recurrence over centuries of pluralist solutions to multicultural dilemmas to the particular decisions of actors in government about immigrants, and ethnic and religious minorities in Britain over the last fifty years. Here I have tried to indicate something of this in the case of the Sikhs and the politics of turbans. Moreover, it remains to be seen in detail how this tradition interacts and articulates with countervailing policies and strategies and, specifically, to the powerful assimilationist strain in British policy-making in the 1950s and 1960s. But despite these qualifications and caveats I do claim that the recurrence of conservative pluralism over three centuries is a neglected and a significant phenomenon. At the very least, we can say that when politicians perceived that there were compelling political reasons to approve pluralist solutions there was a ready history – one that combined empire and toleration, two central figures in the national imaginary – that could be drawn upon to support this course of action.

The structural feature of pluralism as a facet of British governance is that it has been used to shore up the established disposition of power – English, Anglican and imperial – within the Union and in the empire. This feature continues to the present. Anxiety and debate about urban crisis and its connection with young black men did not disappear after the 1980s, but these concerns began to figure less centrally in public debate. The initiatives that briefly focused attention on employment and equal opportunities in local government lost funding and political vitality in the 1990s.[64] At the same time, the appearance of politicised Islamic voices addressing domestic issues such as blasphemy, the state funding of faith schools, and the absence of a law against religious discrimination, as well as wars overseas, has given religion a new prominence. In some respects, this has generated a backlash against multiculturalism. Multiculturalism is held responsible for allowing the self-segregation of Muslims that contributed to serious civil unrest in northern towns in the summer of 2001. Elsewhere it is blamed for the rise of domestic terrorism. It is now easy to find references to Britishness, citizenship, shared values and cohesion, as politicians, think tanks and commissions of inquiry focus on the goal of social integration.

---

[64] This needs more research, but see the comment in Anthias and Yuval-Davis, *Race, Nation*, at p. 169.

However, this has not led to a revival of the idea of assimilation nor of the idea that somehow a monocultural future is within reach. Rather, over the last two decades the rhetoric and practice of multiculturalism have been revised. At the beginning of the twenty-first century religion has again become central to the politics of multiculturalism. Now we are as likely to be told that we live in a multi-faith society as that we live in a multicultural society.[65]

In this way the politics of multiculturalism has returned to terrain easily accommodated by the practice of conservative pluralism. This has been registered across political parties and at different levels of government. In 1991 the Conservative government established the Inner Cities Religious Council. In 1997 the handbook *Involving Communities in Urban and Rural Regeneration*, published by the Department of Environment, Transport and the Regions, asserted that 'churches, mosques, temples, synagogues and gurdwaras have as much right to contribute to discussions concerning regeneration as residents' or tenants' organisations'. Similar initiatives have been pursued at regional and local levels. Development agencies and assemblies such as Yorkshire Forward and Advantage West Midlands have reserved places for representatives of churches and other faiths, or else have co-opted representatives. By 2006, 44 per cent of local authorities had an officer responsible for liaison with faith communities.[66]

Following the election of Labour in 1997, Anglican, Catholic and Jewish faith schools were supplemented by Muslim, Hindu, Greek Orthodox and Seventh Day Adventist schools. As history might predict, the Church of England has supported state aid for Muslim schools. Advocates of Islamic faith schools recognise the Church as an ally. Dr Fatma Amer, Director of Education and Inter Faith Relations at the Islamic Cultural Centre, London Central Mosque, argued in 2001: 'The religious establishment makes possible a recognition of a person's right to put into action what he most sincerely believes in ... There is much good in keeping the religious establishment intact.'[67] But this

---

[65] Home Office, *Community Cohesion: A Report of the Independent Review Team* (London, 2003); Tariq Modood and Nasar Meer, 'The multicultural state we're in: Muslims, "multiculture" and the civic re-balancing of British multiculturalism', *Political Studies*, 57, (2009), pp. 473–497.

[66] L. Betherton, 'A new establishment? Theological politics and the emerging shape of church-state relations', *Political Theology*, 7(3), (2006), pp. 371–392; Richard Farnell, Robert Furbey, Stephen Shams, Al-Haqq Hills, Marie Macey and Greg Smith, *'Faith' in Urban Regeneration? Engaging Faith Communities in Urban Regeneration* (Bristol, 2003), pp. 1–8. See too Home Office Faith Communities Unit, *Working Together: Co-operation Between Government and Faith Communities* (London, 2004).

[67] Cited in Fetzer and Soper, *Muslims and the State*, at p. 25.

remains a vastly unequal relationship. The number of state-funded Muslim schools is disproportionately tiny: just seven in 2007 for a Muslim population that numbered 1.54 million at the start of the decade. That is just one school for, roughly, every 200,000 Muslims in England. By contrast, there is one Anglican school for every 8,000 people who returned themselves as Christian in the 2001 census.[68] In this way the politics of multiculturalism as it is practised in the UK is doubly conservative. It buttresses the position of an otherwise beleaguered Anglican establishment and at the same time it buttresses the position of religious hierarchies and their religious identities within minority communities.

[68] www.dcsf.gov.uk//DB/SBU/b000rsgateway796/TheCompositionOfSchoolsInEnglandFinal. pdf, p. 15; Office for National Statistics, *Census, 2001 National Report for England and Wales*, (London, 2003), p. 247.

Index

Aberystwyth (Wales), 290
abolitionism, 189–90, 193
  feminist critiques, 190
Abraham, Karl (1877–1925), 218
Abrams, Philip (1933–81), 'Notes on the
  Difficulty of Studying the State'
  (1977), 78–9
absent centre, 231–2
  concept of, 232–3
accountability, 76
Addington, Henry, 1st Viscount Sidmouth
  (1757–1844), 95
administration, use of term, 79
Administrative Reform Association, 173
Adorno, Theodor W. (1903–69), 214–15
Adrianople (Turkey), 196
Advantage West Midlands, 301
Afghan war, 183–4
Africa
  British policies in, 292
  West, 177–8
  see also South Africa
agency, 264–5
aggregate demand, 31–2
agrarian capitalism, 126–7
agricultural improvement, 121–2
agricultural involution, 35–6
  use of term, 32–3
agricultural labourers
  defence of, 130–1
  unemployment, 35–6
agriculture
  employment, 49–50
  labour demand, 47
  and population change, 33–5
  productivity increase, 51
Albert, Frances [Fanny] Ellen (*fl.* 1877),
  198, 200–2
  'On Turkish Ways and Women'
  (1876–7), 198
Albert, Prince Consort (1819–61),
  marriage, 167–8

Aldermaston (West Berkshire), 271–2
Alexander, Sally, 234
Ali, Tariq (1943–), 279
alienation, and capitalism, 152–3
alterity, 108–9
  class-based, 112–13
  racial, 100–1, 115–16
Althusser, Louis (1918–90), 8–9, 229–30,
  231–3
  structuralism, 268–9
  and Thompson, 217–18
Amalgamated Society of Gas, Municipal
  and General Workers, 241–2
ambulances, 196
Amer, Fatma, 301–2
American Civil War (1861–5), 189–90
American Historical Association, 222–3
Americanisation, 173–5
Amery, Leopold Charles Maurice Stennett
  (1873–1955), 259–60
Amos, Sarah Sheldon (d. 1908), 196,
  200–2
anarchism, revisionist, 272–3, 277–8
Anarchy (journal), 272–3
ancestry, and social status, 101–2
ancien regime, 164, 169–70, 212–13, 244, 293
Anderson, Elizabeth Garrett
  (1836–1917), 199
Anderson, Perry (1938–), 8–9, 17–18,
  214–17, 232–3, 267–8
  'Components of the National Culture'
  (1968), 212–14, 231–2
  and Stedman Jones, 9–10
Anglicans, 173–5, 179–80, 290–1, 293
  Conservative, 297
  and Sikhs, 294
Anglo India, and familial proto-state,
  100–17
Anglo-Armenian Association, 203
Anglo-Marxists, 2
Annales School, 1, 8–9, 13–14, 211, 228
anthropology, 229–30

anthropology (cont.)
    as socialism, 146
anti-Catholicism, 191–2
Anti-Corn Law League, 124–5
anti-Muslim prejudice, 198
anti-Turkish prejudice, 198
antiquarianism, 220–1
apprenticeships, 148
Arch, Joseph (1826–1919), 137, 138
archaeology, of slums, 161–2
armed services, and labour, 47–8
Armenia, 201, 203, 206–7
Armenian Christians, 201
Armenians, 201–3, 204, 208
Armistice (1918), 242–3
army, political standing of, 178–9
army reforms, 167–8, 169–71, 178–9
    goals, 172–3
Artaud, Antonin (1896–1948), 270
Ashanti War (1873), 178–9
Ashdown Forest (East Sussex), 132–3
    Board of Conservators, 133
    commoner associations, 133–4
    illegal commoner activities, 134–5
    middle-class residences and, 133–4
Ashley-Cooper, Anthony, 7th Earl of
        Shaftesbury (1801–85), 191–2
Asia, British policies in, 292
Askern, William, 131
Asquith, Herbert Henry (1852–1928),
        183–4
assimilation
    Conservative Party and, 299
    immigrants, 285–8, 298
    Labour Party and, 286–7
atrocities, Turks, 195–6, 208
Attlee, Clement Richard (1883–1967), 257
Auden, W. H. (1907–73), 236
Auerbach, Berthold (1812–82), 147
Australia, 173
Austria, 192, 193, 197
authoritarianism, 211
avant garde, 271, 273
Aveling, Edward (1849–98), 156

backbenchers, roles, 91, 95, 96
Baines, Edward (1800–90), 175–6
Baker, Kenneth (1934–), 297
Balabanov, Marko (1837–1921), 199
Baldwin, Peter, 258
Baldwin, Stanley (1867–1947), 259
Balgarnie, Florence (1856–1928),
        201–2
Balkan Christians, 197
Balkan women, 200–1

Balkans, 197, 200
bands, psychedelic, 271–2
Banstead (Surrey), 136
Baptista, Joseph (1864–1930), 242
Bardonneau, Elizabeth Ann Ashurst
        (1820–50), 193
Barmen-Elberfeld (Germany), 144,
        149–52
Barnett, Henrietta (1851–1936), 203
Barnett, Samuel (1844–1913), 17–18
Barry, Alexander (fl. 1800), 111–16
Barry, George (fl. 1800), 111–13
Barry, Leonore (née Auclair) (fl. 1811),
        114–15
Barry, Mrs (fl. 1800), 111–12
Barry, Robert (fl. 1800), 111–12
Barry family, 111–15, 116–17
Batavia, 113–14
Bateson, Gregory (1904–80), 277–8
Bayly, C. A., 100–1
Beaconsfieldism, destruction of, 183–4
Beard, John (fl. 1917), 242–3
beards, 281
    ban on, 281–2, 294
Beare, Mrs, 67
Beck, Julian (1925–85), 277–8
Becker, Lydia Ernestine (1827–90), 199
Beckett, Samuel (1906–89), 270
beggars, 73
    18th century, 56–7
Belfast Agreement (1998), 290
Belford, Paul, 161–2
Belgium, 206–7
Bengal, 113–15
Bentham, Jeremy (1748–1832), 86
Benthamism, 75–6
Benthamite utilitarianism, 85
Berke, Joseph, 279
Berkhampstead [Berkhamsted]
        (Hertfordshire), 129
Berlin (Germany), 144–5
    British embassy, 171–2
Berlin, University of, 145–6
Berne (Switzerland), 191–2
Bevin, Ernest (1881–1951), 244–5
Bidwell, Sydney James (1917–97), 294–5
Big Business, 266–7
Big Government, 266–7
Biggs, Caroline Ashurst (1840–89),
        198–9
Biggs, Matilda Ashurst (c. 1816–66),
        193
Biggs-Davison, John (1918–88), 294
Bindar, Singh, 287–8
Bion, Wilfred Ruprecht (1897–1979), 228

Birmingham (West Midlands), 143, 283–4
    Edgbaston, 246
    Erdington, 251
    nonconformists, 184–5
    relief organisations, 201–2
Birmingham Daily Post, 134
birth, privilege of, 252
Black Papers on Education, 264–5
Black Sea crisis, 177–8
black separatism, 274–5
Blackheath (London), 129
blacks, South Africa, 208
Blair, Eric (*pseud.* George Orwell)
    (1903–50), 235–6
Blair, Tony (1953–), 264–5
Blanc, Louis (1811–82), 193–4
Blind, Mathilde (1841–96), 193–4
Board of Deputies of British Jews, 291–2
Board of Education, 290
Boer War (1899–1902), 187–8, 202–3
    opposition to, 203–5
Boers, 204–5, 206–7, 208
Bolshevik Revolution (1917), 261
Bolsheviks, 279
Bondfield, Margaret (1873–1953),
    253–4
Booth, Catherine (1829–90), 203
Booth, Charles (1840–1916), 153–4
Booth, William (1829–1912), *In Darkest
    England and the Way Out* (1890),
    156–7
Borsay, Peter, 54, 60
Boserup, Ester (1910–99), 32–3
Bosnia, 197
Bosnians, 200–1
Bourbon, Ile [Réunion], 113–14
Boyle, Sir Edward (1923–81), 286
Boyson, Sir Rhodes (1925–), 264–5
Bradlaugh, Charles (1833–91),
    129–31
Braudel, Fernand (1902–85), 13–14
Brewer, John, 76–8
brickfields, on commons, 136
Briggs, Asa (1921–), 143
Bright, John (1811–89), 171–2, 175–6
Brighton (East Sussex), market
    place, 59
Bristol Mercury, 124–5
Britain
    class feeling in, 237–41
    family solidarity, 101–2
    global trade, 21
    institutional reform, decline, 164–86
    see also England; Scotland; Wales
British Empire, 158, 293

conflicted modernities of, 100–1
    transnational networks, 20, 21
    women of, and feminists, 187–8
British fathers, mixed-race children of,
    100–1
British historiography
    empiricism in, 8–9
    positivism in, 8–9
    structure in, 1–23
    transformations in, 1–23
British history
    current situation, 18–19
    multicultural politics in, 281–302
    Stedman Jones and, 8–9
British Psychoanalytical Society, 215–16
British women
    activist, 188–9
    and cultures of internationalism, 209
    international interests, 187–8
    opposition to Boer War, 203–5
    and pacifism, 187–8, 200, 206–7
    and religion, 188–9
    responses to Eastern question, 195–203
    roles, 189
British Workers League, 241–2
Brixton riots (1981; 1985; 1995),
    296–7, 299
Bromley (Kent), 254, 255
Brook, Peter (1925–), 270
Brotherton, Joseph (1783–1857), 123
Bruce, Henry, 1st Baron Aberdare
    (1815–95), 170–1
Bryce, Elizabeth Marion (1854–1939),
    203
Bryce, James (1838–1922), 203
Budapest (Hungary), 207
Buddhism, 279, 281–2
Bulgaria, 194–6, 197, 199, 203
Bulgarians, 195–6, 201–2, 204, 208
bull-rings, 65
Burdett-Coutts, Angela, 1st Baroness
    (1814–1906), 196, 197
bureaucracies, Weberian, 74–5
Burns, John (1858–1943), 156
Burns, Mary (d. 1863), 148, 150
Burns, Robert (1759–96), 240
Burroughs, William Seward II
    (1914–97), 271
bus drivers, and turbans, 281, 282, 283
buses, turbans on, 286–7
bussing, 286
butchers, 69
Butler, Josephine (1828–1906), 190–5,
    196, 198, 200–1, 202–7, 208
Butterfield, Sir Herbert (1900–79), 220–1

Calcutta (India), 104, 114–15
Calvin, Robert (*fl.* 1808), 66
Calvinism, 144–5
Cambridge Population Group,
    20–1
Cambridge School, 16–17, 231
Cambridge Social History of Britain, The
    (1990), 2–3
Cambridge Social History Seminar, 11–12
Cambridge, University of, 11–12, 17–18,
    211–21
    King's College, 14–15, 16–17
Camden (London), Roundhouse, 274
Cameron, Sir Donald Charles
    (1872–1948), 292
Campaign for Nuclear Disarmament
    (CND), 262–3, 267, 269, 271–2
Canada, 173
Canning Town Women's Settlement, 157
capitalism
    agrarian, 126–7
    and alienation, 152–3
    and commons, 138–9
    consumer, 211
    costs of, 149–50
    critiques
        Engels's, 147
        Marxist, 142–3
    development of, 140
    families and, 100–1
    global liberal, 15–16
    industrial, 15–16
    and marriage, 100
    opposition to, 146
capitalist production, vs. socialist
    production, 257–8
Cardwell, Edward (1813–86), 176
Caribbean
    immigrants from, 283–4
    slavery, 189–90
Carlisle (Cumbria), 252–3
    market place, shambles, 63
Carlyle, Thomas (1795–1881), 240
Carmichael, Stokely (1941–98),
    274–5, 279
Carpenter, Edward, 138–40
Carpenter, Mary (1807–77), 199
Casamaijor, James Henry (1745–1815),
    104–7
Casamaijor, Jane Amelia (1789–1809),
    105–6
Casamaijor family, 105–6
Catholics *see* Roman Catholics
Catt, Carrie Chapman (1859–1947), 206
Cavell, Edith Louisa (1865–1915), 206–7

Cecil, Robert, 3rd Marquess of Salisbury
    (1830–1903), 180–1, 184–5
celebrations, civic, 65
censuses, 35, 93–4
central government, 78–9
    roles, 84
    use of term, 79–80
central state, 78–9
    broadening, 96–7
Ceylon, 111–12
Chadwick, Edwin (1800–90), 86
Chahal, Baldev Singh, 289
Chalmers, Thomas (1780–1847), 86
Chamberlain, Arthur Neville (1869–1940),
    260
Chamberlain, Joseph (1836–1914), 130–1,
    138, 173, 177–8, 181, 184–5, 204
Chambers, Jonathan David (1898–1970),
    119–20
Chambers of Commerce, 181
Chant, Laura Ormiston (née Dibbin)
    (1848–1923), 201–2
Charing Cross (Greater London), pillories,
    67–8
Charity Organisation Society, 173–5
Chartism, 3–4, 14–15, 126, 164–5, 170–1
    meetings, 72
    programmes, 129–30
    rallies, 150–1
Chartists, 125
    and landed property, 126–7
Chase, Malcolm, 126
Chatterjee, Indrani, 100–1
Chelmsford (Essex), pillories, 67–8
Chester, market place, shambles, 63
Chesterfield (Derbyshire), market place, 60
Chicago School, 142–3
Chichester (West Sussex), market cross, 62
Chief Rabbinate, 291–2
child poverty, 163
Childers, Hugh (1827–96), 178–9
children
    mixed-race, of British fathers, 100–1
    see also illegitimate children
Christianity
    British women and, 188–9
    criticisms of, 144–5
    providentialist, 85
    and spiritual freedom, 207–8, 209
    see also Church of England; Church of
        Ireland; nonconformism;
        Protestantism; Roman Catholics
Christians
    Armenian, 201
    Balkan, 197

non-Anglican, 290–1
in Ottoman Empire, 187–8, 195–203
Slavonic, 197
and world affairs, 191
see also Anglicans; Quakers; Roman
    Catholics
Church of England, 173–5, 290–1
disestablishment, 177
and Muslim schools, 301–2
women and, 189
see also Anglicans
Church of Ireland, 167–8, 173–5
disestablishment, 175–6
church reform, 93, 94, 172–3
churches, 301
Churchill, Sir Winston Leonard Spencer
    (1874–1965), 248, 250, 255–6, 260
cities
doughnut, 162
Engels and, 163
see also towns
civic centres, urban renaissance, 54
civic improvement
18th century, 54–73
London, 156
Paris, 154–5
research sources, 68–9
use of term, 73
civic spaces
codified, 142
see also public spaces
Civil Administration of the Army, 169–70
civil disobedience, 289
civil government
spending, 83–4
use of term, 84
civil rights liberalism, 87–8
civil rights movement, 274–5
civil service, 176, 184–5, 298–9
expansion, 74–5
limited competition in, 170–1
organisation, 169–70
Clapham, Sir John (1873–1946), *An
    Economic History of Modern Britain*
    (1926), 119–20
Clare, John (1793–1864), 120, 122–3, 140
Clare (Suffolk), political protests, 70–1
class
concept of, 2–3
industrious, 239–40
polarisation, 239
in social history, 2–8
use of term, 4, 230–1
yeoman, and enclosure, 118
see also elites; middle class; working class

class analysis, Marxism and, 2
class conflict, 150–1
class-consciousness, 14
class feeling
in Britain, 237–41
issues, 242–3
Labour Party and, 239–40
politicisation, 239
post-World War I, 238–9
and World War I, 237–8
class identities, Victorian, 100
class parties, 243–4, 250
class politics
and Conservative Party, 244
and Labour Party (1900–40), 237
rejection, 241–5
class prejudice, 244, 253
class privilege, 158–9
critiques, 259
class struggle, 243–4
class war, 242, 250
class zoning
Engels's studies, 151–2
criticisms, 153–4
class-based alterity, 112–13
class-consciousness, 153
Clause Four, 264–5
Clent Hills (Staffordshire), 134
Clifton (Bristol), 246
Clive, Robert (1725–74), 102
Clode, Charles M., 178–9
CND (Campaign for Nuclear
    Disarmament), 262–3, 267, 269,
    271–2
co-operative movement, 247
coal industry, strikes, 238–9
coalition governments, 170–1, 185–6,
    248, 250
Cobbe, Frances Power (1822–1904), 199
Cobden, Richard (1804–65), 164, 169–70,
    171–5, 177–8, 184–5
cogito, 232–3
Cohn, Norman (1915–2007), *Europe's
    Inner Demons* (1975), 221–2
Cold War, 225–6, 262–3
Cole, Margaret Isabel (1893–1980), 8–9
Cole, W. A., 25–6
collective security, 257
collectivism, 75–6
Colley, Linda, 100–1
Collings, Jesse (1831–1920), 138
Collingwood, Robin George (1889–1943),
    214–15
Collini, Stefan (1947–), *Absent Minds*
    (2006), 231

colonial India
  illegitimate children in, 100–1, 102–3,
    111–16
  racial prejudice in, 105–6
Colonies, pluralism, 292
Combination Act (1799), repeal, 86–7
Committee of Inquiry into the Education of
    Children from Ethnic Minority
    Groups, 295–6
common rights, 137
  wastes, 119–20
commoners
  associations, 133–4
  regulation, 134
  see also illegal commoners
commons
  administration, 133
  brickfields on, 136
  capitalism and, 138–9
  enclosure, and radical histories, 118–41
  extent of, 121
  grazing, 135
  and land ownership, 118–19
  metropolitan, 136
  middle-class residences and, 133–4
  mineral rights, 136
  perspectives, 136–7, 139–40
  pre-enclosure useage, 119–20
  public access, 127–8
  as public amenities, 122–3
  radicalism and, 129–30
  resources, vs. commoners, 118–19
  riots, 133–4
  roles, 129
  Select Committee investigations, 123–4
  socialism and, 138–40
  squatting, 135
  upland areas, 132–3
  and urban development, 129–30
  useage, 132, 134–5, 136
  see also wastes
Commons Preservation Society (CPS),
    130–1, 133, 135–6, 137, 139–40
  activities, 129, 136
  establishment, 128
  goals, 129–30
  perspectives, 136–7
  and regulation, 134–5
Commons Protection League (CPL)
  establishment, 129–30
  goals, 129–30
  militancy, 130–1
  perspectives, 136–7
communalism, 283–4
communism, 12–13

development, 146
Communist Party, 226–7, 262–3
Communist Party Historians Group
    (CPHG), 210–11, 223
  activities, 217–18
  legacies, 228
  publications, 224–5
communitarianism, 242–4, 251
Community Relations Commission, 287–8
Community Relations Councils, 294
Condorcet, Marie-Jean-Antoine-Nicholas
    de Caritat, Marquis de (1743–94),
    15–18
consciousness, revolutionary, 276–7
Conservatism, 259, 263, 264–5
  institutional, 183–4
  inter-war, 248–9
Conservative governments, 296–7, 301
  goals, 286
Conservative Party, 168–9, 176, 181–2,
    183–4, 185–6, 247
  and assimilation, 299
  and class politics, 244
  conferences, 299
  criticisms, 239–40, 250, 252–3
  education policies, 290–1
  elections, 254, 284–5
  on ethnic minorities, 298–9
  historiography, 248–9
  Labour opposition, 240–1
  on Labour Party, 248
  revival, 179–80
conservative pluralism, 288, 294, 301
Conservative policies, ethnic minorities,
    296–7
Constantinople (Turkey), 198, 201
  British embassy, 169–70, 171–2
constitutional reform, 185–6
consumer capitalism, 211
consumerism, ethical, 269
Contagious Diseases Acts, 189–91
  opposition to, 198
Cooper, David (1931–86), 276–7, 279
Corfu, 114–15
Cork (Eire), 129–30
Corn Laws, 125
Cornhill Magazine, 198
Cornwall, population growth, 41–2
corporal punishment, 68
corruption, 77–8
Cosgrove, Richard, 75–6
counter-culture
  concept of, 269–70
  and New Left, 261–80
  and Old Left, 261–80

Courtney, Kate (1847–1929), 203
Cousins, Frank (1904–86), 286–7
CPHG *see* Communist Party Historians
     Group (CPHG)
CPL *see* Commons Protection League
     (CPL)
CPS *see* Commons Preservation Society
     (CPS)
Crafts, N. F. R., 25–6
Creoles, 114–17
Crimean War, 170–3, 197, 200
criminal justice, administration, 91–2
Cripps, Stafford (1889–1952), 257
Croatia, 197
Crosland, Anthony (1918–77),
     261–2, 286
crowds, in history, 226–7, 229–30
Crown
     criticisms, 183–4
     direct political power, 165–6
     reform, 164–5
Cruise missiles, 269
cultural diversity, 297
cultural history, Foucauldian, 16–17
cultural pluralism, 295–6
cultural politics, 21–2
     and social change, 20
cultural revolution, 271
cultural turn, and sciences, 76
culture, 7–8, 264–5
     popular, 2–3
     see also counter-culture; national
          culture
cutcherries, 102

Dadaism, 269–70
Daily Herald, 251
daily life, social history studies, 2–3
Daily Mail, 260
Daily News, 199
Daily Telegraph, 260
Dangerous Drugs Act (1964), 273
Dartmoor (Devonshire), 133
Darwin, Charles (1809–82), 218
Davidoff, Leonore, 100, 115–16
Davies, Albert Emil (1875–1950), 250,
     251–2
Davis, Jennifer, 159–60
Davis, Mike (1946–), 159, 160
     Planet of Slums (2006), 158–9
de Morgan, John (*fl.* 1872), 129–31
Deane, P., 25–6
demand
     aggregate, 31–2
     income elasticity of, 31–2

labour, 47
for raw materials, 29–30
demographic growth *see* population
     growth
demography, research, 20–1
demonstrations
     market places and, 71
     mass, 227–8
     see also protests; riots
Department of Education, 286, 297
Department of the Environment,
     Transport and the Regions, 301
depressions, 167–8
Deutsch-Französische Jahrbücher, 147
dialectics, of liberation, 261–80
Dialectics of Liberation Congress (1967),
     271–2, 274, 279–80
Dicey, Albert Venn (1835–1922), 85
     *Lectures on the Relations between Law and
          Public Opinion in the Nineteenth
          Century* (1905), 75–6
Dickens, Charles (1812–70), 240
     Little Dorrit (1856), 173
Dilke, Sir Charles (1843–1911), 173,
     177–8
discourses, 7–8, 19–20, 230–1, 268–9
     of radicalism, 22
disestablishment, 173–6, 177, 184–5
Disraeli, Benjamin (1804–81), 176,
     178–81, 184–5, 195–6
     criticisms, 183–4
Disraelianism, 152
Dissenters, 293
district councils, 138–9
Dockers' Union, 241–2
Dodds, Eric Robertson (1893–1979),
     The Greeks and the Irrational (1951),
     221–2
domestic terrorism, 300–1
donkey racing, 129
Dorset, population growth, 41–2
doughnut cities, 162
Dover (Kent), political protests, 70–1
Drinkwater, John Bethune (1762–1844),
     103–4
Ducie Bridge (River Irk), 149–50
Dunn, John (1940–), 16–17
Dunning, John, 1st Baron Ashburton
     (1731–83), 165–6
dynasties, Celtic and English,
     intermarriage, 100–1

East India Company, 100–1, 108–9
     and state power, 102
Easter Rising (1916), 290

Eastern question, British women's
    responses to, 195–203
Eastern Rumelia (Bulgaria), 195–6
Easthope, Anthony, 225–6
economic development, and family
    formations, 100
economic growth
    Industrial Revolution, 25–6
    and raw materials, 29–30
economic history, issues, 2
economies
    organic, 28, 29–30, 48
    political, 16–17
Edgbaston (West Midlands), 246
Edinburgh (Scotland), 289–90
    relief organisations, 201–2
education
    compulsory, 74–5
    free, 74–5
    and multiculturalism, 295–6
    Privy Council grants, 74–5
    secular, 290–1
Education Acts
    1902, 290–1
    1903, 290–1
    1988, 297
education reforms, 170–1
Edward I (1239–1307), 290
Edward VII (1841–1910), 173–5
ego, 218
Eichmann, Adolf (1906–62), 270
eight-hour day, 238–9
electioneering, stratified, 255–6
elections
    18th century, 55–6
    Conservative Party, 254, 284–5
    Labour Party, 254, 257–8, 261–2,
        301–2
    Liberal Party, 290
Elias, Norbert (1897–1990), *The Civilizing
    Process* (1939), 221–2
Eliot, T. S. (1888–1965), 222–3
elites
    encroachments, 135–6
    and institutional reform, 185–6
    popular entertainment, 56–7
    and public spaces, 55–6, 73
Elizabethan period, population growth,
    36–9
Elliot, Amelia (née Casamaijor) (d. 1872),
    104–9, 110–11, 112–13,
    114–17
Elliot, Anna Maria (née Amyand), Lady
    Minto (d. 1829), 103–4, 106–11,
    112–13, 114–15, 116–17

Elliot, Eliza (née Ness) (d. 1848), 104–5,
    108–13, 114–17
Elliot, Sir George (1784–1863), 103–4,
    112–13
    education, 111–12
    marriage, 104–5, 108–11
Elliot, Gilbert, 1st Earl of Minto
    (1751–1814), 102–17
    illegitimate children, 111–17
Elliot, Gilbert, 2nd Earl of Minto
    (1782–1859), 107–8
    education, 111–12
Elliot, John (1788–1862), 103–4, 112–13
    education, 111–12
    marriage, 104–9
Elliot, William (*fl.* 1814), 108–9
Elton, Sir Geoffrey Rudolph (1821–94),
    211–12
Ely, Isle of, population growth, 46
emancipation
    female, 188, 198
    Jews, 295
    Roman Catholics, 94, 295
    sexual, 194–5
embassies, British, 169–70, 171–2
empiricism, in British historiography, 8–9
employment
    agriculture, 49–50
    indices, 82
    primary, 49
    secondary, 49
    tertiary, 49
    see also unemployment
employment opportunities, hundreds, 44
enclosure
    commons, and radical histories,
        118–41
    desirability, 119–20
    illegal, 135–6
    impacts, 121–2
    last phase of, 120
    legislation, 121
    moorland, 132–3
    opposition to, 122, 124–5, 140–1
    and peasant class, 118
    perspectives, 139–40
    promoters of, 127
    reversing the process of, 137
    socialism and, 140
    and yeoman class, 118
enclosure awards, opposition to, 128
encroachments, 135
    elites, 135–6
Endowed Schools Commission, 173–5,
    179–80

energy economies, mineral-based, 35, 49
Engels, Friedrich (1820–95), 4
    and cities, 163
    *The Condition of the Working Class in
        England* (1845), 142–4, 147,
        148–54, 159, 160–1
        criticisms, 153–4
    early thinking, 144
    and Hegelianism, 144–5
    The Housing Question (1872–3), 154–5,
        160–1
    legacies, 159–62
    Letters from Wuppertal (1839), 144,
        149–50
    *Origins of the Family, Private Property and
        the State* (1884), 100
    'Outlines of a Critique of Political
        Economy' (1843), 147–8
England
    common land, 121
    multiculturalism, 289–90
    population growth, 50
        from 1541, 24–53
        1750–1850, 24–53
        1760–1840, 25–6
    social welfare, 89–99
    socialism, 146
    Stuart, 55–6
    see also Georgian England
English Historical Review (journal), 219–20
Englishwoman's Review (journal), 192,
    198–9, 200–1
environmental movement, 269
environmentalism, second-wave, 266–7
Epping Forest, 129
Epsom (Surrey), 136
Equal Opportunities Commission, 298
Erdington (West Midlands), 251
Erikson, Erik (1902–94), 222–3
Ermen & Engels, 147
ethical consumerism, 269
ethnic minorities
    British-born members, 298–9
    Conservative policies, 296–7
ethnicity, 298–9
Europe
    population growth, 33–5, 49–50
    prostitution, 190–1, 209
European Jewry, 270
Evans, Sir Arthur John (1851–1941), 197
Evans, Margaret (née Freeman)
    (c. 1851–1893), 196
Evelyn, John (1620–1706), 60–1
Everitt, Alan, 119–20
evolutionary theory, 218

executions, public, 68
Exeter (Devon), slaughter houses, 69
Exmoor, squatting, 135
experience, 14
experimentalism, modernist, 218
Eysenck, Hans (1916–97), 213–14

Factory Acts
    1802, 74–5
    1833, 74–5
faith-based schools, 290–1, 301–2
familial proto-state, and Anglo India,
    100–17
families
    and capitalism, 100–1
    nuclear, 100
    and race, 116
family formations, 100–17
    and economic development, 100
family solidarity, in Britain, 101–2
farm workers
    unionisation, 130–1
    see also agricultural labourers
fascism, historiography of, 222–3
Faucher, Léon (1803–54), 152
Fawcett, Henry (1833–84), 129–30
Fawcett, Dame Millicent Garrett
    (1847–1929), 199, 200–1,
    204–5, 206
Feldman, David, 21
female emancipation, 188, 198
female imagination, Italy and, 192–5
female internationalism, 21
    British women, historiography, 207–8
    vs. male internationalism, 187–8
females *see* women
feminism, 21, 200
    consequences, 298
    development, 188, 206, 207–8
    and Freud, 234
    impacts, 5–6
    and liberalism, 202–3
    national movements, 187–8
    and psychoanalysis, 234
    second-wave, 266–7
feminists, and women of the British
    Empire, 187–8
fences, destruction of, 129
Ferenczi, Sándor (1873–1933), 218
fertility, 24
    rates, 51–2
Feuerbach, Ludwig Andreas (1804–72),
    146, 148
    The Essence of Christianity (1841), 144–5
    on Hegel, 145–6

Feuerbach, Ludwig Andreas (1804–72)
  (cont.)
  materialism, 147
Feuerbachianism, 160–1
Field, John, 131
finance, kin-based, 102
Financial Reform Association, 169–70
Finn, Margot, 21
First International, 129–30
First World War *see* World War I (1914–18)
fiscal-military state, 77–8
  use of term, 76–8
flogging, military, 181
Flower Power, 280
Foley, Sir Thomas (1757–1833),
  111–13
food, income elasticity of demand, 31–2
food riots, 70–1
Ford, Henry (1863–1947), 214–15
Foreign Office, 177–8, 183–5
foreign policies, 184–5
Forest of Dean, 132–3
Foster, John, *Class Struggle and the
  Industrial Revolution* (1974), 4
Foucauldianism, 16–17
Foucault, Michel Paul (1926–84), 6–7,
  229–30
France, 173, 191
  political activism, 146
  political revolution, 148
  protests, 265–6, 279–80
  socialist movements, 206
  universities, 276
  see also Paris (France)
franchise
  distortions, 239
  extension, 175–6
Franco-Prussian War, 177–8
Frankfurt School, 211
Frederick, Prince, Duke of York and
  Albany (1763–1827), 172–3
Freedom Press Group, 272–3
freedom to roam, 122–3
Freeman, Arnold (*fl.* 1923), 251–2
Freeman, Edward Augustus (1823–92),
  196, 197
French, 114–15
French Revolution, 15–16, 83, 153,
  231–2
  impacts, 93
  and subsistence crisis, 20–1
French Situationists, 271
Freud, Sigmund (1856–1939), 21–2,
  214–23, 233
  Beyond the Pleasure Principle (1920), 218

biographies, 213–14
Civilization and its Discontents (1930),
  218
criticisms, 211–12, 213–14, 231–3
death, 218, 236
early reception of, 221–2
and feminism, 234
Hobsbawm's views of, 217–18
identity theories, 225–6
The Interpretation of Dreams (1899),
  219
mass psychology, 228
Moses and Monotheism (1939), 218
'Mourning and Melancholia' (1917),
  218
*New Introductory Lectures on Psycho-
  Analysis* (1933), 218
sexual theory, 215–16
terminology, 235–6
theories, 210–11, 218, 223
  neglect of, 216–17
friendly societies, 97–8
Friends of the Earth, 266–7
Friends of Italy, 191–2
Fromm, Erich Seligmann (1900–80),
  225–6
Fry, Roger (1866–1934), 214–15

Gaitskell, Hugh (1906–63), 287
Gallipoli (Turkey), 294
Gallup Poll, 248
Garibaldi, Giuseppe (1807–82), 193–4
Garibaldini, 192
gated communities, 142
Gay, Peter (1923–), 223
Geddes, Sir Patrick (1854–1932), 158
Geertz, Clifford (1926–2006), 32–3,
  229–30
gender differences, 6–7
gender equality, feminism and, 188
gender stereotypes, 106–7
General Enclosure Act (1845), 121,
  138–9
  criticisms, 124
  impacts, 121–2
  opposition to, 124, 126, 127–8
  provisions, 127–8
George II (1683–1760), 126–7
George IV (1762–1830), 165
George, Prince, Duke of Cambridge
  (1819–1904), 172–5, 178–9,
  184–5
Georgian England
  towns, 55–6
  versions of, 73

Gerassi, John, 274–7, 278, 280
German missions, 171–2
Germany
   communism, 146
   philosophical revolution, 148
   socialist movements, 206
Gestalt psychotherapy, 277–8
Ghosh, Durba, 100–1, 102
Gilbert, John (1927–), 294–5
Ginsberg, Irwin Allen (1926–97), 277–8,
      279, 280
Gladstone, William Ewart (1809–98),
      169–76, 177–81, 183–5, 251
   *Bulgarian Horrors and the Question of the
      East* (1876), 195–6
   criticisms, 179–80
   on Mackenzie, 197
   and 'Old Corruption', 176
   and Turkey, 197
Glasgow (Scotland), Independent Labour
      Party, 259–60
global liberal capitalism, 15–16
global trade, Britain, 21
Gloucester
   Barley-Market House, 59–60
   High Cross, 59–60
   Kings Board, 59–60
   market place, 59–60
   Wheat-Market House, 59–60
Glyn, George, 2nd Baron Wolverton
      (1824–87), 180–1
Gobind Singh, Guru (1666–1708), 281
Goldmann, Lucien (1913–), 276
golf, and commons riots, 133–4
Gombrich, Ernst (1909–2001), criticisms,
      213–14
Goodman, Paul (1911–72), 277–8, 279
Gough, Richard (1735–1809), 43
government
   big, 266–7
   coalition, 170–1, 185–6, 248, 250
   integration, 90
   Liberal, 290
   overgrown, 82
   roles, 92–3, 98–9
      in promoting social welfare,
         89–99
   shrinkage, 85, 88–9
   use of term, 79, 99
   and wars, 83
   see also central government; civil
      government; Conservative
      governments; Labour governments;
      local government; National
      Government
government growth
   1780–1830, 74–99
   conceptual issues, 78
   Dicey's views, 75–6
   quantifying, 82–5
   studies
      early, 74–6
      recent, 76–8
government interference, arguments
      against, 99
government salaries, 169–70
governmentality, and kinship, 102
Gramsci, Antonio (1891–1937), 8–9,
      267–8
Grassby, Richard, 100
grazing
   commons, 135
   rights, 132–3
Great Britain *see* Britain
Great Exhibition (1851), 170–1
Great War *see* World War I (1914–18)
Greater London Council, 296
Greece
   independence, 191–2
   liberation, 191
Greek Orthodox Church, 197
Green movement, 120
Green Party, 269
Greenpeace, 266–7
Greenwood, Arthur (1880–1954), 259–60
Grenville, William Wyndham
      (1759–1834), 93, 94, 95
Grey, Charles, 2nd Earl Grey, Viscount
      Howick (1764–1845), 169–70
   army reforms, 167–8
Griffiths, Clare, 139–40
Guardian, The, 15, 142
guilds, 148
Gunn, Simon, 143
Gutzkow, Karl Ferdinand (1811–78), 144

Hackney (Greater London), 296
Hackney Downs (London), 129–30
Halifax (West Yorkshire), market place, 60
Hall, Catherine, 100
Hall, Stuart (1932–), 8–9, 264–5
Hallas, Eldred (1870–1926), 241–2
Hamilton, Harriet Baillie (c. 1812–1884),
      193–4
Hamilton-Gordon, Ishbel Maria,
      Marchioness of Aberdeen and
      Temair (1857–1939), 206
Hammond, Barbara (née Bradby)
      (1873–1961), 118–19
   The Village Labourer (1911), 139–40

Hammond, John Lawrence (1872–1949), 118–19
  The Village Labourer (1911), 139–40
Hampstead Heath (London), 128, 129, 136
Hapsburg Empire, 192–4, 200, 208
harems, 195–6, 198, 200–1, 209
Harling, Philip, 77–8, 82, 83–4, 85
Harvey Lewis, John (b. 1812), 173–5
Haussmann, Georges-Eugène (1809–91), 154–5, 159
  legacies, 155–6
Haussmannisation, 156–7, 158, 160, 162
Hawes, Christopher, 100–1
Hegel, Georg Wilhelm Friedrich (1770–1831), 265
  Feuerbach's criticisms, 145–6
Hegelianism, 144–6, 150–1
hegemony, 267
Henderson, Arthur (1863–1935), 242–3, 244–5
Hendrix, Jimi (1942–70), 271–2
Henry VIII (1491–1547), 290
Henry, Jules (1904–69), 274–5
Herbert, Auberon (1838–1906), 173–5
Hereford, market place, shambles, 63
Herzegovinians, 200–1
Heseltine, Michael (1933–), 296–7, 299
Hess, Moses (1812–75), 146, 147, 148
Hey, D., 43
Highland Clearances, 120
Hill, Christopher (1912–2003), 217–18
Hill, Octavia (1838–1912), 199
Hilton, Boyd, 87–8
  Age of Atonement (1988), 85–6
  Oxford History of England (2006), 85
Hindus, 293
Hippies, 278
l'histoire totale see total history
historical biographers, Freudian, 223–4
historiography
  of British womens' internationalism, 207–8
  Conservative Party, 248–9
  of fascism, 222–3
  Labour Party, 248–9
  Marxist, 1
  and modernism, 234–5
  see also British historiography
history
  as craft, 217–18
  crowds in, 226–7, 229–30
  economic, 2
  field of study, 219–20
  Foucauldian cultural, 16–17
  politicised, 21
  and psychoanalysis, 210–36
  serious, 220–1
  theoretical foundations, 8–9
  theories of, 4
  urban, 2–3
  use of term, 219–20
  see also British history; social history; total history
history seminars, 11–12
History Workshop Journal (*HWJ*), 5, 10–11
  emergence, 234
History Workshop movement, 5, 10–11, 234
Hitchcock, Tim, 56–7
Hobhouse, Emily (1860–1926), 203, 204–7, 208
Hobsbawm, Eric (1917–), 1, 14–15, 211, 216–17, 222–3, 224–5
  Captain Swing (1968), 228–9
  crowds in history theory, 226–7, 229–30
  and Freud, 217–18
  Interesting Times (2002), 227–8
Hobson, John Atkinson (1858–1940), *The Psychology of Jingoism* (1901), 226–7
Hoey, Frances Cashel (1830–1908), 198–9
Hoggart, Richard (1918–), *The Uses of Literacy* (1957), 12–13
Holocaust, 278
Home Counties, encroachments, 135–6
Home Office, 74–5
Home Rule (Ireland), 180–2, 204–5, 290, 293
Honor Oak (London), 133–4
honours system, 180–1
Hopkins, S. V., 26
Hoppit, Julian, 83
Hornsey School of Art, 265–6
Horowitz, Michael (1935–), 'Live New Departures', 271–2
Horse Guards, 176
Houghton, Douglas, Baron Houghton of Sowerby (1898–1996), 286–7
House of Commons, 122–3, 127–8, 290, 294–5, 299
  petitions to, 128
House of Lords, 290, 297
Housing Market Renewal Funds, 162
Howick, Viscount *see* Grey, Charles, 2nd Earl Grey, Viscount Howick (1764–1845)
Howkins, Alan, 22
Huddersfield (West Yorkshire), market place, 69–70

humanism, 10–11, 240
   socialist, 225–6
humanitarianism, 251–2
Hume, Joseph (1777–1855), 124, 169–70
hundreds
   employment opportunities, 44
   population change, 35
   population growth, 36–43
      fast, 44–8, 52
      slow, 44–8, 52
Hungary
   crisis (1956), 225–6, 262–3
   independence movements, 192–3
Hunt, Margaret, 101–2
Huskisson, William (1770–1830), 86–7
Hutton, William (1723–1815), 67
Huxley, Aldous (1894–1963), 214–16
HWJ see *History Workshop Journal* (*HWJ*)
Hyde Park (London), 129–30
Hyndman, Henry (1842–1921), 156

Ibrahim Pasha of Egypt (1789–1848),
   191
ICW (International Council of Women),
   205–6
id, 218
identity, Freud's theories, 225–6
ideology
   and Marxism, 16–17
   vs. political decisions, 86–7
idlers, vs. producers, 239–40
IGR (intrinsic growth rate), 24–5
Iliffe, John, 293
illegal commoners
   activities, 134–5, 141
   rights, 134–5
illegitimate children, in colonial India,
   100–3, 111–17
ILP see Independent Labour Party (ILP)
IMF (International Monetary Fund), 159
immigrants
   assimilation, 285–8, 298
   British reactions to, 283–4
   and conservative pluralism, 288
   exclusion, 281–5
   Irish, 150
   and multiculturalism, 294–9
   trade union resistance to, 286–7
immigration controls, 285
imperialism, 21, 157, 278
Inclosure Commission, 121, 136
income elasticity of demand, food, 31–2
Independent Labour Party (ILP)
   Glasgow, 259–60
   pamphlets, 238–9, 256–7

India, 198, 279, 294
   19th century, and British family
      functions, 100–17
   British women in, 187–8
   sanitary policies, 158
   suttee, 209
   see also colonial India
Indian Army, 293
Indian Muslims, 197
Indian Mutiny (1857), 102, 293
individualism, 75–6, 85
industrial capitalism, 15–16
Industrial Revolution, 4, 226–7
   economic growth, 25–6
   Engels's views, 148
   histories of, 5–6
   population growth, 25–6, 51
industrialisation, 5–6
   critiques, Engels's, 144
   nuclear family and, 100
   and public spaces, 122–3
industrious classes, 239–40
information, access issues, 208–9
Inland Revenue Staff Federation, 286–7
Inner Cities Religious Council, 301
Innes, Joanna, 22
innovation, lack of, 91
Institute for Economic Affairs, 264–5
Institute of Historical Research, 234
Institute of Phenomenological Studies, 274
institutional conservatism, 183–4
institutional reform
   1867 and new politics, 177–8
   decline, in 19th century Britain, 164–86
   elites and, 185–6
   historical background, 164–5
   Liberal, 183–4
   redefining (1850–70), 171–7
instrumentalism, 12–13
interconnections, 18–19
interference, principle of, 74–5
International Council of Women (ICW),
   205–6
International Marxist Group, 265–6
International Monetary Fund (IMF), 159
International Poetry Incarnation (1965),
   271–2
International Times (*IT*), 271–2, 273
International Woman Suffrage Alliance
   (IWSA), 205–6, 207
internationalism
   British womens', historiography, 207–8
   cultures of, British women and, 209
   limitations, 205–7
   male vs. female, 187–8

internationalism (cont.)
  see also female internationalism
intrinsic growth rate (IGR), 24–5
inversion, 283–4
*Involving Communities in Urban and Rural
  Regeneration* (1997), 301
Ionesco, Eugène (1909–94), 270
Ipswich (Suffolk), 138
Iraq, 269
Irby, Adeline Pauline (1831–1911), 197
Ireland
  Home Rule, 180–2, 204–5, 290, 293
  nationalism, 290
Irish, prejudices against, 108–9
Irish Famine, 120
Irish immigrants, 150
Irish Nationalists, 125
Irish republicanism, 129–30
Irk, River, Ducie Bridge, 149–50
Ironfounders' Society, 242–3
Islam, 197
  politicised, 300–1
  schools, 301–2
  see also Muslims
Islamic Cultural Centre, 301–2
Islington (London), Campbell Bunk,
  159–60
Israel, 270
IT (*International Times*), 271–2, 273
Italian unification movement, 187–8,
  192–5, 208–9
Italy, and female imagination, 192–5
IWSA (International Woman Suffrage
  Alliance), 205–6, 207

Jacquerie (1358), 226–7
Jakobsen, Roman (1896–1982), 214–15
Jarvis, David, 246
Jenkinson, Robert, 2nd Earl of Liverpool
  (1770–1828), 79, 95
  and 'Old Corruption', 165–6
Jerusalem, 201
Jesuits, 197
Jews, 191, 192, 208, 270, 293, 294
  emancipation, 295
  marriage, 291–2
  schools, 290–1
jingoism, 200, 226–7
Johnson, Samuel (1709–84), 116
Johnston, Priscilla (d. 1912), 197
Jolly, Sohan Singh, 281–2, 289
Jones, Alfred Ernest (1879–1958), 213–14,
  215–16
Joyce, Patrick (1945–), 7–8
Judea, 201

Jupp, Peter (1940–2006), 82
  'The Landed Elite and Political
    Authority in Britain, c. 1760–1850'
    (1990), 77–8

Karrenbinder, 144
Kay-Shuttleworth, James Phillips
  (1804–77), 149–50
Kendal (Cumbria), pillories, 66–7
Kennington Common (London), 129
Kensington (London), Jennings' Buildings,
  159–60
Kent, evictions, 130–1
Kent and Sussex Labourers Union,
  130–1
kesh, 281
Keynes, John Maynard (1883–1946), *The
  Economic Consequences of the Peace*
  (1919), 214–15
Khalsa, 293
kin
  financial mechanisms, 102
  loyalty to, 101–2
King, Anthony D., *Colonial Urban
  Development* (1976), 158
King's College (Cambridge), 16–17
  Centre for History and Economics,
    14–15
Kingsley, Charles (1819–75), 220–1
Kingsley Hall (London), 271–2
kinship, and governmentality, 102
Kitson Clark, George Sidney Roberts
  (1900–75), 2–3
Klein, Melanie (1882–1960), 218
Kleinian psychoanalysis, 223, 234
Knight, Anne (1786–1862), 189–90
Knight, Charles (1791–1873), 69–70
Kortright, Fanny Aikin (1821–1900),
  198–9

laagers, 142
labour
  and armed services, 47–8
  dignity of, 240, 253
  nobility of, 240
  and ownership, 147–8
  representation of, 5
  wage, 119–20, 256–7
labour demand, agriculture, 47
Labour governments, 263, 281–2, 294–5
  goals, 286
  and immigration, 288
labour history, 2
Labour Leader, 242
labour movement, growth of, 5

Labour Party, 17–18, 138–9, 183–4
    and assimilation, 286–7
    and class feeling, 239–40
    as class party, 243–4
    and class politics (1900–40), 237
    and commons, 139–40
    Constitution (1918), 241–2
    decline, 248
    elections, 254, 257–8, 261–2, 301–2
    emergence, 3–4
    heartlands, 246–7
    historiography, 248–9
    leaders, 244–5
    membership, 242
    and middle class, 253–8
    modernisation, 264–5
    and National Government, 259
    political visions, 22
    politics, language of, 248–53
    popular alliances, 247
    propaganda, 243–4, 249–50
    and rail strikes, 238–9
    reconstruction, 274
    roles, 5
    strategies, 240–1
    and working class, 240, 253–8, 259
    and World War II, 259–60
    see also Independent Labour Party (ILP)
Labour Representation Committee,
    241–2
labourers
    poverty, 137
    studies, 228
    see also agricultural labourers
Labourism, 8–9
Lacan, Jacques (1901–81), 268–9
Laing, Ronald David (1927–89), 271–2,
    274, 277–8, 279
Lambeth (London), South London
    Chartist Hall, 126
Lancashire, 143
    commons, 129
    population growth, 49
land
    nationalisation, 129–30, 138
    pressure on, 31–2
    see also commons
land acquisition, parish councils, 138
Land Inquiry, 138
land ownership, and commons, 118–19
land reform, 138
land taxes, 129–30
land use, and population growth, 48
landed property, 126
    Chartists and, 126–7

Langer, William L. (1898–1977), 222–3
language, of Labour Party politics, 248–53
Lansbury, George (1859–1940), 251–2
Lawrence, D. H. (1885–1930), 214–19,
    238–9
Lawrence, Jon, 22
Layard, Austen Henry (1817–94), 170–1,
    175–6
Le Bon, Gustave (1841–1931), 226–7
Leary, Timothy Francis (1920–96), 271
LEAs (local education authorities), 295–6,
    297
Leavis, Frank Raymond (1895–1978),
    217–18
Leeds (West Yorkshire), 129–30, 247
Lefebvre, Henri (1901–91), 142–3
legal system
    administration, 91–2
    expenditures, 83–4
legislation, science of, 93
Leicester
    market crosses, 61–2
    market place, 60–1
Leipzig (Germany), 160–1
Lenin, Vladimir (1870–1924), 279
Leninism, 10–11
Leonard, Graham Douglas (1921–2010),
    297
Lessing, Doris (1919–), 272
Lévi-Strauss, Claude (1908–2009), 214–15
Liberal coalition, 170–1, 185–6
Liberal governments, 290
Liberal institutional reformism, 183–4
liberal modernity, 19–20
Liberal Party, 138, 181–2, 183–5
    causes, 252
    criticisms, 250
    elections, 290
    miners' legislation, 237–8
liberal radicalism, 179–80
    and proto-socialism, 129–30
Liberal sectionalism, 181–3
Liberal Tories, 165–6, 170–1
    strategies, 168–9
liberalism, 4, 239–40
    civil rights, 87–8
    and feminism, 202–3
    socio-economic, 87–8
    use of term, 87–8
    varieties of, 85–9
liberals
    feminist, 202–3
    use of term, 87–8
liberation, dialectics of, 261–80
linguistic theory, structuralist, 14–15

linguistic turn, 13–15, 22–3, 248–9, 268–9
Little Ireland (Greater Manchester), 148, 155–6
Liverpool, Lord see Jenkinson, Robert, 2nd Earl of Liverpool (1770–1828)
Liverpool (Merseyside), 169–70
    Croxteth, 162–3
    Gold Zone regeneration, 162–3
    Norris Green, 162–3
Lloyd George, David (1863–1945), 138, 252
local education authorities (LEAs), 295–6, 297
local government, 78–9
    expenditures, 84
    use of term, 79–80
Local Government Acts
    1858, 79–80
    1966, 288
Local Government Board, 79–80
London, 261
    Cannon Street Hotel, 198
    class zoning, 152
    commons, 129–30, 136
        mineral rights, 136
    East End, 156–7, 163
    encroachments, 135–6
    ethnic minorities, 296
    Grosvenor Square, 265–6
    Hyde Park, 129–30
    immigrants, 283–4
    Kensington Girls' School, 198–9
    Kingsley Hall, 271–2
    Labour Party control of, 255
    Pall Mall, 176
    Piccadilly, St James's Hall, 201
    poor, 12–13
    population growth, 33–5
    poverty, 163
    Primrose Hill, 154–5
    protests, 265–6, 267–8
    radical Islam, 163
    regeneration, 156
    Roundhouse, 274
    Royal Albert Hall, 271–2
    St Giles, 152
    St Pancras North, 251–2
    spatial authority, 157
    street life, 56–7
    Theatre of the Absurd, 270
    toryism, 9–10
    Trafalgar Square, 142
    West End, 246
    Westminster, 289–90

London Central Mosque, 301–2
London Education Authority, 295–6
London Free School, 271–2
London Labour Party, 255
London School of Economics (LSE), 265–6
Lowe, Robert, Viscount Sherbrooke (1811–92), 170–1, 176
LSE (London School of Economics), 265–6
Luddism, 226–7
Lukács, Georg (1885–1971), 8–9, 13–14
lumpenproletariat, 150, 153–4, 161–2
    use of term, 144
Lyttle, John, 287

MacDonald, James Ramsay (1866–1937), 239–40, 243–4, 250, 251–2, 253–4, 255–6
Macfarlane, Alan, 100
McGovern, John (1887–1968), 259–60
Mackenzie, Georgina Muir (1833–74), 197
    Travels in the Slavonic Provinces of Turkey-in-Europe (1867), 197
McKibbin, Ross, 246, 248
MacLaughlin, Louisa (1836–1921), 196
MacMaster, Neil, 134
Madras (India), 105, 158
magistrates, salaries, 91–2
male internationalism, vs. female internationalism, 187–8
Malinowski, Bronislaw Kasper (1884–1942), 214–15
Malleson, Elizabeth (1828–1916), 196, 200–1
Malta, 183–4
Maltby (North Yorkshire), 131
Malthus, Thomas Robert (1766–1834), 20–1, 30–1, 44, 93–4
    Essay on the Principle of Population (1798), 93
Manchester (Greater Manchester), 4, 137, 143, 147, 148, 160–1
    and British Empire, 158
    Broughton, 151
    Cheetham Hill, 151
    Chorlton, 151, 152
    city centre, 162–3
    class zoning, 151–2
    de Tocqueville's views, 153
    Deansgate, 151
    Engels and, 143–4, 150–1
    Gorton, 162–3
    Hulme, 152
    hypocritical planning of, 153

insanitary conditions, 149–50
Irish immigrants, 150
Moss Side, 162–3
multicultural education, 295–6
Oxford Road, 155–6
Pendleton, 151
spatial authority, 157
turbans on buses, 286–7
Mandler, Peter, 77–8, 82, 83–4, 85
manners, reform, 97–8
Marcus, Steven, 143
Marcuse, Herbert (1898–1979), 276–7
Mario, Jessie White (1832–1906), 193
market crosses
medieval, 61
preservation, 62
removal, 61–2
market-places
and demonstrations, 71
historical background, 58–9
improvements, 57–65, 64–5
medieval, 58–9
new, 59
political meetings in, 72
and political protests, 70–1
political significance, 72
and popular entertainment, 69–70
and public punishment, 66
renewal, 63–4
reorganisation, 64–5, 67
roles, 57–8
shambles, 63, 71
sheds, tenements and encroachments,
    62–3
and traffic, 62–3
and urban renaissance, 73
useage, 60–1
Marley, James (1893–1954), 251–2
marriage, 35
and capitalism, 100
and fertility rates, 51–2
Jews, 291–2
legitimate, 100–1
and slavery, 190
Marriage Registration Act (1836), 291–2
Marx, Eleanor (1855–98), 156
Marx, Karl (1818–83), 4, 126–7, 154,
    193–4, 265
Das Kapital (1867), 150–1
early obscurity, 212–13
Marxism, 211–13, 217–18
capitalist critiques, 142–3
and class analysis, 2
early, 147
European, 274–5

history of, 17–18
and ideology, 16–17
and psychoanalysis, 229–30
and social history, 2–3
and Stedman Jones, 15–16
Western, 267–8
Marxism Today (journal), 264–5
Marxism–Leninism, 4
Marxist historians, 8–9, 210–11, 216–17
Marxist historiography, 1
Marxist models, 267–8
Mason, Tim (1940–90), and Stedman
    Jones, 11–12
mass demonstrations, 227–8
mass hysteria, 226
mass meetings, 72
mass psychology, 228
mass violence, 227–8
Masschaele, James, 58–9
masses, approaches to, 226–7
material turn, 161–2
materialism, Feuerbach's, 147
Matterdale Common (Cumbria), 132–3
Mayhew, Henry (1812–87), 153–4
Mayne, Alan, Imagined Slum (1993),
    159–62
Mazzini, Giuseppe (1805–72), 191–2,
    192–5
    I doveri delluomo (1860), 194
Mazzinism, 192–5
meaning, 7–8
meetings, public, 72
Mellor, Rosemary, 162–3
Members of Parliament (MPs), Scottish,
    289–90
mental illness, 271
Methodism, 225–6
    iconography, 226
metropolitan commons, 136
Metropolitan Police Act (1829), 96
M'Grath, Philip (fl. 1845), 126
Miall, Edward (1809–81), 175–6
middle class
    brain workers of, 258
    Labour Party and, 253–8
    radicalism, 248
    socialism and, 257
middle-class residences, and commons,
    133–4
Middleton, Sir George (1876–1938),
    252–3
Midgley, Clare, 190
Milgram, Stanley (1933–84), 278
militarism, 200
    critiques, 207–8

Military Cantonments Act (1864), 158
military flogging, 181
military policies, 184–5
Mill, John Stuart (1806–73), 131, 164
    On the Subjection of Women (1869), 190
millennialism, 191–2
Milligan, George Jardine (1868–1925),
    241–2
mineral rights, commons, 136
mineral-based energy economies, 35, 49
miners, legislation, 237–8
miners' strikes, 238–9
Mingay, Gordon Edmund (1923–2006),
    119–20
ministers, roles, 91, 92–3, 96
minorities
    religious, 291–2
    see also ethnic minorities
Minto (Scotland), 104, 116
Misuse of Drugs Act (1970), 273
Mitchell, Juliet (1940–), *Psychoanalysis and
    Feminism* (1974), 234
mixed-race children, of British fathers,
    100–1
mobs
    and pillories, 67–8
    and urban renaissance, 54–7
modernism, 219, 221–2
    and historiography, 234–5
modernist experimentalism, 218
Modeste (ship), 103–4
monarchy, reform, 164–5
moorland, enclosure, 132–3
Moral Reform Union, 200–2
Mordaunt, Sir Charles, 10th Baronet
    (1836–97), 173–5
More, Hannah (1745–1833), 189
More, Sir Thomas (1478–1535), 29–30, 32
Morris, Jan (1926–), 157
Morris, R. J., 101–2
Morrison, Herbert (1888–1965), 255
mortality, 24
motor cycle helmets, Sikhs and, 283,
    284, 287–8, 294–5
Mousehold Heath (Norwich), 134
Mulley, Frederick William (1918–95),
    287–8
multicultural politics, in British history,
    281–302
multiculturalism, 21
    antecedents, 299–300
    dilemmas, 283
    and education, 295–6
    emergence, 284–5
    immigrants and, 294–9

United Kingdom, 289–90
    use of term, 289
    vs. religion, 300–1
Municipal Corporations Act (1835), 167
Muslim schools, 297
    Church of England and, 301–2
    state-funded, 301–2
Muslims, 198
    Indian, 197
    self-segregation, 300–1
    see also Islam
Myddle (Shropshire), population
    growth, 43

Nairn, Tom (1932–), 8–10
Namier, Sir Lewis Bernstein (1888–1960),
    221–2
Naples (Italy), 192, 208–9
Napoleon III (1808–73), 154–5, 171–2,
    173
Napoleonic Wars, 88–9, 165
Nathan, Sarah, 192
national culture
    and psychoanalysis, 210–36
    use of term, 212
National Curriculum Council, 297
National Education League, 181
National Education Union, 181
National Front, 284
National Government, 248, 289–90
    Labour Party and, 259
national institutions, reform, 164–5
National Insurance, establishment, 74–5
National Liberal Federation, 181–2
National Republican League, 129–30
National Society for Aid to the Sick and
    Wounded in War, 196
National Viewers' and Listeners'
    Association, 264–5
nationalisation, of land, 129–30, 138
nationalism
    Irish, 290
    Scottish, 289–90
native law, 292
Navarino, Battle of (1827), 191
Navickas, Katrina, 129
Nazis, 221–2, 270
Neeson, Jeanette, 134–5, 140
    Commoners (1993), 119–20
Negroes, 278
Neighbourhood Renewal Strategies, 162
networks, transnational, 20, 21
New Deal for Communities, 162
New Forest (Hampshire), 132–3
    commoner associations, 133–4

Court of Verderers, 133
illegal commoner activities, 134–5
middle-class residences and, 133–4
New Labour, 264–5
New Left, 8–10
and counter-culture, 261–80
New Left Review (NLR) (journal), 9–11,
212, 267
establishment, 262–3
and student movement, 267–8
New Liberals, 226–7
New Moral World, The (journal), 147–8
New Poor Law (1834), 74–5, 84
'New Power in Politics, The' (1936), 256
New Society (journal), 272–3
Newark (Peterborough), butchers, 69
Newcastle Programme (1891), 181–2
Nietzsche, Friedrich Wilhelm
(1844–1900), 218, 221–2
Nightingale, Florence (1820–1910), 197,
199
NLR see New Left Review (NLR) (journal)
nonconformism, 172–3, 175–6, 179–80,
184–5, 263, 293
Norman Invasion (1066), 58
Norman Yoke, concept of, 126
North America, 266–7
Northcote–Trevelyan Report (1854),
169–70
Northern Echo, 195
Northern Star, 132
Norwich
Mousehold Heath, 134
Pockthorpe, 134, 136
Nottingham
market crosses, 61–2
market place, 60–1, 68–9
pillories, 66
political protests, 70–1
nuclear family, and industrialisation, 100
Nuffield College (Oxford), 10–11
nuptiality, 24
nursing, 196, 197

Obscene Publications Acts (1959; 1964),
273
obscenity offences, 273
Oedipus complex, 215–16, 226
O'Gorman, Frank, 55–6
Old Age Pension, establishment, 74–5
'Old Corruption', 173, 176
decline of, 165–71
Gladstone and, 176
language of, 177–8
Old Left, and counter-culture, 261–80

Olivier, Laurence (1907–89), 215–16
One Tree Hill, Battle of (1897), 133–4
open spaces *see* public spaces
open-field system, 118
Orange Free State (South Africa), 203
Orders in Council (1920), 292
organic economies, 28, 29–30, 48
Orwell, George (*pseud.*) (Eric Blair)
(1903–50), 235–6
Osborne, Ralph Bernal (1808–82), 169–70
Ossoli, Margaret Fuller (1810–50), 193
Oswald, Friedrich *see* Engels, Friedrich
(1820–95)
Ottoman Empire, 191, 193–4, 208
Christians in, 187–8, 195–203
overgrown government, 82
overseers of the poor, salaries, 91–2
Owenites, 147–8
ownership, and labour, 147–8
Oxford, University of, 11–12, 219–20,
262–5
Nuffield College, 10–11
Ruskin College, 10–11
Oz (magazine), 273

pacifism, British women and, 187–8, 200,
206–7
Paine, Thomas (1737–1809), 15–16,
17–18
Palestine, 191
Palmerston, Henry John Temple, 3rd
Viscount Palmerston (1784–1865),
168, 170–2
Pankhurst, Christabel (1880–1958), 202–3
Paris (France), 146, 268–9
British embassy, 169–70, 171–2
post-war, 270
regeneration, 154–5
riots, 265–6
spatial authority, 157
parish councils, 138–9
land acquisition, 138
Parish Register Abstract (PRA), 35
parish registers, 24, 35
parishes
policy-making, 91–2
population change, 35
'Parliamentary Enclosure by Private Bill',
120–1
Parliamentary Labour Party, 286–7
parliamentary reform, 185–6
Parliamentary Select Committee on Open
Spaces (Metropolis), 128
parochial schools, 92–3
Parry, Jonathan, 22

Parsons, Talcott (1902–79), 100, 214–15
Past and Present (journal), 224–5, 226–7
patriarchy, critiques, 198
patriotism, 185–6, 203, 204–5, 220–1, 250, 251
patronage, and honours system, 180–1
Pavlov, Ivan (1849–1936), 214–15
Pearson, Emma Maria (1828–93), 196
peasant class, and enclosure, 118
Peckham Rye (London), 136
Peel, Sir Robert, 2nd Baronet (1788–1850), 96, 168–9
Peelites, 168–9, 185–6
Pelling, Henry Mathison (1920–97), 8–9
Penson, L. M., 184–5
people, state of the, 98
People's Political Union, 129–30
Perceval, Spencer (1762–1812), 95
Perham, Dame Margery (1895–1982), 292
Perkin, Harold James (1926–2004), 4
Peterloo Massacre (1819), 72
Petertavy Common (Devonshire), 133
petitions, 126, 128, 131, 198
Phelan, Laura, 133–4
Phelps Brown, E. H., 26
Philadelphia Association, 274
philosophical revolutions, 148
Pick, Daniel, 21–2
pillories, 59–60, 66
    decline, 66, 67, 68
    escape from, 67
    mobs and, 67–8
    removal, 60
    survival, 66–7
    see also stocks
Pink Floyd (band), 271–2
Pinter, Harold (1930–2008), 270
Pitt, William, the Younger (1759–1806), 79, 93–4, 95, 98, 165–6
Pittite-Peelite reforms, 171–2
plebeians
    consumption, 69–70
    popular entertainment, 56–7
    and public spaces, 55–6, 73
    sociability, 69–70
Plumstead (London), 130–1
pluralism, 13–14, 283–4, 298–9
    barriers to, 298
    in Colonies, 292
    conservative, 288, 294, 301
    cultural, 295–6
    history of, 284–5
    justifications, 299–300
    religious, 291–2

and religious diversity, 290–1
    structural features, 300–1
Pockthorpe (Norwich), 134
    brickfields, 136
Pocock, John Greville Agard (1924–), 16–17
pogroms, Russian, 208
Poland, independence movements, 192–3
policemen, and turbans, 282, 283
policies
    Conservative, 296–7
    foreign, 184–5
    military, 184–5
    public, 98
    sanitary, 158
    see also social policy
policy-making, 95, 96
    parishes, 91–2
    processes, 90
political activism, 146
political celebrations, in Stuart England, 55–6
political decisions, vs. ideology, 86–7
political economy, 16–17
political imagery, transformations in, 22
political meetings, in market places, 72
political protests, and market places, 70–1
political revolutions, 148
politics
    social, 184–5
    street, 55–6
    of turbans, 281–302
    see also class politics; cultural politics; radical politics
poor law expenditure
    and population growth, 45, 46–8
    regional differences, 84
poor laws, 44
    1834, 74–5, 84
Popes, 191–2
populace, improvements, 65–72
popular culture, history of, 2–3
popular entertainment
    18th century, 56–7
    and market places, 69–70
popularism, 12–13
population change
    and agriculture, 33–5
    hundreds, 35
    parishes, 35
    and urbanisation, 33–5
    and wage change, 27–9, 31
population growth, 290–1
    Elizabethan period, 36–9
    geographical differences, 40–2

hundreds, 36–43
    fast, 44–8, 52
    slow, 44–8, 52
    and land use, 48
    percentage rise, 41–2
    and poor law expenditure, 45, 46–8
    rapid, 20, 24–53
    simplified models, 43
    sustained, 20–1, 28–9
population growth rate, peak, 51–2
populism, 252–3
Portsmouth (Hampshire), 131
positivism, in British historiography, 8–9
post-modernism, 7–8
post-structuralism, 14–15, 229–30, 268–9
Potter, Richard ('Radical Dick')
    (1778–1842), 123
Potter, Thomas Bayley (1817–98), 184–5
poverty
    child, 163
    ending, 15–16
    experience of, 11–12
    labourers, 137
Powell, Enoch (1912–98), 264–5, 284, 294
    'rivers of blood' speech, 283–4, 288
Powellism, 298–9
power, images of, 211
PRA (Parish Register Abstract), 35
pre-modern states, 81
prejudice
    against Irish, 108–9
    anti-Muslim, 198
    anti-Turkish, 198
    class, 244, 253
    racial, 105–6
Preston (Lancashire), 137
primary employment, 49
Primrose, Archibald, 5th Earl of Rosebery
    (1847–1929), 183–4
Primrose Hill (London), 123
Primrose League, 202–3
prison reforms, 189–90
privatisation, of public spaces, 142
privilege, 244, 253
    of birth, 252
    urban, 246
    of wealth, 252
    see also class privilege
Privy Council, education grants, 74–5
process, use of term, 19–20
producers, vs. idlers, 239–40
production
    capitalist vs. socialist, 257–8
    means of, and urban analysis,
        142–3

social relations of, and spatial
    function, 142
propaganda, Labour Party, 243–4, 249–50
property
    Engels's views, 148
    Proudhon's views, 147–8
    see also landed property
property relations, analyses, 101–2
prostitution, 209
    and slavery, 190
    state registration, 190–1
protectionism, 252
Protestantism, 290–1
    British, 191–2
    British women and, 188–9
    opposition to slavery, 190
    virtual, 192
    see also Christianity
protests, 271–2
    France, 265–6, 279–80
    London, 265–6, 267–8
    political, 70–1
    Sikhs, 281–2, 288
    single-issue, 271–2
    see also demonstrations; riots
proto-socialism, and liberal radicalism,
    129–30
Proudhon, Pierre-Joseph (1809–65), *What
    is Property?* (1840), 147–8
Proudhonism, 154–5
Provisional Orders, 121
psychedelic bands, 271–2
psychiatrists, radical, 277–8
psycho-historians, 222–3, 226
psychoanalysis, 21–2
    criticisms, 276–7
    and feminism, 234
    and history, 210–36
    history of, 218
    importance of, 233
    Kleinian, 223, 234
    and Marxism, 229–30
    and national culture, 210–36
    relevance, 231
    theories, 268–9
Psychoanalysis and History (journal), 234
psychologism, 213–14
psychology, mass, 228
public, concepts of, 256
public access
    commons, 127–8
    wastes, 127–8
public acts, decline in, 83
public amenities, commons as, 122–3
public executions, 68

public expenditure, trends, 83
public policies, goals, 98
public punishment, 66
  see also pillories; stocks
public services, financing, 90
public spaces
  18th century, 73
  control of, 142
  elites and, 73
  and industrialisation, 122–3
  plebeians and, 55–6, 73
  privatisation, 142
  provision, 122–3
  and urbanisation, 122–3
  useage, 65
  see also market-places
public speaking, 72
public walks, 123–5, 128
punishment
  corporal, 68
  public, 66
  see also pillories; stocks
Punjab (India), 293

Quakers, 189–90, 201–2

race
  definitions of, 116
  and families, 116
race relations, 285
Race Relations Act (1976), 298
Race Relations Board, 284, 287–8
racial alterity, 100–1, 115–16
racial disadvantage, 296–7, 298–9
racial discrimination, 286–7
racial prejudice, in colonial India,
    105–6
racialism, opposition to, 287
radical campaigns, 177
radical histories, and enclosure of
    commons, 118–41
radical Islam, 163
radical politics, 21–2, 169–70
  and social change, 20
Radical Programme (1885), 184–5
radical psychiatrists, 277–8
radicalism
  and commons, 129–30
  discourses of, 22
  middle class, 248
  popular, 252
  see also liberal radicalism
radicals, 86–7, 185–6
  and commons, 136–7
  political meetings, 72

religious, 167–8
  sinecure lists, 165
rail strikes, 238–9
Railway Clerks Association (RCA), 253–4
raw materials, demand for, 29–30
RCA (Railway Clerks Association), 253–4
Readman, Paul, 138–9
Rees, Merlyn (1920–2006), 298–9
Reform Acts, 185–6
  1832, 77–8, 167–8
Reform crisis (1832), 2, 167–8
reformers, 89–90, 98
reforming manners, use of term, 97–8
reformism, 12–13, 97–8
reforms
  church, 93, 94, 172–3
  constitutional, 185–6
  educational, 170–1
  land, 138
  manners, 97–8
  monarchy, 164–5
  parliamentary, 185–6
  Pittite-Peelite, 171–2
  prison, 189–90
  see also army reforms; institutional reform
Regents Park (London), 123, 128
registration of births, deaths, and
    marriages, 24
Reich, Wilhelm (1897–1957), 222–3
Reid, Alastair, 21–2
relief organisations, 196, 200–2
religion
  British women and, 188–9
  vs. multiculturalism, 300–1
  see also Christianity; Islam; Jews
religious diversity, and pluralism, 290–1
religious minorities, 291–2
religious pluralism, 291–2
religious radicals, 167–8
rents, control of, 237–8
representation, field of study, 7–8
republicanism, 129–30, 173
residences, middle-class, 133–4
Restoration of Pre-War Practices Act
    (1919), 242–3
revisionism, 261–2
revisionist anarchism, 272–3, 277–8
revolutionary consciousness, 276–7
revolutions
  Bolshevik, 261
  cultural, 271
  philosophical, 148
  political, 148
  see also French Revolution; Industrial
    Revolution

Reynold's News, 138
Reynold's Newspaper, 126, 135–6
Reynolds, Stephen (1888–1919), 237
Rhodesia, 265–6
Ricardo, David (1772–1823), 29–30, 86
Riccall (North Yorkshire), 131
rich, stereotypes, 252
Richards, Graham, 218
  'Britain on the Couch' (2000), 235–6
Rickman, John (1771–1840), 35, 93–4
riots, 131, 226–8
  Brixton, 296–7, 299
  commons, 133–4
  food, 70–1
  urban, 295–6
  see also demonstrations; protests
risk management, familial strategies, 101–2
Risorgimento see Italian unification
  movement
Roberts, Robert (1905–79), 237
Robinson, George Frederick, 1st Marquess
  of Ripon, Viscount Goderich
  (1827–1909), 170–1
Rogers, James Edwin Thorold (1823–90),
  130–1
Rolls-Royce, 252
Roman Catholics, 290–1, 293
  emancipation, 94, 295
Romford (London), 250, 251–2
Roper, Lyndal, 234
Rose, Sir George (1744–1818), 93–4
Ross, Ellen, 157
Roundhouse (Camden), 274
Rousseau, Jean-Jacques (1712–78), 192–3
Royal Albert Hall (London), 271–2
Royal Commission, 161–2, 167–8
Royal Historical Society, 219–20
Royal Institution of Chartered Surveyors,
  142
Royal Shakespeare Company, 270
Rudé, George (1910–93), 226–7
  Captain Swing (1968), 228–9
Ruskin, John (1819–1900), 240
Ruskin College (Oxford), 10–11
Russell, Sir Henry (1751–1836), 105–6
Russell, Sir Henry II (1783–1852), 105–6
Russell, John (1792–1878), 123
Russia, 183–4, 191, 195–6
  pogroms, 208
Russian Orthodox Church, 197
Rylands, Peter (1820–87), 173–5, 177–8,
  184–5

sado-masochism, 226
Saffi, Georgina Craufurd (1827–1911), 193

Saigon (Vietnam), 281–2
St Albans (Hertfordshire), 254, 255
  market place, 69–70
St Petersburg (Russia), British embassy,
  171–2
salaries, 256–7
  government, 169–70
  reduction, 171–2
Salford (Greater Manchester), 143,
  147, 148
Samuel, Raphael (1934–96), 7–8, 9–10,
  230–1
  and History Workshop movement,
    10–11, 234
  and Stedman Jones, 11–12
Sandhu, Tarsem, 281
Sandwich (Kent), market place, 59
Sanitary Commissions, 158
sanitary policies, India, 158
Sartre, Jean-Paul (1905–80), 8–9
Sasun (Turkey), 201
Saussure, Ferdinand de (1857–1913), 14
Save the Turban Action Committee, 287–8
Saville, John (1916–2009), 262–3
Sax, Emil (1845–1927), *The Housing
  Conditions of the Working Classes and
  their Reform* (1869), 154–5
Schofield, Jonathan, 143
Schofield, R. S., *Population History of
  England* (1981), 25–6
School Kids' Issue (magazine), 273
school uniforms, Sikhs and, 283
schools
  faith-based, 290–1, 301–2
  parochial, 92–3
sciences, and cultural turn, 76
Scotland
  Members of Parliament, 289–90
  nationalism, 289–90
Scottish Nationalist Party (SNP), 289–90
Scottish Office, 289–90
Scutari (Turkey), 196
SDF (Social Democratic Federation),
  139–40, 241–2
SDP (Social Democratic Party of
  Germany), 247
Second World War *see* World War II
  (1939–45)
second-wave environmentalism, 266–7
second-wave feminism, 266–7
secondary employment, 49
secular education, 290–1
security, 257–8
  collective, 257
  social, 257, 258

Seeley, Sir John Robert (1834–95), 220–1
segregation, urban, 159
Select Committee on Official Salaries,
    169–70
Select Committees, 122–4, 134–5, 136,
    138, 171–2, 177–8
    on sinecures, 167
Selson (Nottinghamshire), 130–1
separation of church and state, 169–70
separatism, black, 274–5
Serbia, 197
Serbs, 195–6
Sewall, May Wright (1844–1920), 206
Sex Discrimination Act (1975), 298
sexual emancipation, 194–5
sexual identity, 6–7
sexual immorality, 198–9
sexual theory, Freud's, 215–16
Shaen, Emily Winkworth (1822–87),
    194–5
Shaftesbury, 7th Earl of (Anthony Ashley-
    Cooper) (1801–85), 191–2
Shakespeare, William (1564–1616)
    Hamlet (1599–1601), 215–16
    Othello (1603), 215–16
shambles, in market places, 63, 71
Sharman Crawford, William (1781–1861),
    125
Shaw, George Bernard (1856–1950),
    241–2
Shaw Lefevre, George, 1st Baron Eversley
    (1831–1928), 129
Shaw-Taylor, Leigh, 119–20, 134–5
sheds, and market places, 62–3
Sheffield (South Yorkshire)
    Crofts district, 161–2
    food riots, 71
    market place, 64–5
    Sheffield Hallam, 251–2
Shore, Arabella (c.1822–c.1899), 198–9,
    200
Shore, Louisa (1824–95), 198–9
Sicily (Italy), 208–9
signs, 230–1
Sikhism, 281
Sikhs
    and Anglicans, 294
    and motor cycle helmets, 283, 284,
        287–8, 294–5
    protests, 281–2, 288
    as soldiers, 293, 294
    and turbans, 281–302
sinecures
    lists, 165
    Select Committee on, 167

Skinner, Quentin (1940–), 16–17, 231
Skocpol, Theda (1947–), 14–15
slaughter houses, 69
slavery, 198–9
    abolition, 167, 189–90
    and marriage, 190
    outlawed, 292
    and prostitution, 190
    Protestant opposition to, 190
Slavonic Christians, 197
slums, 160–1, 237
    archaeology of, 161–2
    codification, 159–62
smallpox, inoculation, 96–7
Smith, Adam (1723–90), 30, 86, 93–4
    Wealth of Nations (1776), 93
Smith, Frank (fl. 1923), 253
Smythe, Emily Anne Beaufort, Lady
    Strangford (d. 1887), 196, 197
snobs, 253
Snowden, Ethel (née Annakin)
    (1881–1951), 251–2
Snowden, Philip (1864–1937), 243–4,
    253–4
SNP (Scottish Nationalist Party), 289–90
sociability, plebeians, 69–70
social change
    and cultural politics, 20
    and radical politics, 20
Social Darwinists, 222–3
Social Democratic Federation (SDF),
    139–40, 241–2
Social Democratic Party of Germany
    (SDP), 247
social democrats, and universalism, 286–7
social elites, 73
social history
    class in, 2–8
    criticisms, 5–6
    field of study
        current situation, 18–19
        daily life studies, 2–3
        expansion of, 6–7
        issues, 1–8
    Marxism and, 2–3
    totalising version of, 11–12
Social History (journal), 1, 230–1
social movements, 272, 278
social policy
    Whigs, 168
    writings on, 2
social politics, 184–5
Social Purity Alliance, 200–1
social sciences, 274–5
    bourgeois, 267

social security, 257, 258
social status, ancestry and, 101–2
social welfare
    government roles in, 89–99
    regional differences, 89
socialism, 139, 243–4, 251–2
    anthropology as, 146
    and commons, 138–9, 139–40
    development, 146
    and enclosure, 140
    and middle class, 257
    renewal, 263
socialist humanism, 225–6
socialist movements, 206
socialist production, vs. capitalist
    production, 257–8
socio-economic change, 20
socio-economic liberalism, 87–8
sociology, bourgeois continental,
    212–13
Sofia (Bulgaria), 196
Soft Machine (band), 271–2
soldiers, Sikhs as, 293, 294
Somerset, Lady Henry (née Isabel Cocks)
    (1851–1921), 201, 206–7
    Woman's Signal, 201, 202–3
Somerset, population growth, 41–2
Somerville, John Southey, 15th Lord
    Somerville (1765–1819), 104
South Africa, 206–7
    blacks, 208
    Boer War, 187, 203
South Africa Conciliation Committee, 203
South African Women and Children
    Distress Fund, 204
South Asia, immigrants from, 283–4
Southall (Greater London), 286, 294–5
Southsea (Hampshire), riots, 131
Southwark (London), 175–6
Soviet Union (former), 225–6
    see also Russia
Spare Rib (magazine), 266–7
spatial authority, 157
spatial function, and social relations of
    production, 142
Speck, Ross, 277–8
spending, indices, 82
spiritual freedom, Christian concept of,
    207–8, 209
squatting, commons, 135
Sri Lanka, 279
Stalin, Joseph (1878–1953), 262–3
Stalinism, 217–18, 225–6
Stalybridge (Greater Manchester), 152
Stamford (Lincolnshire), squatting, 135

Standing Advisory Councils for Religious
    Education, 297
Stanley, Henry Morton (1841–1904),
    156–7
Stansfeld, Caroline (née Ashurst)
    (1822–85), 193
Stansfeld, Sir James (1820–98), 193
state
    changing forms of, 76
    concepts of, 80–1
    definitional issues, 78–81
    pre-modern, 81
    separation of church and, 169–70
    shrinkage, 77–8
    studies, 76
    use of term, 79
    see also central state; fiscal-military state
state power, 80–1
Stead, William Thomas (1849–1912),
    195–6, 203
    'Maiden Tribute' (1885), 198
Stedman Jones, Gareth (1942–), 20, 22–3,
    144–5
    biographical notes, 17–18
    and British history, 8–9
    on Chartism, 170–1
    on East End, 156
    An End to Poverty (2004), 15–16, 17–18
    on Engels, 148
    on institutional reform, 164–5
    Languages of Class (1983), 14–15, 230–1
    and Marxism, 15–16
    ed. *Metropolis: London* (1989), 14–15
    Outcast London (1971), 9–10, 11–12,
        13–15, 17–18, 22–3
    'Rethinking Chartism' (1983), 17–18
    on student protests, 267–8
    'Working-class Culture and Working-
        class Politics in Victorian London'
        (1974), 12–13
stereotypes
    gender, 106–7
    rich, 252
Stockport (Greater Manchester), 152
stocks, 59–60, 66
    removal, 60
    in rural areas, 68
    see also pillories
Stockton-on-Tees (County Durham;
    North Yorkshire), market place,
    shambles, 63
Stokes, Adrian (1902–72), 214–15
Stone, Lawrence (1919–99), 222–3
Stormont (Northern Ireland), 290
Strachey, Giles Lytton (1880–1932), 221–2

stratified electioneering, 255–6
street politics, 18th century, 55–6
strikes, 237–8, 238–9
structuralism, 268–9
    and linguistic theory, 14–15
    see also post-structuralism
structure
    in British historiography, 1–23
    use of term, 19–20
Stuart England, political celebrations, 55–6
Stubbs, William (1825–1901), 220–1
student movement, 265–6, 267–8
subordination, popular mentalities of, 211
subsistence crisis, 20–1
Suez Canal, 183–4
    crisis (1956), 262–3
Suffolk, labourers, 137
suffrage movement, 198–9, 204, 206,
    207–8
Summer of Love (1967), 274
Summers, Anne, 21
Sunday schools, 97–8
superego, 211, 218
Surrealism, 269–70
suttee, 209
Swann Report (1985), 295–6
Sweezy, Paul Marlor (1910–2004), 274–5
Swing Rising, 139–40, 228–9

Tanganyika (former), 292, 293
Tate, W. E., 121
Tavistock (Devonshire), 133
taxes, 171–2, 175–6
    land, 129–30
    reduction, 165, 169–70, 255–6
    repeal, 180–1
Taylor, Alan John Percival (1906–90),
    222–3
Taylor, Anthony, 129
Taylor, Barbara, 226, 234
Teesside, 129–30
Telegraph für Deutschland, 144
Temperley, H. W. V., 184–5
tenements, and market places, 62–3
terrorism, domestic, 300–1
tertiary employment, 49
Thatcher, Margaret (1925–), 264–5, 284,
    297
Theatre of the Absurd, 270
Theatre of Cruelty, 270
Themes in Modern History Seminar,
    11–12
Third World, 274–5, 277–8
Thomas, James Henry ('Jimmy')
    (1874–1949), 238–9

Thomas, Sir Keith Vivian (1933–), *Religion
    and the Decline of Magic* (1971), 231
Thompson, Edward Palmer (1924–93),
    5–6, 8–9, 17–18, 211, 229–30,
    262–3
    and Althusser, 217–18
    criticisms, 14
    crowd in history theory, 226–7
    Customs in Common (1991), 118–19
    on enclosure, 118, 140
    legacies, 11–12
    The Making of the English Working Class
        (1963), 12–13, 118–19, 225–6
    on Methodism, 226
    on Reform crisis, 2
    and Stedman Jones, 9–10
Thorne, Will (1857–1946), 156
Throsby, John (1740–1803), 68–9
Tichbourne Claimant, 129–30
Times, The, 124, 292
Tiratsoo, Nick, 255
Titmuss, Richard Morris (1907–73), 2
Tocqueville, Alexis de (1805–59), 153
toleration, models of, 295
Tonna, Charlotte Elizabeth (1790–1846),
    191–4
Tories, 167–8
    criticisms, 169–70
    see also Conservative Party; Liberal
        Tories
toryism, 9–10
    old, 170–1
total history, 12–13
    lack of return to, 18–19
    theories, 13–14
Towers, Peter (*fl.* 1801), 66–7
towns
    18th century, urban renaissance, 54–73
    Georgian, 55–6
    see also cities
Toynbee, Arnold (1852–83), 17–18
trade, and market places, 58–9
Trade Union Act (1913), 253–4
Trade Union Labour Party, 241–2
trade unions, 226–7, 241–2
    and assimilation, 286–7
    growth of, 5
    pioneers, 253–4
    and rail strikes, 238–9
    resistance to immigrants, 286–7
    and turbans, 283
traffic, and market places, 62–3
transformations
    in British historiography, 1–23
    in political imagery, 22

transnational networks, 20, 21
Transport and General Workers Union, 281–2, 286–7
Transvaal (South Africa), 203, 204
Treacher, Mrs E. M., 284
Treasury, 180–1, 184–5
Trevelyan, Sir Charles (1807–86), 169–70, 178–9
Trevelyan, Sir George Otto (1838–1928), 173–5
tribes, 293
Trocchi, Alexander (1925–84), 271–2
  Sigma Portfolio (1963–8), 271
Trotsky, Leon (1879–1940), 279
Trotskyism, 265–6, 267–8, 279
Turban Action Committee, 289
turbans
  ban on, 281–2, 294
  on buses, 286–7
  politics of, 281–302
Turkey, 183–4, 191–2, 197, 199
  British policies, 191
  critiques, 198
  harems, 195–6, 198, 200–1, 209
Turkish Compassionate Fund, 197
Turks, 198, 201–2, 203
  atrocities, 195–6, 208
Turner, Michael, 120–1
Tzankof, Dragan Kiriakov (1828–1911), 199

Ulster (Ireland), 290
UN-HABITAT (United Nations Human Settlements Programme), State of the World Cities (2008), 159
Underground movement, 271–2
unemployment, 238–9
  agricultural labourers, 35–6
unionisation, 139
  farm workers, 130–1
Unionism, 290
Unitarians, 189
United Kingdom (UK)
  Union (1707), 289–90
  see also Britain
United Nations Human Settlements Programme (UN-HABITAT), State of the World Cities (2008), 159
United States (US), 173
  administration, 79
  Civil War, 189–90
  social sciences, 274–5
  universities, 276
universalism
  decline of, 298

opposition to, 287
  social democrats and, 286–7
upper class see elites
urban analysis, and means of production, 142–3
urban development, commons and, 129–30
urban ethnography, field of study, 159–62
Urban Fund, 296–7
urban history, 2–3
urban hypocrisy, philosophy and practice of, 163
urban life, 18th century, 54
urban privilege, 246
Urban Programme, 288
urban renaissance
  18th century towns, 54–73
  concept of, 54
  historical sanitisation, 57
  issues, 69
  and market places, 73
  and the mob, 54–7
  see also civic improvement
urban riots, 295–6
urban segregation, 159
urban spaces, conflicting interests, 142
urbanisation, 20–1
  and population change, 33–5
  and public spaces, 122–3
utilitarianism, Benthamite, 85

Venturi, Emilie Ashurst (1826–93), 193, 194–5
Victoria (1819–1901), 172–3
  activities, 184–5
  criticisms, 183–4
  marriage, 167–8
  petitions, 198, 199, 200
  political influence, 173–5
Victoria League, 204
Victorian City, The (1973), 2–3
Victorianism, 219
Vienna (Austria), British embassy, 171–2
Vietnam Solidarity Campaign, 265–6, 267–8
Vincent, John (1937–), How Victorians Voted (1967), 2
Vinkenoog, Simon (1928–2009), 277–8
violence, mass, 227–8
virtual Protestantism, 192
Vorwärts (newspaper), 247

Wade, John (1788–1875), Black Book (1820), 165
wage change, and population change, 27–9, 31

wage labour, 119–20, 256–7
Waites, Bernard, 237–8
Wales
    disestablishment, 184–5
    historical background, 290
Walkden, Alexander George (1873–1951),
    253–4
walks, public, 123–5, 128
Wallis, John (*fl.* 1809), 66–7
Walworth (London), 139–40
War Office, 176, 178–9
Ward, Colin (1924–2010), 272–3
Warrington (Cheshire), 177–8
wars
    Afghan, 183–4
    Ashanti, 178–9
    civil, 189–90
    class, 242, 250
    Franco-Prussian, 177–8
    government and, 83
    Napoleonic, 88–9, 165
    see also Boer War (1899–1902); Crimean
        War; World War I (1914–18); World
        War II (1939–45)
wartime coalition, 248
wastes
    common, 118–19
    common rights, 119–20
    extent of, 121
    former forests, 132–3
    improvements, 123–4
    pre-enclosure useage, 119–20
    public access, 127–8
    useage, 134–5
    see also commons
Waters, Chris, 245
wealth, privilege of, 252
Webb, Martha Beatrice (née Potter)
    (1858–1943), *English Local
    Government* (1906–29), 89–90
Webb, Sidney James, 1st Baron Passfield
    (1859–1947), 242, 255
    English Local Government (1906–29),
        89–90
Weberian bureaucracies, 74–5
Weiss, Peter Ulrich (1916–82), *Marat/Sade*
    (1963), 261, 270
welfare
    direct vs. indirect control, 76
    financing, 74–5
    see also social welfare
Wells, Herbert George (1866–1946),
    241–2
Wells (Somerset), 284
Welsh language, 290

Wertheimer, Egon (1894–1957), 247
Wesleyan hymns, 226
Wesleyans, 290–1
West Africa, 177–8
West Bromwich (West Midlands), 242–3
West London Synagogue of British Jews,
    291–2
Western Marxism, 267–8
Westminster (London), 289–90
Whiggery, 77–8
    narratives, 248–9
    old, 170–1
Whigs, 86–7, 165–6, 167–8, 170–1,
        184–6
    activist social policies, 168
    criticisms, 169–70
    fall of, 168–9
whipping posts, 66
White, Jerry, 159–60
White, Jessie (1832–1906), 193–4
Whitehouse, Mary (1910–2001), 264–5
Whitelaw, William (1918–99), 299
'Who are the patriots?' (1931), 250
Williams, Raymond Henry (1921–88), 8–9,
    262–3
    Keywords (1976), 227–8
Williams, Shirley (1930–), 287
Wilson, James Harold (1916–95), 263
Wiltshire, population growth, 49
Wimbledon Common (London), 128
witches, women as, 231
Withypool (Somerset), squatting, 135
Wittgenstein, Ludwig (1889–1951),
    214–15
Wolverhampton (West Midlands), 281,
    286–7
    market place, 62–3
    protests, 281–2, 283–4, 289
Wolverhampton Corporation, 281–2,
    283–4
Wolverhampton Transport Committee,
    281–2
Woman's Signal (journal), 201–3
women
    Balkan, 200–1
    of the British Empire, and feminists,
        187–8
    emancipation, 188, 198
    as witches, 231
    see also British women; female
        internationalism
Women's Liberal Federation, 202–3, 208
    Armenia Bureau, 201–2
    Cambridge Resolution, 204
Women's Liberation Movement, 266–7

Women's Memorial (petition), 198–9
   goals, 200
women's movement, 269
Women's Social and Political Union, 206
Woolf, Adeline Virginia (1882–1941), 219
Wordie, J. R., 120–1
workerism, 252–3
Workers' Union, 242–3
working class, 12–13, 253–4
   condition of, 142–4
   Labour Party and, 240, 253–8, 259
world affairs, Christians and, 191
World Anti-Slavery Convention, 189–90
World Bank, 159
World War I (1914–18), 206, 207–8,
      215–16, 245
   aftermath, 218, 247
   and class feeling, 237–8
World War II (1939–45), 222–3, 270

Jews and, 270
Labour Party and, 259–60
Sikhs in, 294
Wrigley, Sir Anthony Edward (1931–), 20–1
   Population History of England (1981), 26
Wupper, River, 144

Yale University (US), 278
Yellow Press, 156
yeoman class, and enclosure, 118
Yorkshire
   commons, 129
   enclosure, 126–7
Yorkshire Forward, 301
Young Europe, 192–3
Young Hegelianism, 144–5, 147,
      148, 154

Zulus, 208–9